4

Eku Takeshima

# Whisper Me A Love Song

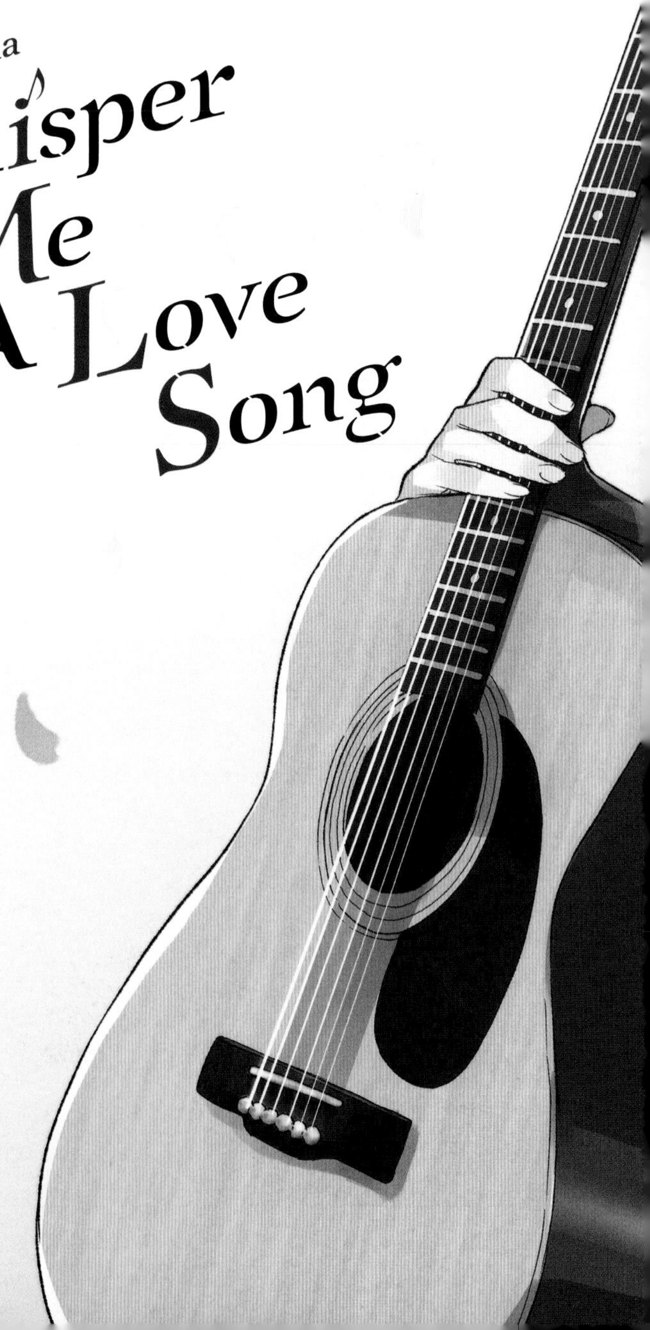

Song 16:
The Roof, a Guitar,
& Girlfriends.

*4*

*contents*

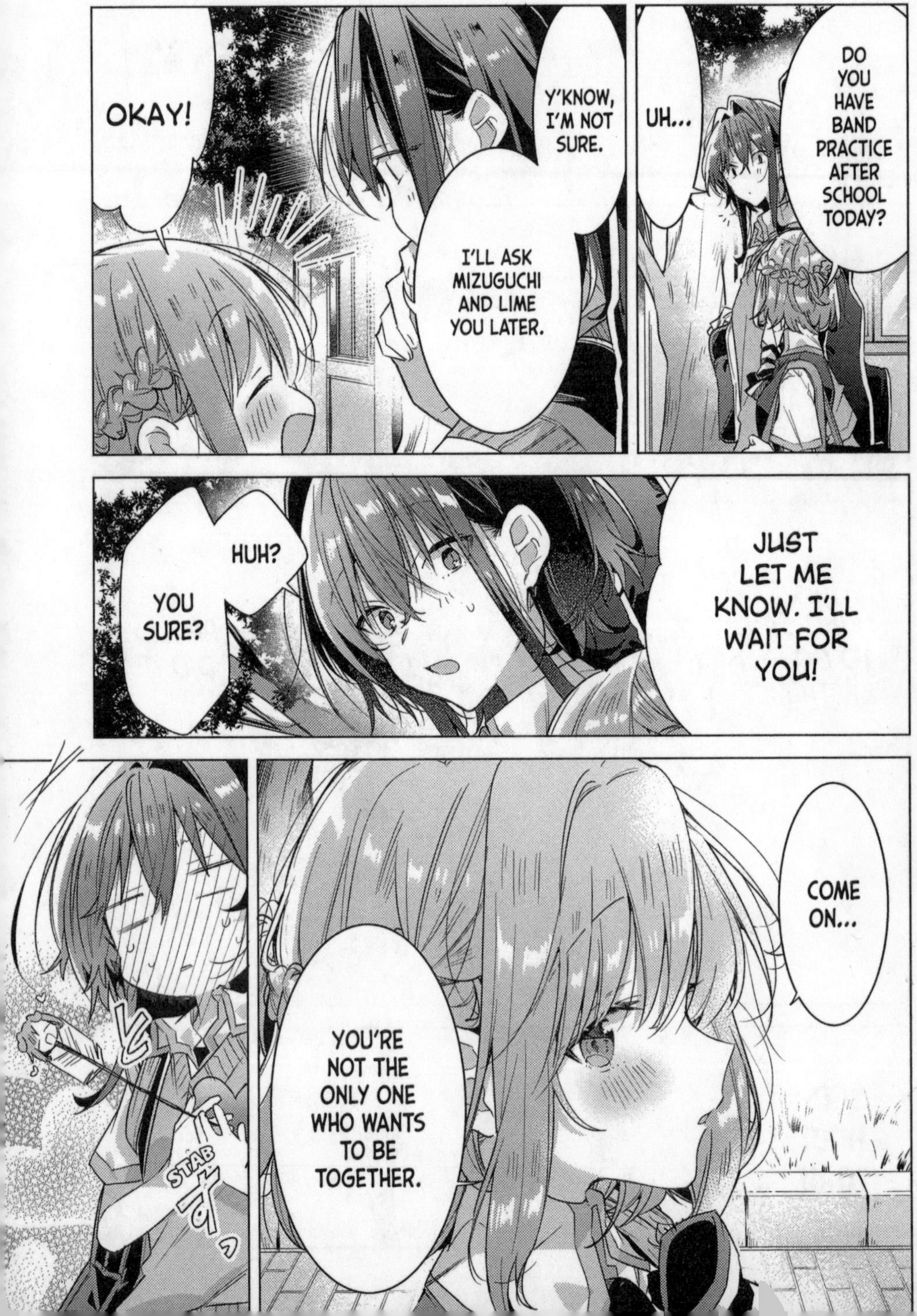
DO YOU HAVE BAND PRACTICE AFTER SCHOOL TODAY?
UH...
Y'KNOW, I'M NOT SURE.
I'LL ASK MIZUGUCHI AND LIME YOU LATER.
OKAY!
JUST LET ME KNOW. I'LL WAIT FOR YOU!
HUH?
YOU SURE?
COME ON...
YOU'RE NOT THE ONLY ONE WHO WANTS TO BE TOGETHER.
STAB

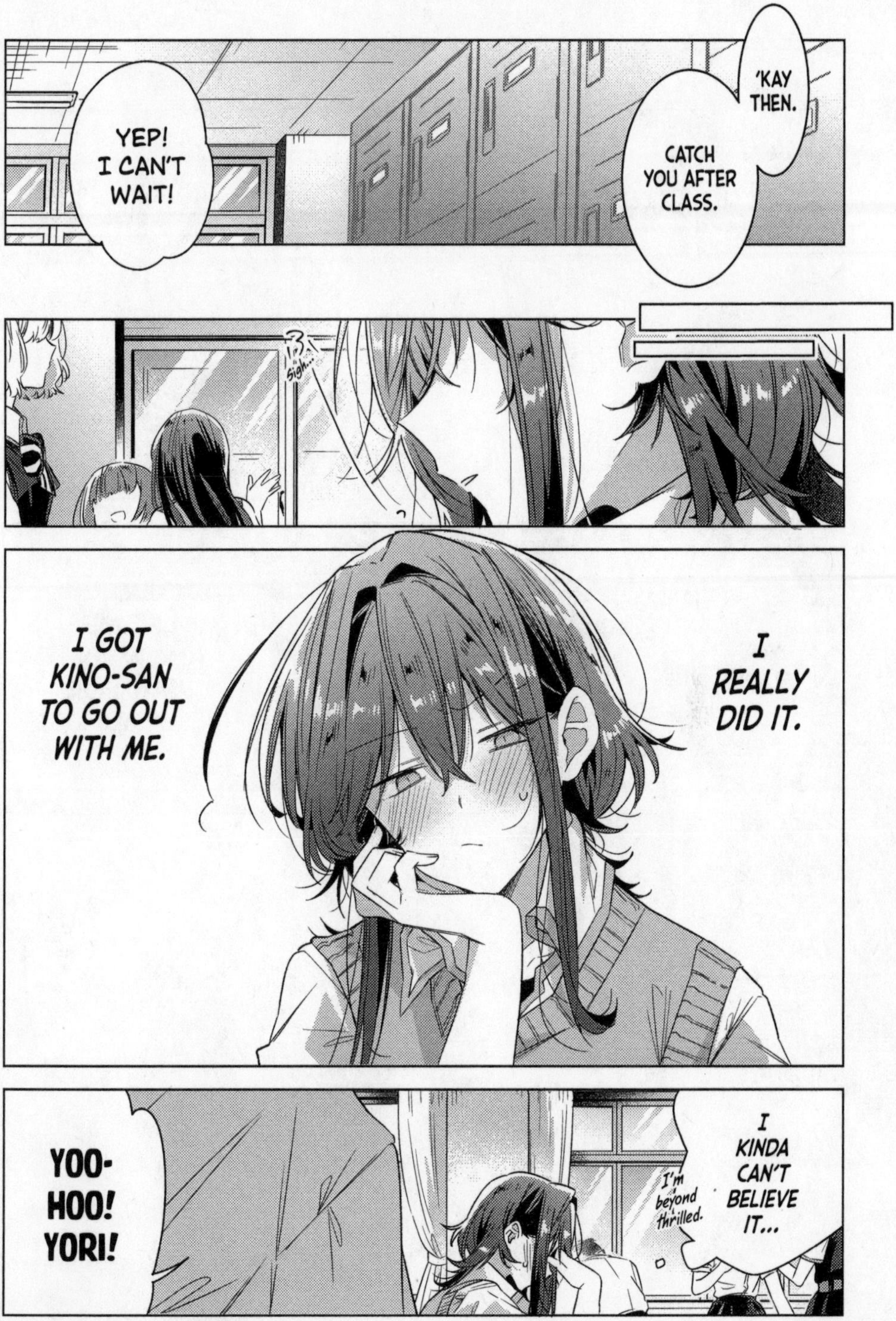
'KAY THEN.
CATCH YOU AFTER CLASS.
YEP! I CAN'T WAIT!
Sigh...
I REALLY DID IT.
I GOT KINO-SAN TO GO OUT WITH ME.
I KINDA CAN'T BELIEVE IT...
I'm beyond thrilled.
YOO-HOO! YORI!

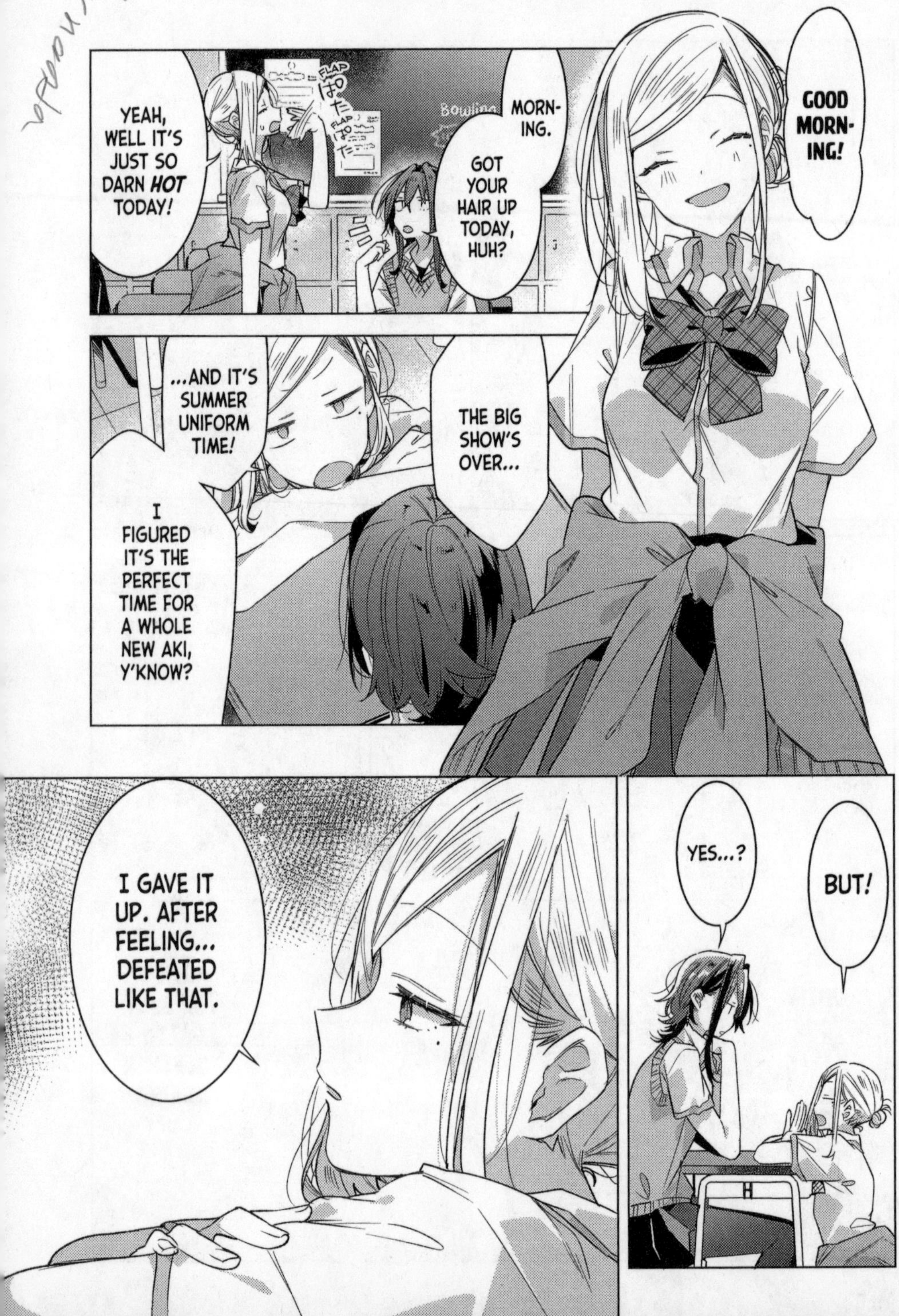
GOOD MORN-ING!
MORN-ING.
GOT YOUR HAIR UP TODAY, HUH?
FLAP ぱた FLAP ぱた
YEAH, WELL IT'S JUST SO DARN *HOT* TODAY!
THE BIG SHOW'S OVER...
...AND IT'S SUMMER UNIFORM TIME!
I FIGURED IT'S THE PERFECT TIME FOR A WHOLE NEW AKI, Y'KNOW?
BUT!
YES...?
I GAVE IT UP. AFTER FEELING... DEFEATED LIKE THAT.

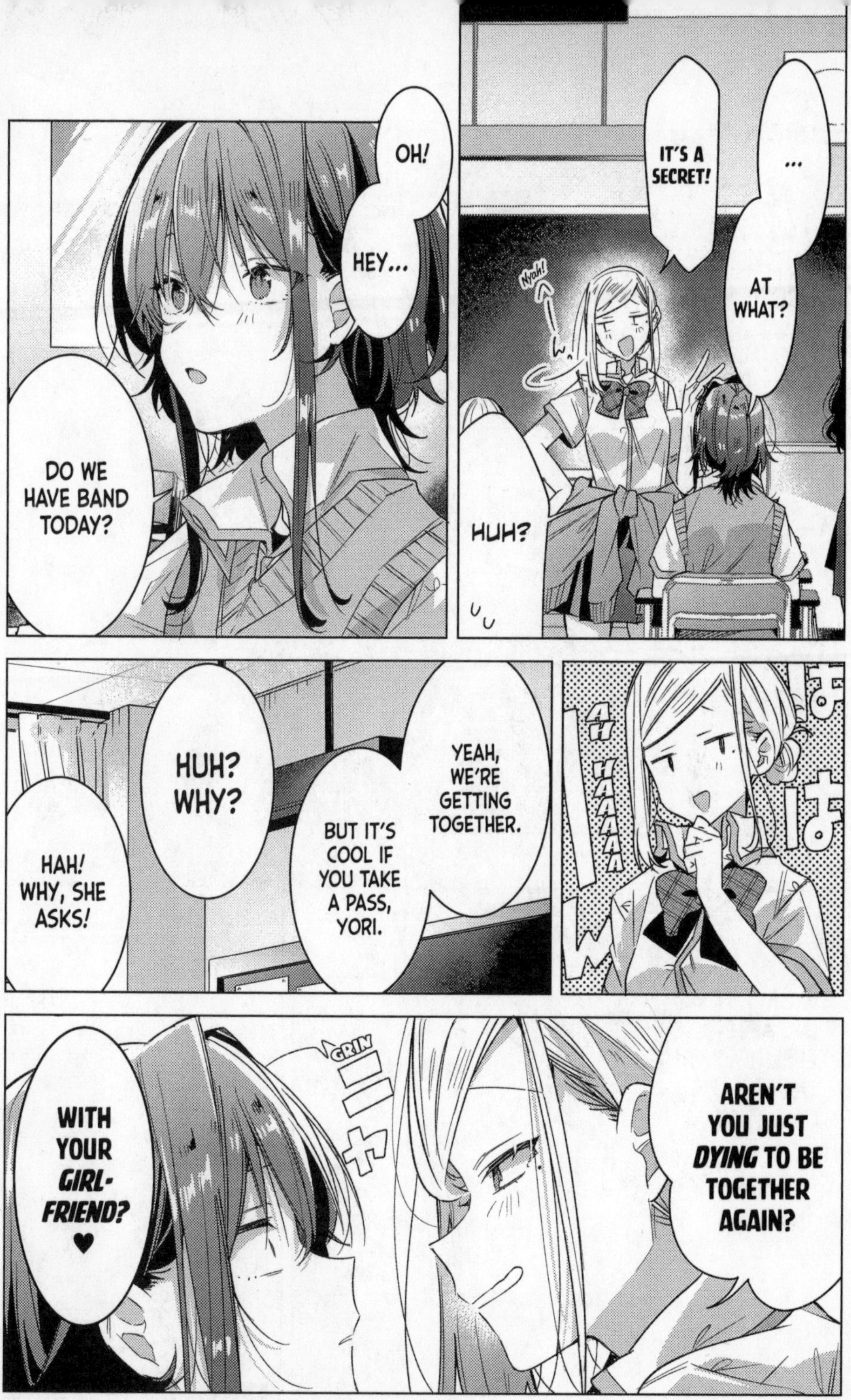
...
AT WHAT?
IT'S A SECRET!
Nyah!
HUH?
OH!
HEY...
DO WE HAVE BAND TODAY?
AH HAHAHAAA
YEAH, WE'RE GETTING TOGETHER.
BUT IT'S COOL IF YOU TAKE A PASS, YORI.
HUH? WHY?
HAH! WHY, SHE ASKS!
AREN'T YOU JUST *DYING* TO BE TOGETHER AGAIN?
GRIN
WITH YOUR *GIRL-FRIEND?* ♥

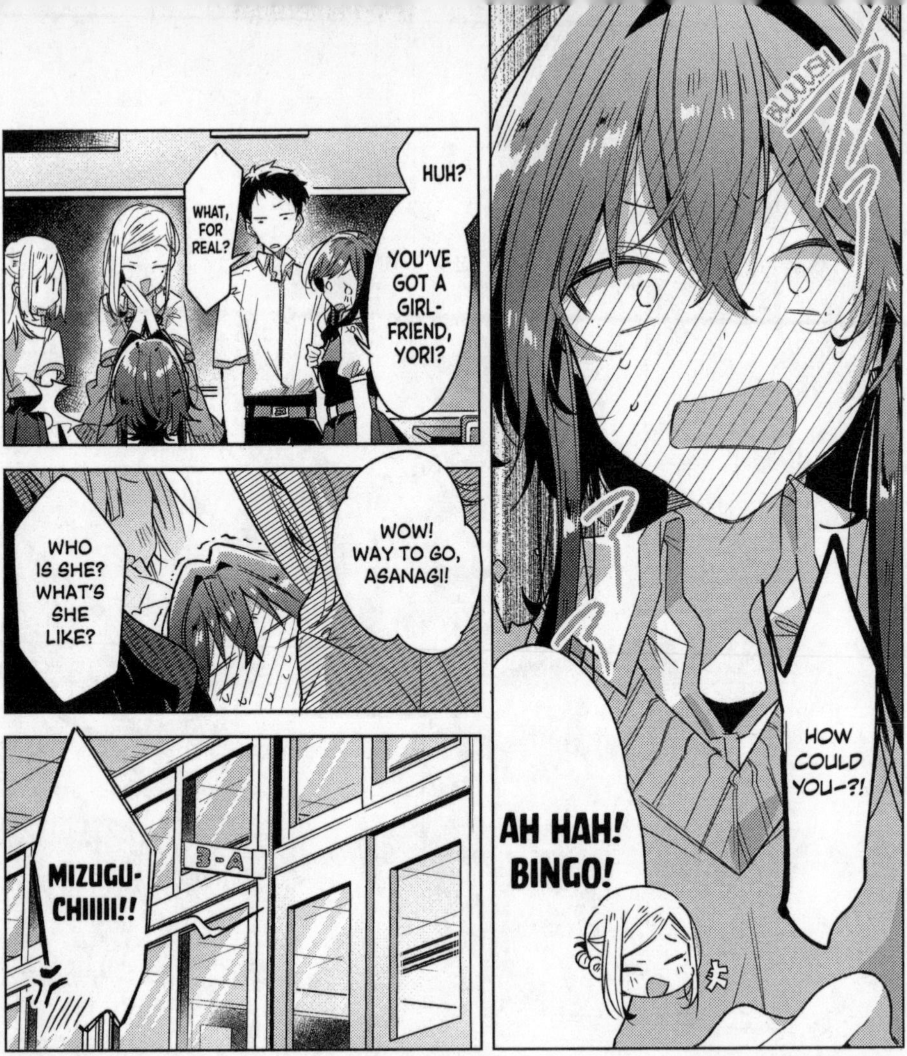
BUUUSH!
HOW COULD YOU-?!
AH HAH! BINGO!
HUH?
YOU'VE GOT A GIRL-FRIEND, YORI?
WHAT, FOR REAL?
WOW! WAY TO GO, ASANAGI!
WHO IS SHE? WHAT'S SHE LIKE?
3-A
MIZUGU-CHIIIIII!!

*SO THERE WE WERE...*

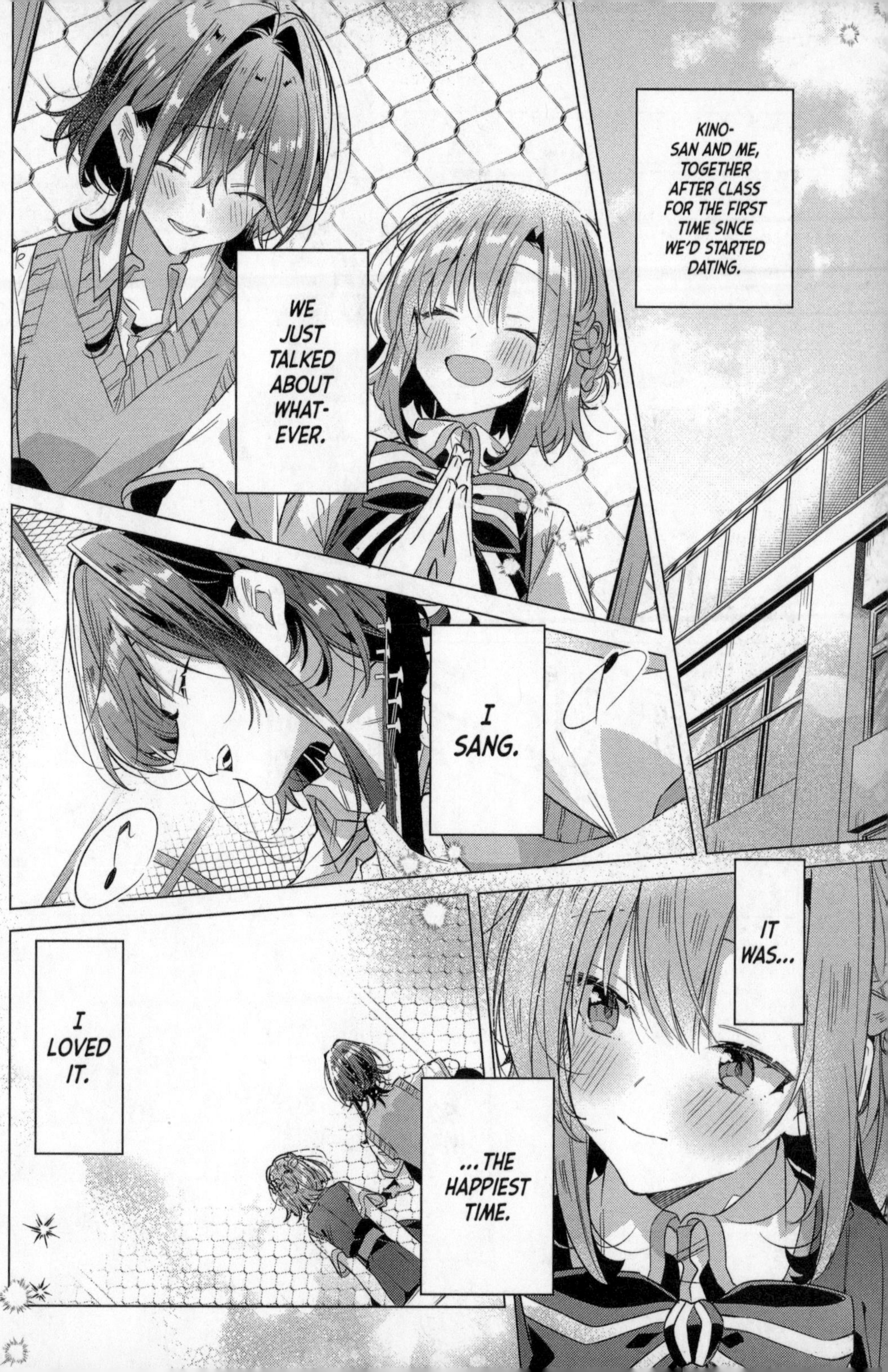
KINO-SAN AND ME, TOGETHER AFTER CLASS FOR THE FIRST TIME SINCE WE'D STARTED DATING.
WE JUST TALKED ABOUT WHATEVER.
I SANG.
IT WAS...
...THE HAPPIEST TIME.
I LOVED IT.

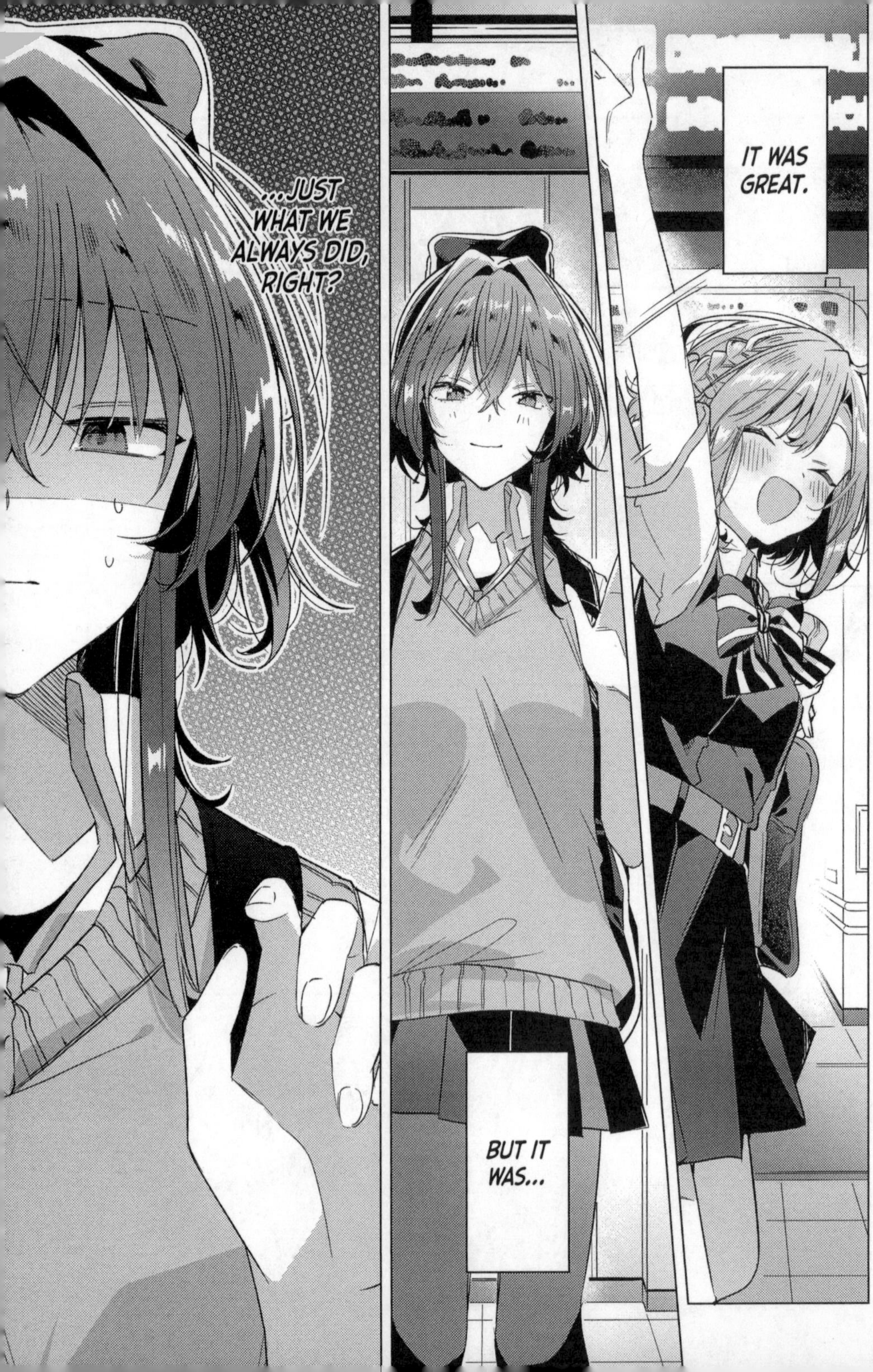
IT WAS GREAT.
BUT IT WAS...
...JUST WHAT WE ALWAYS DID, RIGHT?

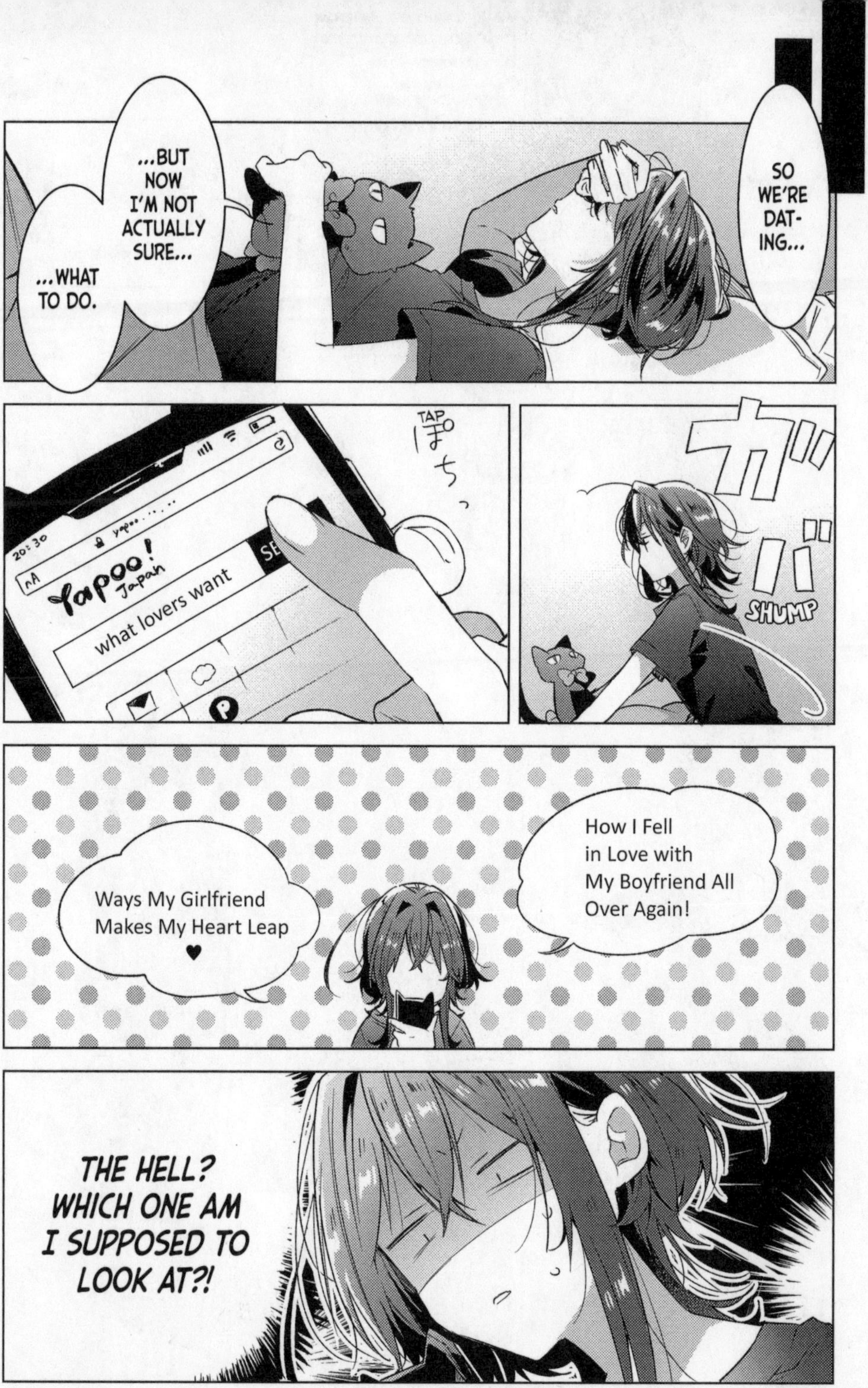
SO WE'RE DATING...
...BUT NOW I'M NOT ACTUALLY SURE...
...WHAT TO DO.
ガバ
SHUMP
TAP
ぽちっ
Yapoo! Japan
what lovers want
How I Fell in Love with My Boyfriend All Over Again!
Ways My Girlfriend Makes My Heart Leap ♥
THE HELL? WHICH ONE AM I SUPPOSED TO LOOK AT?!

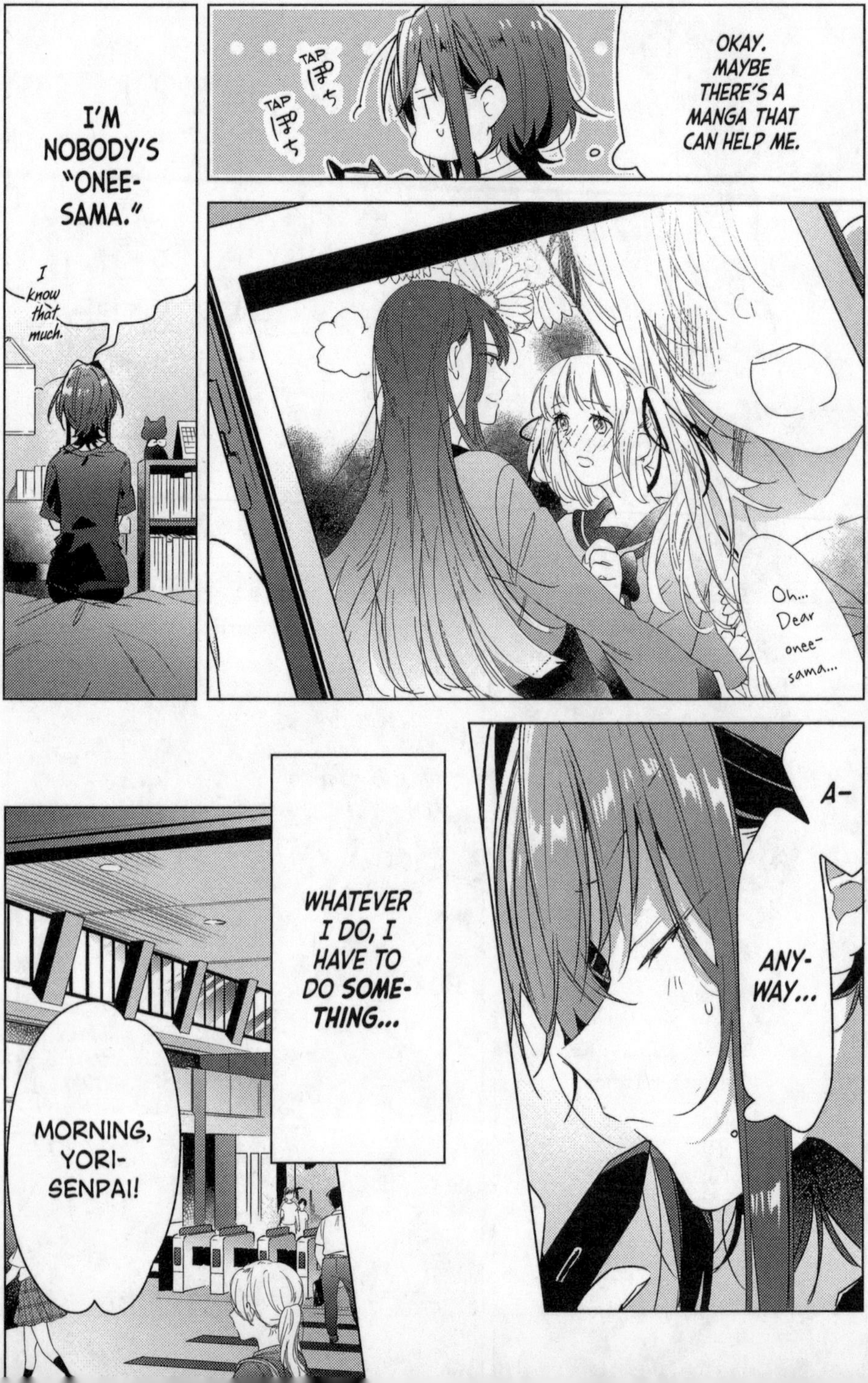
OKAY. MAYBE THERE'S A MANGA THAT CAN HELP ME.
TAP ぽち
TAP ぽち
Oh... Dear onee-sama...
I'M NOBODY'S "ONEE-SAMA."
I know that much.
A-
ANY-WAY...
WHATEVER I DO, I HAVE TO DO SOME-THING...
MORNING, YORI-SENPAI!

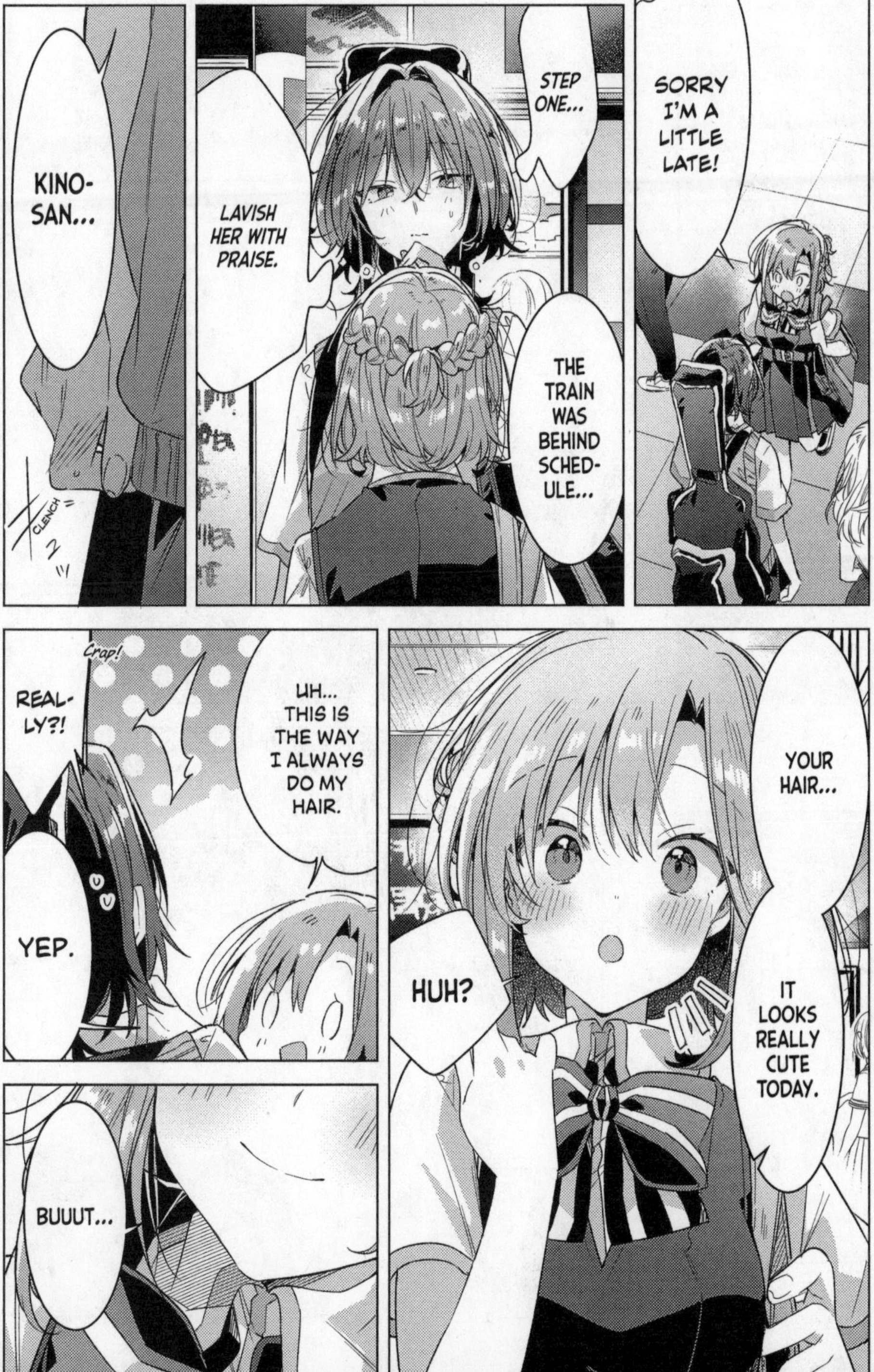
SORRY I'M A LITTLE LATE!
STEP ONE...
THE TRAIN WAS BEHIND SCHED-ULE...
LAVISH HER WITH PRAISE.
KINO-SAN...
CLENCH
YOUR HAIR...
IT LOOKS REALLY CUTE TODAY.
HUH?
UH... THIS IS THE WAY I ALWAYS DO MY HAIR.
Crap!
REAL-LY?!
YEP.
BUUUT...

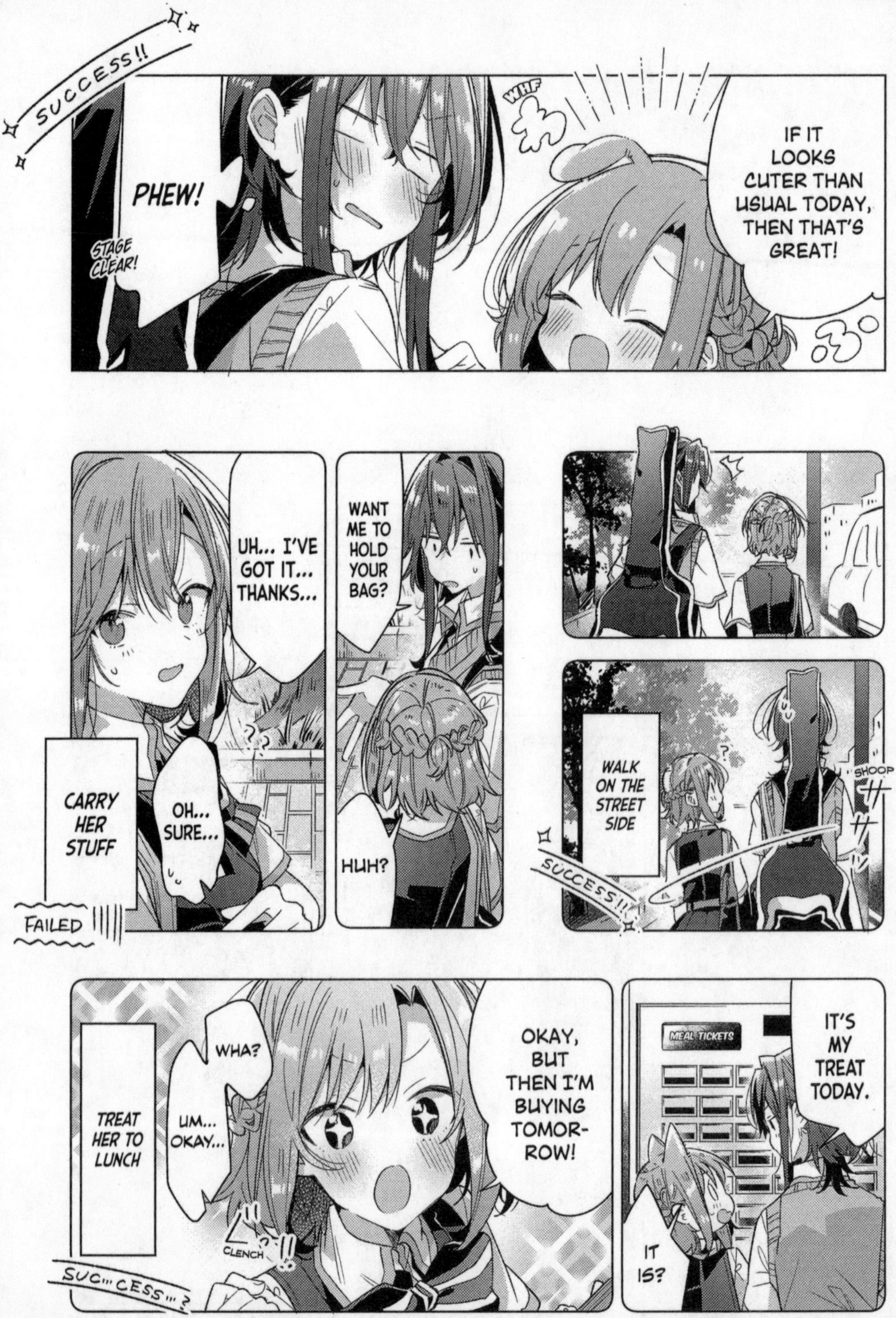

IF IT LOOKS CUTER THAN USUAL TODAY, THEN THAT'S GREAT!
WHF
PHEW!
STAGE CLEAR!
SUCCESS!!
WALK ON THE STREET SIDE
SHOOP
SUCCESS!!
WANT ME TO HOLD YOUR BAG?
HUH?
UH... I'VE GOT IT... THANKS...
OH... SURE...
CARRY HER STUFF
FAILED
IT'S MY TREAT TODAY.
MEAL TICKETS
IT IS?
OKAY, BUT THEN I'M BUYING TOMORROW!
WHA?
UM... OKAY...
TREAT HER TO LUNCH
CLENCH
SUC... CESS...?

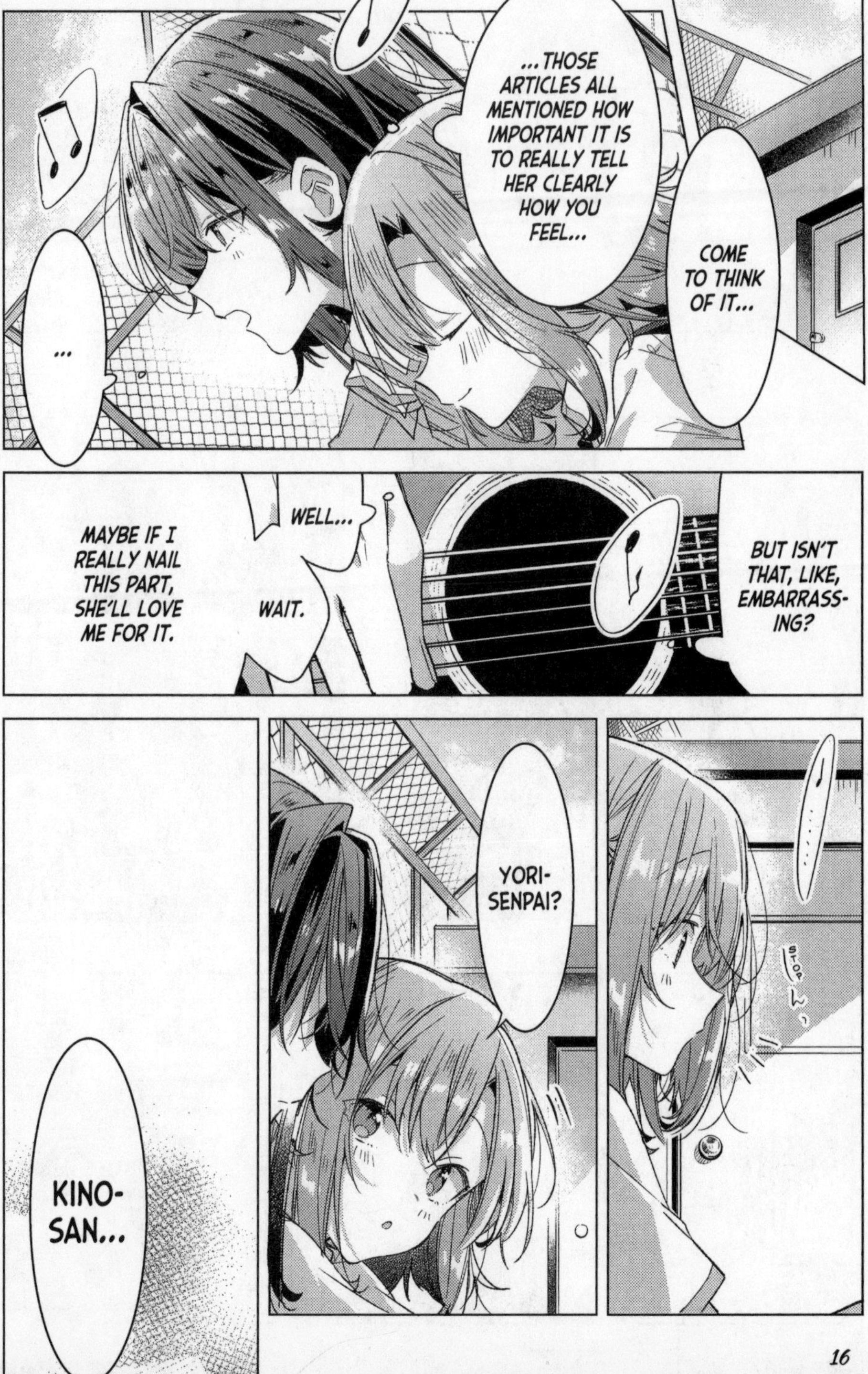
COME TO THINK OF IT...
...THOSE ARTICLES ALL MENTIONED HOW IMPORTANT IT IS TO REALLY TELL HER CLEARLY HOW YOU FEEL...
...
BUT ISN'T THAT, LIKE, EMBARRASS-ING?
WELL...
WAIT.
MAYBE IF I REALLY NAIL THIS PART, SHE'LL LOVE ME FOR IT.
......
STOP
YORI-SENPAI?
KINO-SAN...

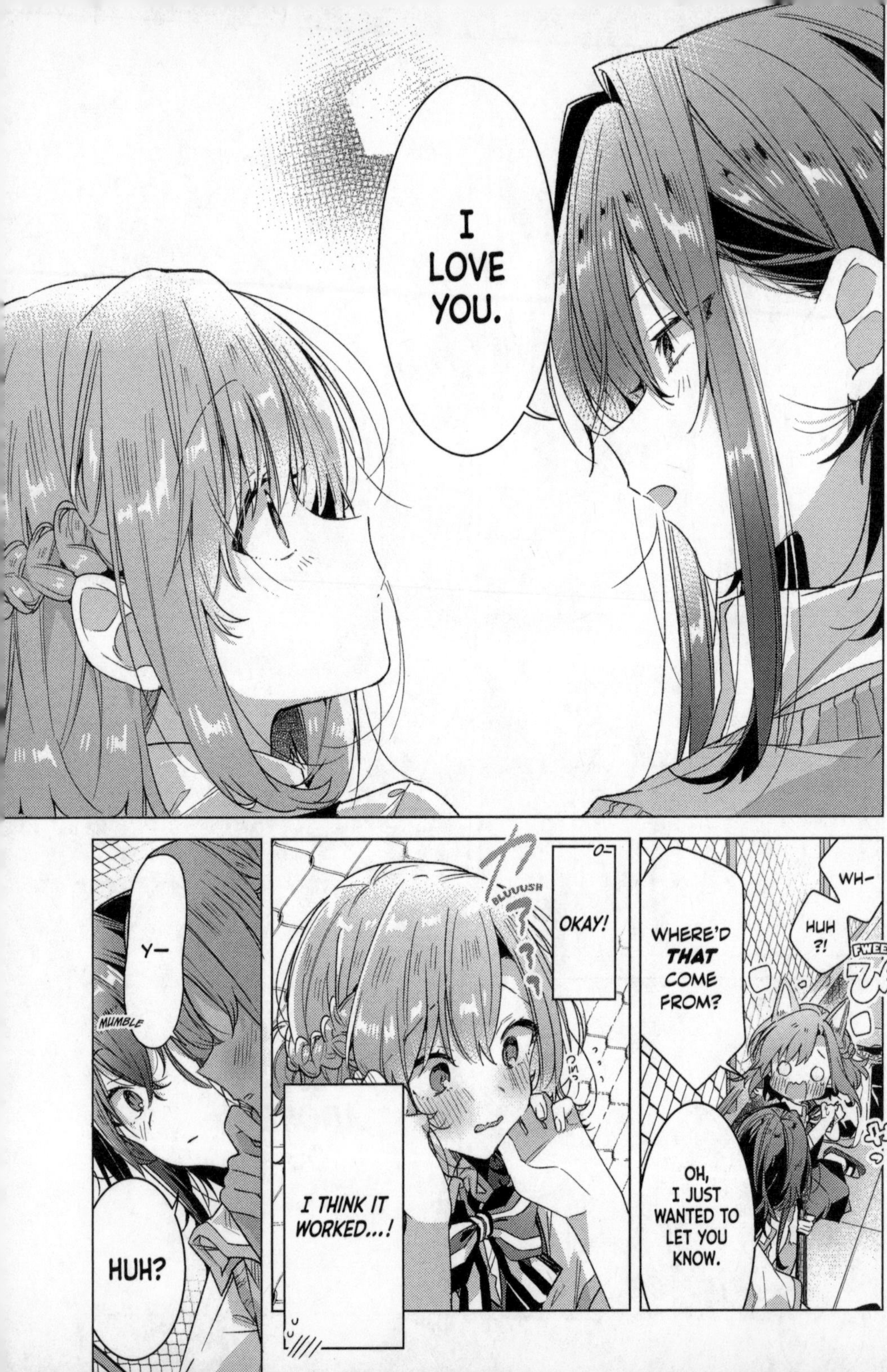
I LOVE YOU.
WH-
HUH ?!
FWEEE
WHERE'D THAT COME FROM?
OH, I JUST WANTED TO LET YOU KNOW.
BLUUUSH
O— OKAY!
I THINK IT WORKED...!
Y—
MUMBLE
HUH?

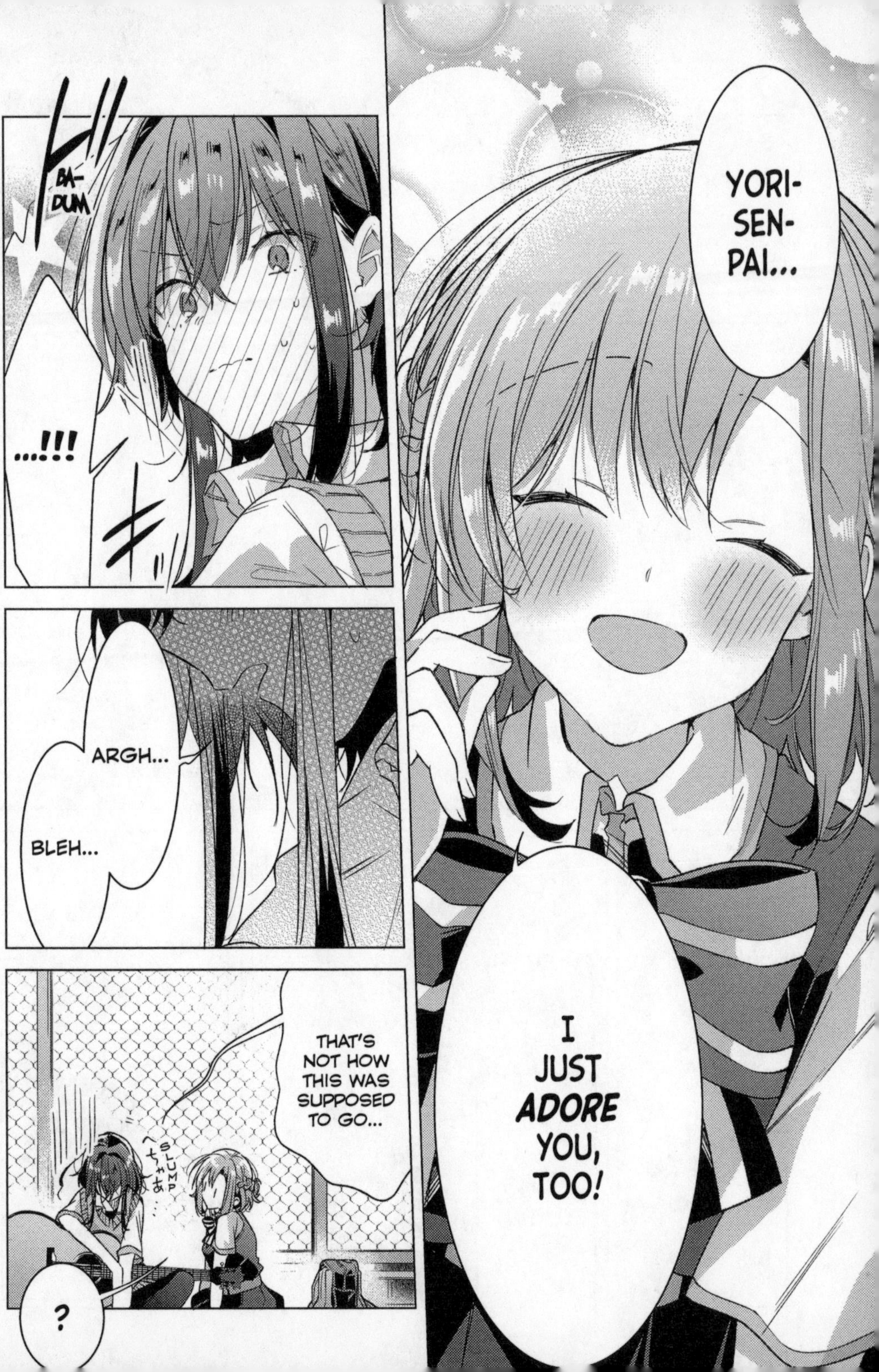

YORI-SENPAI...
I JUST ADORE YOU, TOO!
BA-DUM
...!!!
ARGH...
BLEH...
THAT'S NOT HOW THIS WAS SUPPOSED TO GO...
SLUMP
?

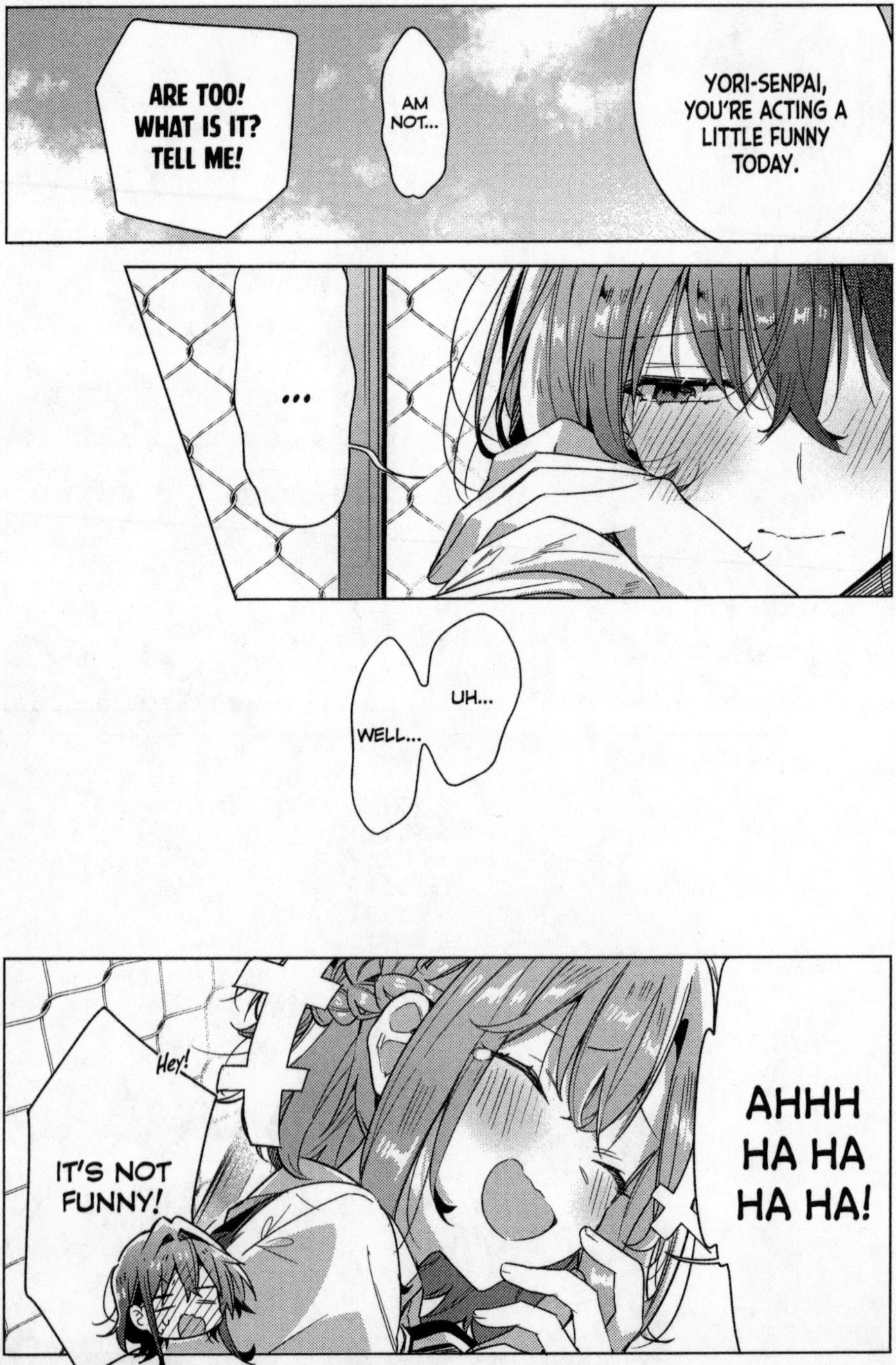
YORI-SENPAI, YOU'RE ACTING A LITTLE FUNNY TODAY.
AM NOT...
ARE TOO! WHAT IS IT? TELL ME!
...
UH...
WELL...
AHHH HA HA HA HA!
Hey!
IT'S NOT FUNNY!

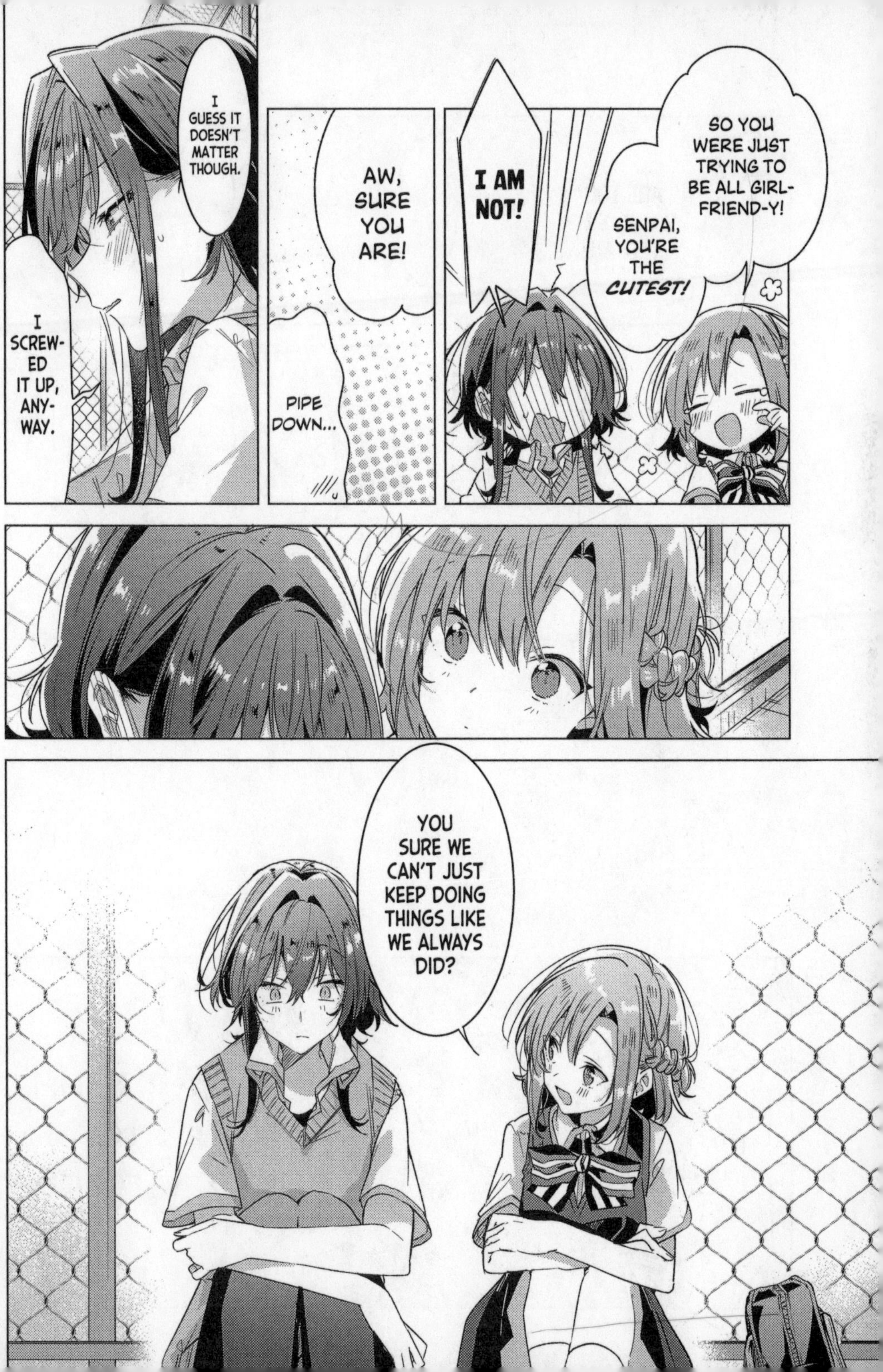
SO YOU WERE JUST TRYING TO BE ALL GIRL-FRIEND-Y!
SENPAI, YOU'RE THE *CUTEST!*
**I AM NOT!**
AW, SURE YOU ARE!
PIPE DOWN...
I GUESS IT DOESN'T MATTER THOUGH.
I SCREWED IT UP, ANYWAY.
YOU SURE WE CAN'T JUST KEEP DOING THINGS LIKE WE ALWAYS DID?

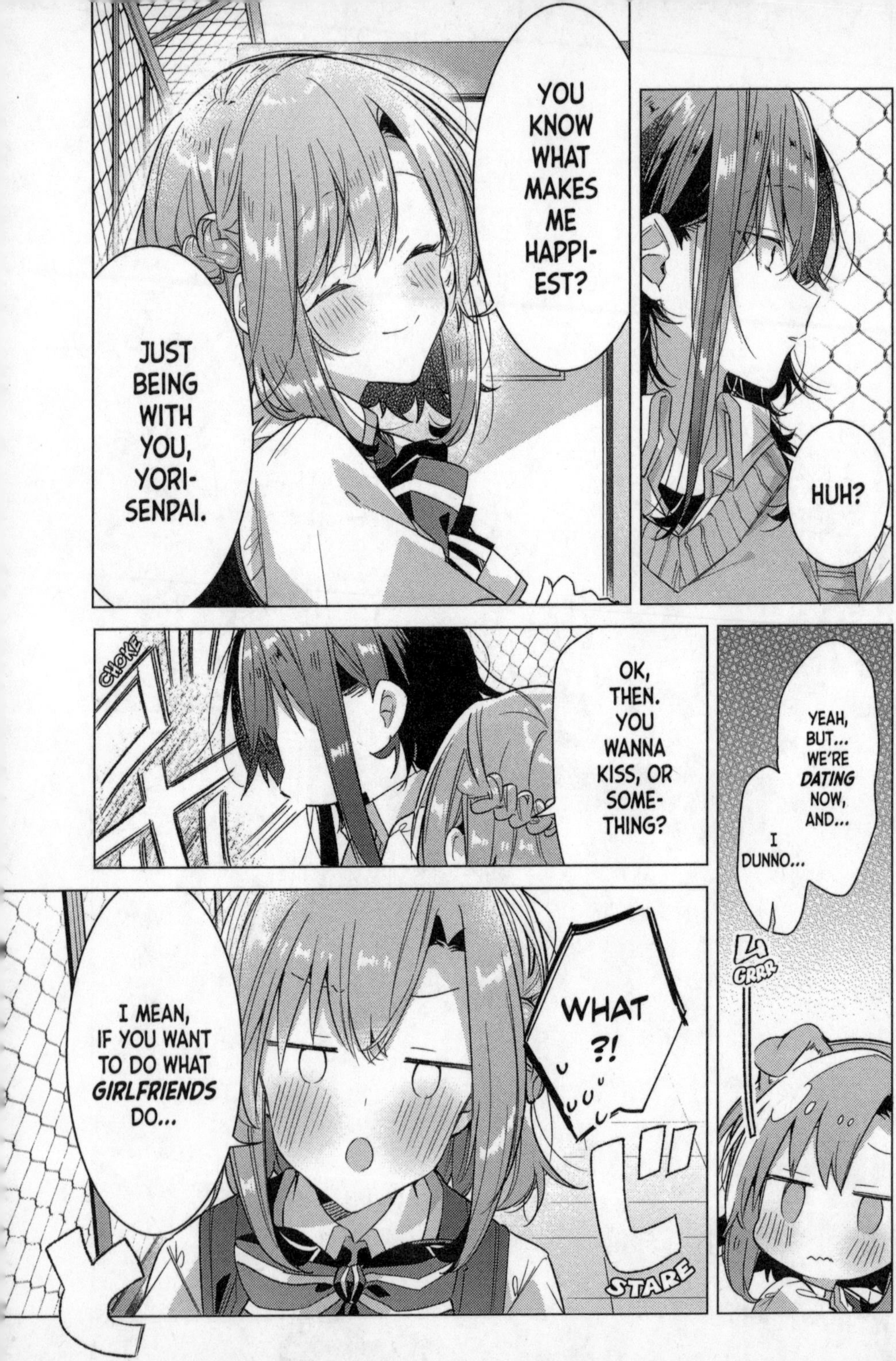

HUH?
YOU KNOW WHAT MAKES ME HAPPI-EST?
JUST BEING WITH YOU, YORI-SENPAI.
YEAH, BUT... WE'RE *DATING* NOW, AND...
I DUNNO...
GRRR
OK, THEN. YOU WANNA KISS, OR SOME-THING?
CHOKE
WHAT ?!
I MEAN, IF YOU WANT TO DO WHAT *GIRLFRIENDS* DO...
STARE

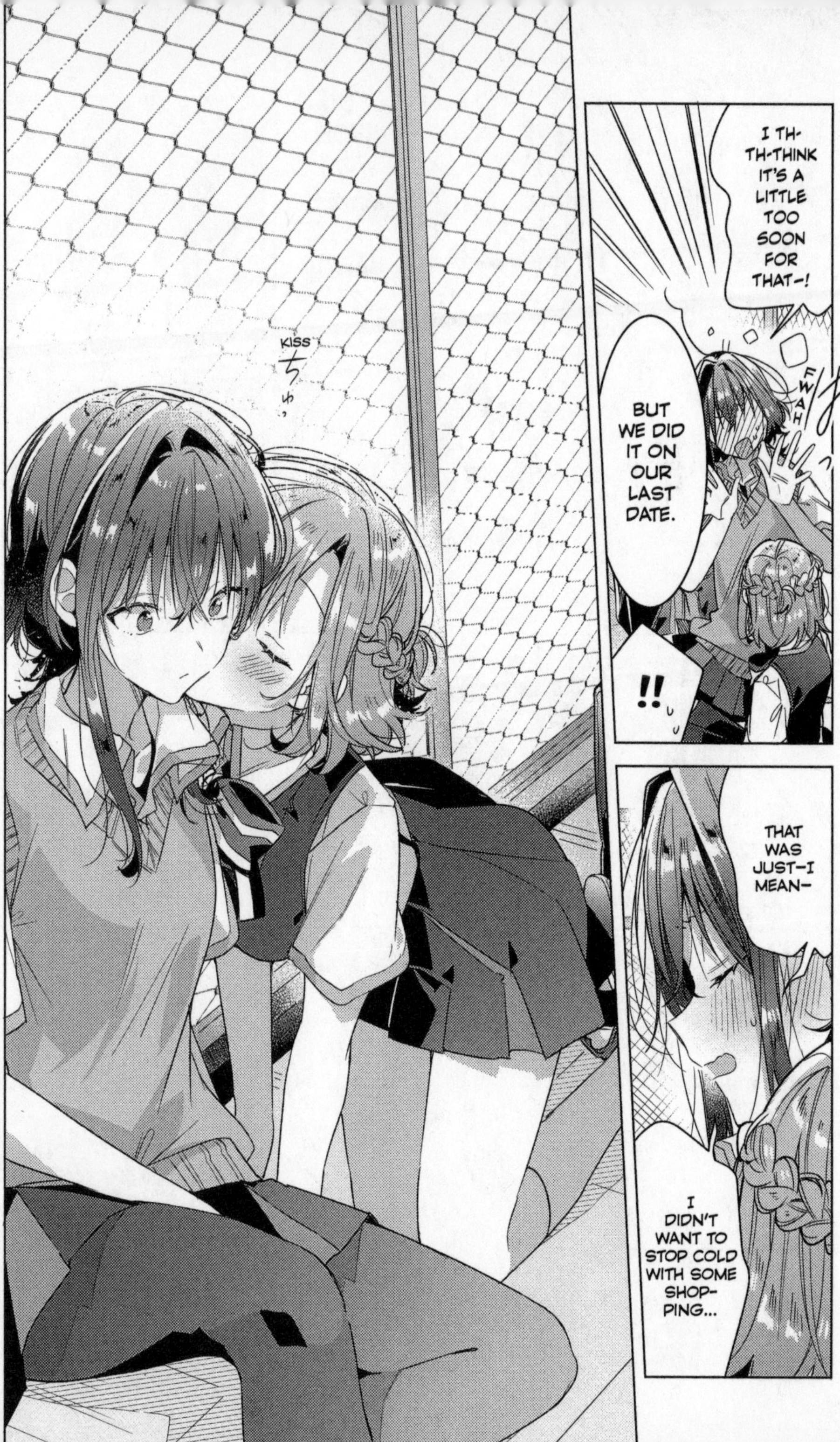
I TH-TH-THINK IT'S A LITTLE TOO SOON FOR THAT—!
FWAH
BUT WE DID IT ON OUR LAST DATE.
!!
THAT WAS JUST—I MEAN—
I DIDN'T WANT TO STOP COLD WITH SOME SHOP-PING...
KISS

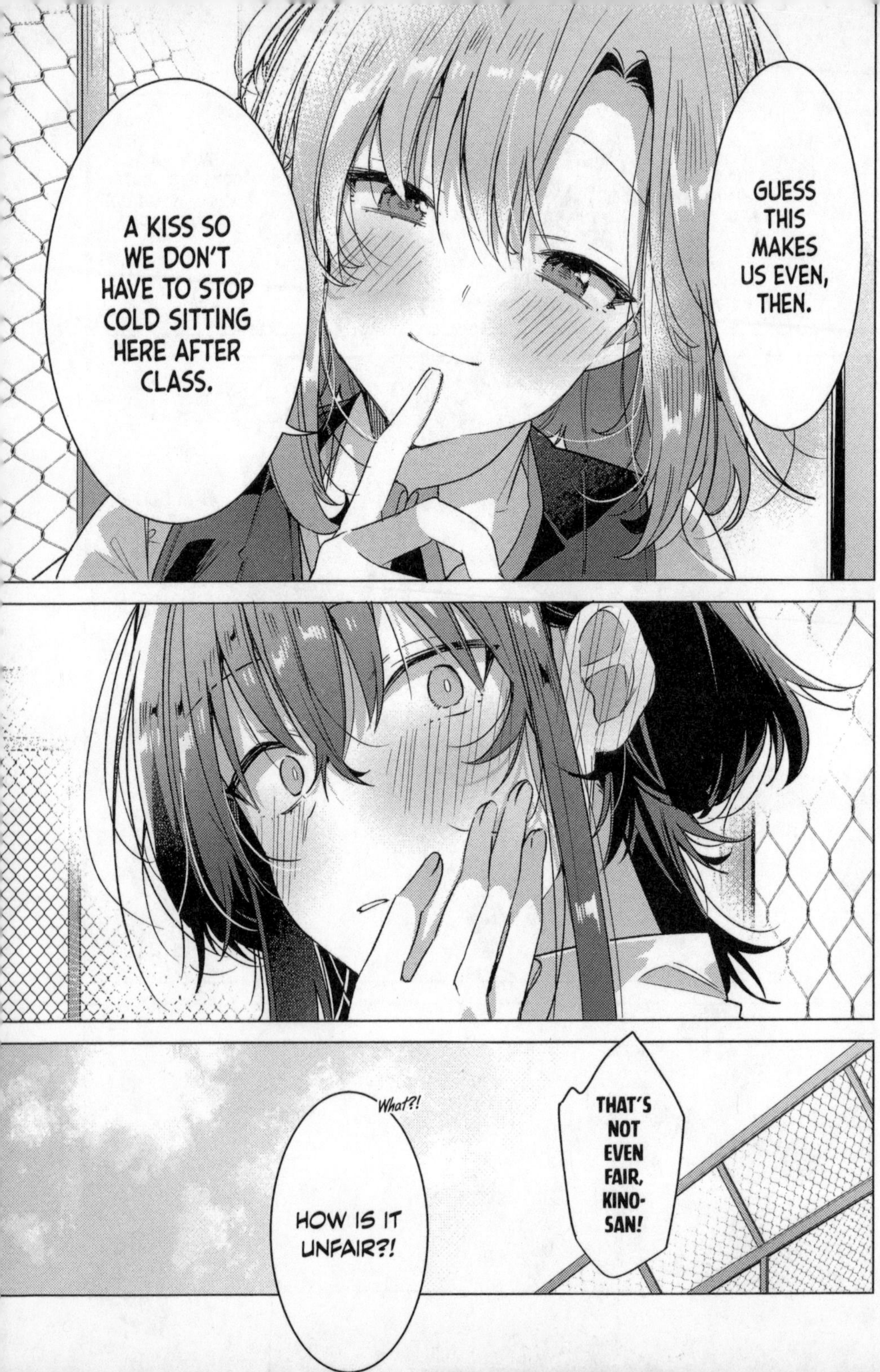
GUESS THIS MAKES US EVEN, THEN.
A KISS SO WE DON'T HAVE TO STOP COLD SITTING HERE AFTER CLASS.
THAT'S NOT EVEN FAIR, KINO-SAN!
What?!
HOW IS IT UNFAIR?!

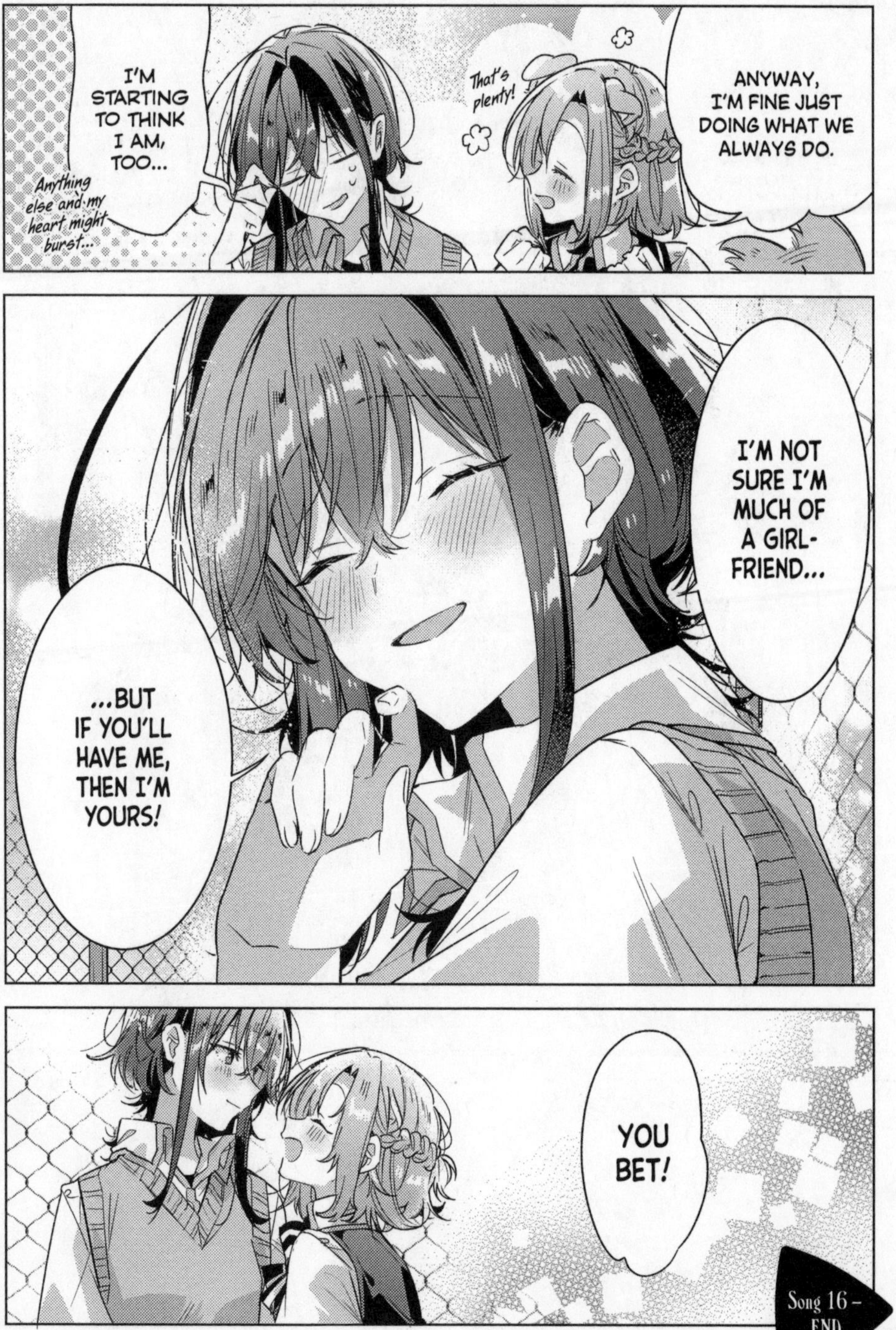
ANYWAY, I'M FINE JUST DOING WHAT WE ALWAYS DO.
That's plenty!
I'M STARTING TO THINK I AM, TOO...
Anything else and my heart might burst...
I'M NOT SURE I'M MUCH OF A GIRL-FRIEND...
...BUT IF YOU'LL HAVE ME, THEN I'M YOURS!
YOU BET!
Song 16 – END

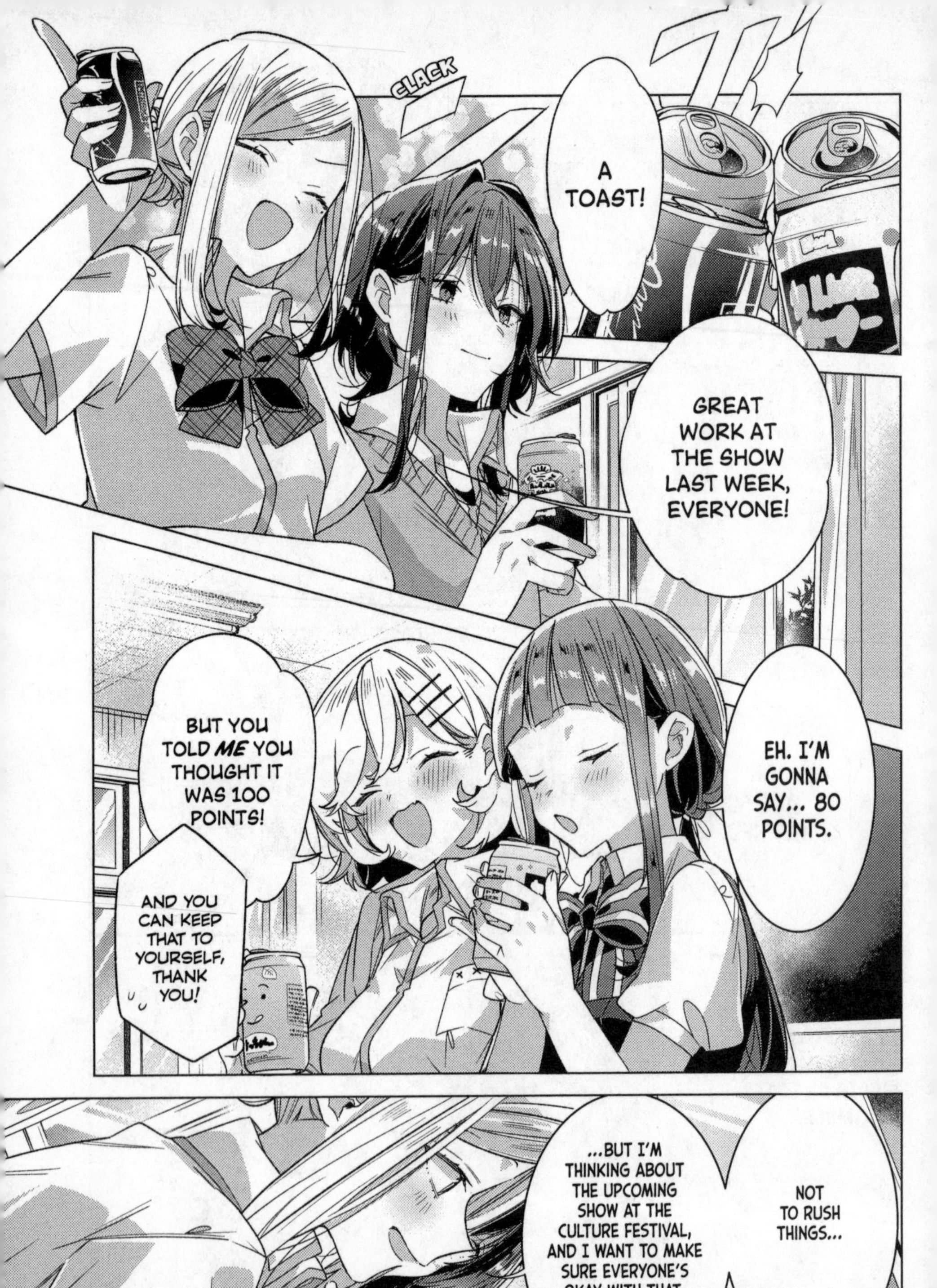

CLACK
A TOAST!
GREAT WORK AT THE SHOW LAST WEEK, EVERYONE!
EH. I'M GONNA SAY... 80 POINTS.
BUT YOU TOLD *ME* YOU THOUGHT IT WAS 100 POINTS!
AND YOU CAN KEEP THAT TO YOURSELF, THANK YOU!
NOT TO RUSH THINGS...
...BUT I'M THINKING ABOUT THE UPCOMING SHOW AT THE CULTURE FESTIVAL, AND I WANT TO MAKE SURE EVERYONE'S OKAY WITH THAT.

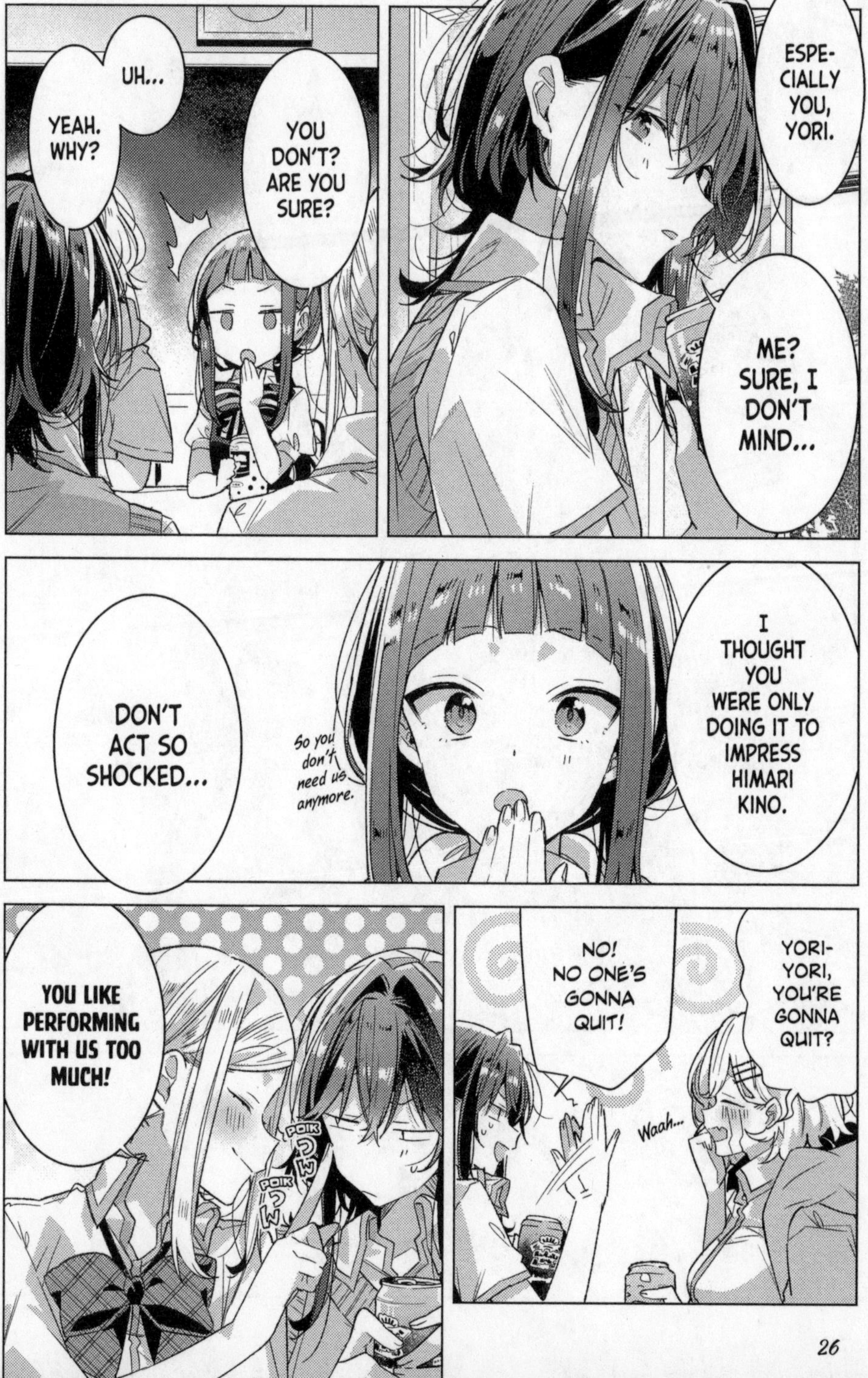
ESPE-CIALLY YOU, YORI.
ME? SURE, I DON'T MIND...
YOU DON'T? ARE YOU SURE?
UH... YEAH. WHY?
I THOUGHT YOU WERE ONLY DOING IT TO IMPRESS HIMARI KINO.
So you don't need us anymore.
DON'T ACT SO SHOCKED...
YORI-YORI, YOU'RE GONNA QUIT?
NO! NO ONE'S GONNA QUIT!
Waah...
YOU LIKE PERFORMING WITH US TOO MUCH!
POIK
POIK

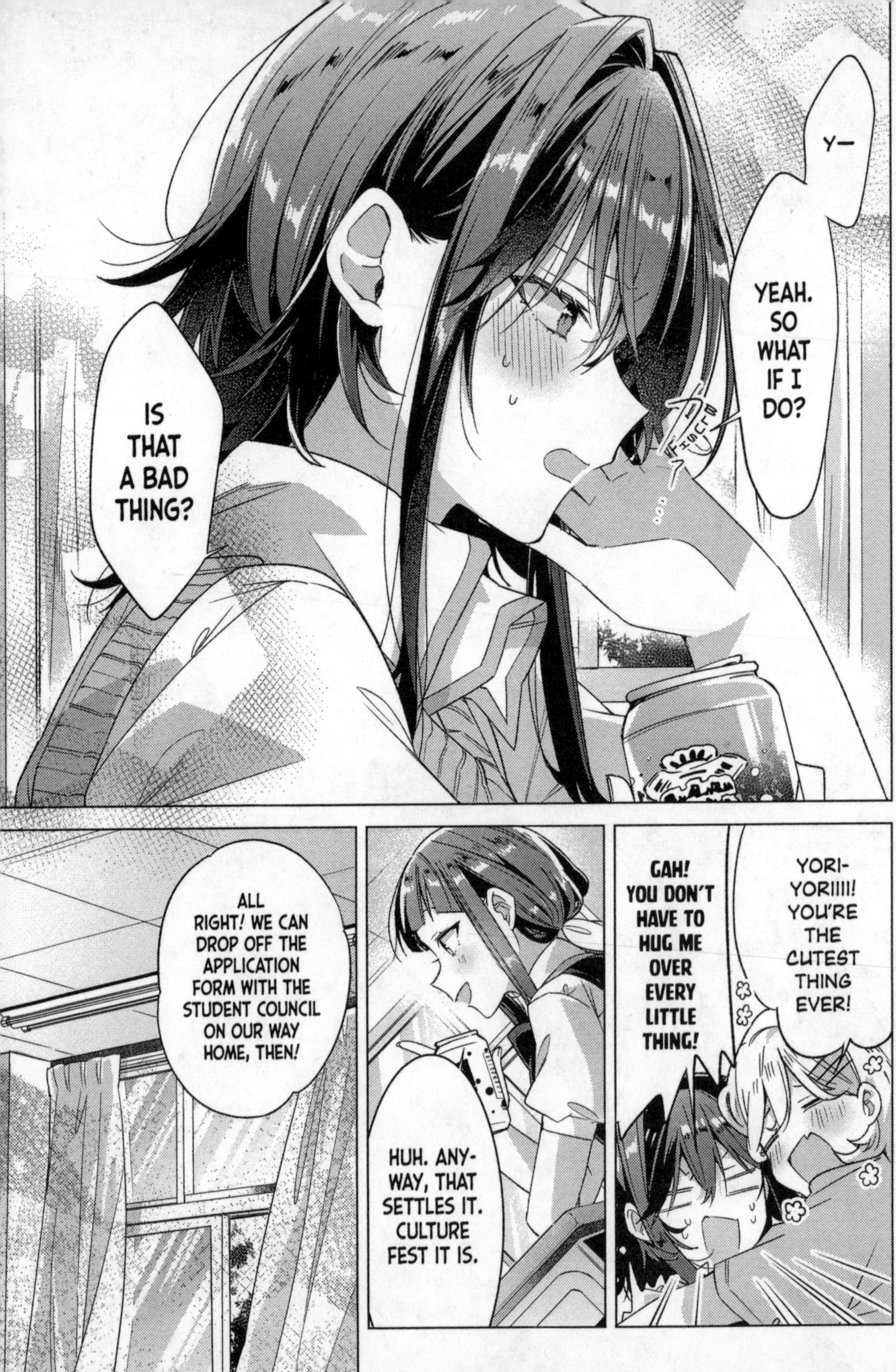
Y—
YEAH. SO WHAT IF I DO?
IS THAT A BAD THING?
YORI-YORIIIII! YOU'RE THE CUTEST THING EVER!
GAH! YOU DON'T HAVE TO HUG ME OVER EVERY LITTLE THING!
HUH. ANY-WAY, THAT SETTLES IT. CULTURE FEST IT IS.
ALL RIGHT! WE CAN DROP OFF THE APPLICATION FORM WITH THE STUDENT COUNCIL ON OUR WAY HOME, THEN!

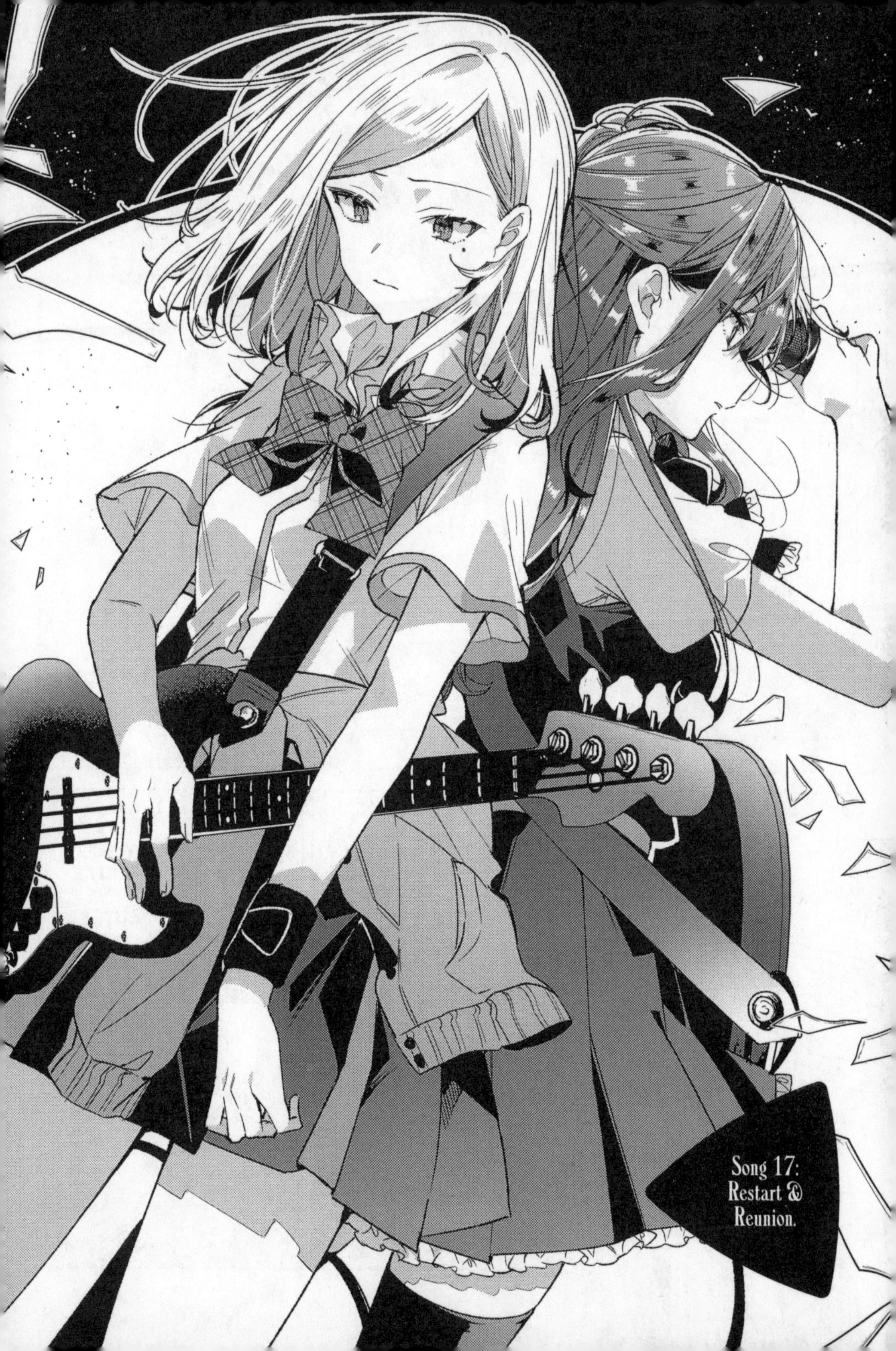
Song 17:
Restart &
Reunion.

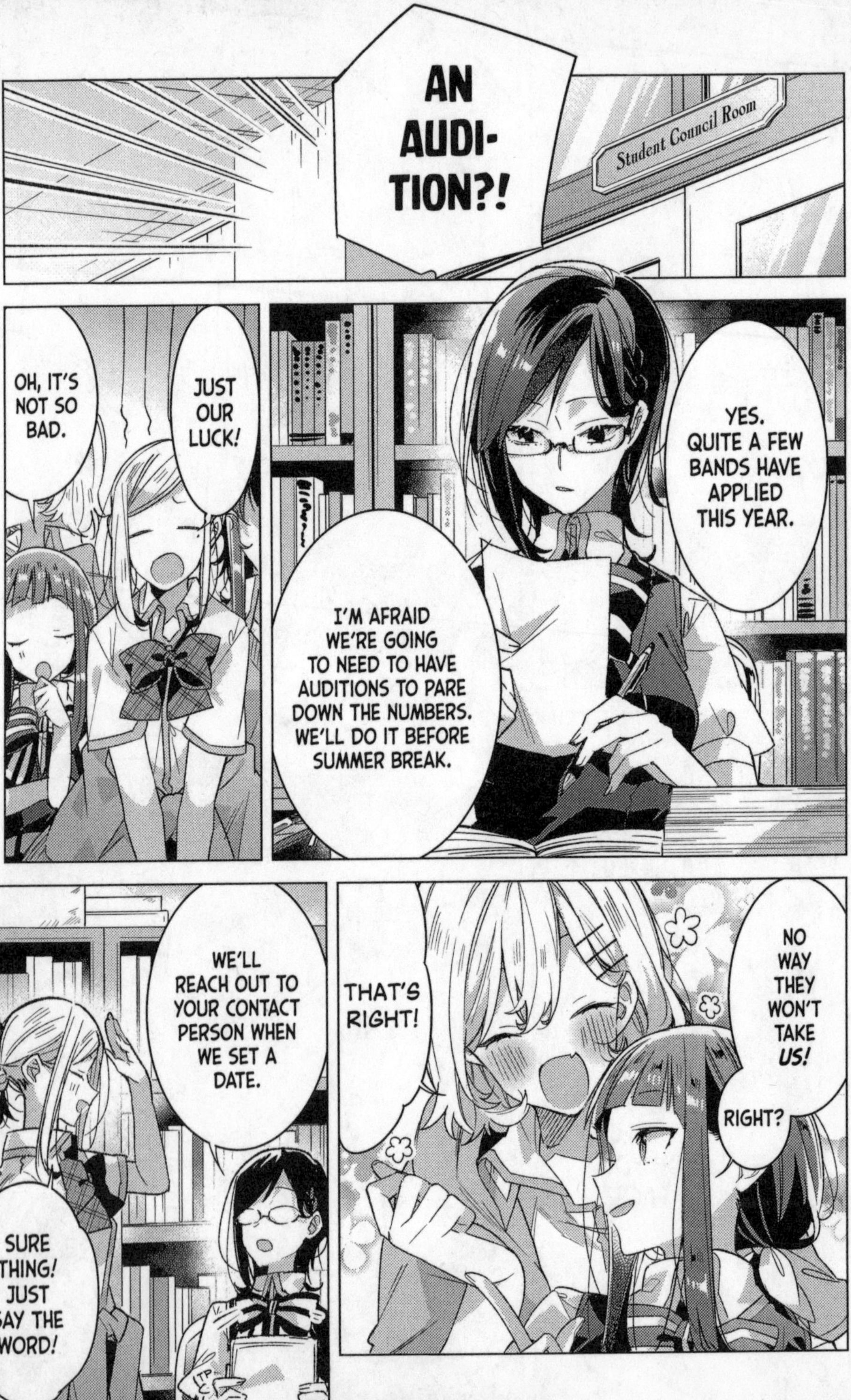
AN AUDI-TION?!
Student Council Room
YES. QUITE A FEW BANDS HAVE APPLIED THIS YEAR.
I'M AFRAID WE'RE GOING TO NEED TO HAVE AUDITIONS TO PARE DOWN THE NUMBERS. WE'LL DO IT BEFORE SUMMER BREAK.
JUST OUR LUCK!
OH, IT'S NOT SO BAD.
NO WAY THEY WON'T TAKE *US!*
RIGHT?
THAT'S RIGHT!
WE'LL REACH OUT TO YOUR CONTACT PERSON WHEN WE SET A DATE.
SURE THING! JUST SAY THE WORD!

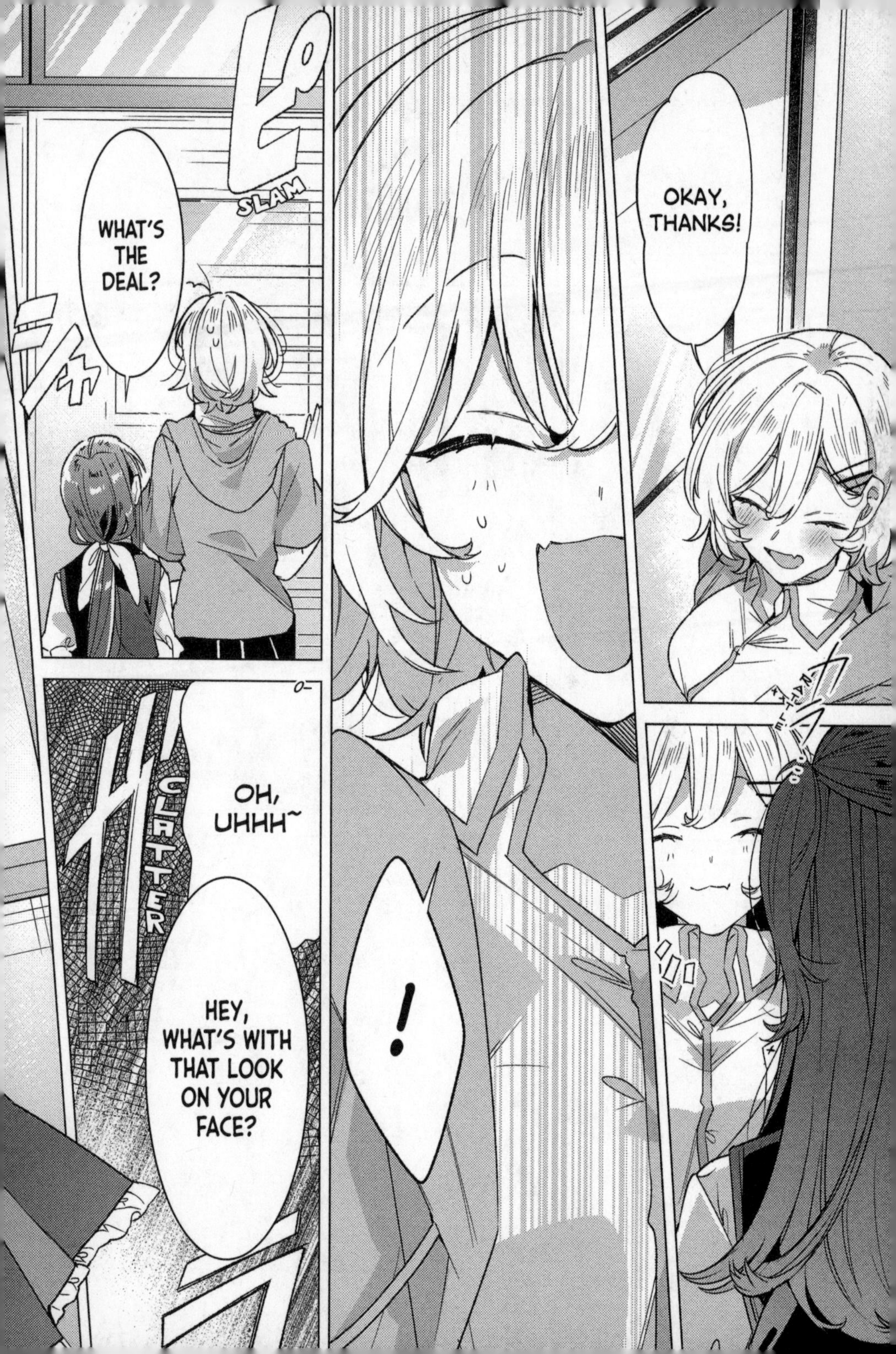
OKAY, THANKS!
RATTLE!
!
WHAT'S THE DEAL?
SLAM
OH, UHHH~
CLATTER
HEY, WHAT'S WITH THAT LOOK ON YOUR FACE?

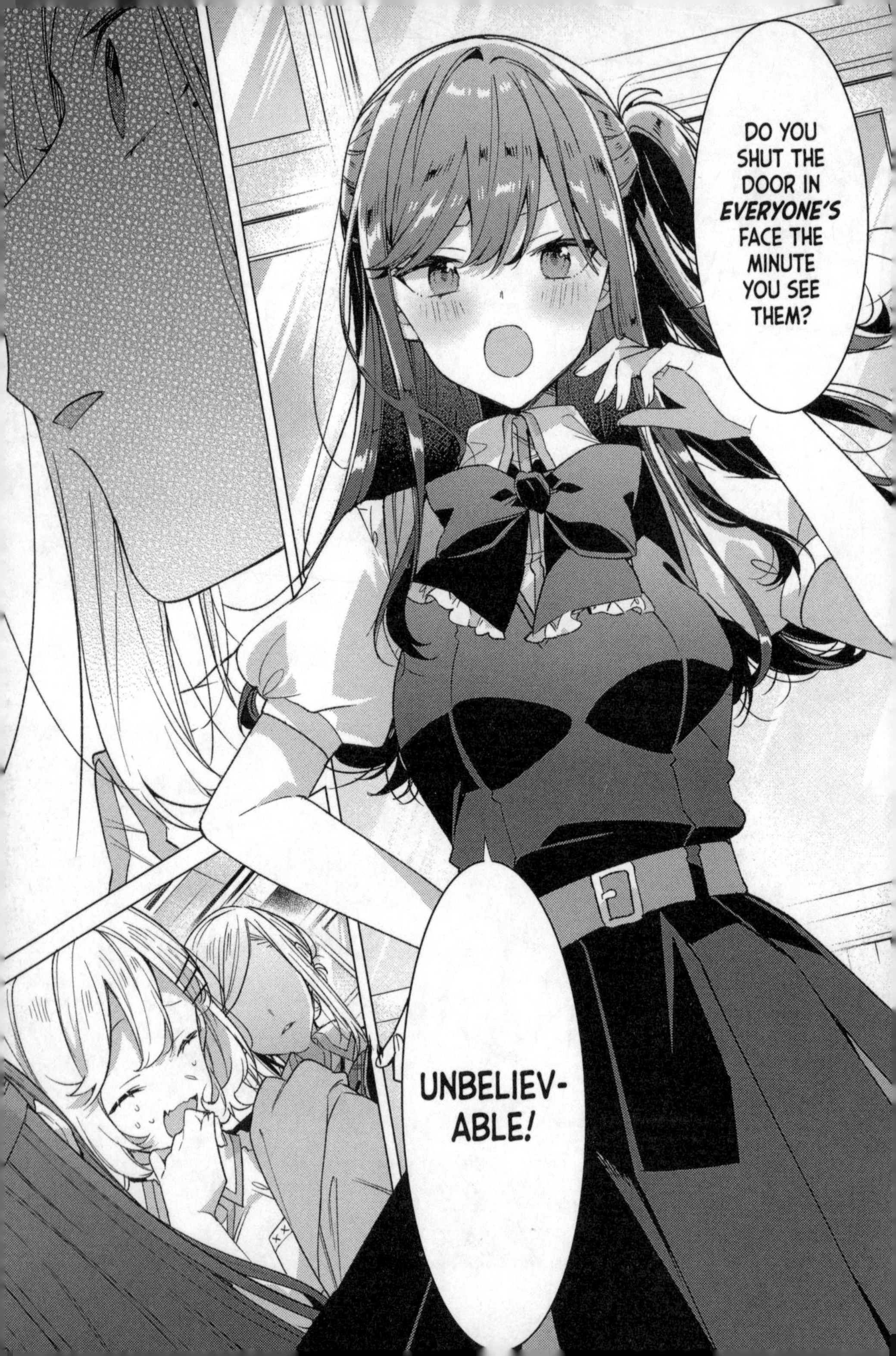
DO YOU SHUT THE DOOR IN *EVERYONE'S* FACE THE MINUTE YOU SEE THEM?
UNBELIEV-ABLE!

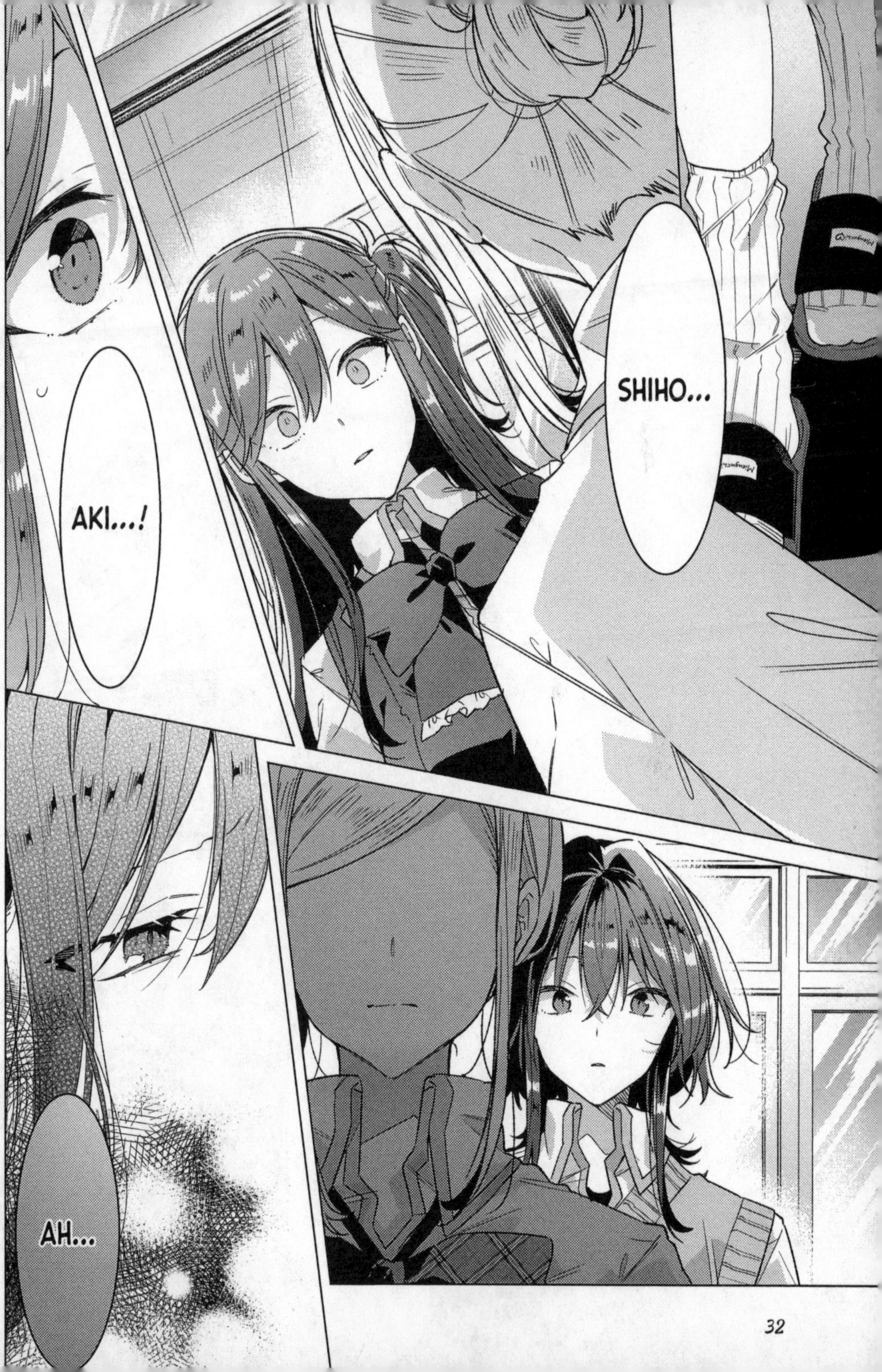
SHIHO...
AKI...!
AH...

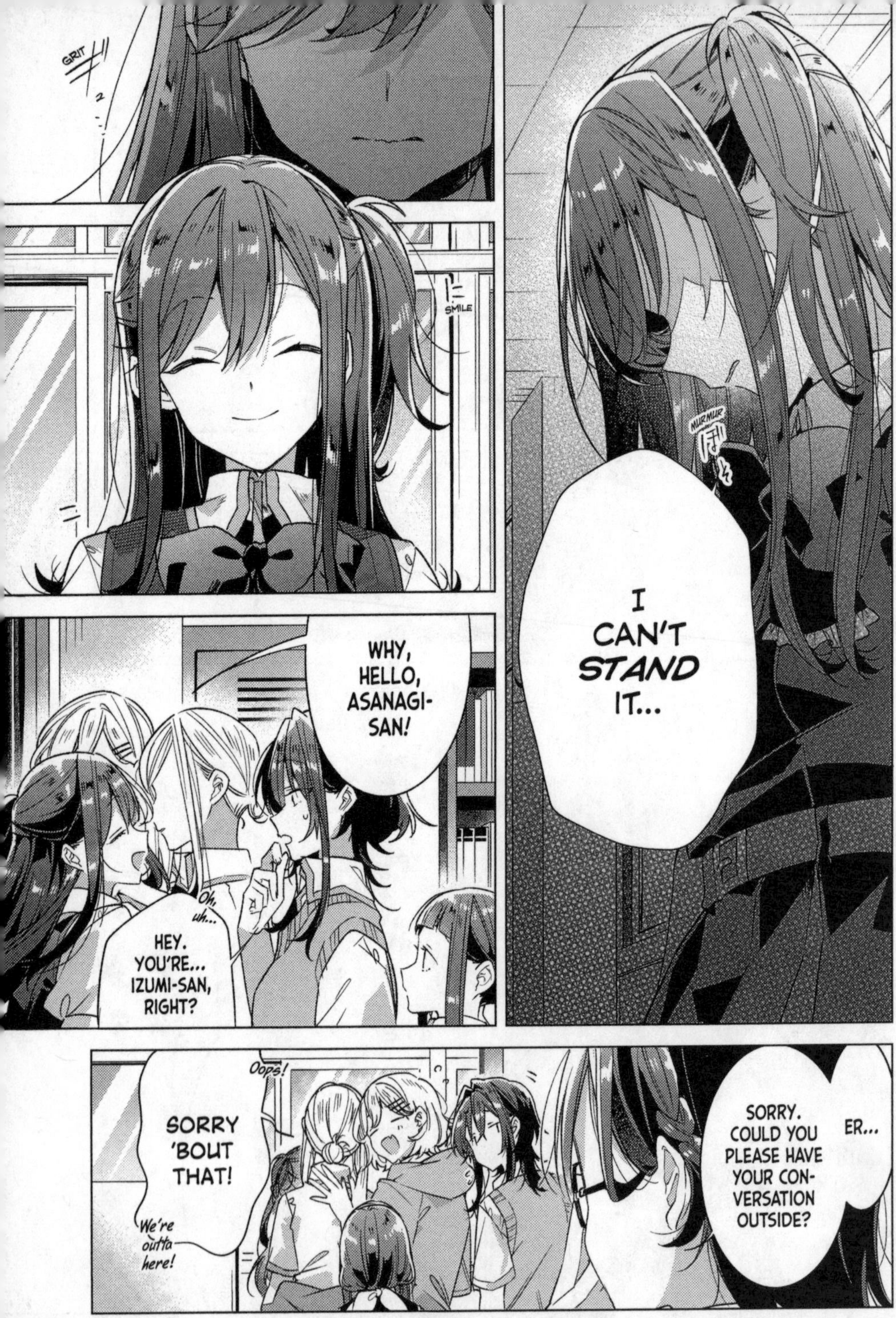
MURMUR
I CAN'T *STAND* IT...
GRIT
SMILE
WHY, HELLO, ASANAGI-SAN!
Oh, uh...
HEY. YOU'RE... IZUMI-SAN, RIGHT?
ER...
SORRY. COULD YOU PLEASE HAVE YOUR CON-VERSATION OUTSIDE?
Oops!
SORRY 'BOUT THAT!
We're outta here!

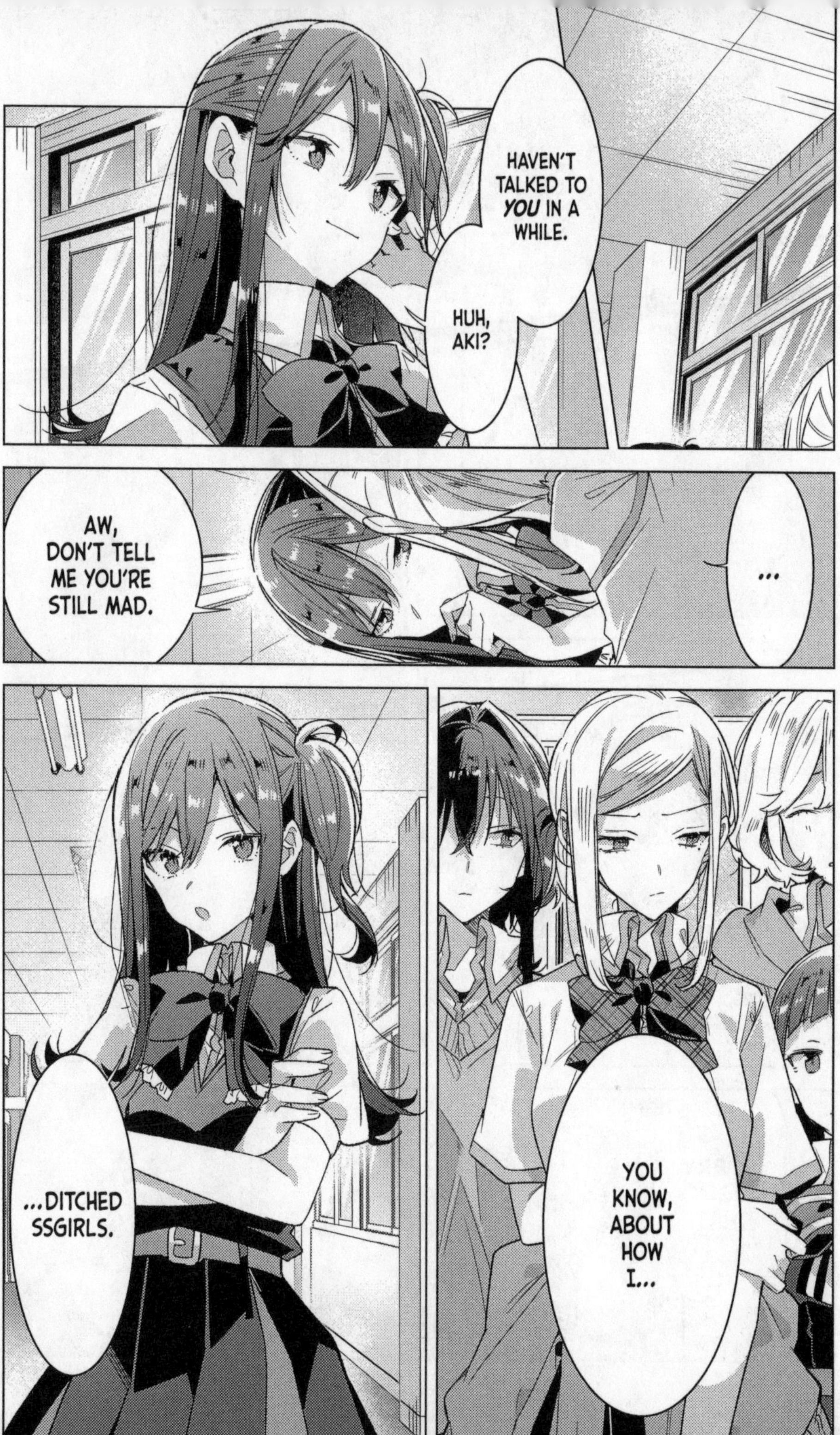
HAVEN'T TALKED TO *YOU* IN A WHILE.
HUH, AKI?
...
AW, DON'T TELL ME YOU'RE STILL MAD.
YOU KNOW, ABOUT HOW I...
...DITCHED SSGIRLS.

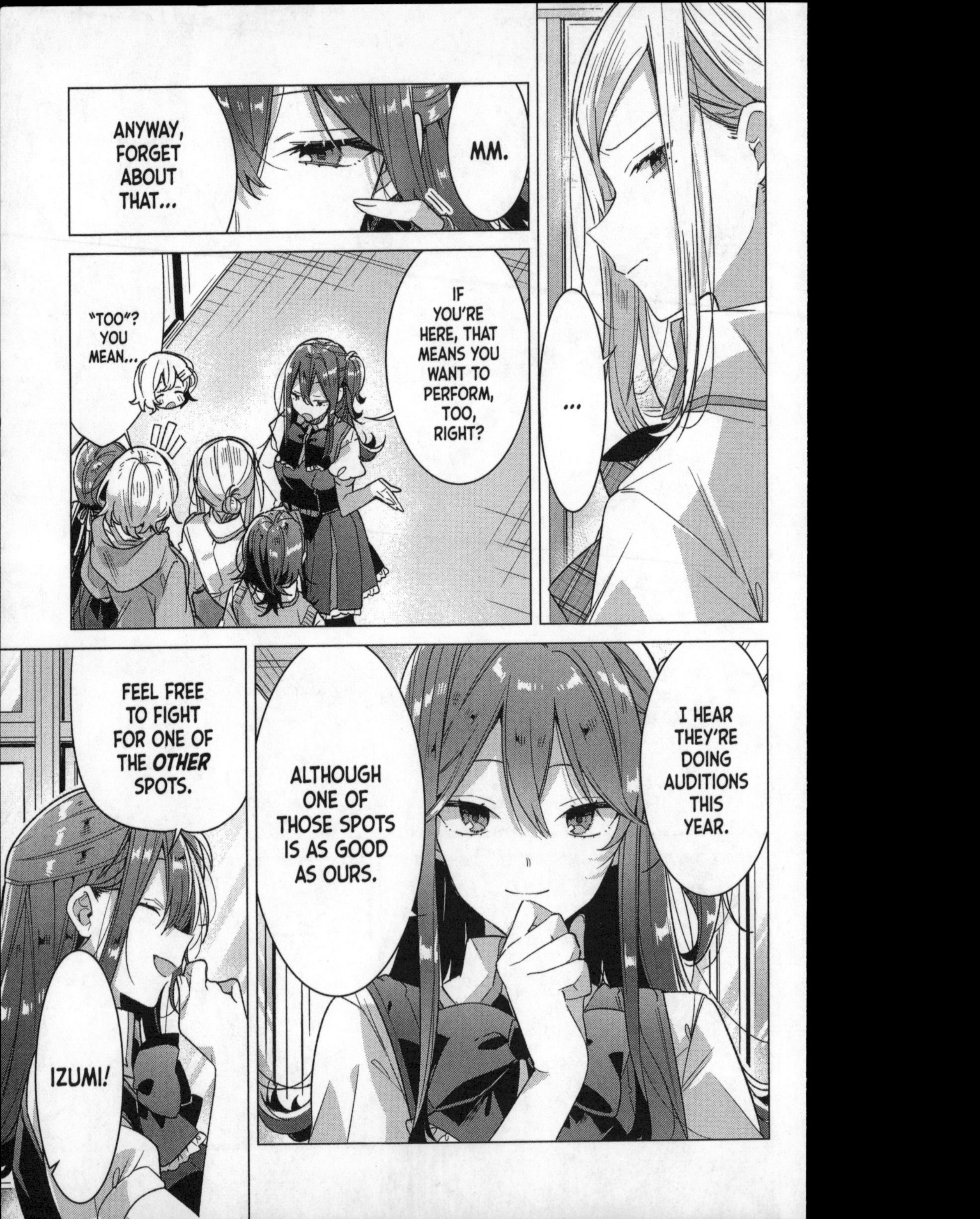
...
MM.
ANYWAY, FORGET ABOUT THAT...
IF YOU'RE HERE, THAT MEANS YOU WANT TO PERFORM, TOO, RIGHT?
"TOO"? YOU MEAN...
I HEAR THEY'RE DOING AUDITIONS THIS YEAR.
ALTHOUGH ONE OF THOSE SPOTS IS AS GOOD AS OURS.
FEEL FREE TO FIGHT FOR ONE OF THE *OTHER* SPOTS.
IZUMI!

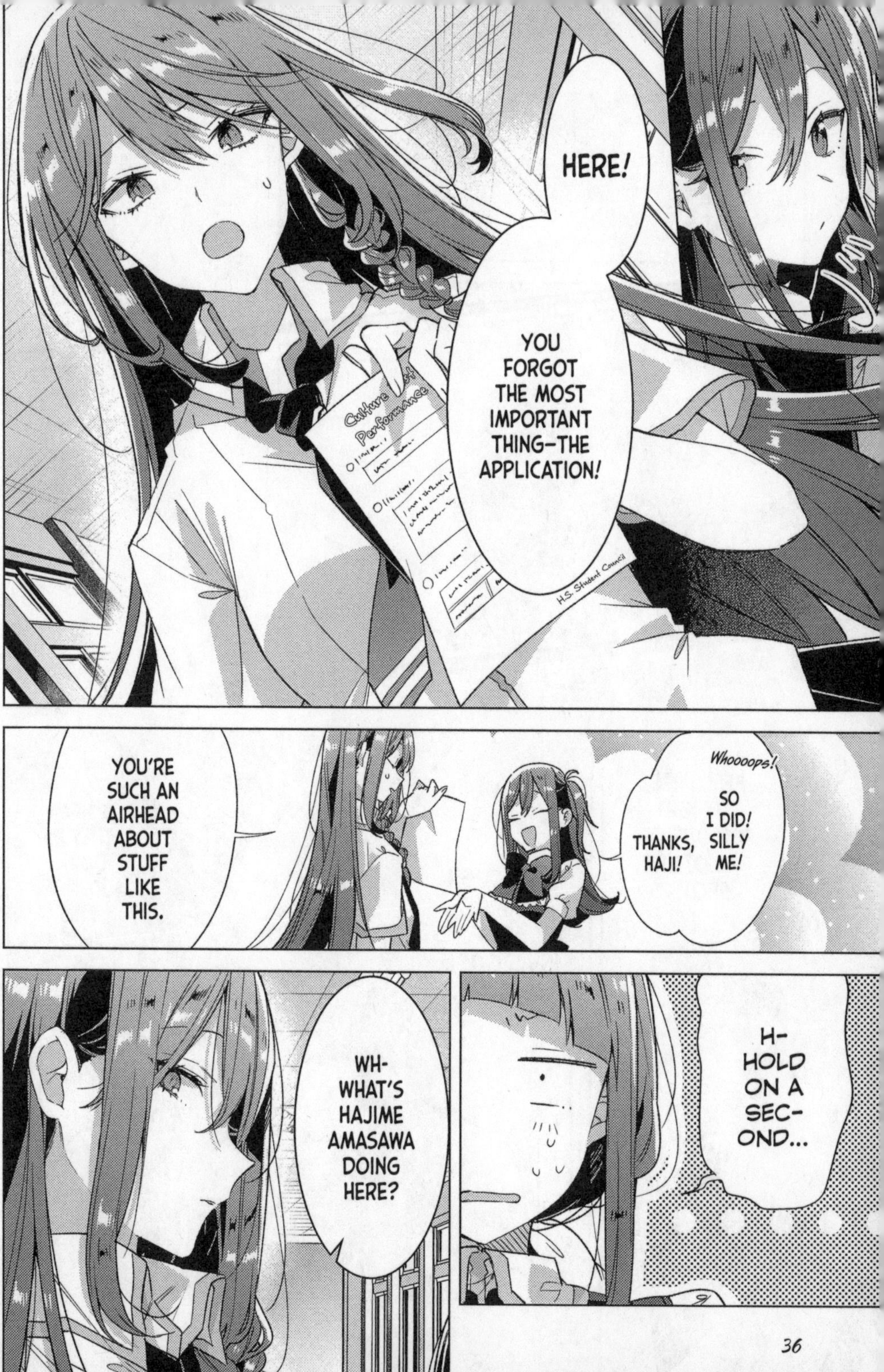
HERE!
YOU FORGOT THE MOST IMPORTANT THING—THE APPLICATION!
Performance
H.S. Student Council
Whoooops!
SO I DID! SILLY ME!
THANKS, HAJI!
YOU'RE SUCH AN AIRHEAD ABOUT STUFF LIKE THIS.
H-HOLD ON A SEC-OND...
WH-WHAT'S HAJIME AMASAWA DOING HERE?

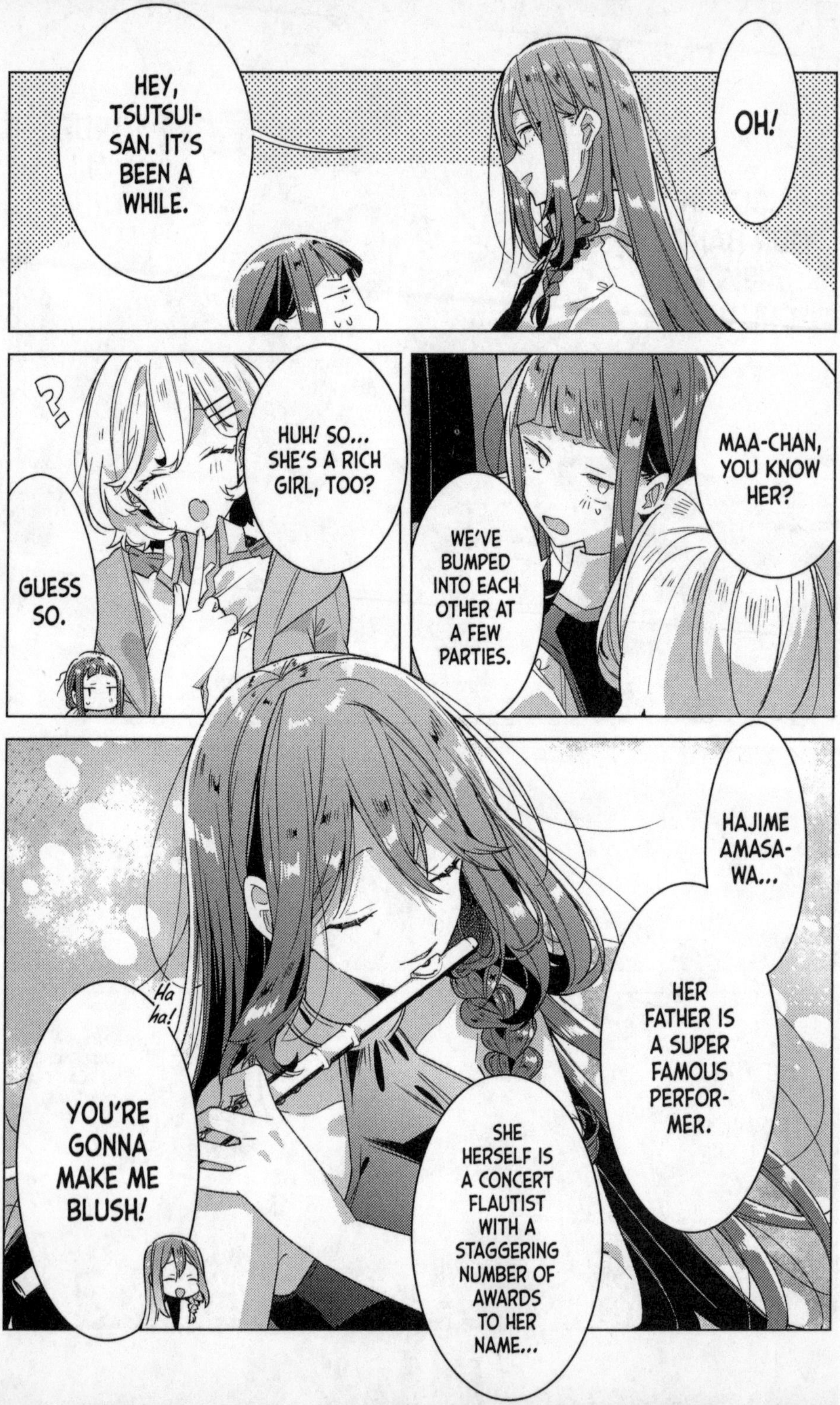
OH!
HEY, TSUTSUI-SAN. IT'S BEEN A WHILE.
MAA-CHAN, YOU KNOW HER?
WE'VE BUMPED INTO EACH OTHER AT A FEW PARTIES.
?
HUH! SO... SHE'S A RICH GIRL, TOO?
GUESS SO.
HAJIME AMASA-WA...
HER FATHER IS A SUPER FAMOUS PERFORMER.
SHE HERSELF IS A CONCERT FLAUTIST WITH A STAGGERING NUMBER OF AWARDS TO HER NAME...
Ha ha!
YOU'RE GONNA MAKE ME BLUSH!

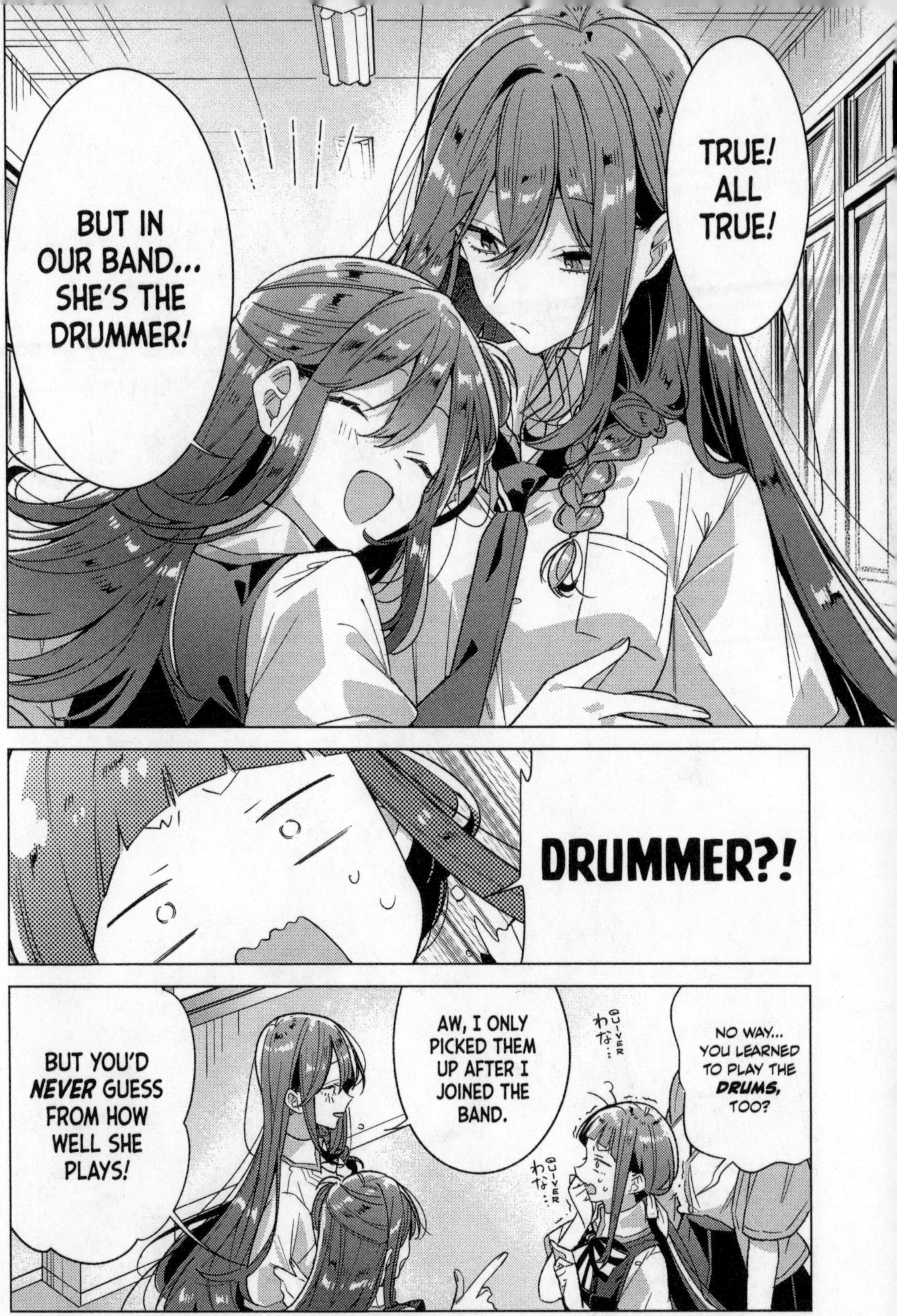
TRUE! ALL TRUE!
BUT IN OUR BAND... SHE'S THE DRUMMER!
DRUMMER?!
NO WAY... YOU LEARNED TO PLAY THE *DRUMS,* TOO?
QUIVER
QUIVER
AW, I ONLY PICKED THEM UP AFTER I JOINED THE BAND.
BUT YOU'D *NEVER* GUESS FROM HOW WELL SHE PLAYS!

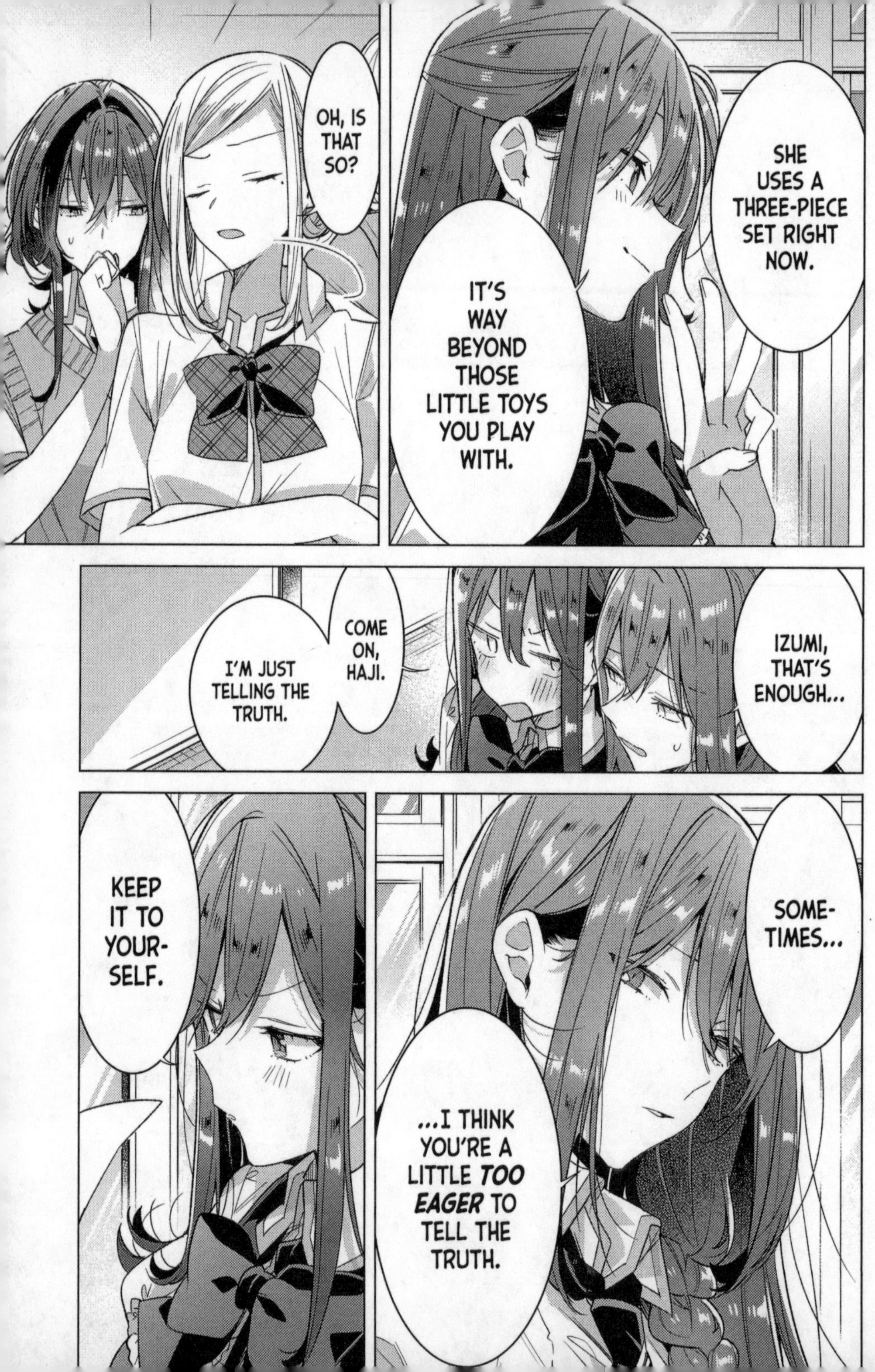

SHE USES A THREE-PIECE SET RIGHT NOW.
IT'S WAY BEYOND THOSE LITTLE TOYS YOU PLAY WITH.
OH, IS THAT SO?
IZUMI, THAT'S ENOUGH...
COME ON, HAJI.
I'M JUST TELLING THE TRUTH.
SOME-TIMES...
...I THINK YOU'RE A LITTLE *TOO EAGER* TO TELL THE TRUTH.
KEEP IT TO YOUR-SELF.

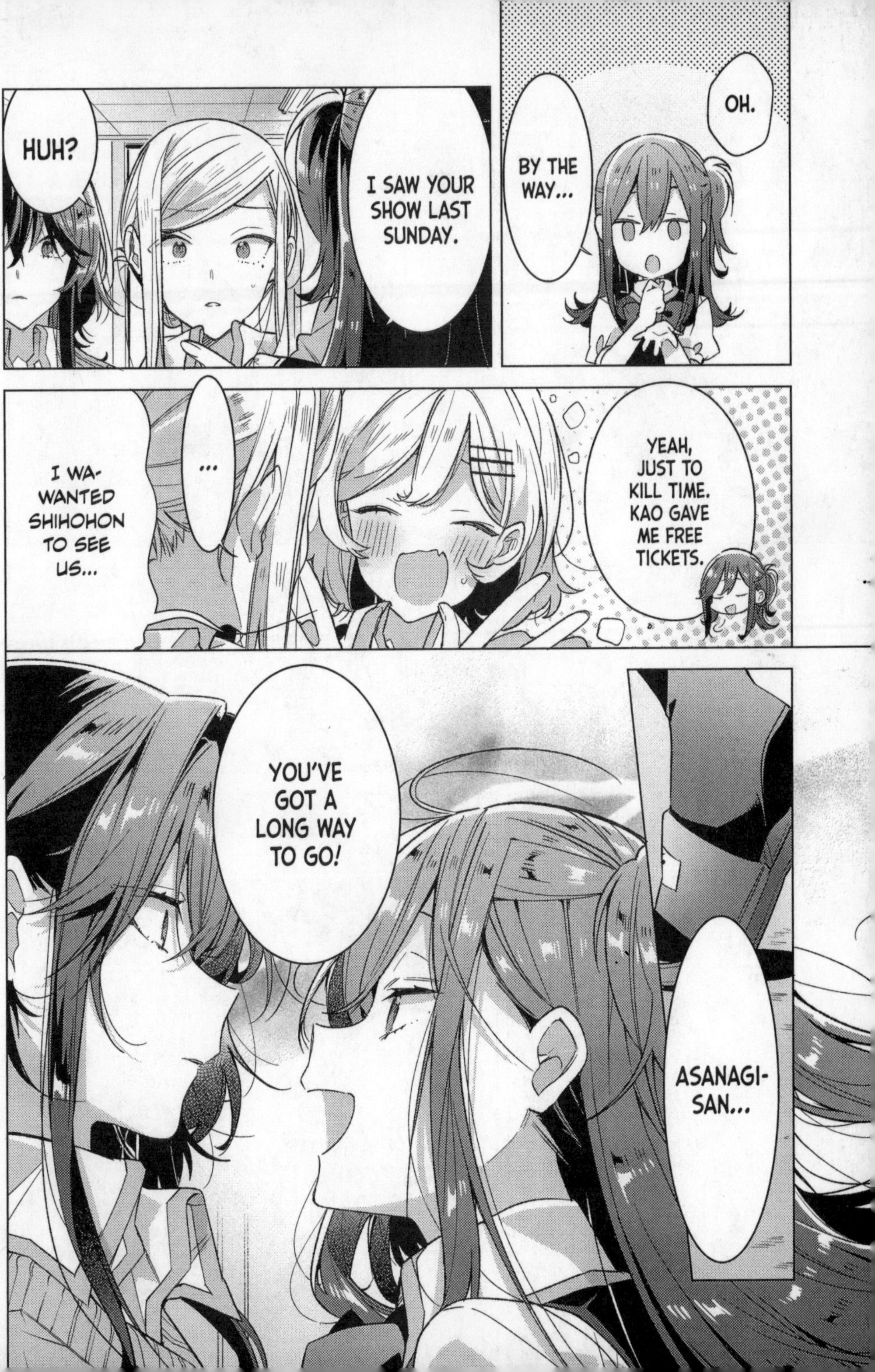
OH.
BY THE WAY...
I SAW YOUR SHOW LAST SUNDAY.
HUH?
YEAH, JUST TO KILL TIME. KAO GAVE ME FREE TICKETS.
...
I WA-WANTED SHIHOHON TO SEE US...
ASANAGI-SAN...
YOU'VE GOT A LONG WAY TO GO!

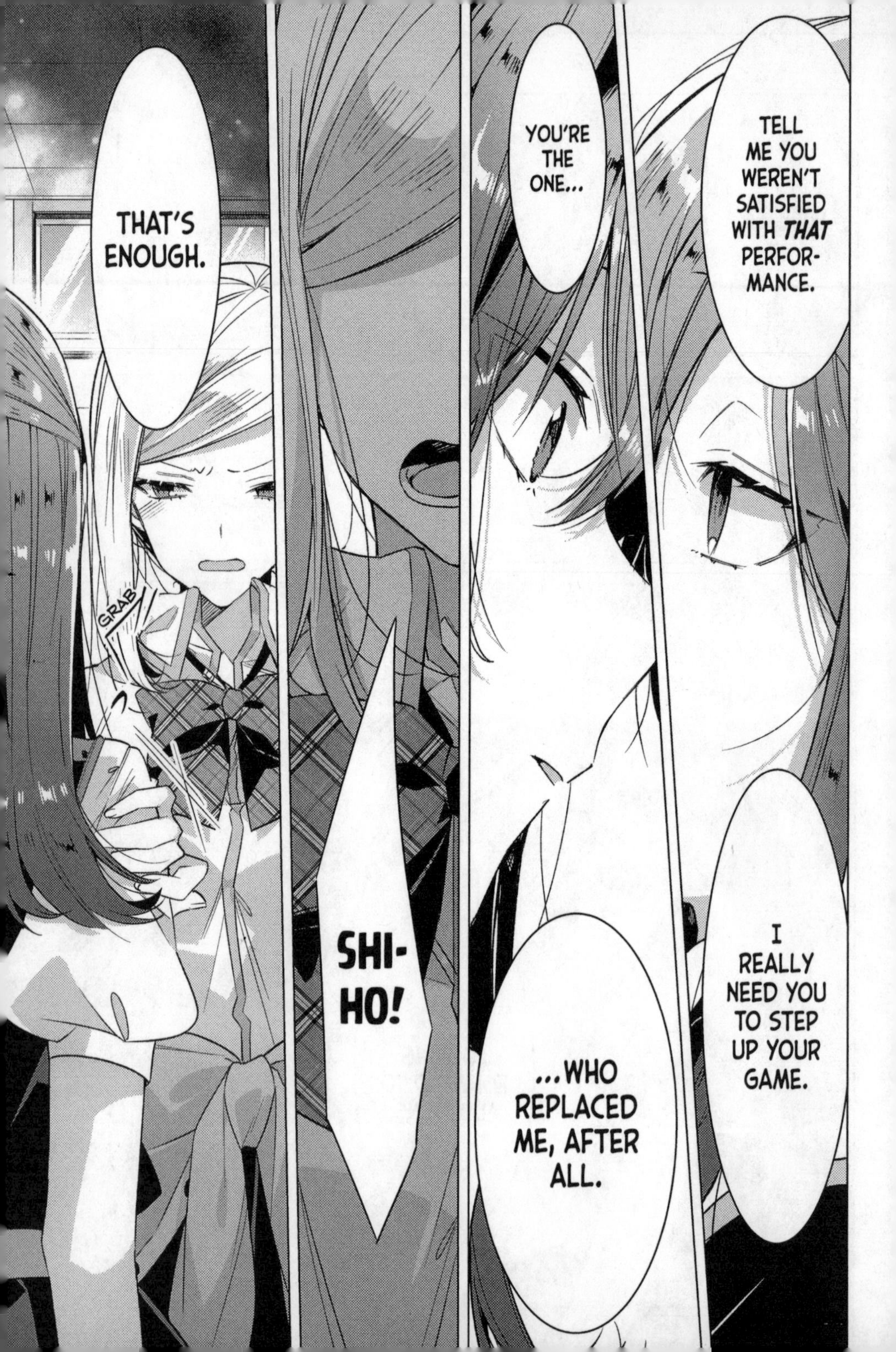
TELL ME YOU WEREN'T SATISFIED WITH *THAT* PERFORMANCE.
I REALLY NEED YOU TO STEP UP YOUR GAME.
YOU'RE THE ONE...
...WHO REPLACED ME, AFTER ALL.
SHI-HO!
THAT'S ENOUGH.
GRAB

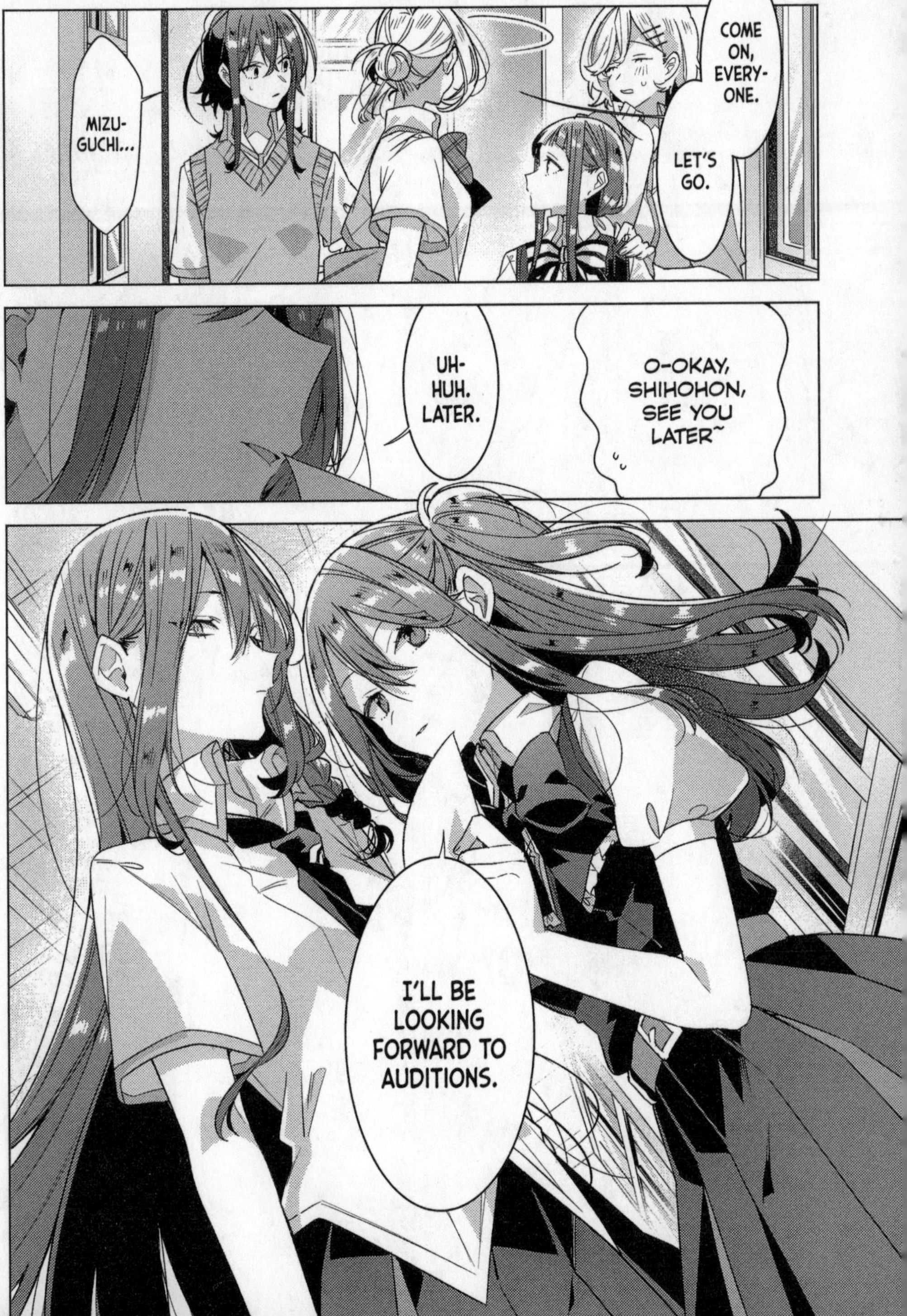
COME ON, EVERY-ONE.
LET'S GO.
MIZU-GUCHI...
O-OKAY, SHIHOHON, SEE YOU LATER~
UH-HUH. LATER.
I'LL BE LOOKING FORWARD TO AUDITIONS.

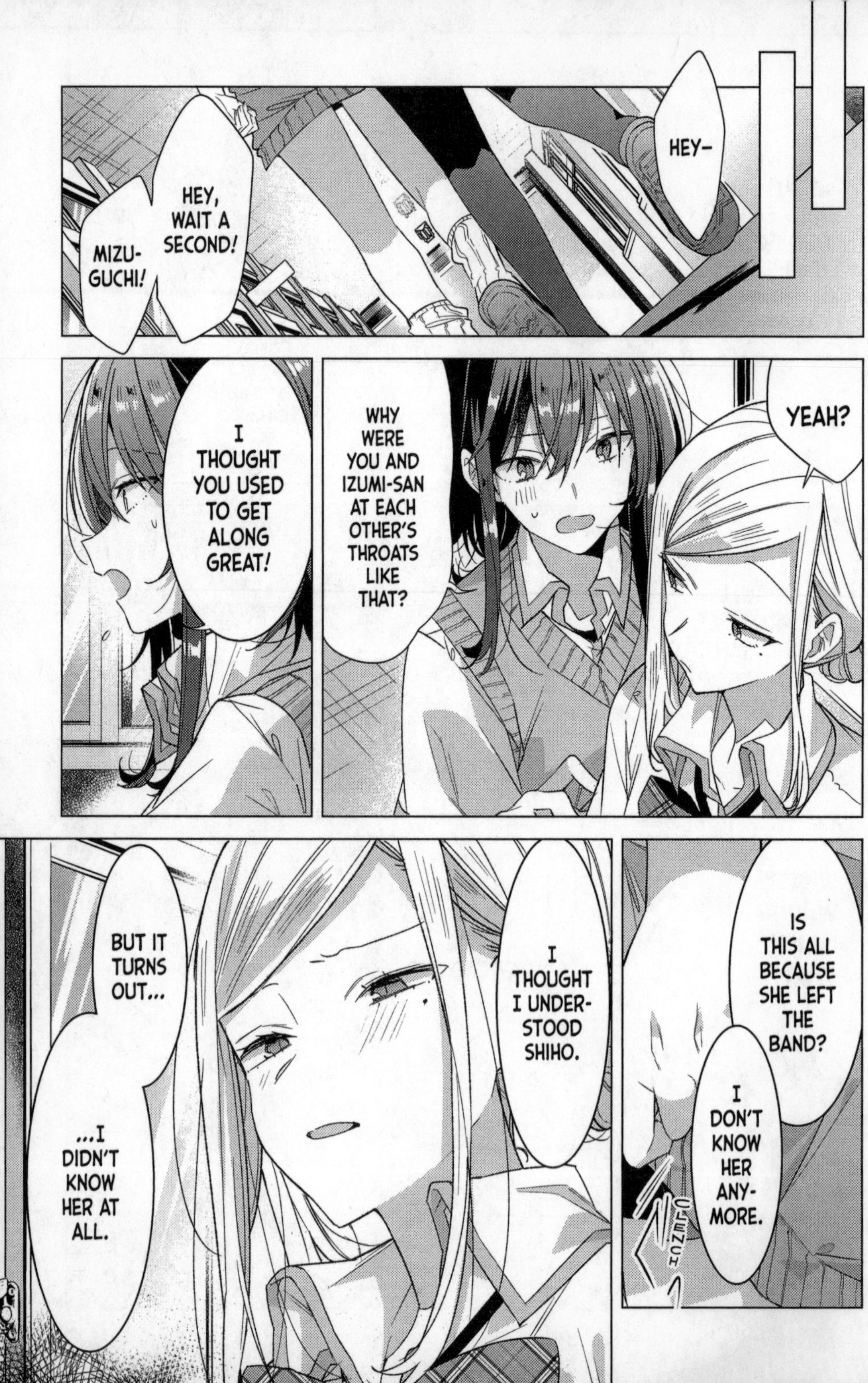

HEY–
HEY, WAIT A SECOND!
MIZU-GUCHI!
YEAH?
WHY WERE YOU AND IZUMI-SAN AT EACH OTHER'S THROATS LIKE THAT?
I THOUGHT YOU USED TO GET ALONG GREAT!
IS THIS ALL BECAUSE SHE LEFT THE BAND?
I DON'T KNOW HER ANY-MORE.
CLENCH
I THOUGHT I UNDER-STOOD SHIHO.
BUT IT TURNS OUT...
...I DIDN'T KNOW HER AT ALL.

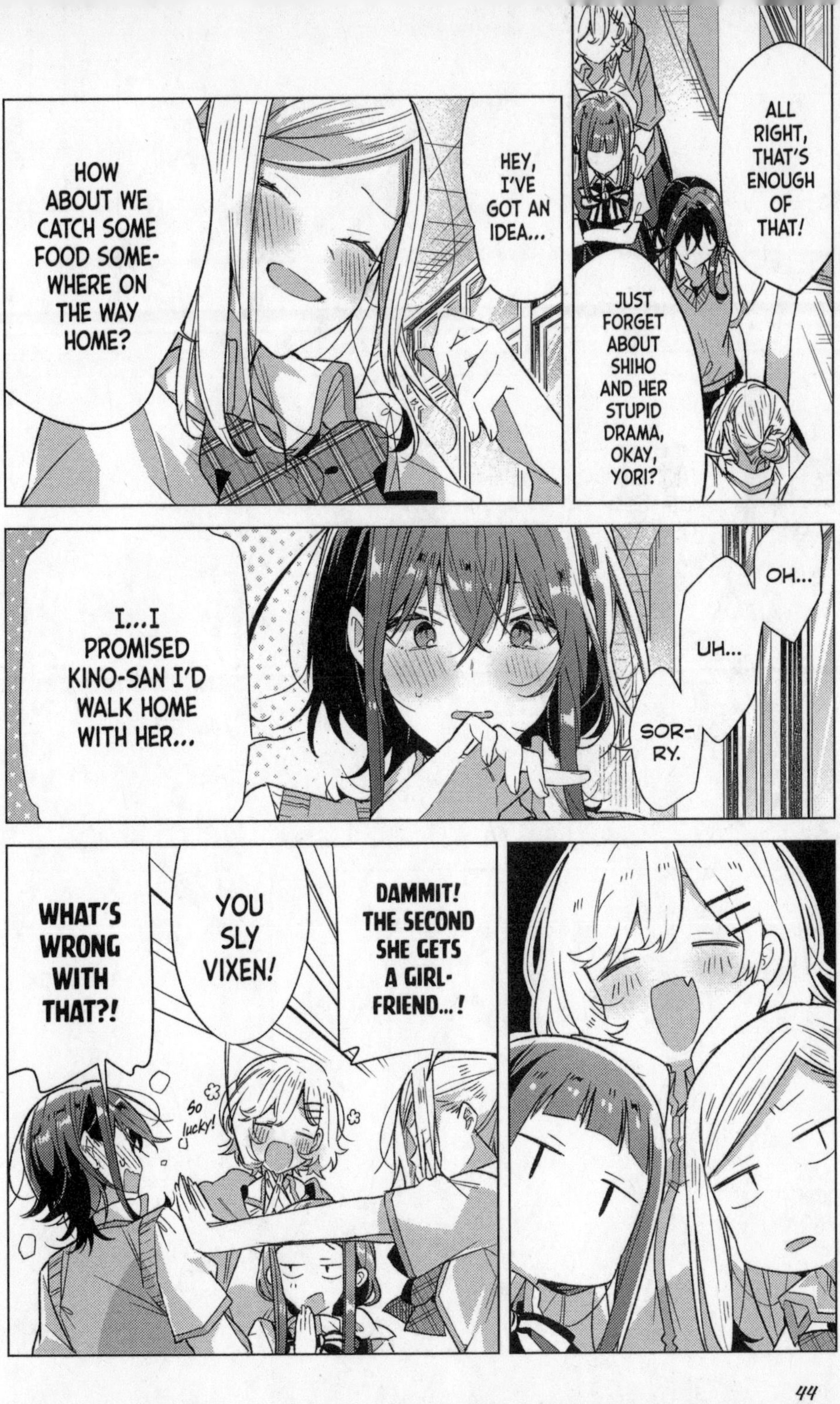
ALL RIGHT, THAT'S ENOUGH OF THAT!
JUST FORGET ABOUT SHIHO AND HER STUPID DRAMA, OKAY, YORI?
HEY, I'VE GOT AN IDEA...
HOW ABOUT WE CATCH SOME FOOD SOME-WHERE ON THE WAY HOME?
OH...
UH...
SOR-RY.
I...I PROMISED KINO-SAN I'D WALK HOME WITH HER...
DAMMIT! THE SECOND SHE GETS A GIRL-FRIEND...!
YOU SLY VIXEN!
WHAT'S WRONG WITH THAT?!
So lucky!

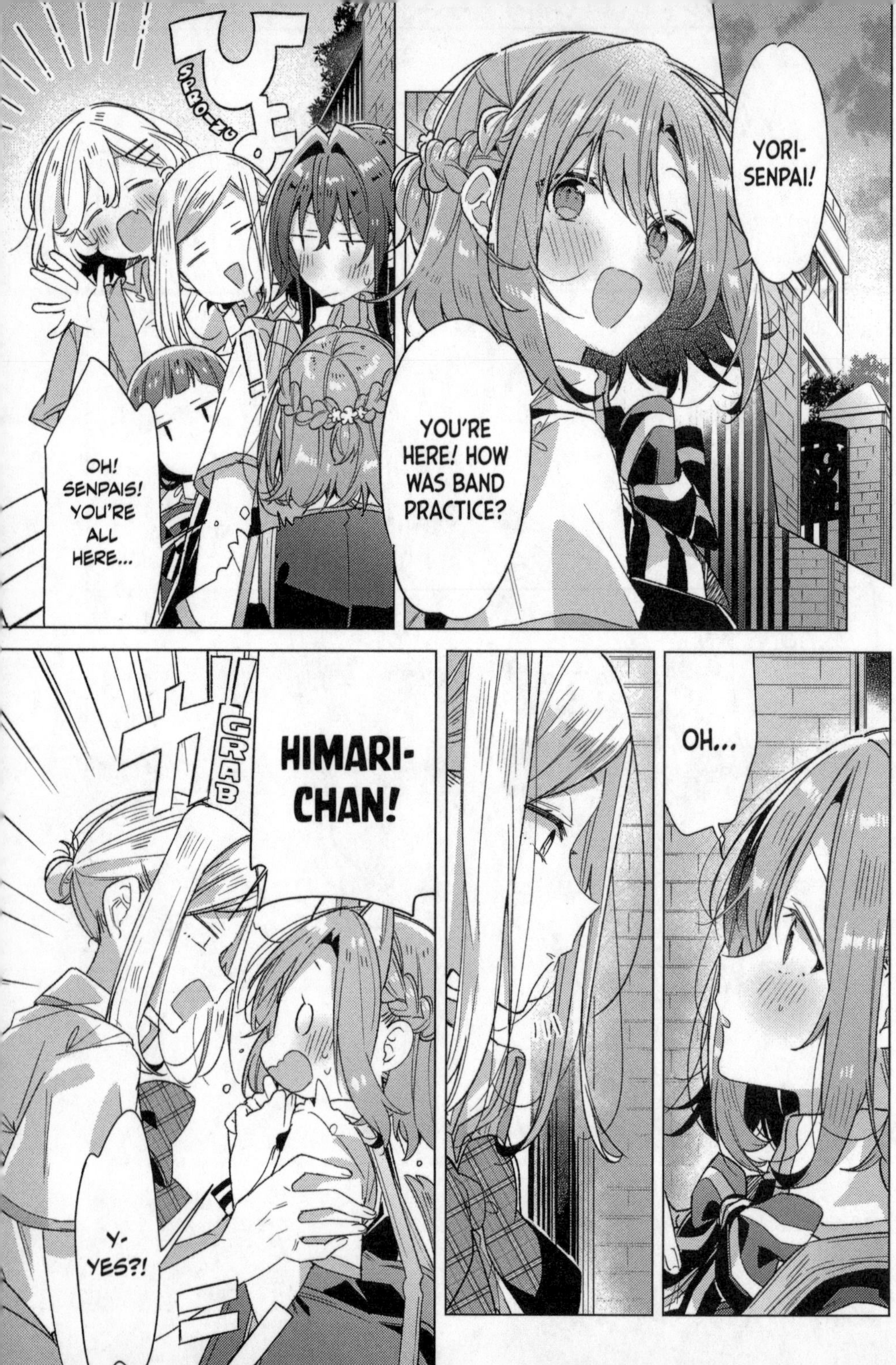
YORI-SENPAI!
YOU'RE HERE! HOW WAS BAND PRACTICE?
SPRO-ZU
OH! SENPAIS! YOU'RE ALL HERE...
OH...
HIMARI-CHAN!
GRAB
Y-YES?!

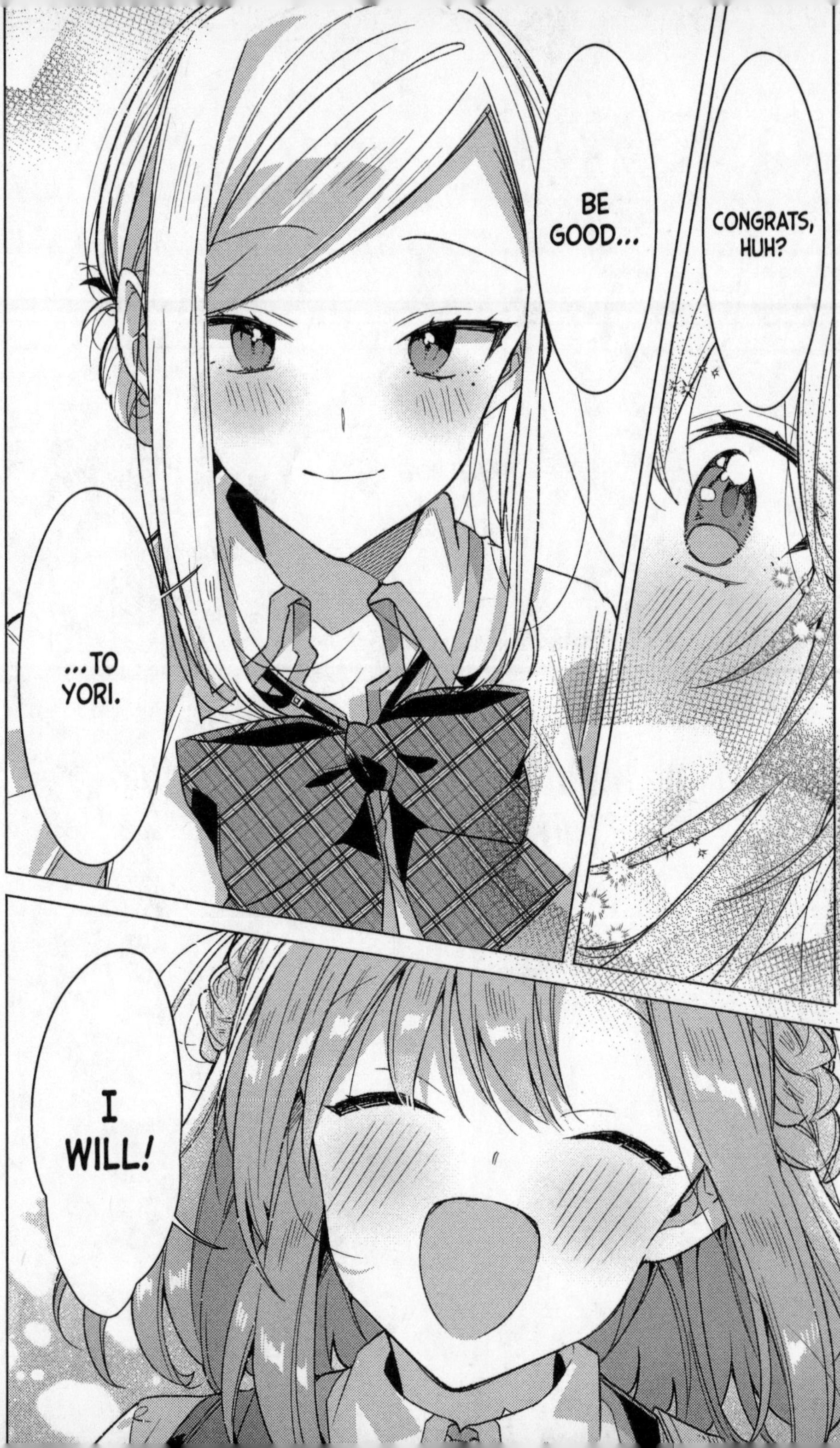
CONGRATS, HUH?
BE GOOD...
...TO YORI.
I WILL!

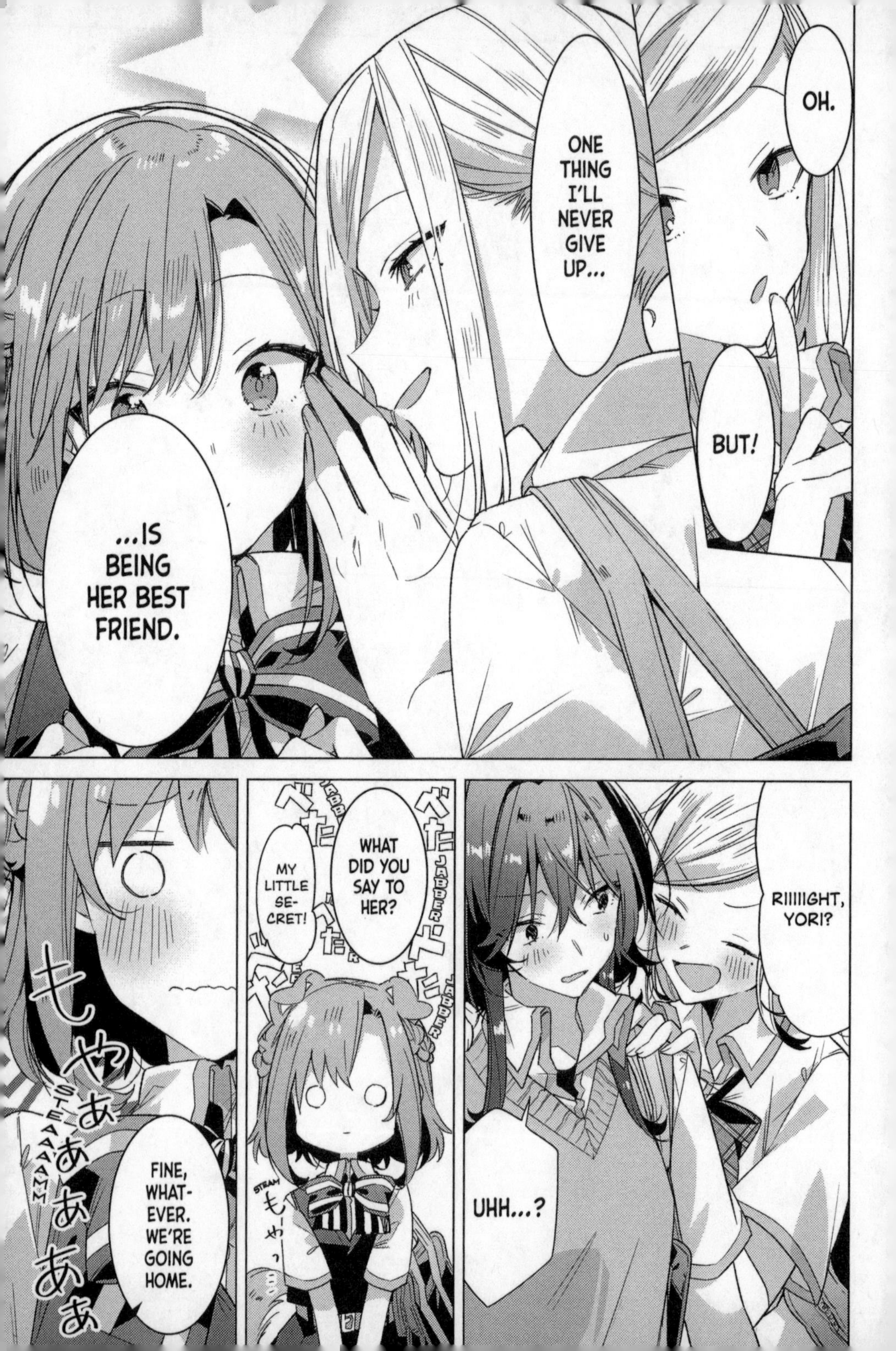
OH.
BUT!
ONE THING I'LL NEVER GIVE UP...
...IS BEING HER BEST FRIEND.
RIIIIGHT, YORI?
UHH...?
WHAT DID YOU SAY TO HER?
MY LITTLE SE-CRET!
JABBER
JABBER
STEAM
もやーっ
FINE, WHAT-EVER. WE'RE GOING HOME.
STEAAAAMM
もやぁぁぁぁ

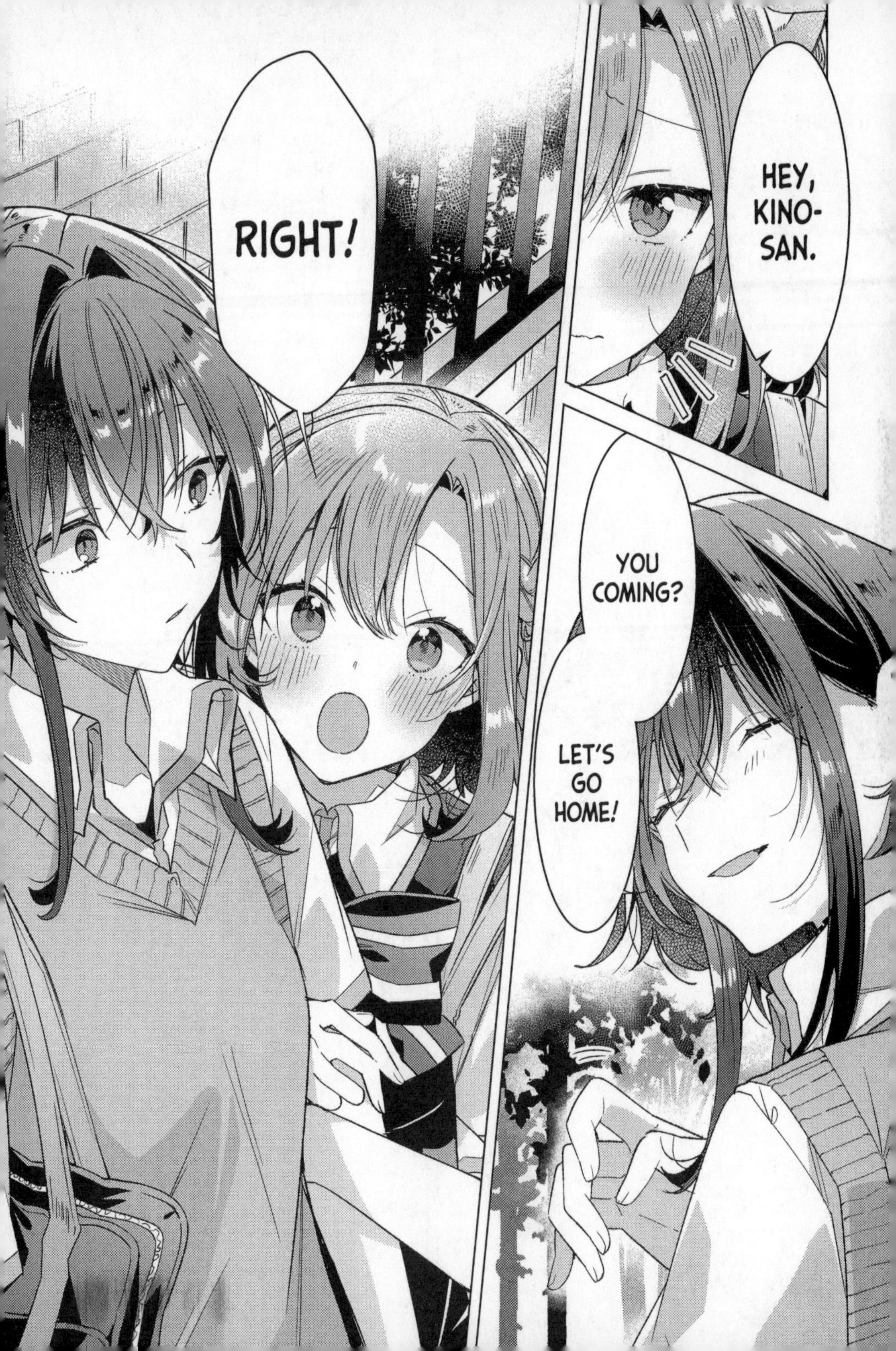
HEY, KINO-SAN.
YOU COMING?
LET'S GO HOME!
RIGHT!

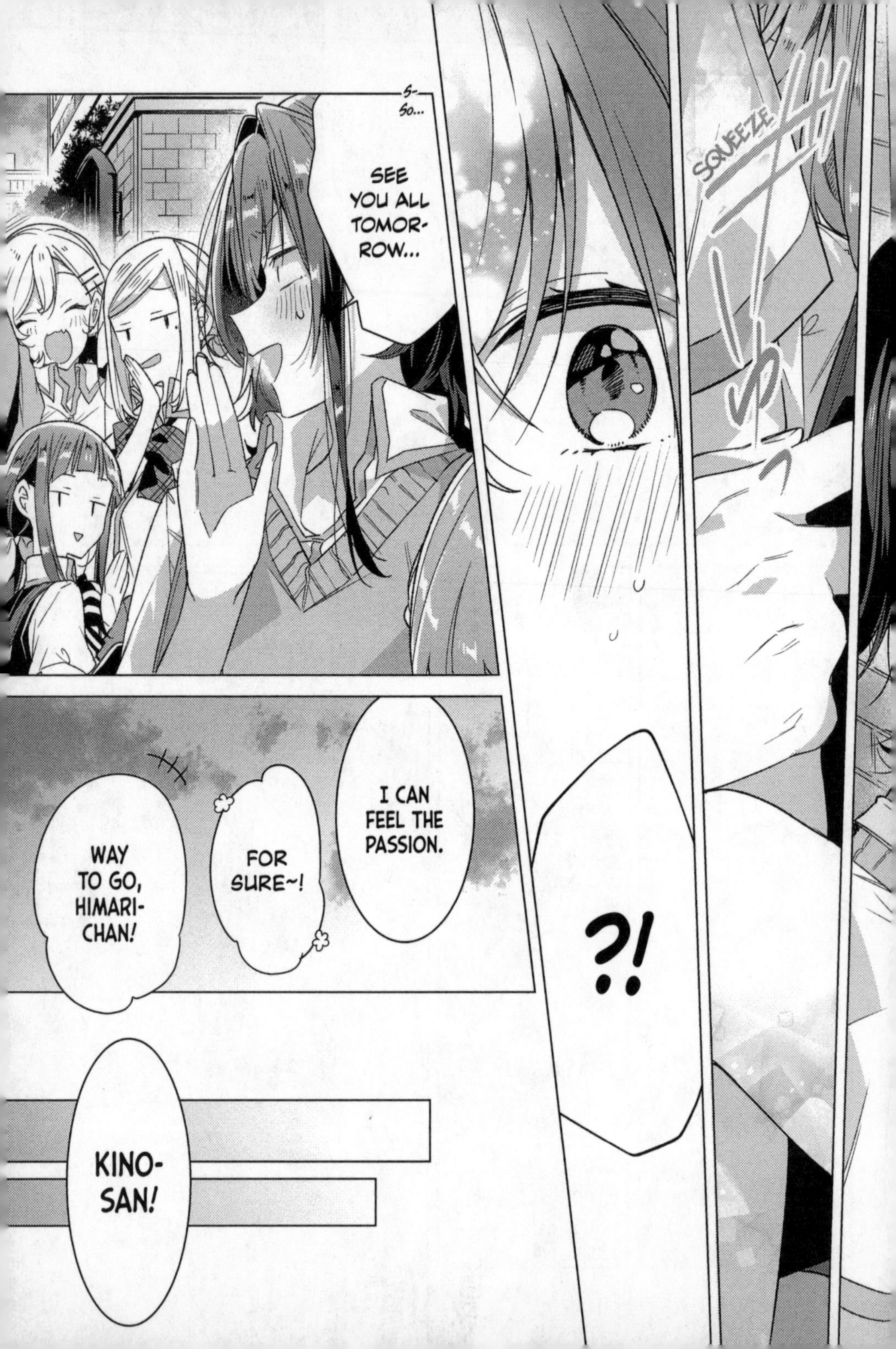
SQUEEZE
?!
S-So...
SEE YOU ALL TOMORROW...
I CAN FEEL THE PASSION.
FOR SURE~!
WAY TO GO, HIMARI-CHAN!
KINO-SAN!

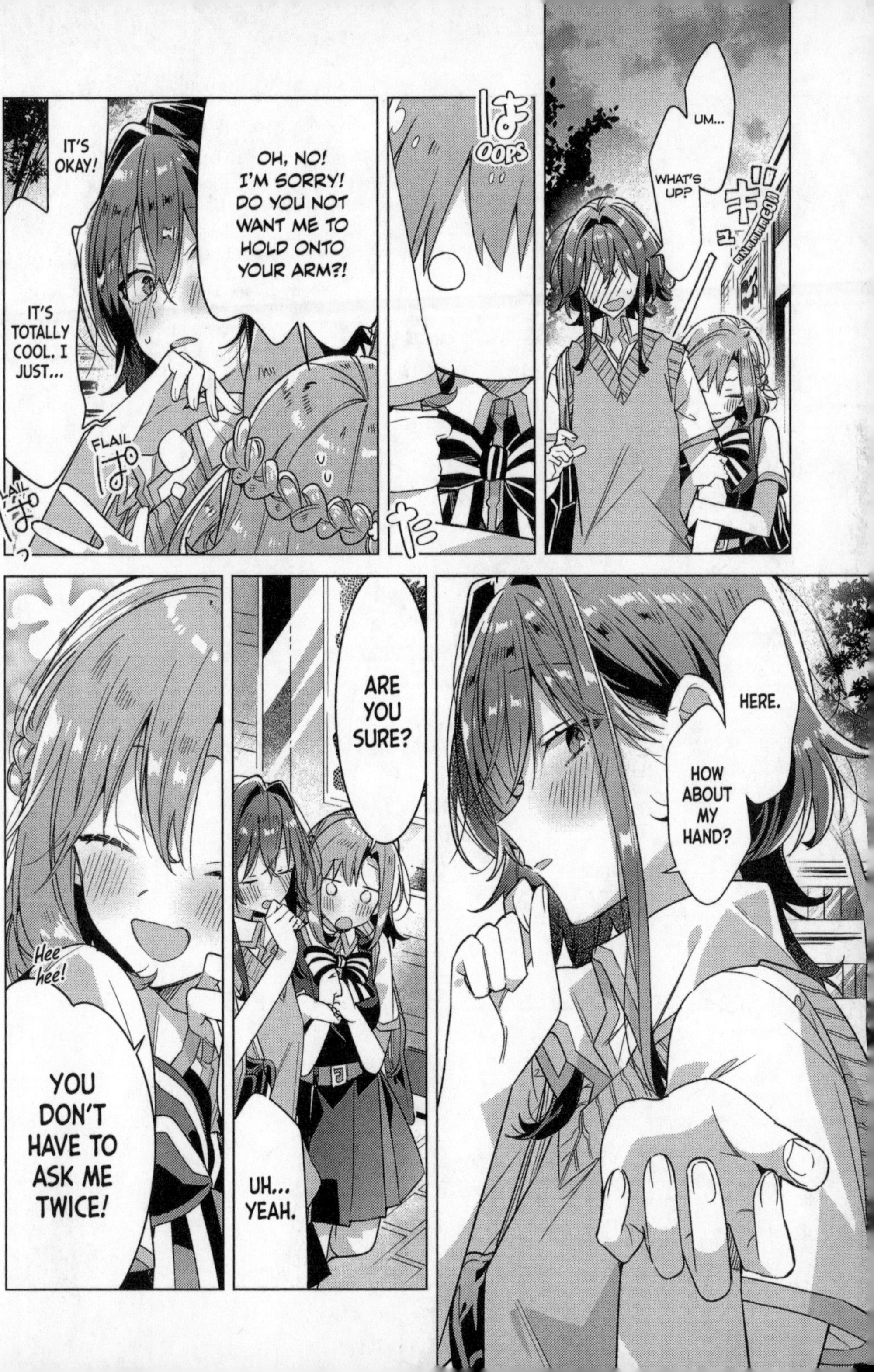
UM...
WHAT'S UP?
OOPS
OH, NO! I'M SORRY! DO YOU NOT WANT ME TO HOLD ONTO YOUR ARM?!
IT'S OKAY!
IT'S TOTALLY COOL. I JUST...
FLAIL
FLAIL
HERE.
HOW ABOUT MY HAND?
ARE YOU SURE?
UH... YEAH.
Hee hee!
YOU DON'T HAVE TO ASK ME TWICE!

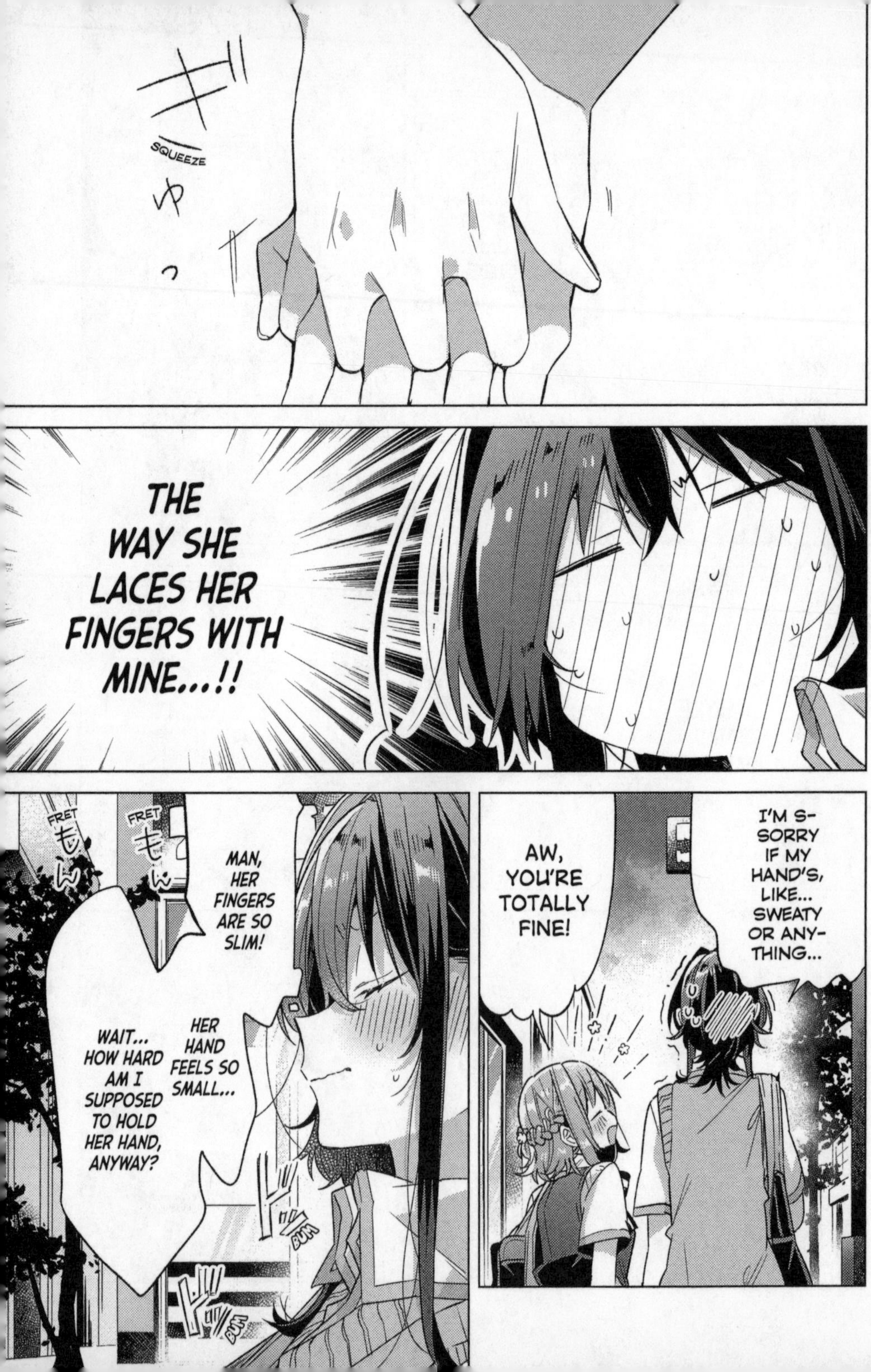
SQUEEZE
THE WAY SHE LACES HER FINGERS WITH MINE...!!
I'M S-SORRY IF MY HAND'S, LIKE... SWEATY OR ANYTHING...
AW, YOU'RE TOTALLY FINE!
FRET
FRET
MAN, HER FINGERS ARE SO SLIM!
HER HAND FEELS SO SMALL...
WAIT... HOW HARD AM I SUPPOSED TO HOLD HER HAND, ANYWAY?
BUM
BUM

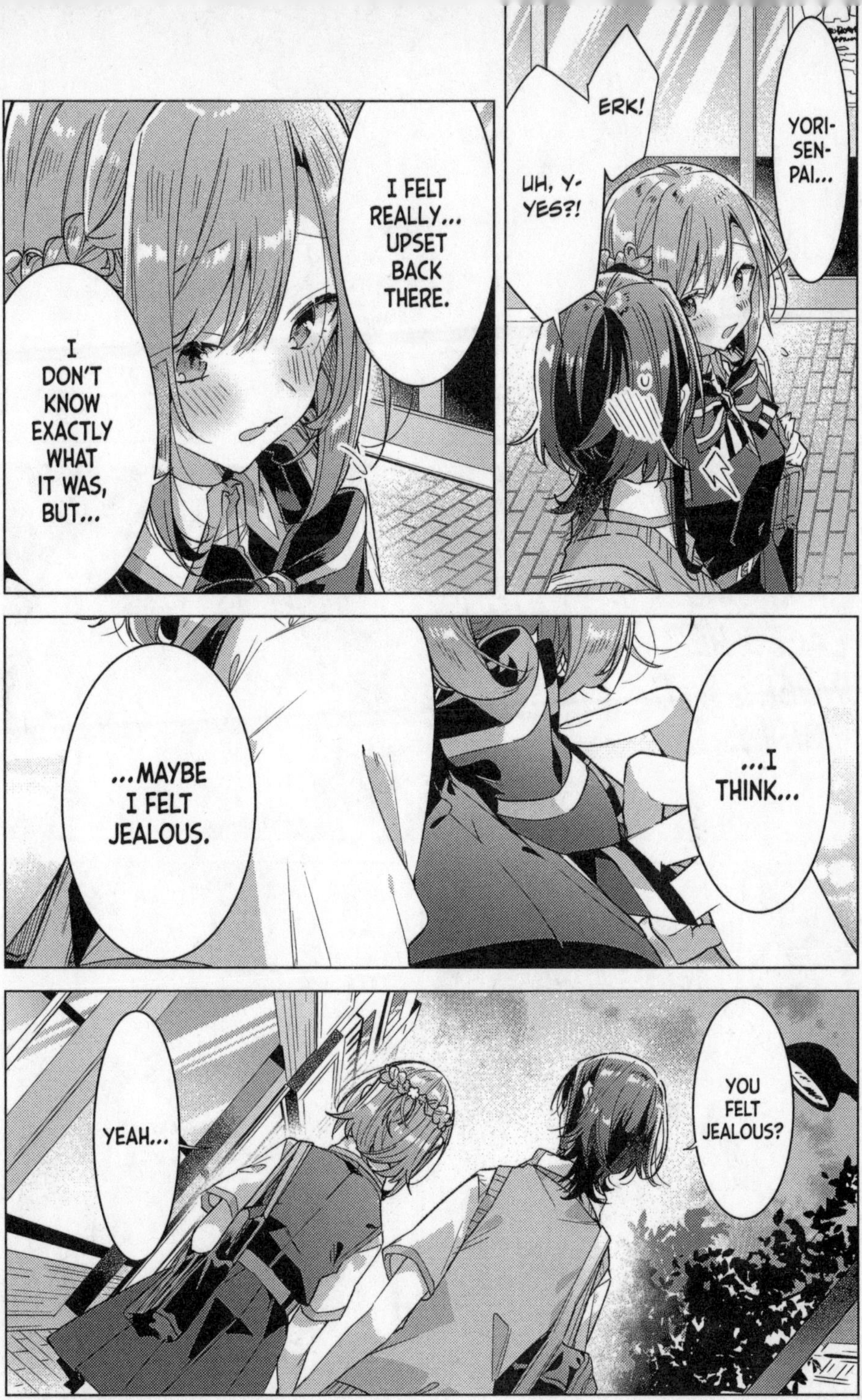
YORI-SENPAI...
ERK!
UH, Y-YES?!
I FELT REALLY... UPSET BACK THERE.
I DON'T KNOW EXACTLY WHAT IT WAS, BUT...
...I THINK...
...MAYBE I FELT JEALOUS.
YOU FELT JEALOUS?
YEAH...

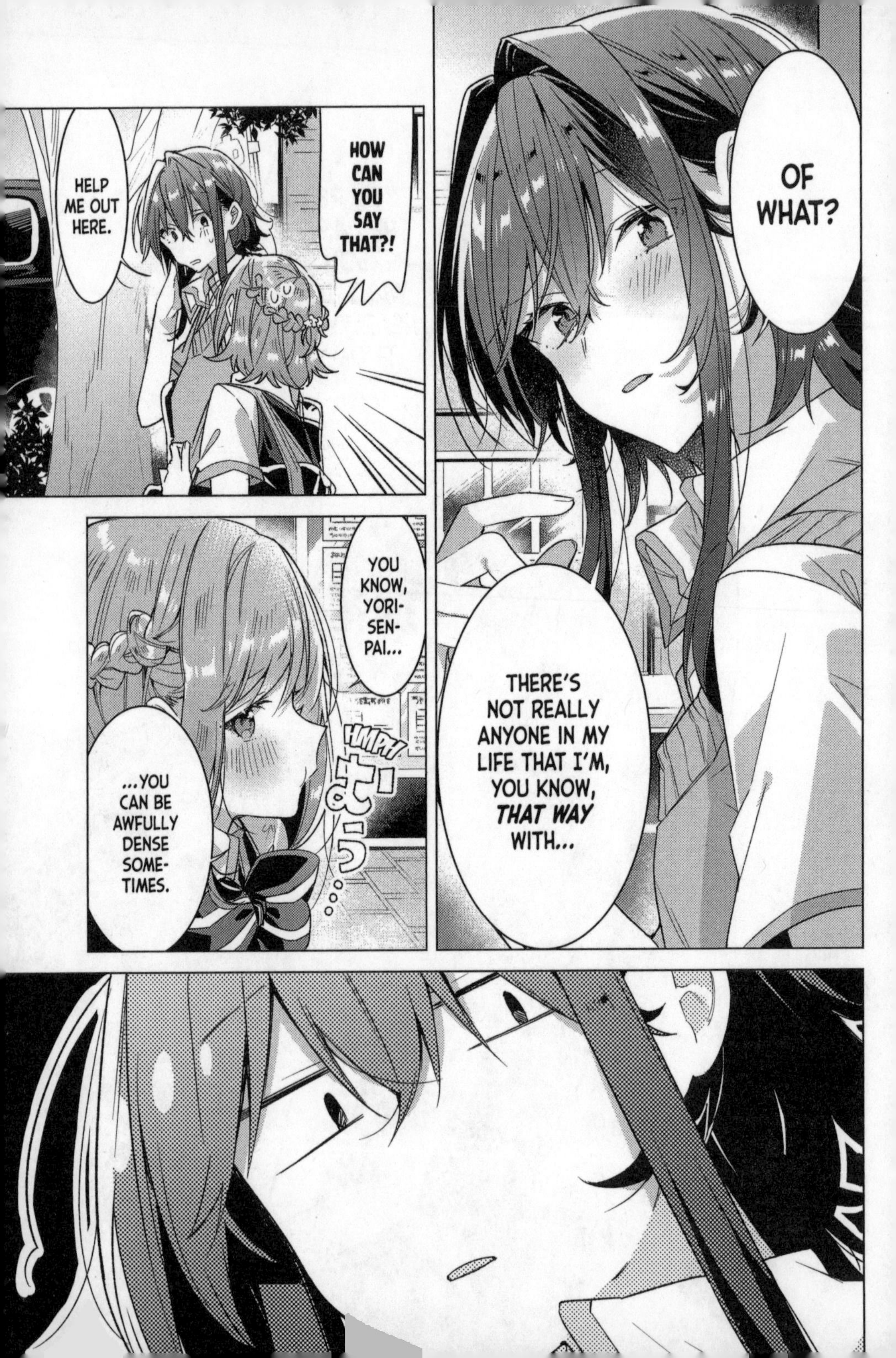
OF WHAT?
THERE'S NOT REALLY ANYONE IN MY LIFE THAT I'M, YOU KNOW, *THAT WAY* WITH...
HOW CAN YOU SAY THAT?!
HELP ME OUT HERE.
YOU KNOW, YORI-SENPAI...
HMPH
...YOU CAN BE AWFULLY DENSE SOMETIMES.

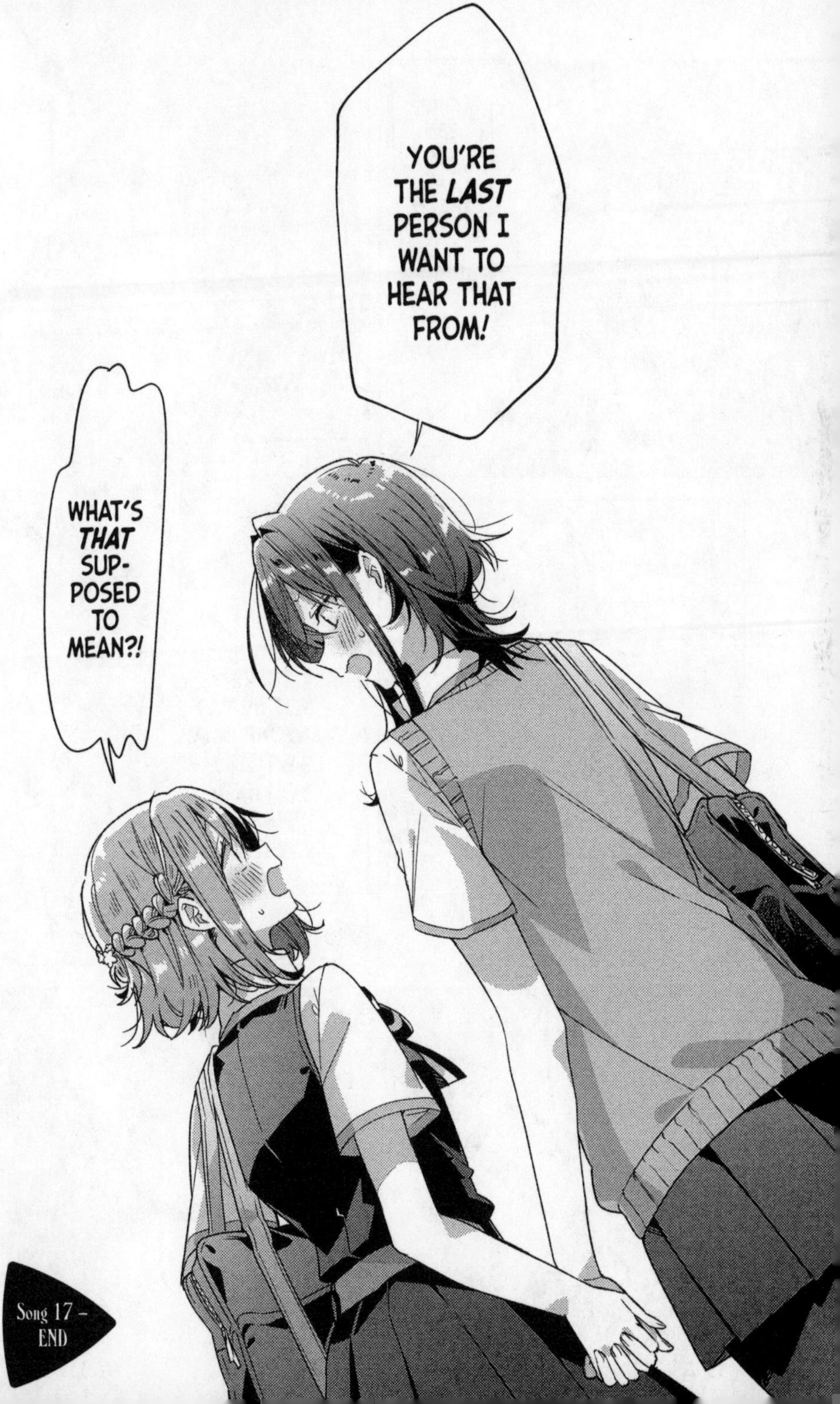
YOU'RE THE *LAST* PERSON I WANT TO HEAR THAT FROM!
WHAT'S *THAT* SUP-POSED TO MEAN?!
Song 17 - END

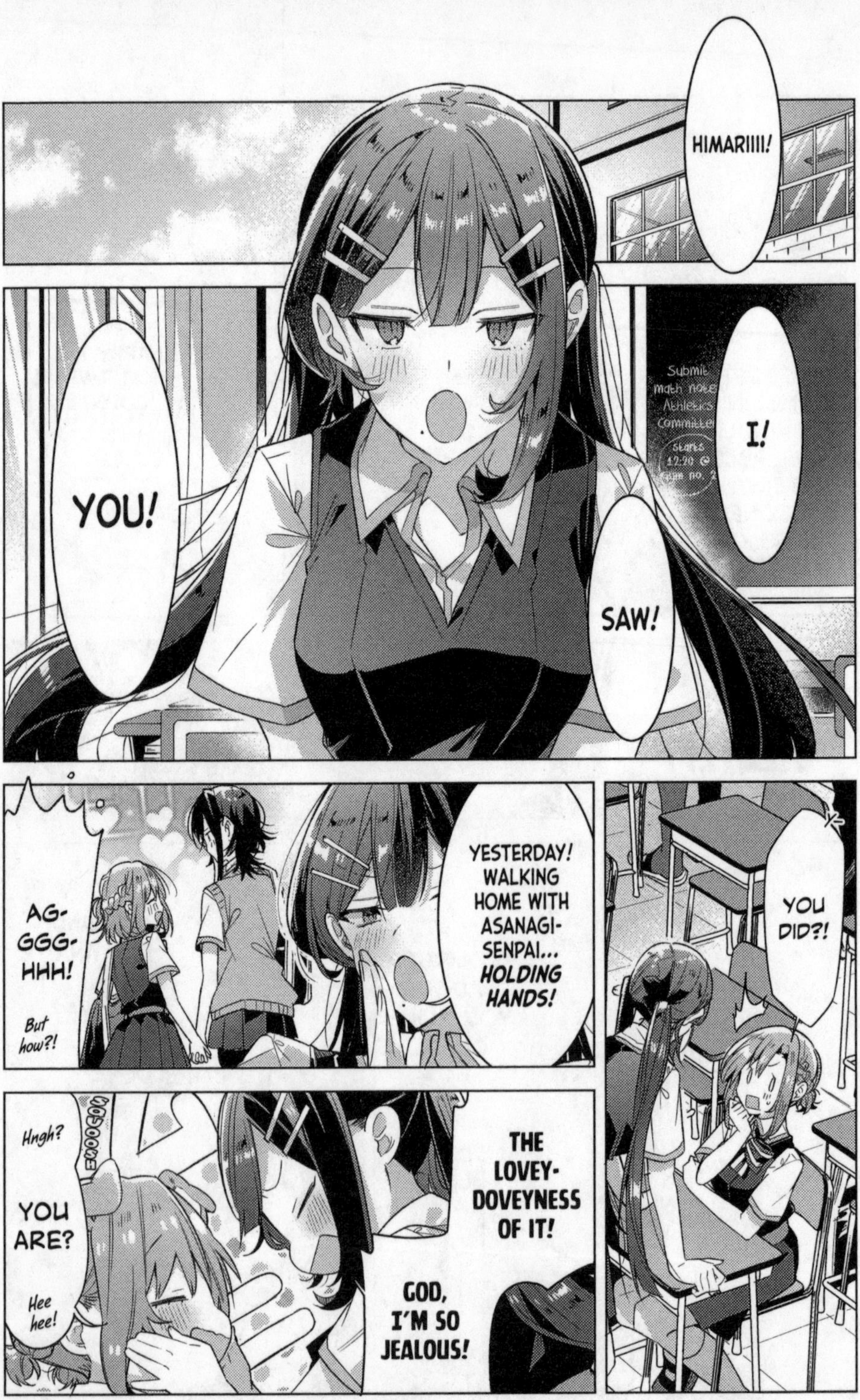
HIMARIIII!
I!
SAW!
YOU!
YOU DID?!
YESTERDAY! WALKING HOME WITH ASANAGI-SENPAI... *HOLDING HANDS!*
AG-GGG-HHH!
*But how?!*
THE LOVEY-DOVEYNESS OF IT!
GOD, I'M SO JEALOUS!
*Hngh?*
YOU ARE?
*Hee hee!*

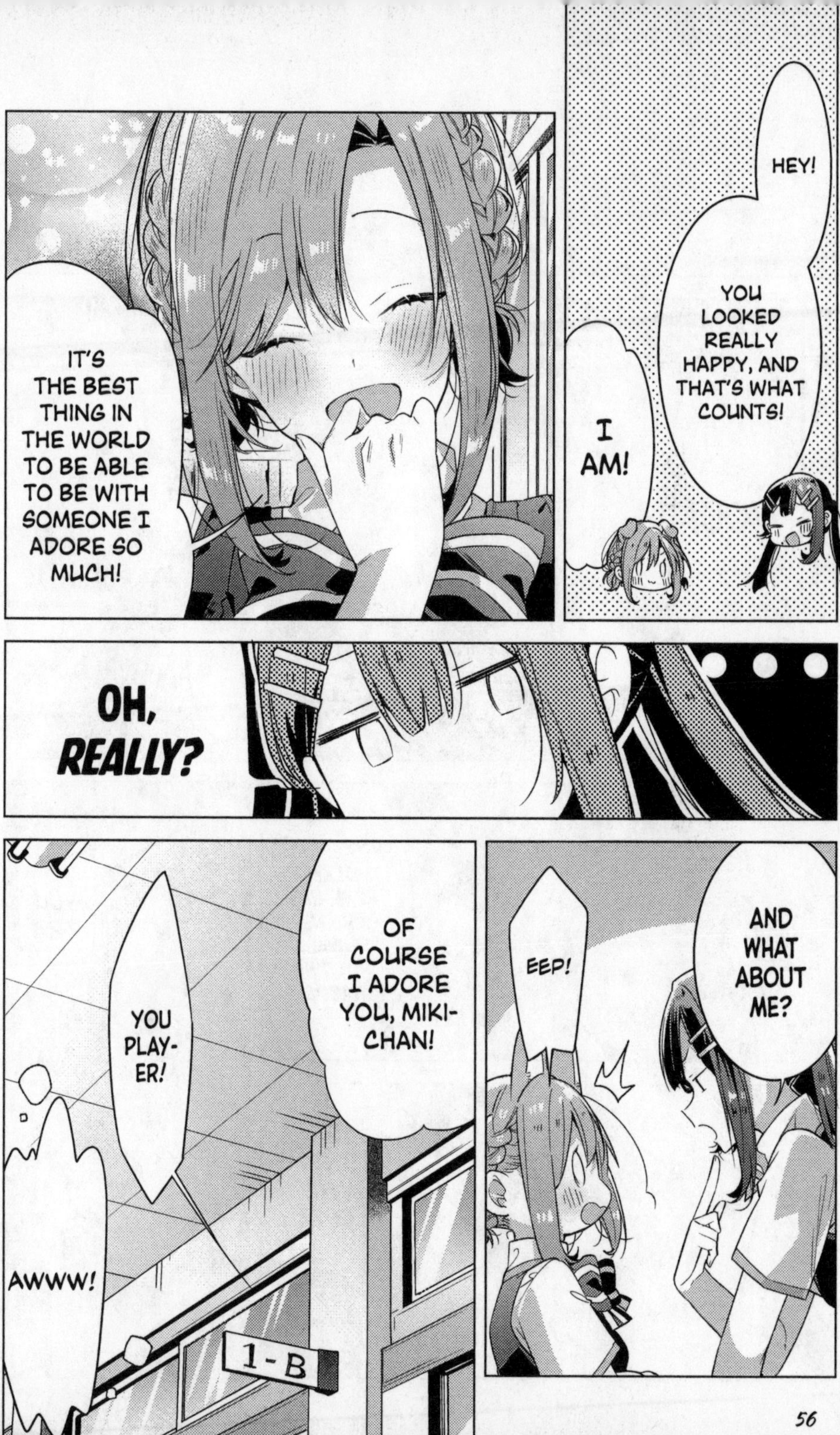
HEY!
YOU LOOKED REALLY HAPPY, AND THAT'S WHAT COUNTS!
I AM!
IT'S THE BEST THING IN THE WORLD TO BE ABLE TO BE WITH SOMEONE I ADORE SO MUCH!
OH, *REALLY?*
AND WHAT ABOUT ME?
EEP!
OF COURSE I ADORE YOU, MIKI-CHAN!
YOU PLAYER!
AWWW!
1-B

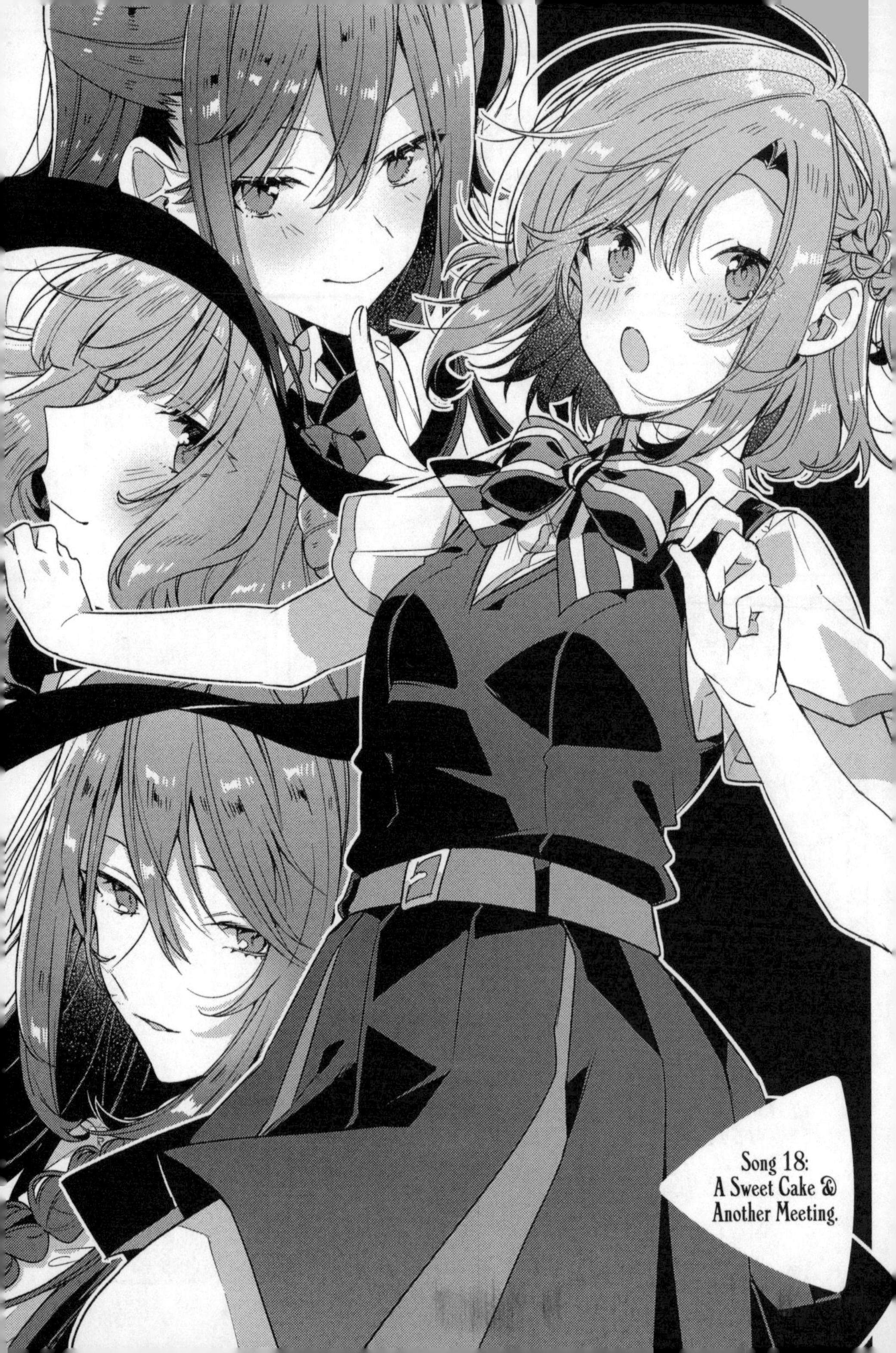
Song 18:
A Sweet Cake &
Another Meeting.

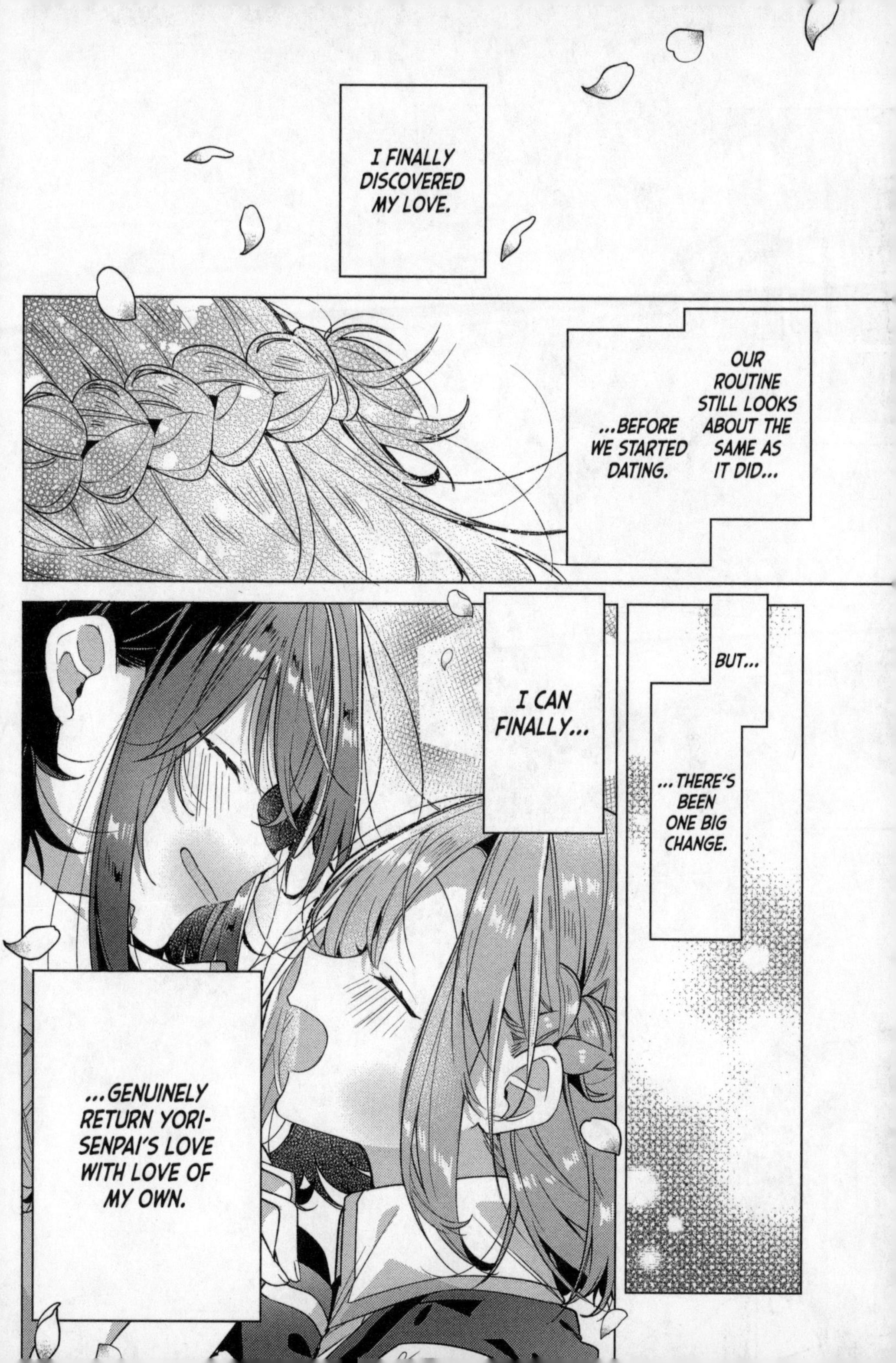
I FINALLY DISCOVERED MY LOVE.
OUR ROUTINE STILL LOOKS ABOUT THE SAME AS IT DID...
...BEFORE WE STARTED DATING.
BUT...
...THERE'S BEEN ONE BIG CHANGE.
I CAN FINALLY...
...GENUINELY RETURN YORI-SENPAI'S LOVE WITH LOVE OF MY OWN.

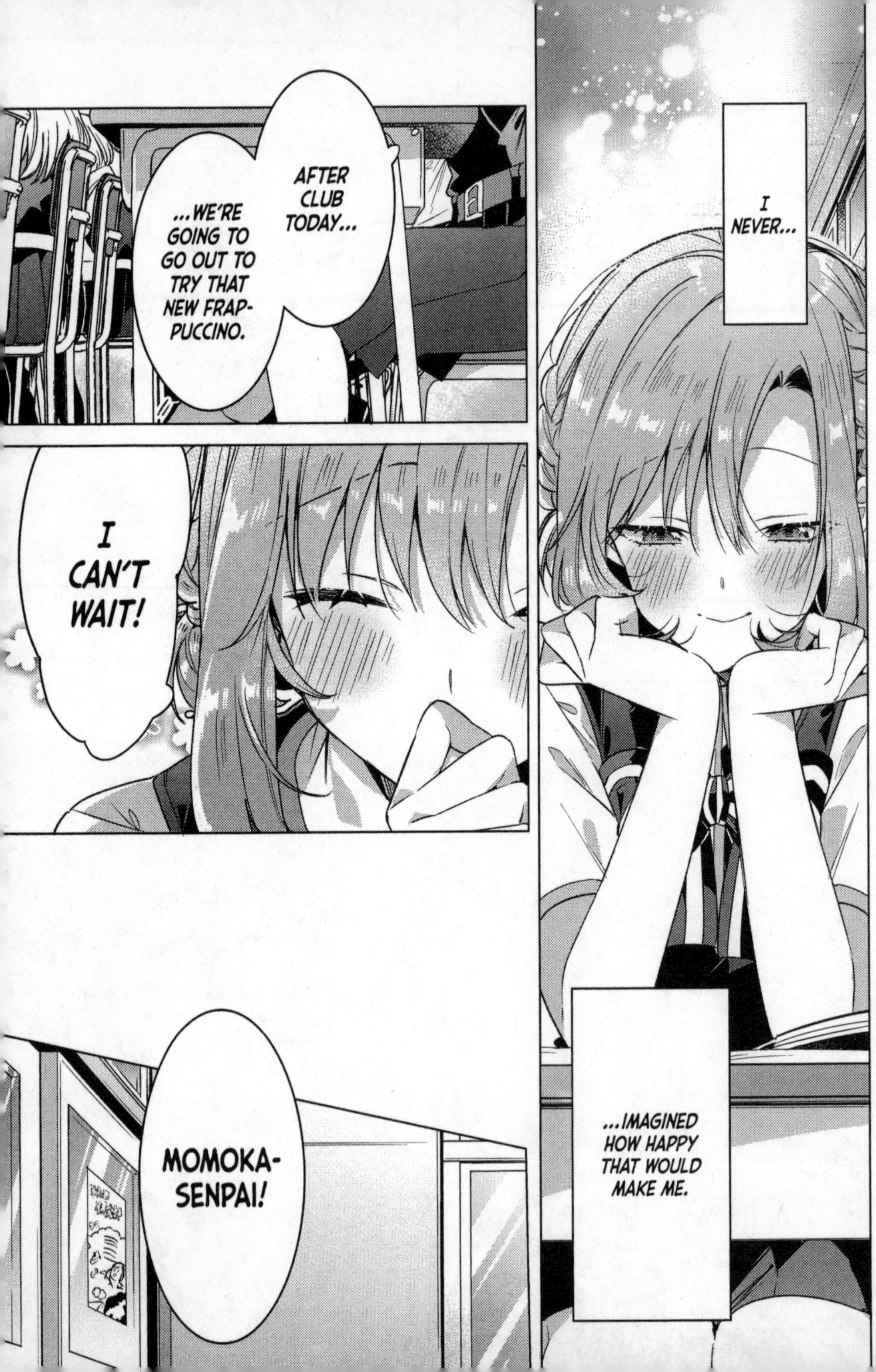
I NEVER...
...IMAGINED HOW HAPPY THAT WOULD MAKE ME.
AFTER CLUB TODAY...
...WE'RE GOING TO GO OUT TO TRY THAT NEW FRAP-PUCCINO.
I CAN'T WAIT!
MOMOKA-SENPAI!

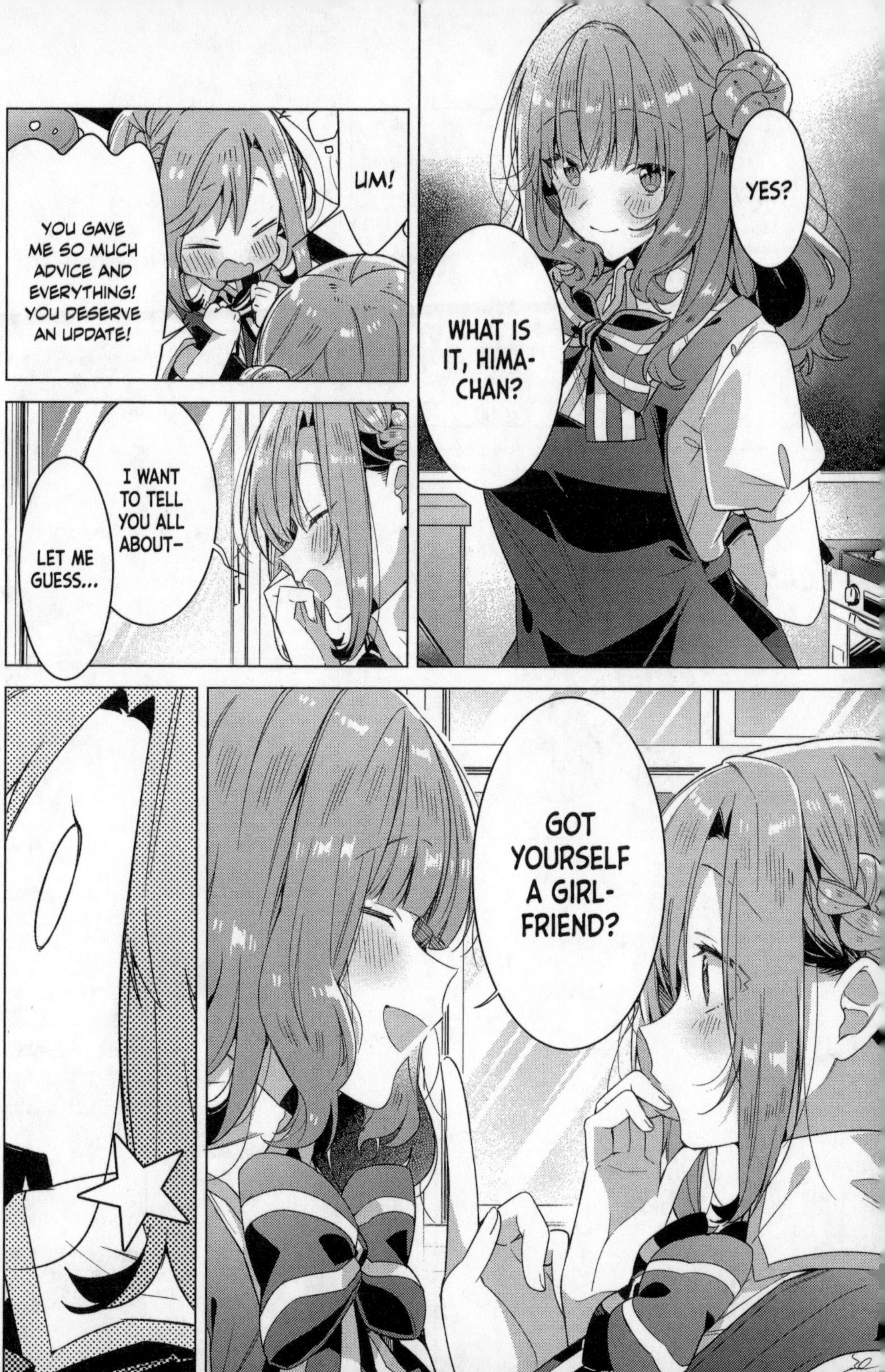
YES?
WHAT IS IT, HIMA-CHAN?
UM!
YOU GAVE ME SO MUCH ADVICE AND EVERYTHING! YOU DESERVE AN UPDATE!
I WANT TO TELL YOU ALL ABOUT-
LET ME GUESS...
GOT YOURSELF A GIRL-FRIEND?

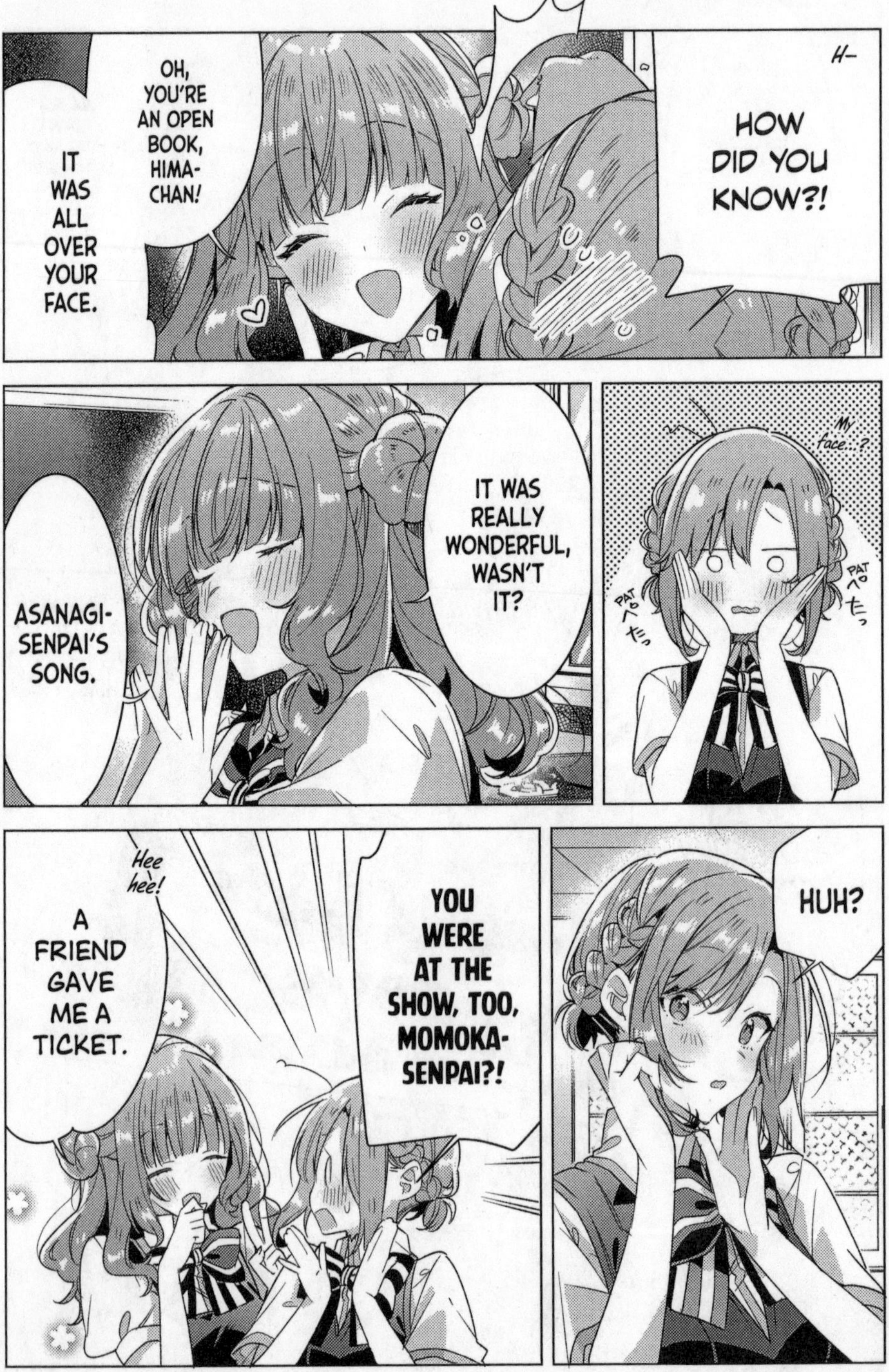
H–
HOW DID YOU KNOW?!
OH, YOU'RE AN OPEN BOOK, HIMA-CHAN!
IT WAS ALL OVER YOUR FACE.
My face...?
PAT ぺたっ
PAT ぺたっ
IT WAS REALLY WONDERFUL, WASN'T IT?
ASANAGI-SENPAI'S SONG.
HUH?
YOU WERE AT THE SHOW, TOO, MOMOKA-SENPAI?!
Hee hee!
A FRIEND GAVE ME A TICKET.

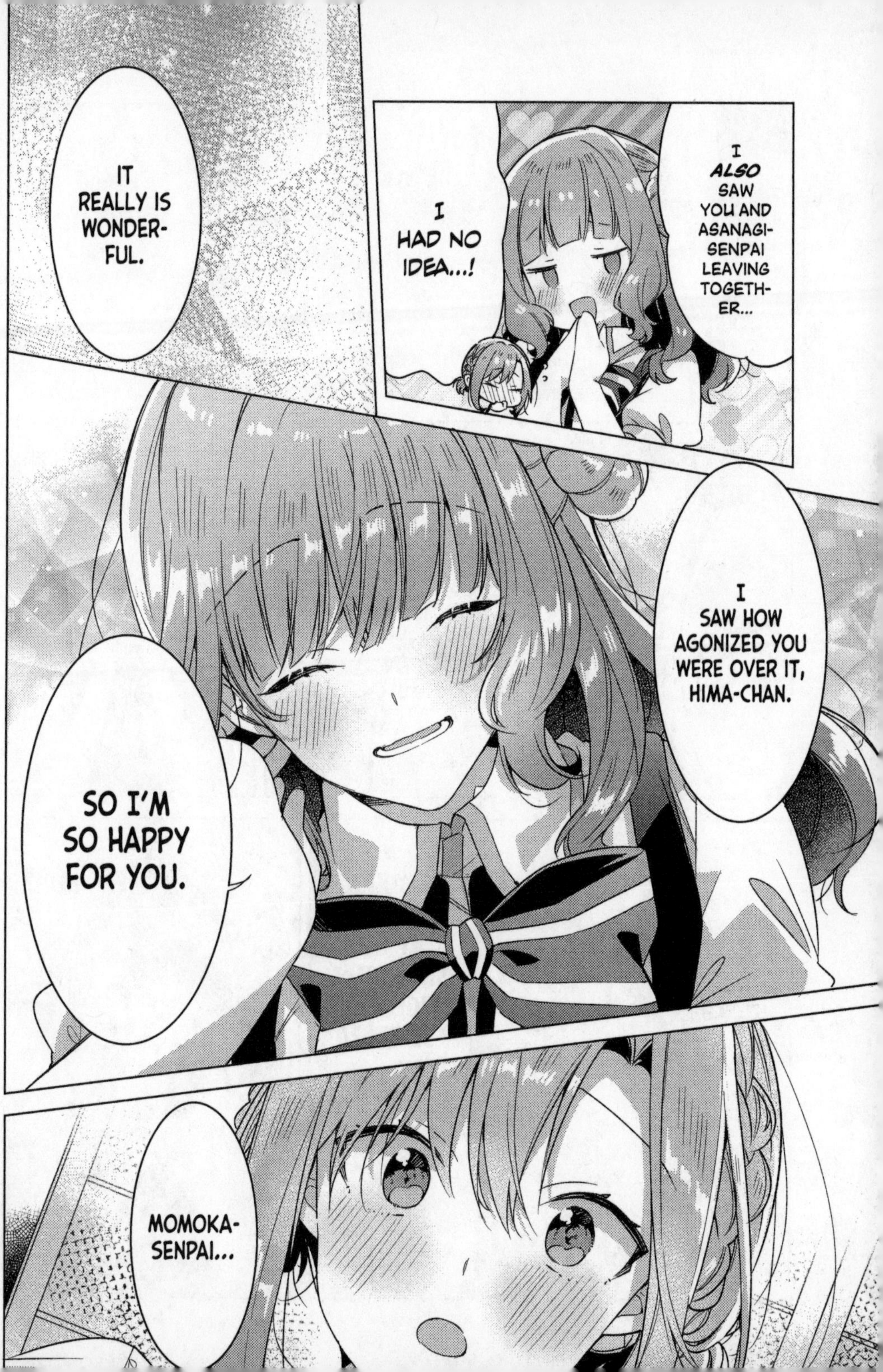
I *ALSO* SAW YOU AND ASANAGI-SENPAI LEAVING TOGETH-ER...
I HAD NO IDEA...!
IT REALLY IS WONDER-FUL.
I SAW HOW AGONIZED YOU WERE OVER IT, HIMA-CHAN.
SO I'M SO HAPPY FOR YOU.
MOMOKA-SENPAI...

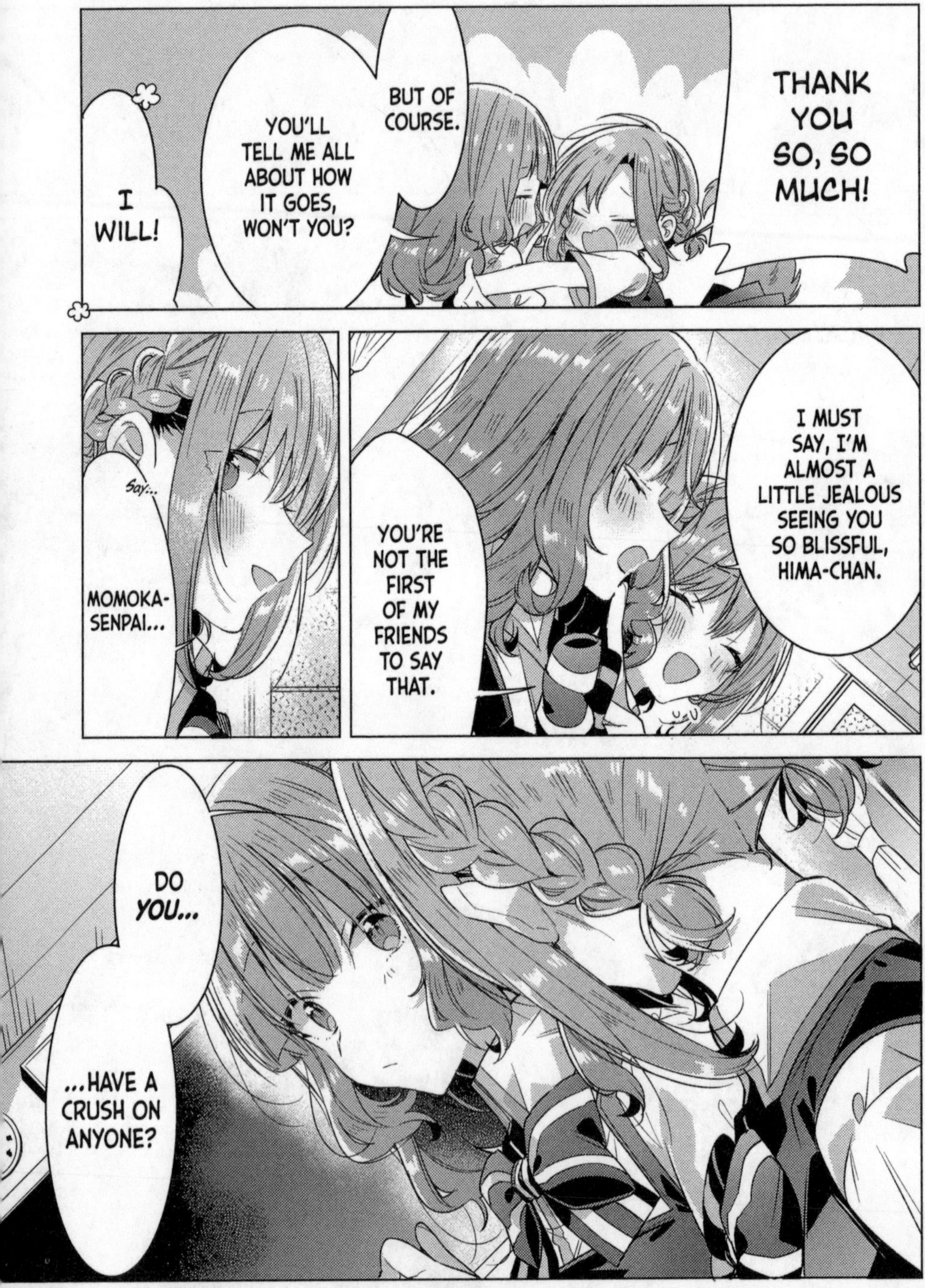
THANK YOU SO, SO MUCH!
BUT OF COURSE.
YOU'LL TELL ME ALL ABOUT HOW IT GOES, WON'T YOU?
I WILL!
I MUST SAY, I'M ALMOST A LITTLE JEALOUS SEEING YOU SO BLISSFUL, HIMA-CHAN.
YOU'RE NOT THE FIRST OF MY FRIENDS TO SAY THAT.
Say...
MOMOKA-SENPAI...
DO *YOU...*
...HAVE A CRUSH ON ANYONE?

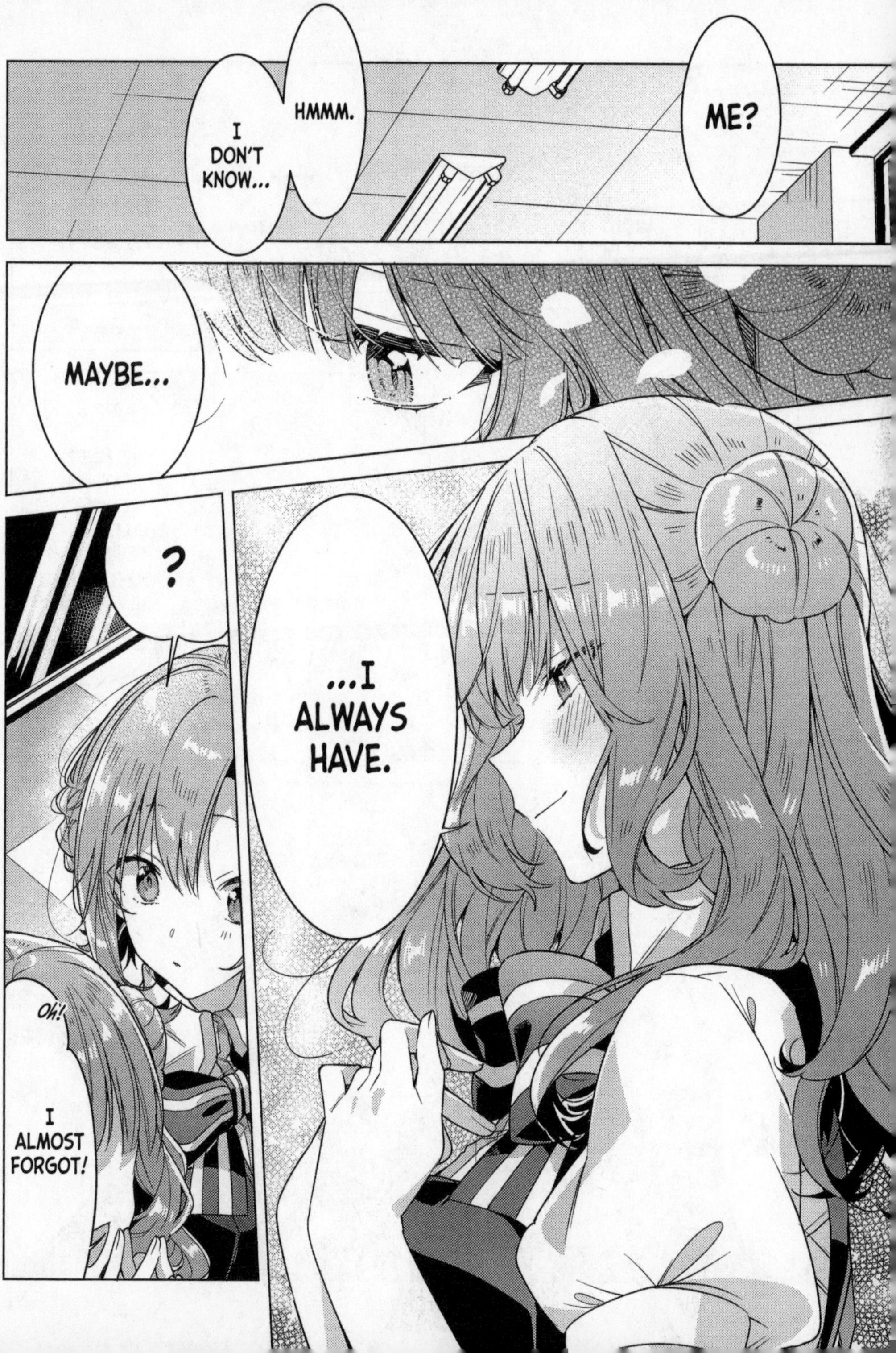
ME?
HMMM.
I DON'T KNOW...
MAYBE...
...I ALWAYS HAVE.
?
Oh!
I ALMOST FORGOT!

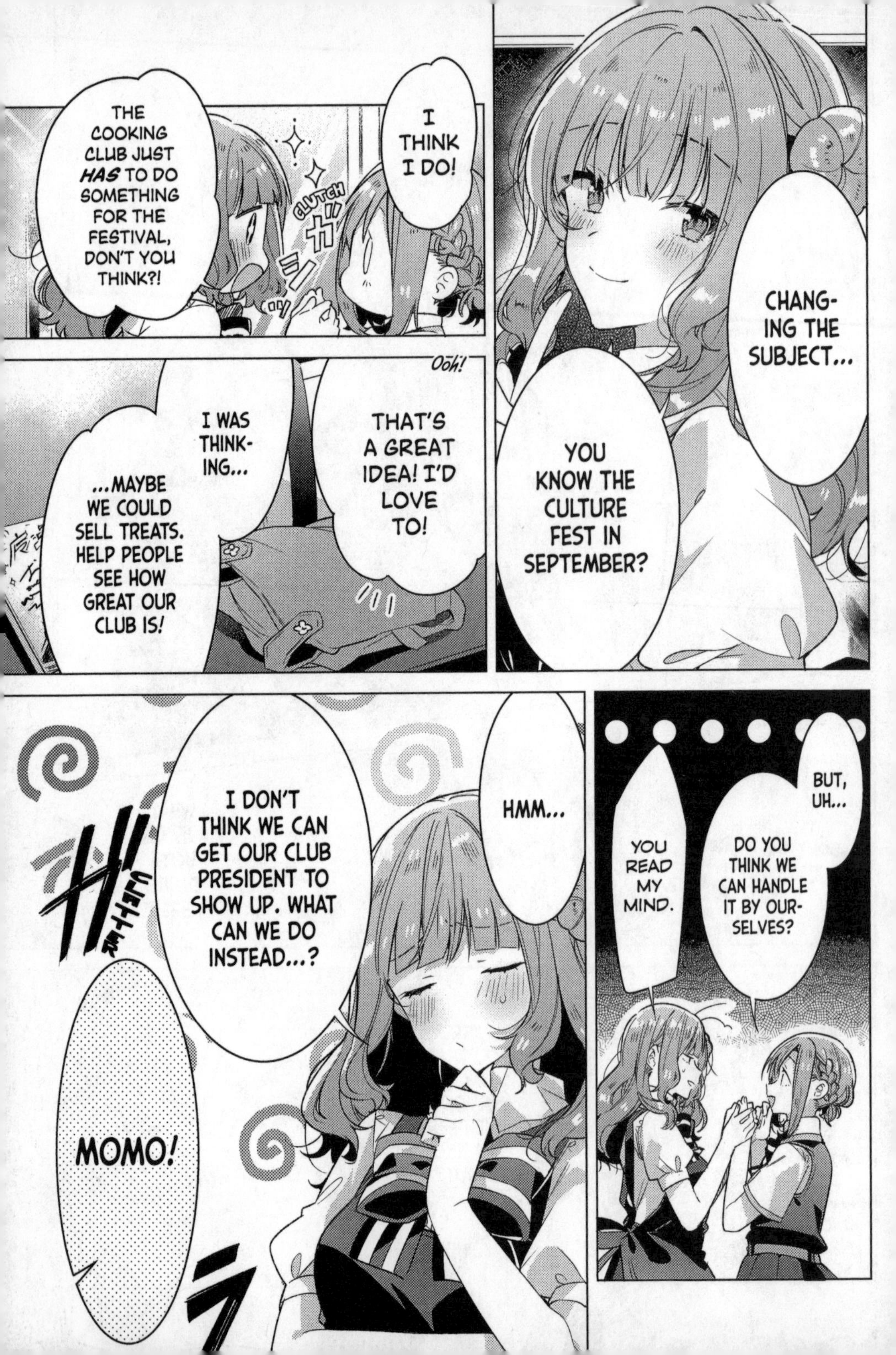

CHANG-ING THE SUBJECT...
YOU KNOW THE CULTURE FEST IN SEPTEMBER?
I THINK I DO!
CLUTCH
THE COOKING CLUB JUST **HAS** TO DO SOMETHING FOR THE FESTIVAL, DON'T YOU THINK?!
Oooh!
THAT'S A GREAT IDEA! I'D LOVE TO!
I WAS THINKING-ING...
...MAYBE WE COULD SELL TREATS. HELP PEOPLE SEE HOW GREAT OUR CLUB IS!
BUT, UH...
DO YOU THINK WE CAN HANDLE IT BY OUR-SELVES?
YOU READ MY MIND.
HMM...
I DON'T THINK WE CAN GET OUR CLUB PRESIDENT TO SHOW UP. WHAT CAN WE DO INSTEAD...?
FLUTTER
MOMO!

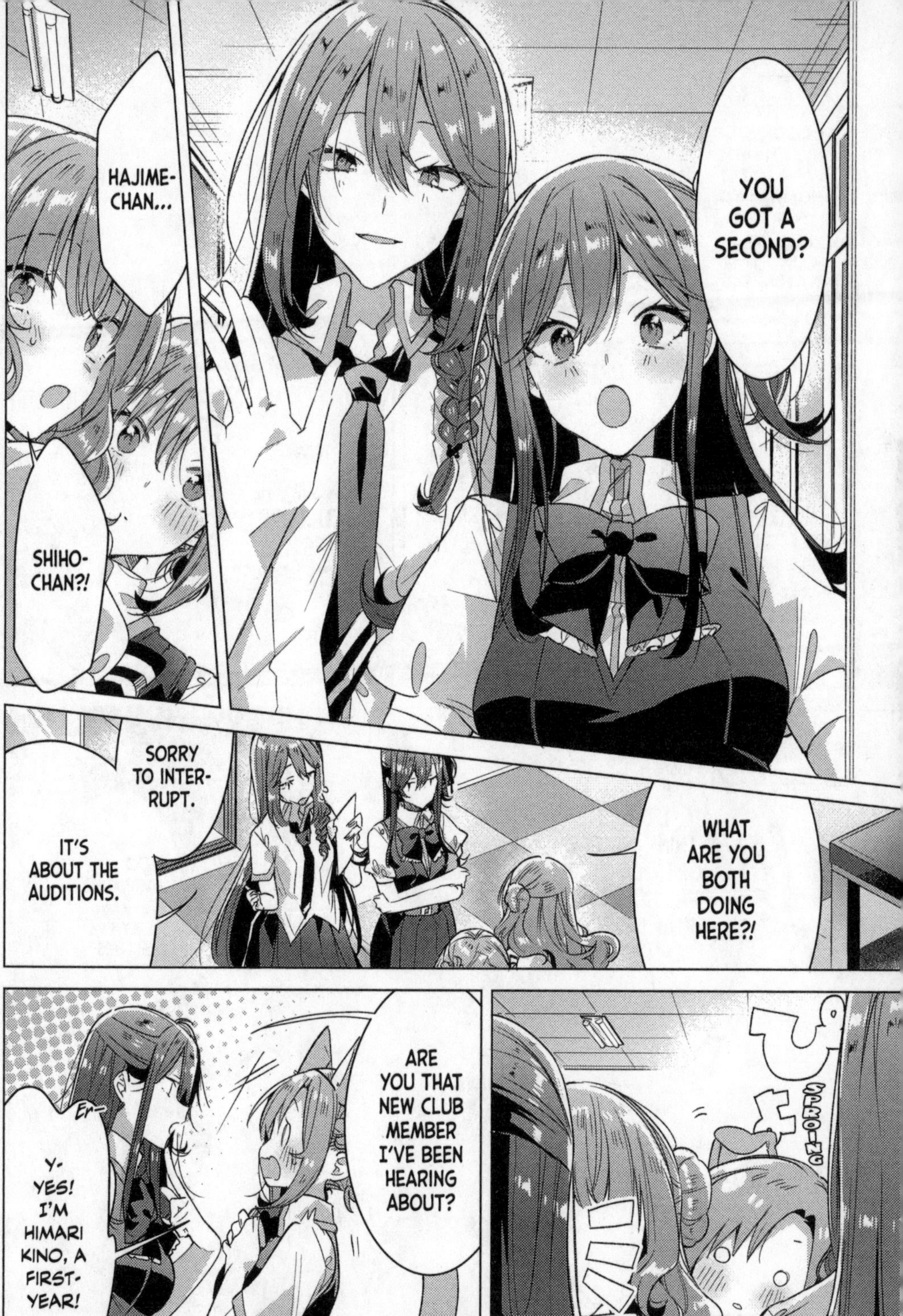
YOU GOT A SECOND?
HAJIME-CHAN...
SHIHO-CHAN?!
WHAT ARE YOU BOTH DOING HERE?!
SORRY TO INTER-RUPT.
IT'S ABOUT THE AUDITIONS.
SPROING
ARE YOU THAT NEW CLUB MEMBER I'VE BEEN HEARING ABOUT?
Er–
Y-YES! I'M HIMARI KINO, A FIRST-YEAR!

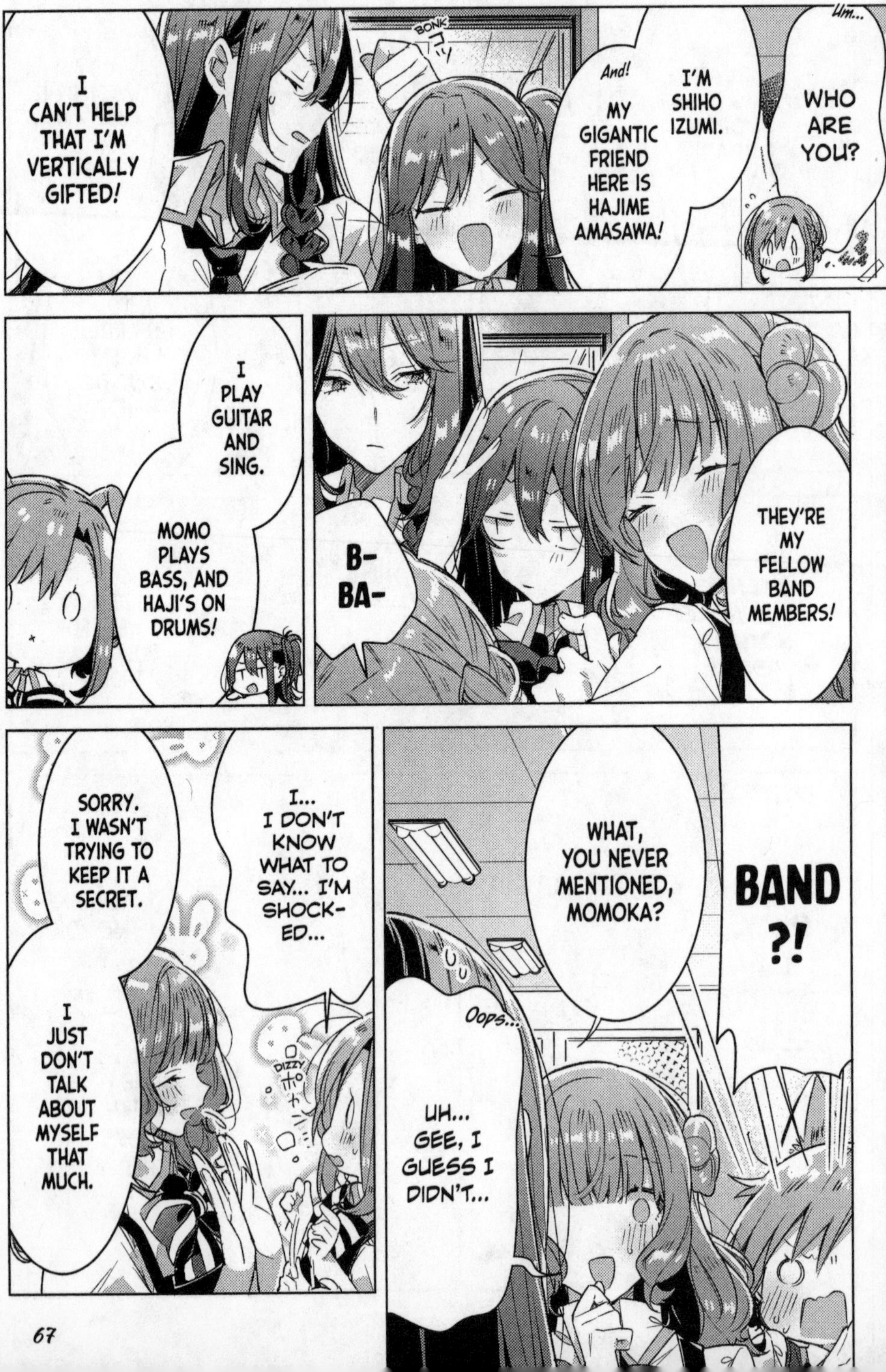
Um...
WHO ARE YOU?
I'M SHIHO IZUMI.
And! MY GIGANTIC FRIEND HERE IS HAJIME AMASAWA!
BONK
I CAN'T HELP THAT I'M VERTICALLY GIFTED!
THEY'RE MY FELLOW BAND MEMBERS!
B- BA-
I PLAY GUITAR AND SING.
MOMO PLAYS BASS, AND HAJI'S ON DRUMS!
BAND ?!
WHAT, YOU NEVER MENTIONED, MOMOKA?
Oops...
UH... GEE, I GUESS I DIDN'T...
I... I DON'T KNOW WHAT TO SAY... I'M SHOCKED...
DIZZY
SORRY. I WASN'T TRYING TO KEEP IT A SECRET.
I JUST DON'T TALK ABOUT MYSELF THAT MUCH.

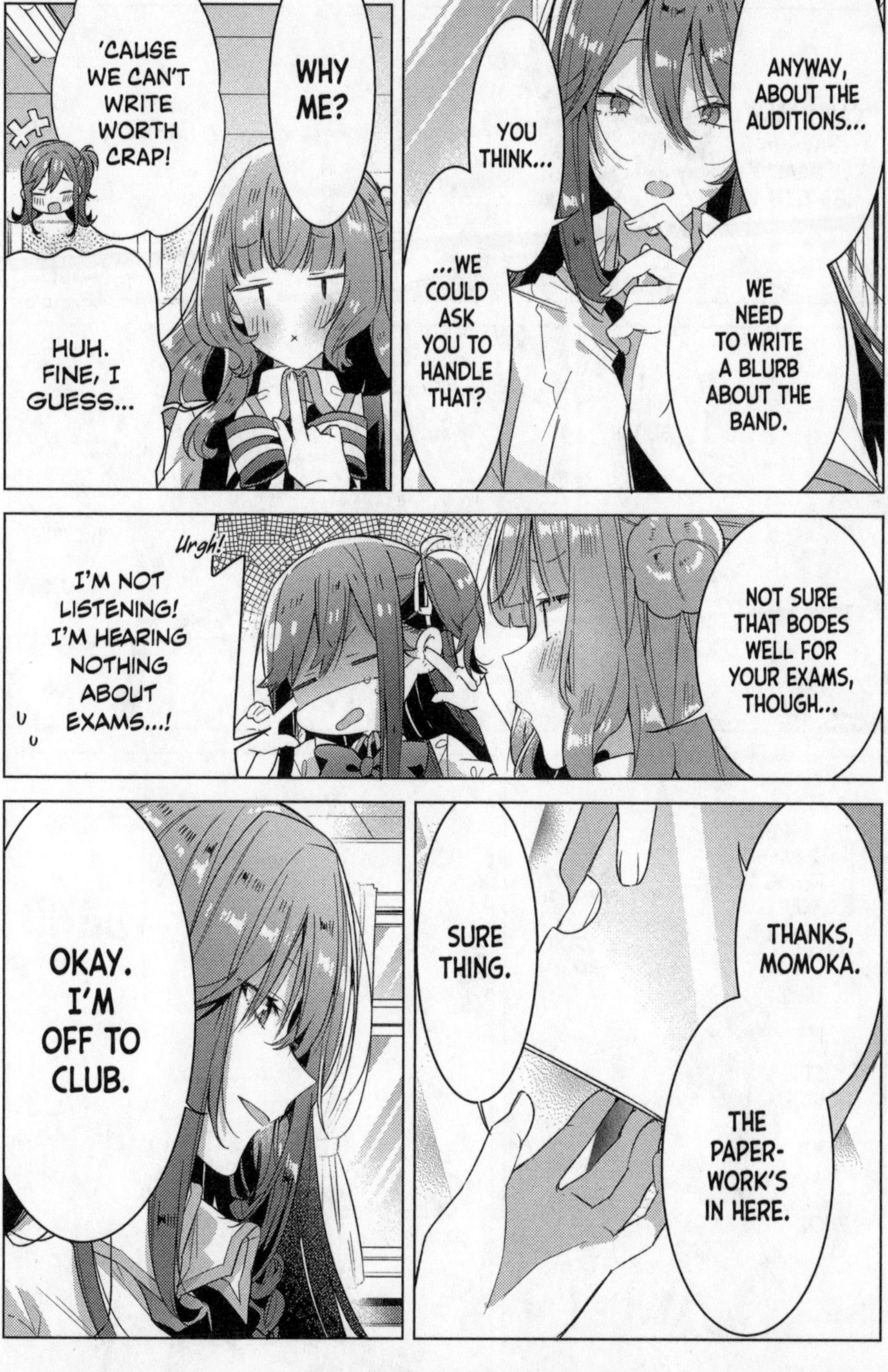
ANYWAY, ABOUT THE AUDITIONS...
WE NEED TO WRITE A BLURB ABOUT THE BAND.
YOU THINK...
...WE COULD ASK YOU TO HANDLE THAT?
WHY ME?
'CAUSE WE CAN'T WRITE WORTH CRAP!
HUH. FINE, I GUESS...
NOT SURE THAT BODES WELL FOR YOUR EXAMS, THOUGH...
Urgh!
I'M NOT LISTENING! I'M HEARING NOTHING ABOUT EXAMS...!
THANKS, MOMOKA.
THE PAPER-WORK'S IN HERE.
SURE THING.
OKAY. I'M OFF TO CLUB.

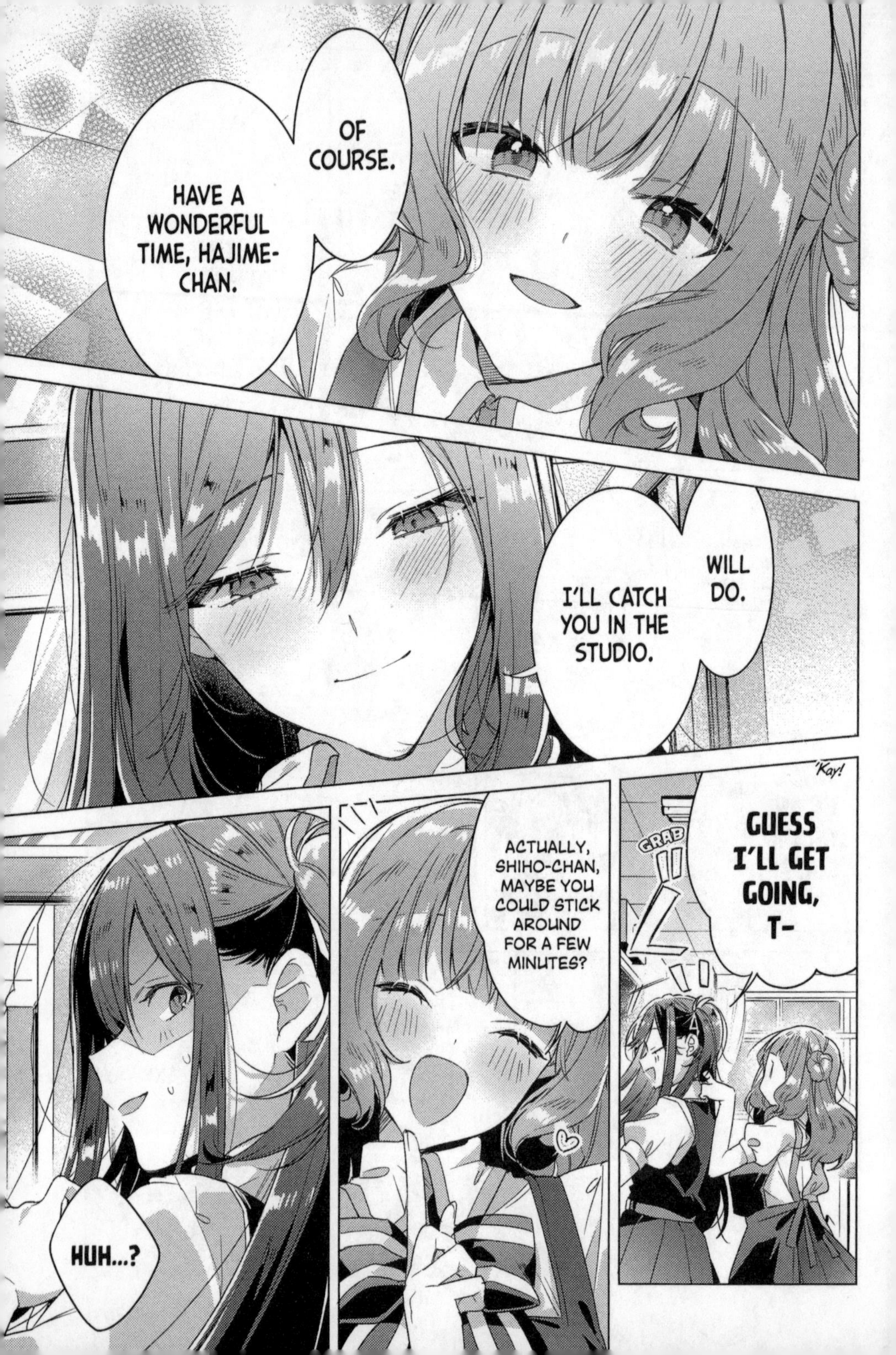
OF COURSE.
HAVE A WONDERFUL TIME, HAJIME-CHAN.
WILL DO.
I'LL CATCH YOU IN THE STUDIO.
'Kay!
GUESS I'LL GET GOING, T-
GRAB
ACTUALLY, SHIHO-CHAN, MAYBE YOU COULD STICK AROUND FOR A FEW MINUTES?
HUH...?

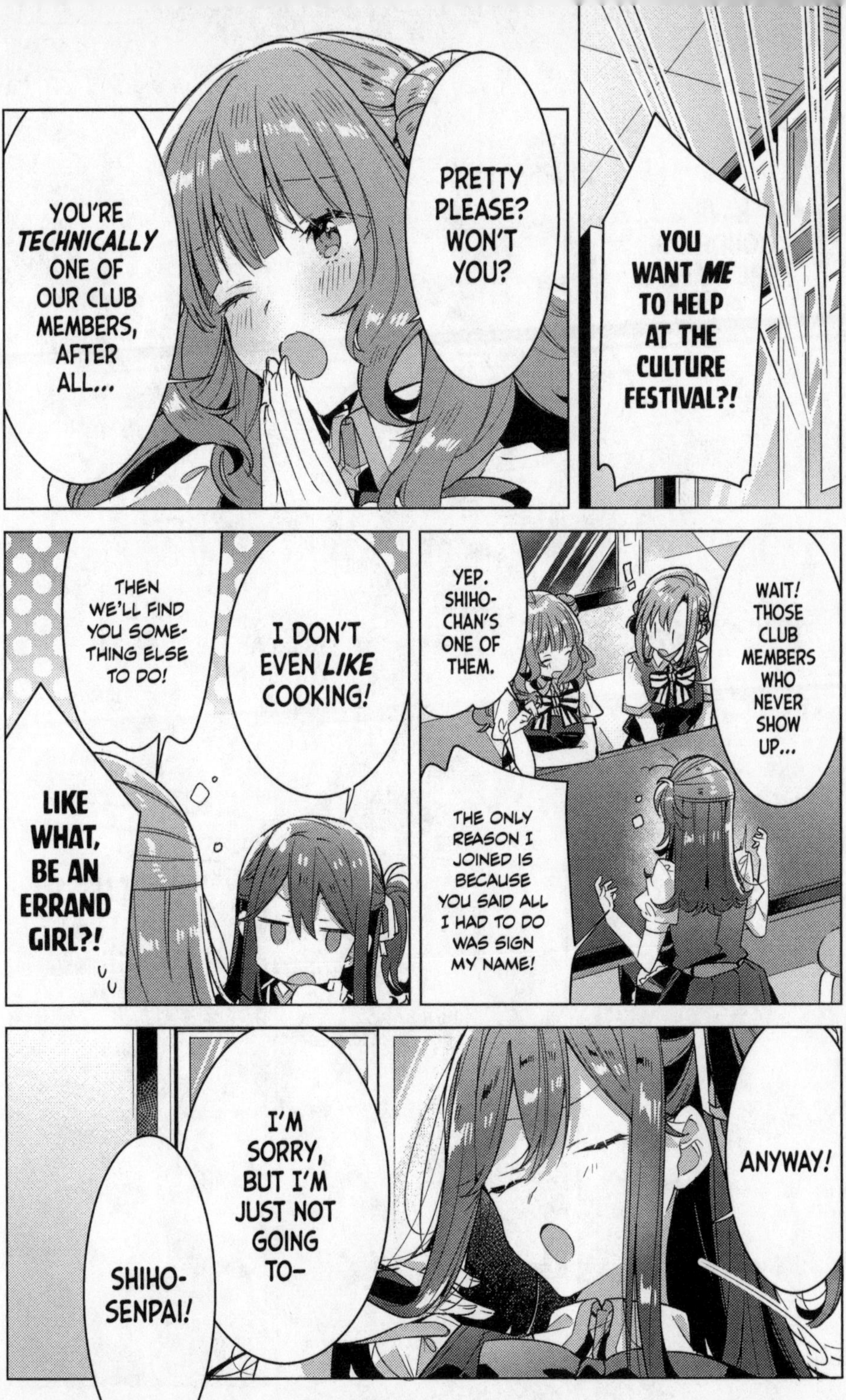
YOU WANT *ME* TO HELP AT THE CULTURE FESTIVAL?!
PRETTY PLEASE? WON'T YOU?
YOU'RE *TECHNICALLY* ONE OF OUR CLUB MEMBERS, AFTER ALL...
WAIT! THOSE CLUB MEMBERS WHO NEVER SHOW UP...
YEP. SHIHO-CHAN'S ONE OF THEM.
THE ONLY REASON I JOINED IS BECAUSE YOU SAID ALL I HAD TO DO WAS SIGN MY NAME!
I DON'T EVEN *LIKE* COOKING!
THEN WE'LL FIND YOU SOME-THING ELSE TO DO!
LIKE WHAT, BE AN ERRAND GIRL?!
ANYWAY!
I'M SORRY, BUT I'M JUST NOT GOING TO-
SHIHO-SENPAI!

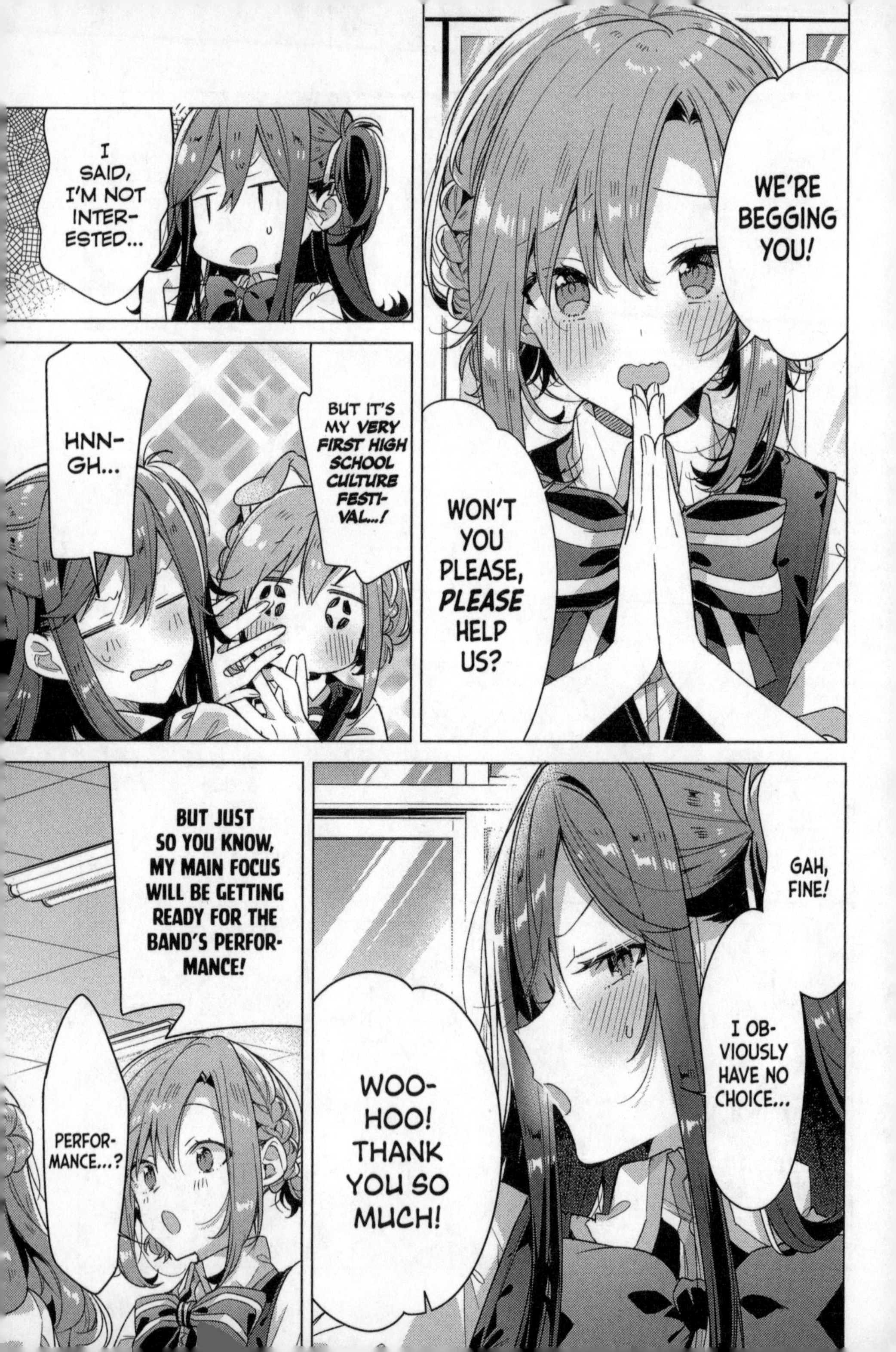
WE'RE BEGGING YOU!
WON'T YOU PLEASE, *PLEASE* HELP US?
I SAID, I'M NOT INTERESTED...
BUT IT'S MY *VERY FIRST HIGH SCHOOL CULTURE FESTIVAL...!*
HNN-GH...
GAH, FINE!
I OBVIOUSLY HAVE NO CHOICE...
WOO-HOO! THANK YOU SO MUCH!
BUT JUST SO YOU KNOW, MY MAIN FOCUS WILL BE GETTING READY FOR THE BAND'S PERFORMANCE!
PERFORMANCE...?

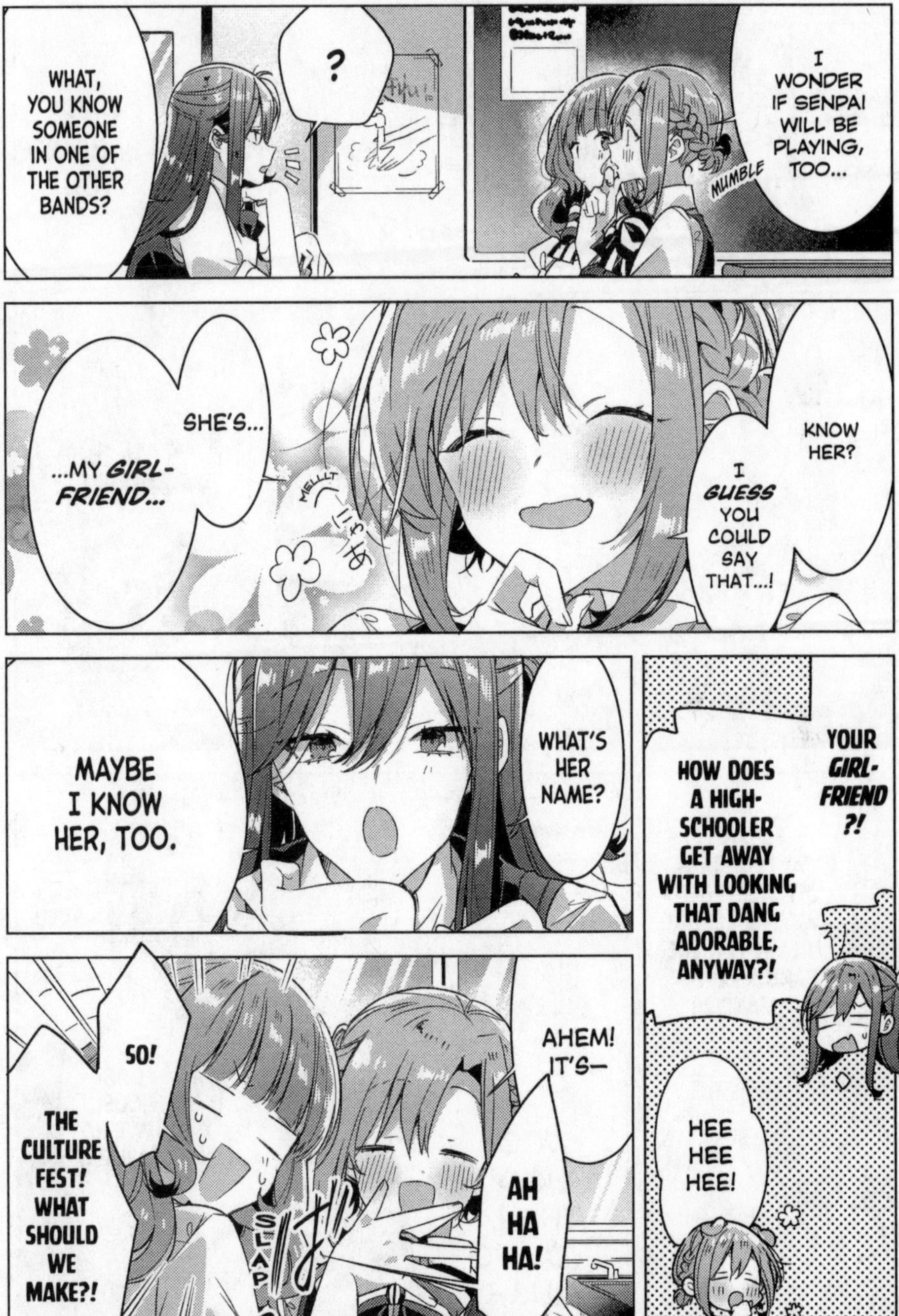
I WONDER IF SENPAI WILL BE PLAYING, TOO...
MUMBLE
?
WHAT, YOU KNOW SOMEONE IN ONE OF THE OTHER BANDS?
KNOW HER?
I *GUESS* YOU COULD SAY THAT...!
MELLLT
にゃあ
SHE'S...
...MY *GIRL-FRIEND*...
YOUR *GIRL-FRIEND* ?!
HOW DOES A HIGH-SCHOOLER GET AWAY WITH LOOKING THAT DANG ADORABLE, ANYWAY?!
HEE HEE HEE!
WHAT'S HER NAME?
MAYBE I KNOW HER, TOO.
AHEM! IT'S—
AH HA HA!
SLAP
SO!
THE CULTURE FEST! WHAT SHOULD WE MAKE?!

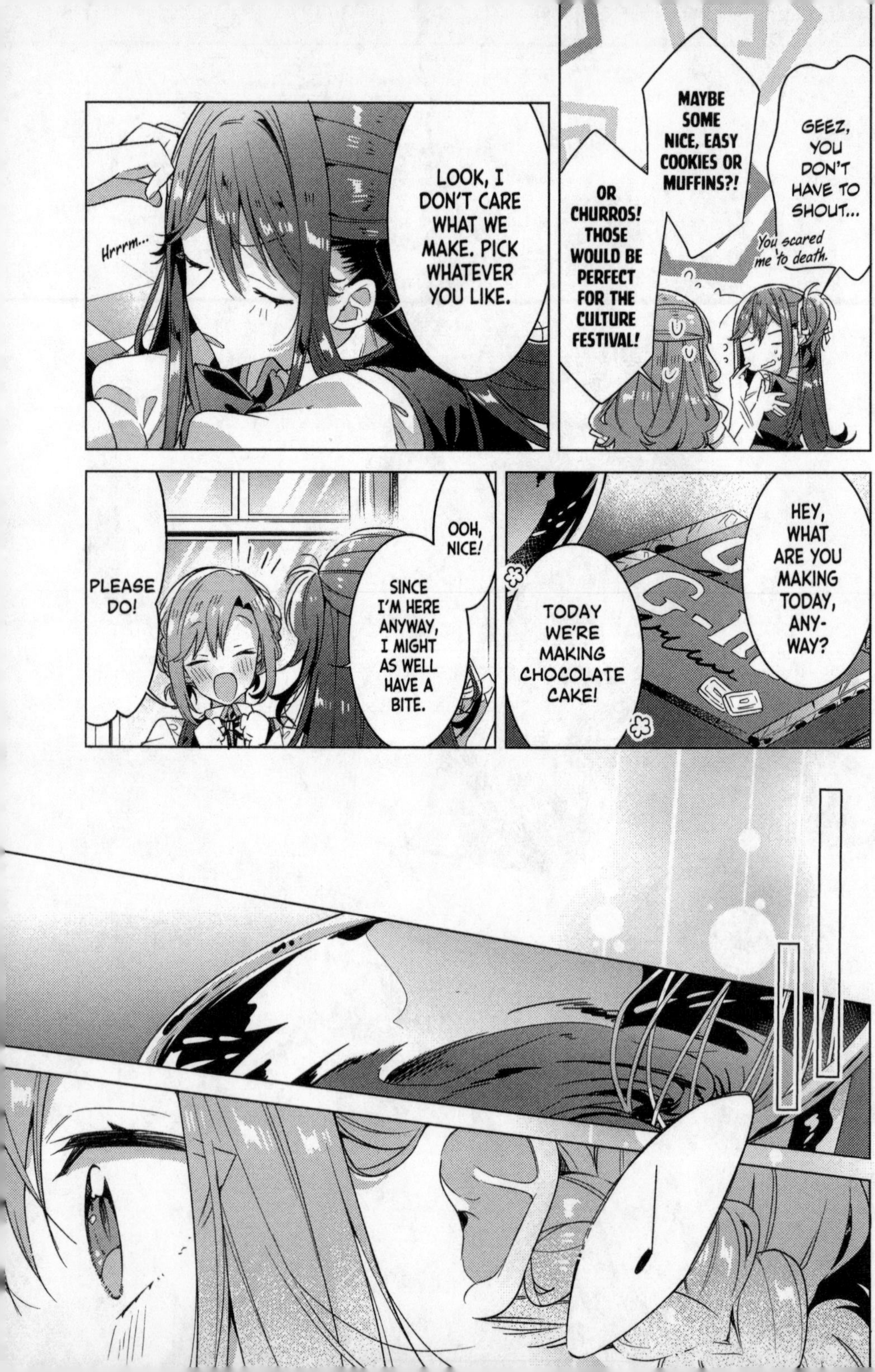
MAYBE SOME NICE, EASY COOKIES OR MUFFINS?!
OR CHURROS! THOSE WOULD BE PERFECT FOR THE CULTURE FESTIVAL!
GEEZ, YOU DON'T HAVE TO SHOUT...
You scared me to death.
LOOK, I DON'T CARE WHAT WE MAKE. PICK WHATEVER YOU LIKE.
Hrrrm...
HEY, WHAT ARE YOU MAKING TODAY, ANYWAY?
TODAY WE'RE MAKING CHOCOLATE CAKE!
OOH, NICE!
SINCE I'M HERE ANYWAY, I MIGHT AS WELL HAVE A BITE.
PLEASE DO!

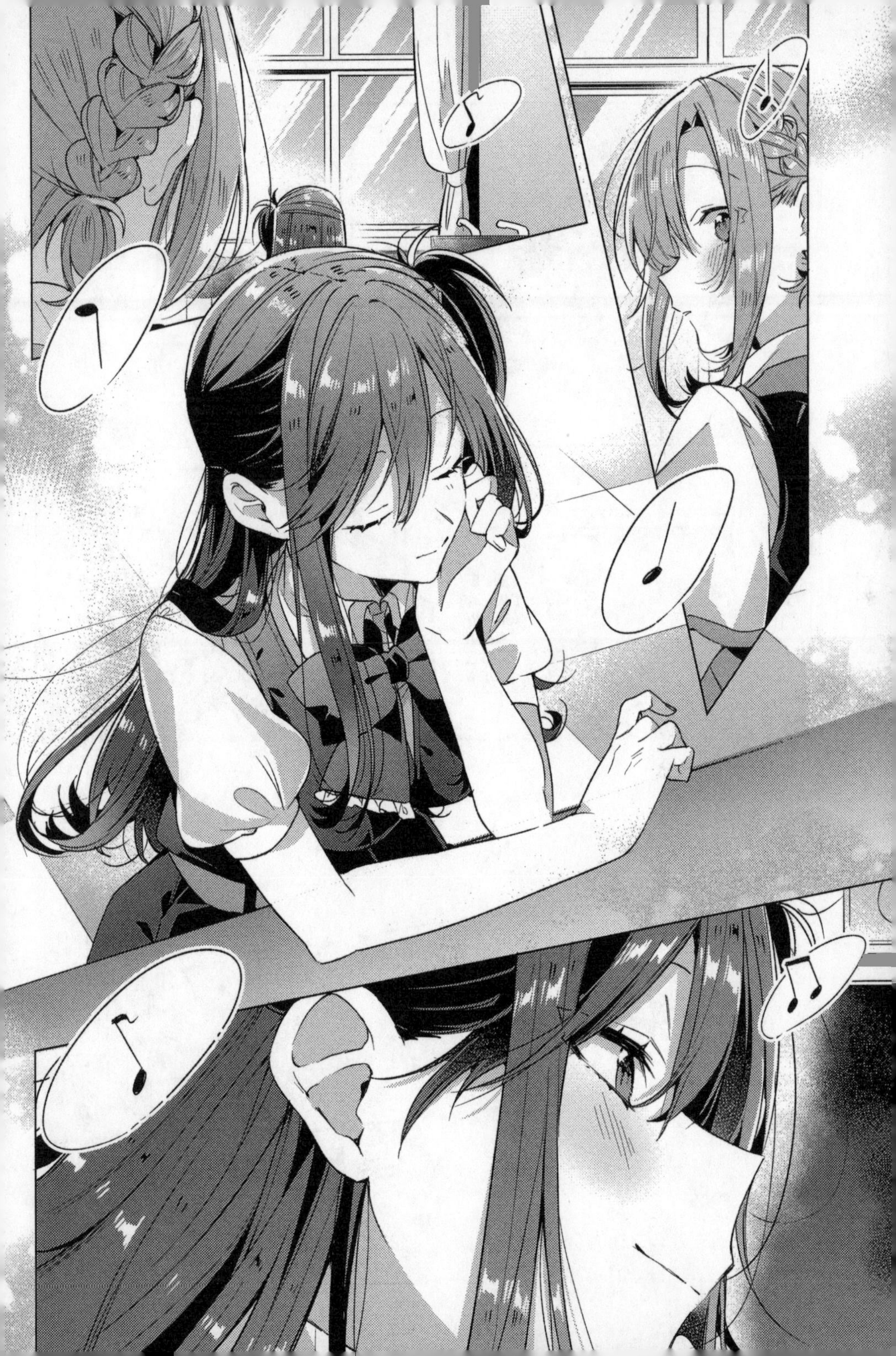

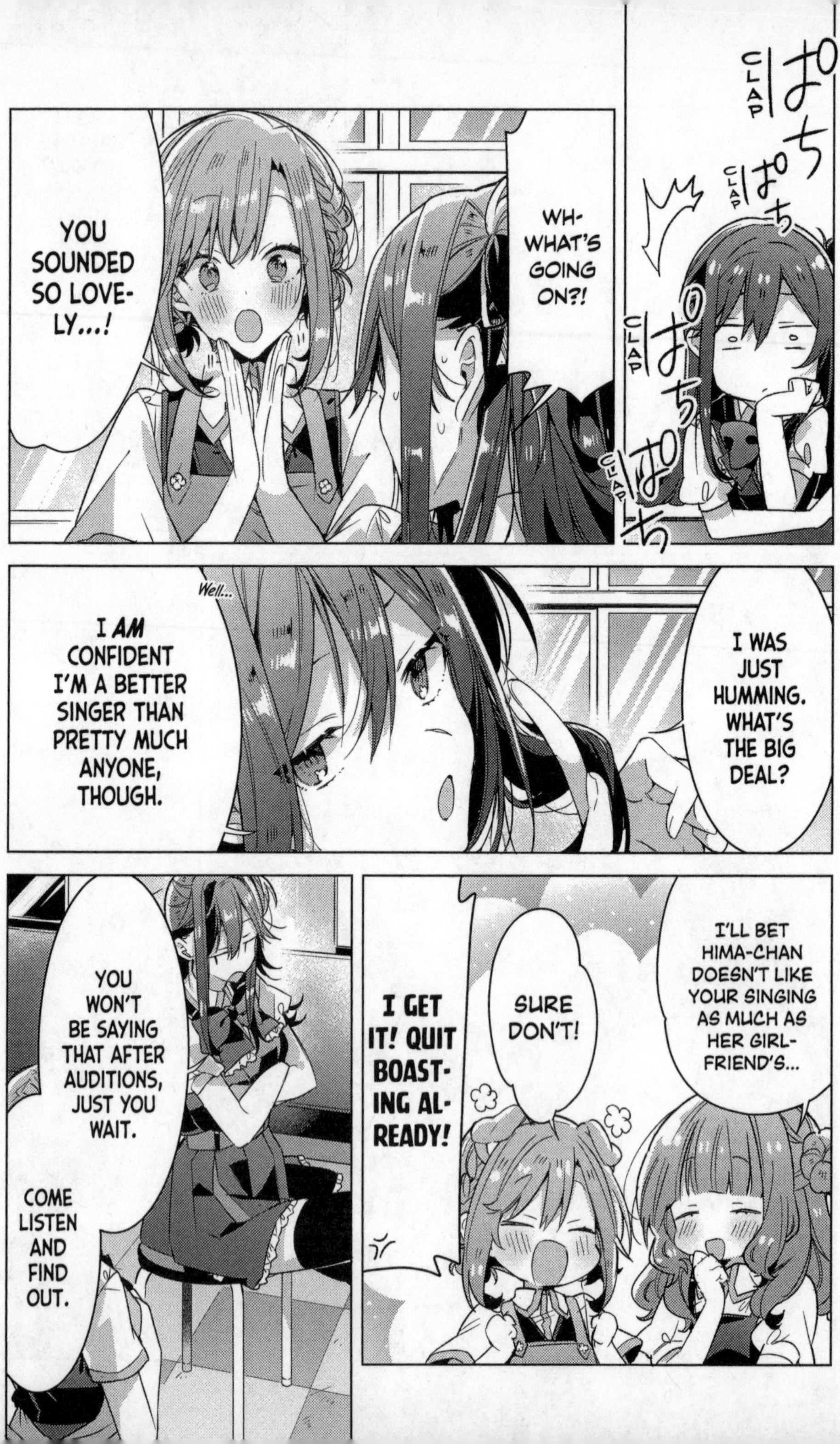
ぱち CLAP
ぱち CLAP
ぱち CLAP
ぱち CLAP
WH-WHAT'S GOING ON?!
YOU SOUNDED SO LOVELY...!
I WAS JUST HUMMING. WHAT'S THE BIG DEAL?
Well...
I *AM* CONFIDENT I'M A BETTER SINGER THAN PRETTY MUCH ANYONE, THOUGH.
I'LL BET HIMA-CHAN DOESN'T LIKE YOUR SINGING AS MUCH AS HER GIRL-FRIEND'S...
SURE DON'T!
I GET IT! QUIT BOAST-ING AL-READY!
YOU WON'T BE SAYING THAT AFTER AUDITIONS, JUST YOU WAIT.
COME LISTEN AND FIND OUT.

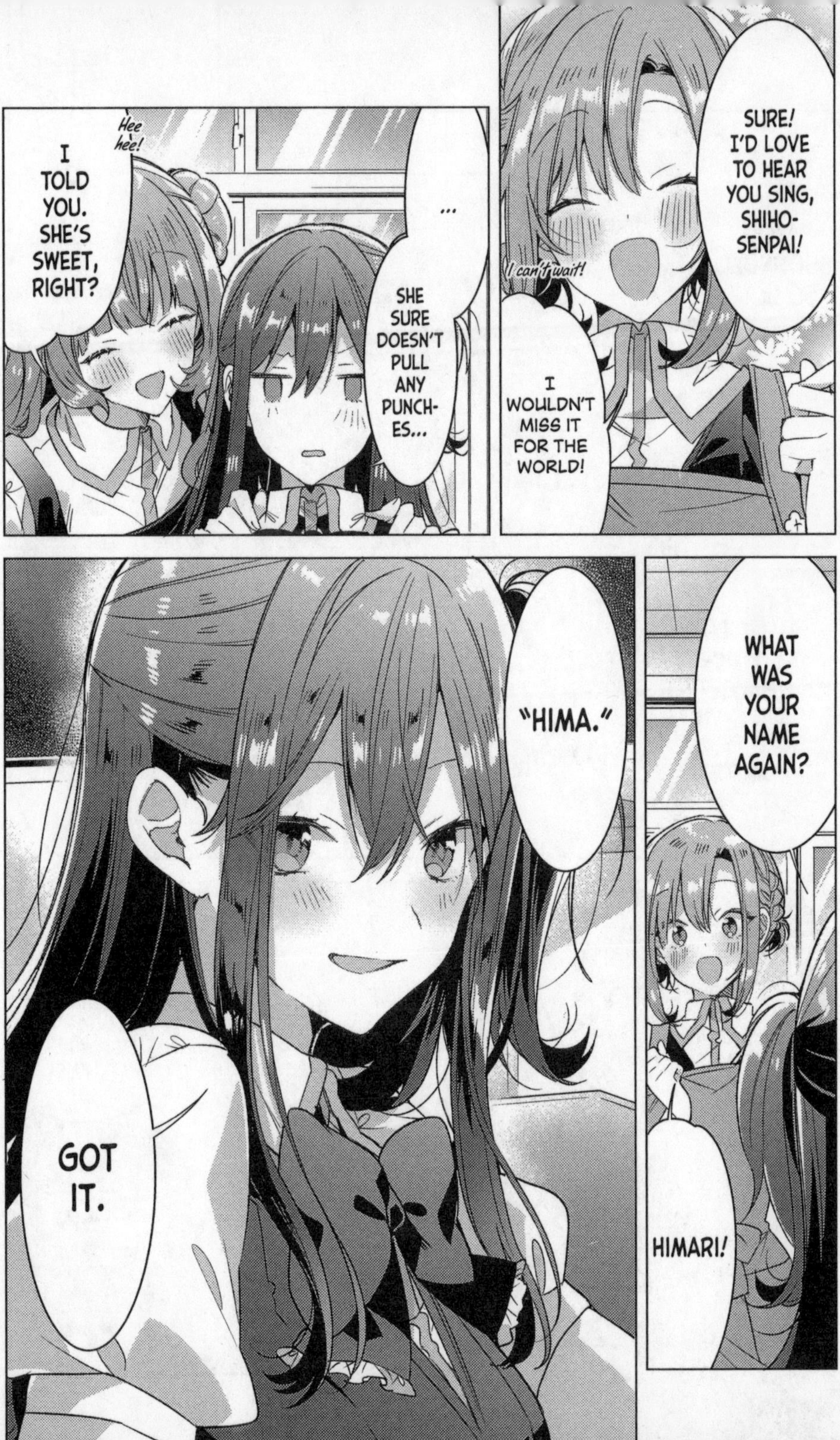
SURE! I'D LOVE TO HEAR YOU SING, SHIHO-SENPAI!
I can't wait!
I WOULDN'T MISS IT FOR THE WORLD!
Hee hee!
I TOLD YOU. SHE'S SWEET, RIGHT?
...
SHE SURE DOESN'T PULL ANY PUNCH-ES...
WHAT WAS YOUR NAME AGAIN?
HIMARI!
"HIMA."
GOT IT.

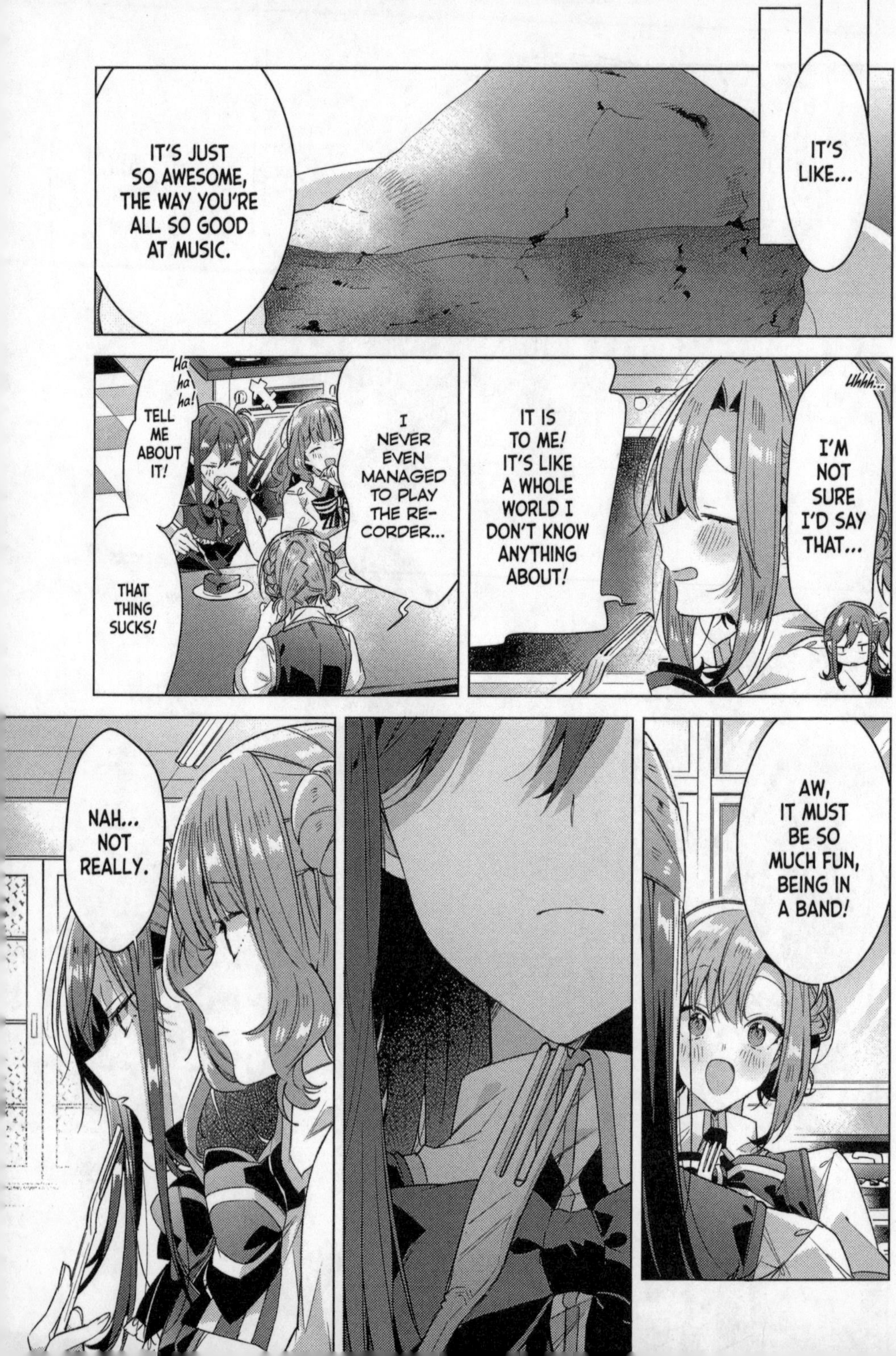
IT'S LIKE...
IT'S JUST SO AWESOME, THE WAY YOU'RE ALL SO GOOD AT MUSIC.
Uhhh...
I'M NOT SURE I'D SAY THAT...
IT IS TO ME! IT'S LIKE A WHOLE WORLD I DON'T KNOW ANYTHING ABOUT!
I NEVER EVEN MANAGED TO PLAY THE RE-CORDER...
Ha ha ha!
TELL ME ABOUT IT!
THAT THING SUCKS!
AW, IT MUST BE SO MUCH FUN, BEING IN A BAND!
NAH... NOT REALLY.

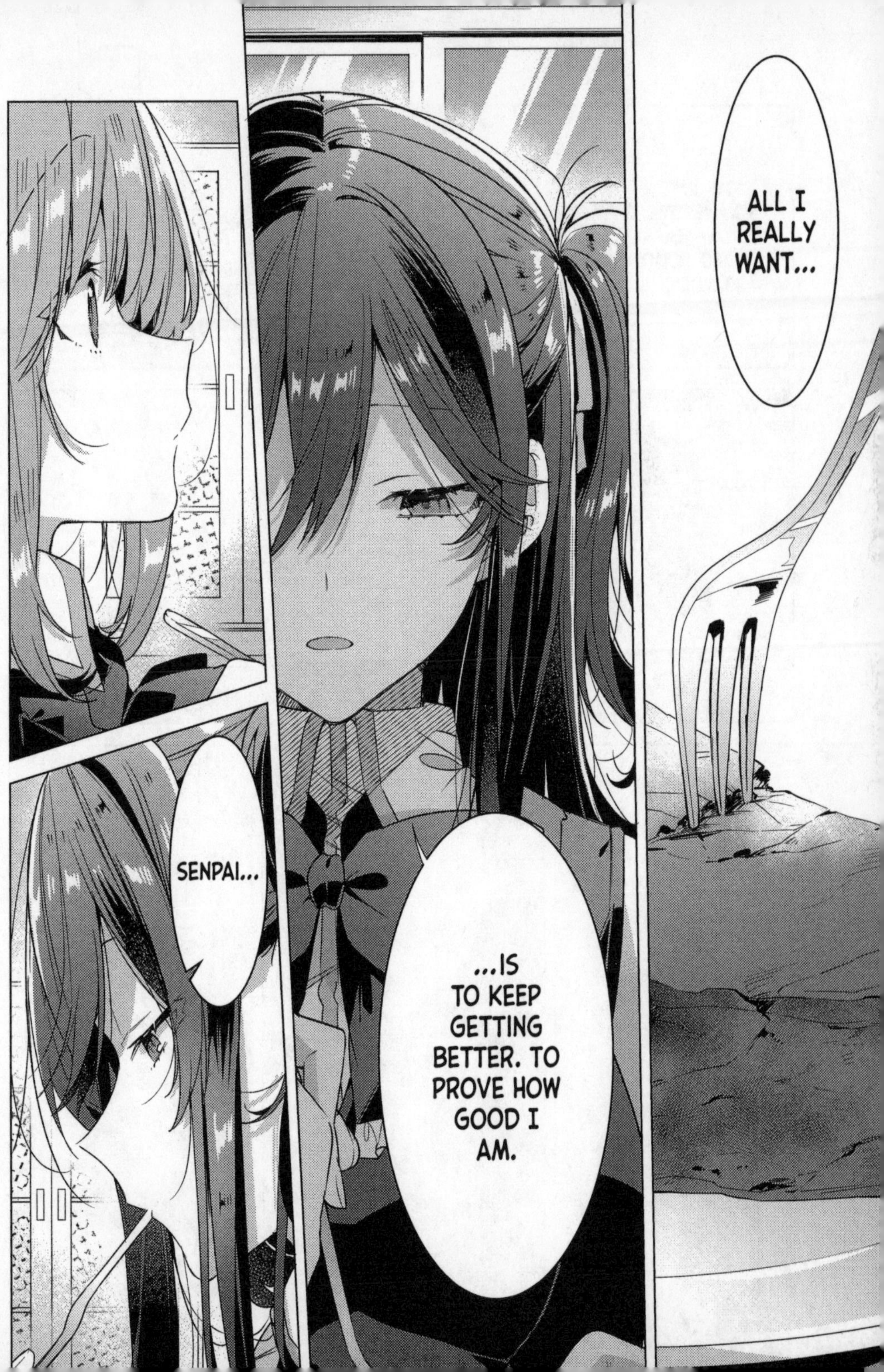
ALL I REALLY WANT...
...IS TO KEEP GETTING BETTER. TO PROVE HOW GOOD I AM.
SENPAI...

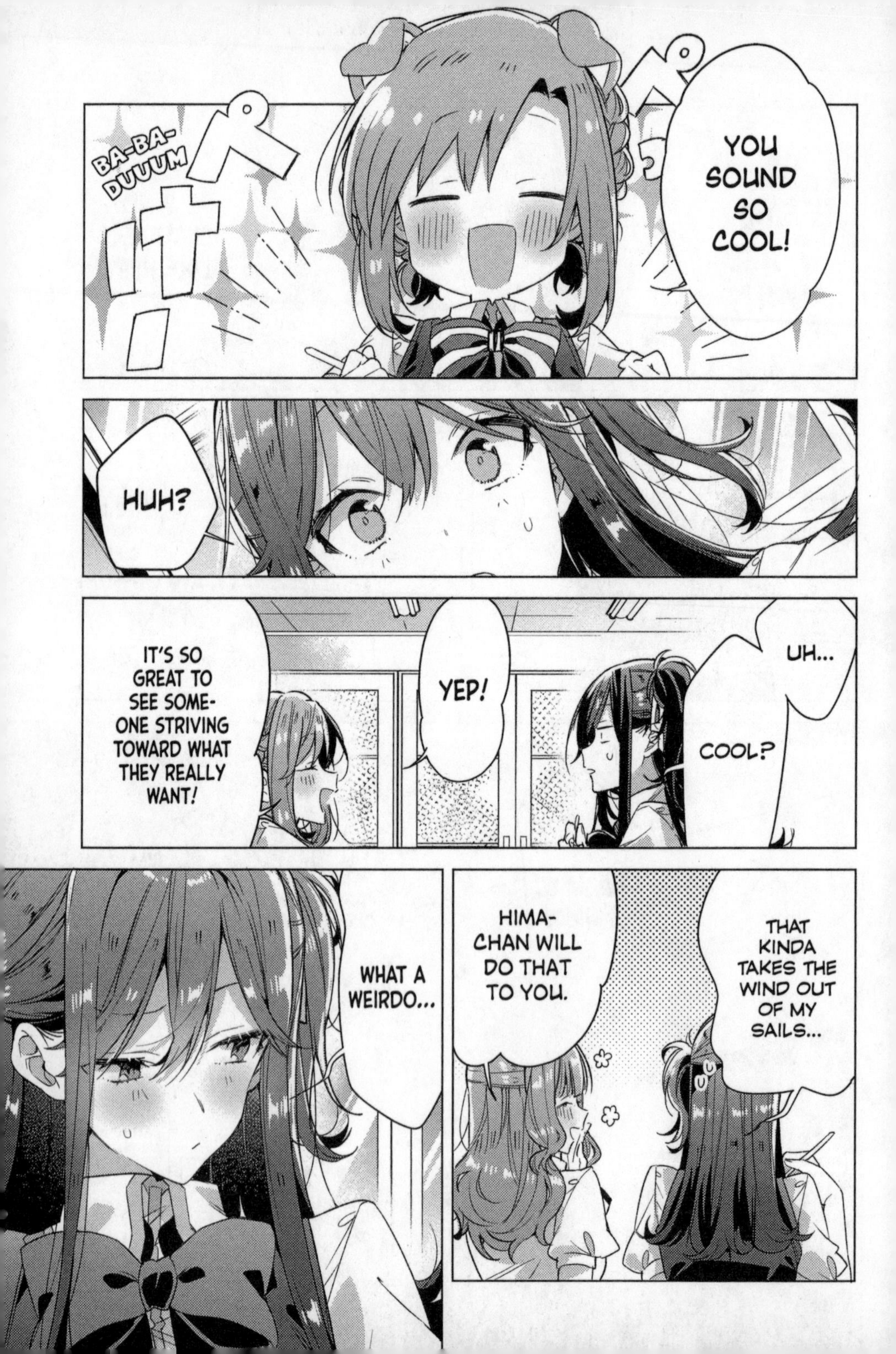
YOU SOUND SO COOL!
BA-BA-DUUUM
HUH?
UH...
COOL?
YEP!
IT'S SO GREAT TO SEE SOME-ONE STRIVING TOWARD WHAT THEY REALLY WANT!
THAT KINDA TAKES THE WIND OUT OF MY SAILS...
HIMA-CHAN WILL DO THAT TO YOU.
WHAT A WEIRDO...

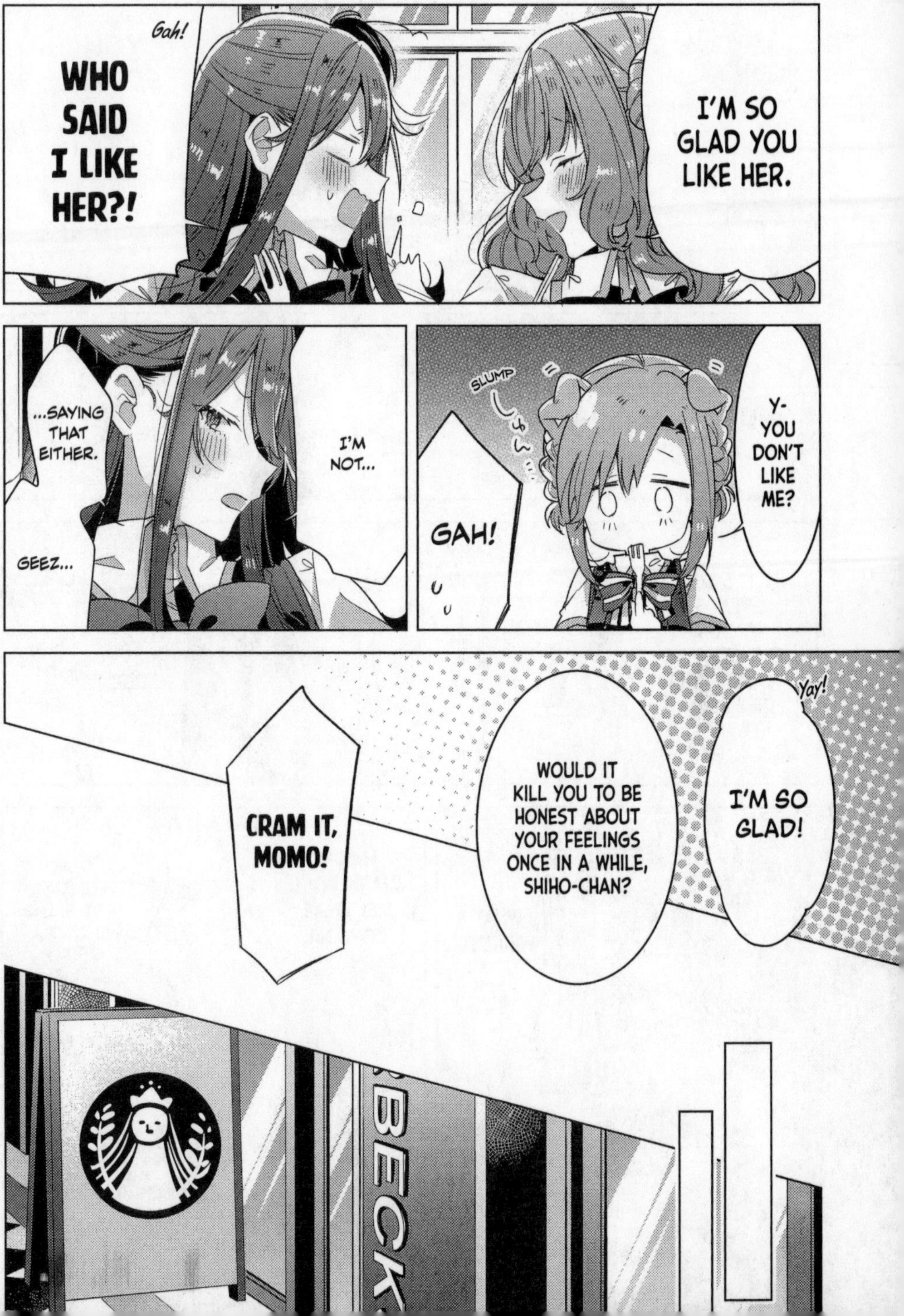
I'M SO GLAD YOU LIKE HER.
Gah!
WHO SAID I LIKE HER?!
Y-YOU DON'T LIKE ME?
SLUMP
GAH!
I'M NOT...
...SAYING THAT EITHER.
GEEZ...
Yay!
I'M SO GLAD!
WOULD IT KILL YOU TO BE HONEST ABOUT YOUR FEELINGS ONCE IN A WHILE, SHIHO-CHAN?
CRAM IT, MOMO!

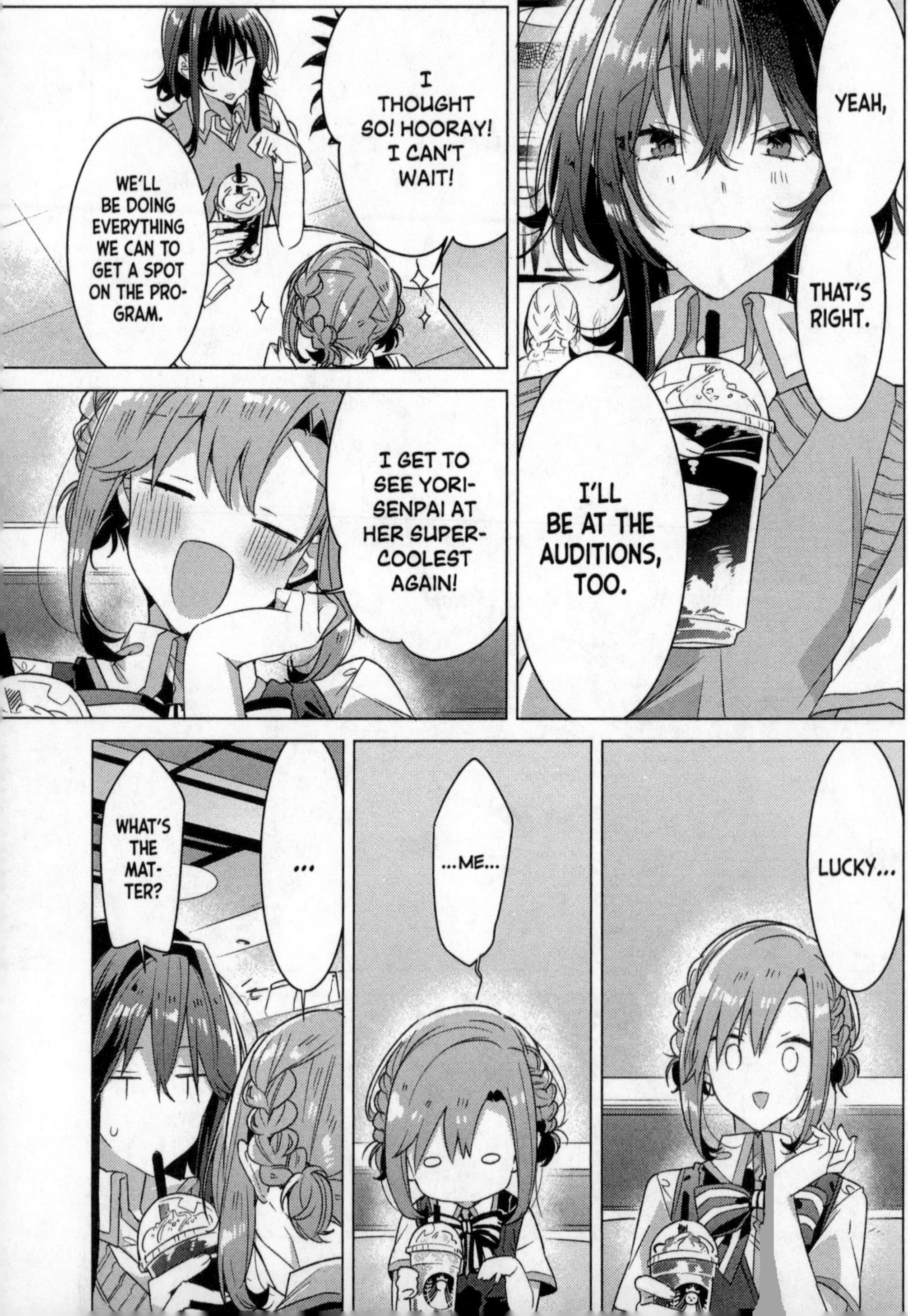
YEAH,
THAT'S RIGHT.
I'LL BE AT THE AUDITIONS, TOO.
I THOUGHT SO! HOORAY! I CAN'T WAIT!
WE'LL BE DOING EVERYTHING WE CAN TO GET A SPOT ON THE PRO-GRAM.
I GET TO SEE YORI-SENPAI AT HER SUPER-COOLEST AGAIN!
LUCKY...
...ME...
...
WHAT'S THE MAT-TER?

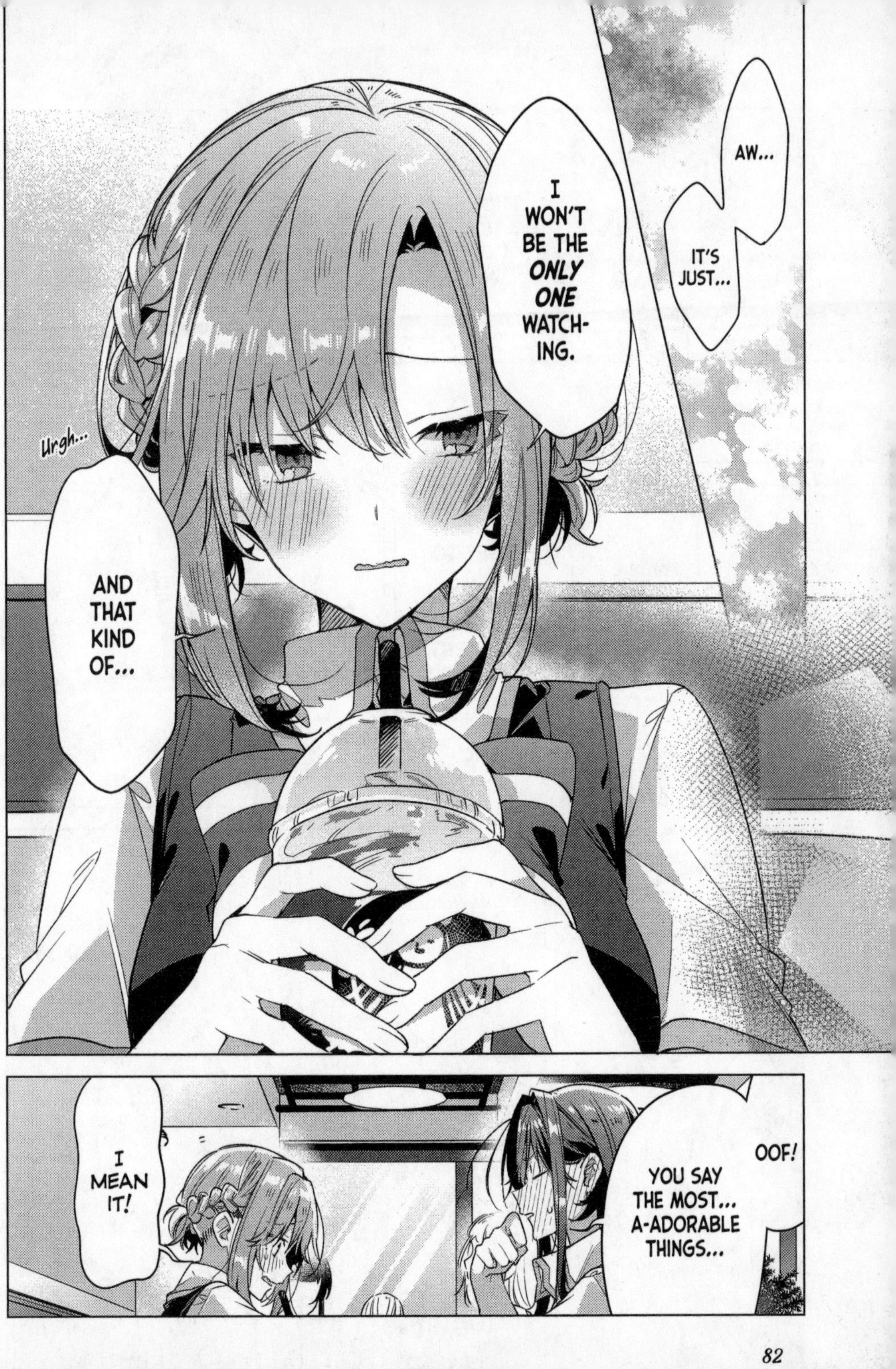
AW...
IT'S JUST...
I WON'T BE THE *ONLY ONE* WATCHING.
Urgh...
AND THAT KIND OF...
OOF!
YOU SAY THE MOST... A-ADORABLE THINGS...
I MEAN IT!

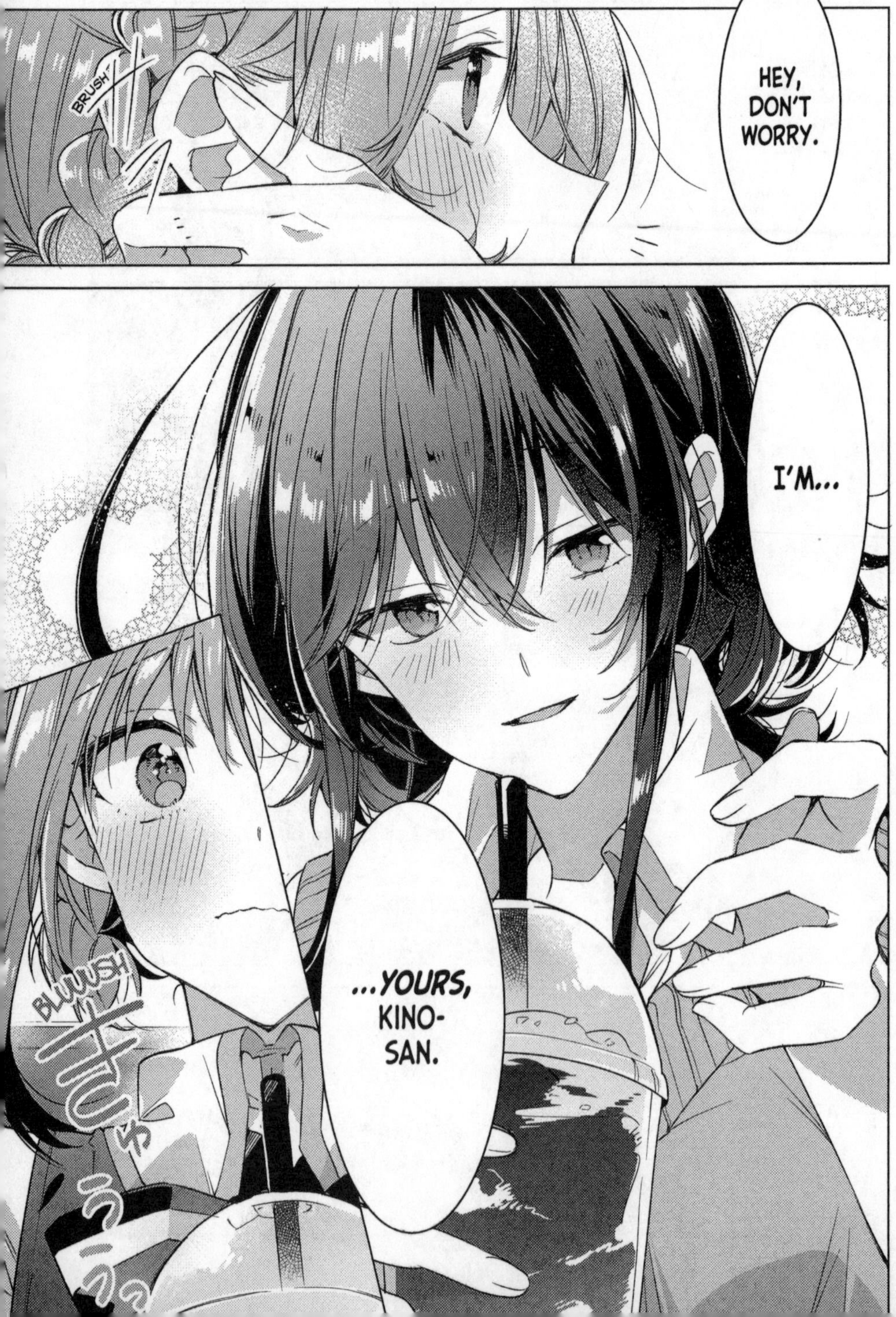
HEY, DON'T WORRY.
BRUSH
I'M...
...YOURS, KINO-SAN.
BLUUUSH

YOU'RE RIGHT! I KNOW YOU ARE!

FWSSHHH

AM I RIGHT, OR AM I RIGHT?

RIGHT! I WON'T!

IT'S SWEET, YOU GETTING JEALOUS AND ALL...

BUT DON'T WORRY, OKAY?

ATTAGIRL.

WIF

'CAUSE YOU'RE *MINE*, YORI-SENPAI!

Song 18 – END

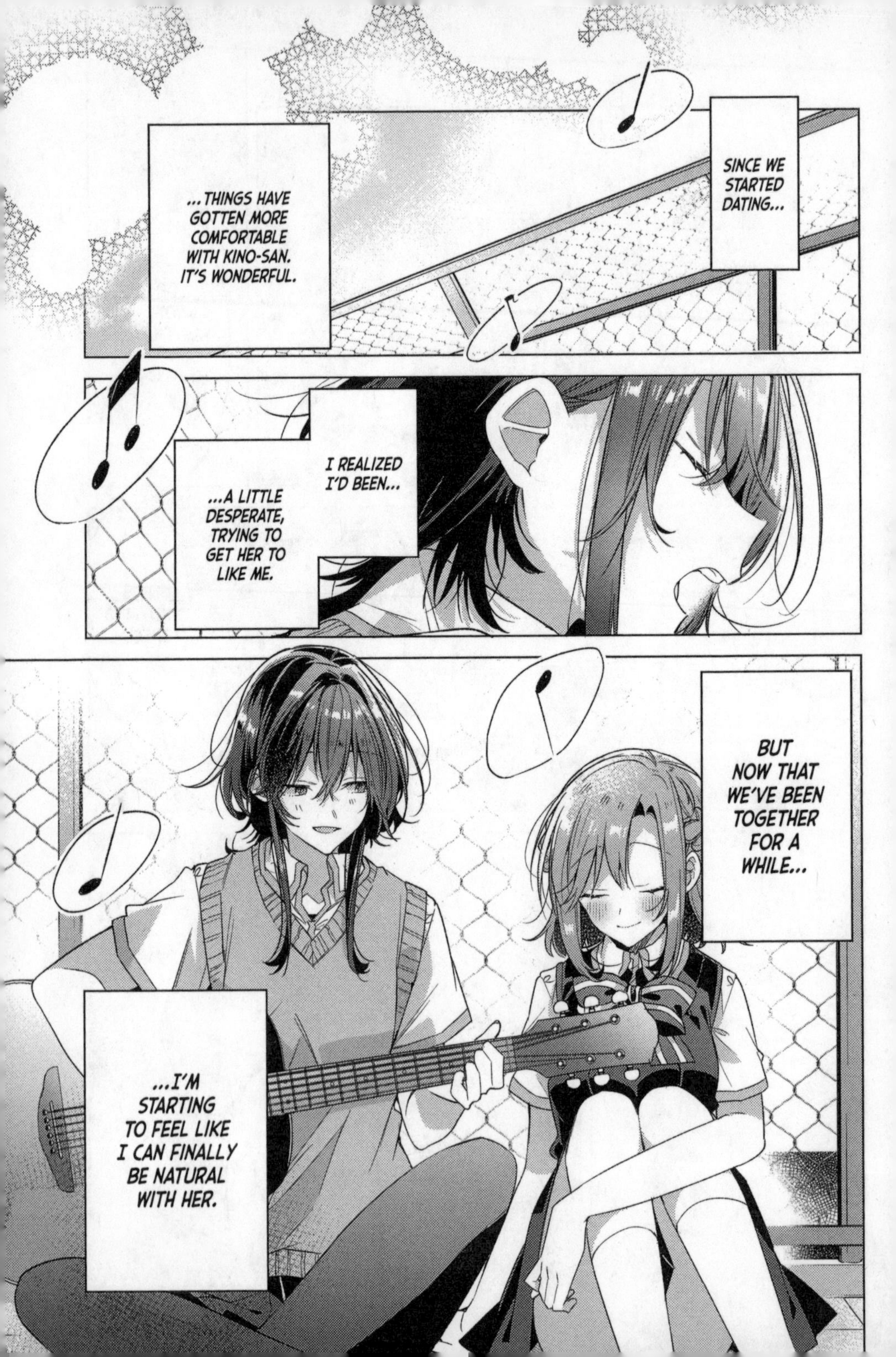
SINCE WE STARTED DATING...
...THINGS HAVE GOTTEN MORE COMFORTABLE WITH KINO-SAN. IT'S WONDERFUL.
I REALIZED I'D BEEN...
...A LITTLE DESPERATE, TRYING TO GET HER TO LIKE ME.
BUT NOW THAT WE'VE BEEN TOGETHER FOR A WHILE...
...I'M STARTING TO FEEL LIKE I CAN FINALLY BE NATURAL WITH HER.

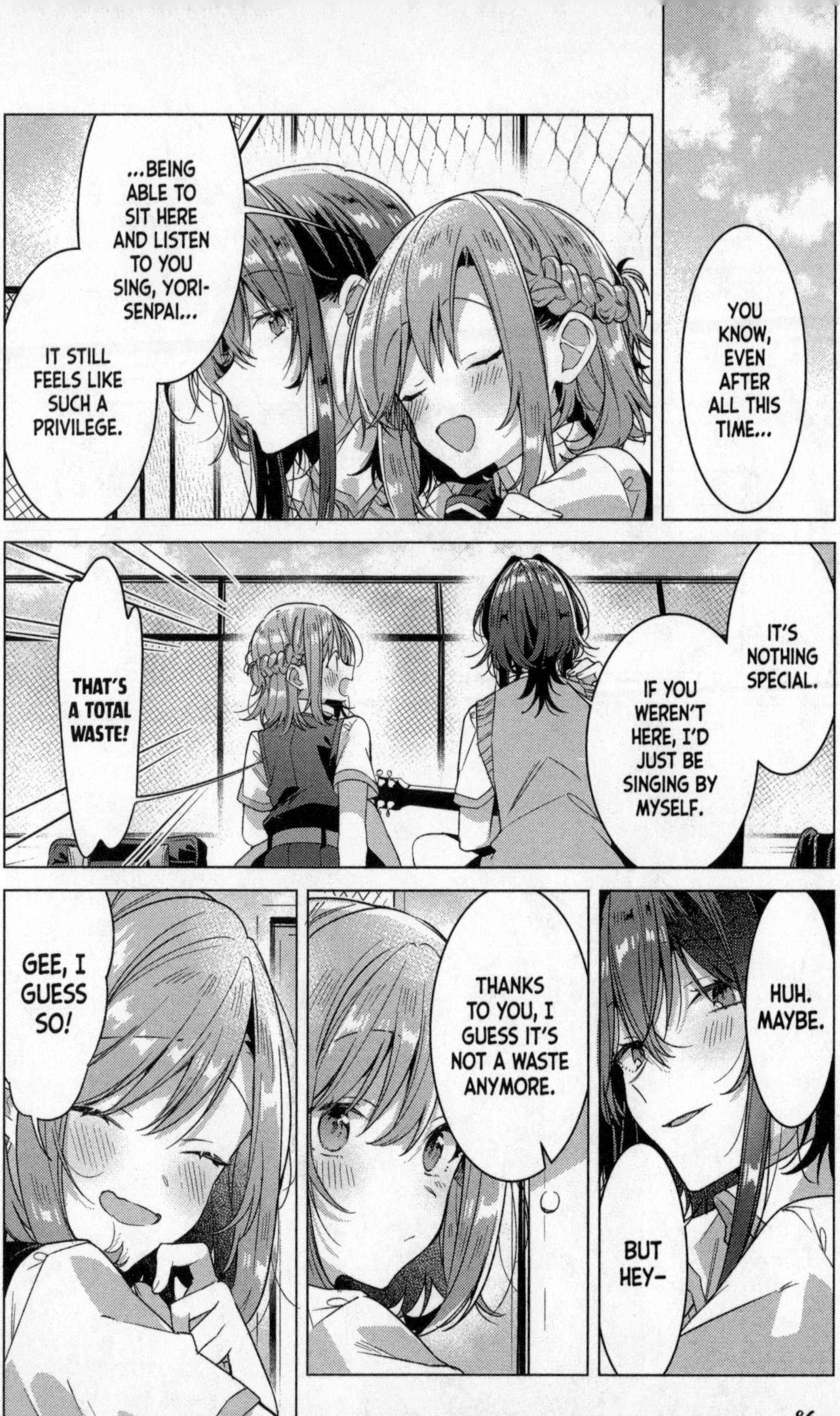
YOU KNOW, EVEN AFTER ALL THIS TIME...
...BEING ABLE TO SIT HERE AND LISTEN TO YOU SING, YORI-SENPAI...
IT STILL FEELS LIKE SUCH A PRIVILEGE.
IT'S NOTHING SPECIAL.
IF YOU WEREN'T HERE, I'D JUST BE SINGING BY MYSELF.
THAT'S A TOTAL WASTE!
HUH. MAYBE.
BUT HEY-
THANKS TO YOU, I GUESS IT'S NOT A WASTE ANYMORE.
GEE, I GUESS SO!

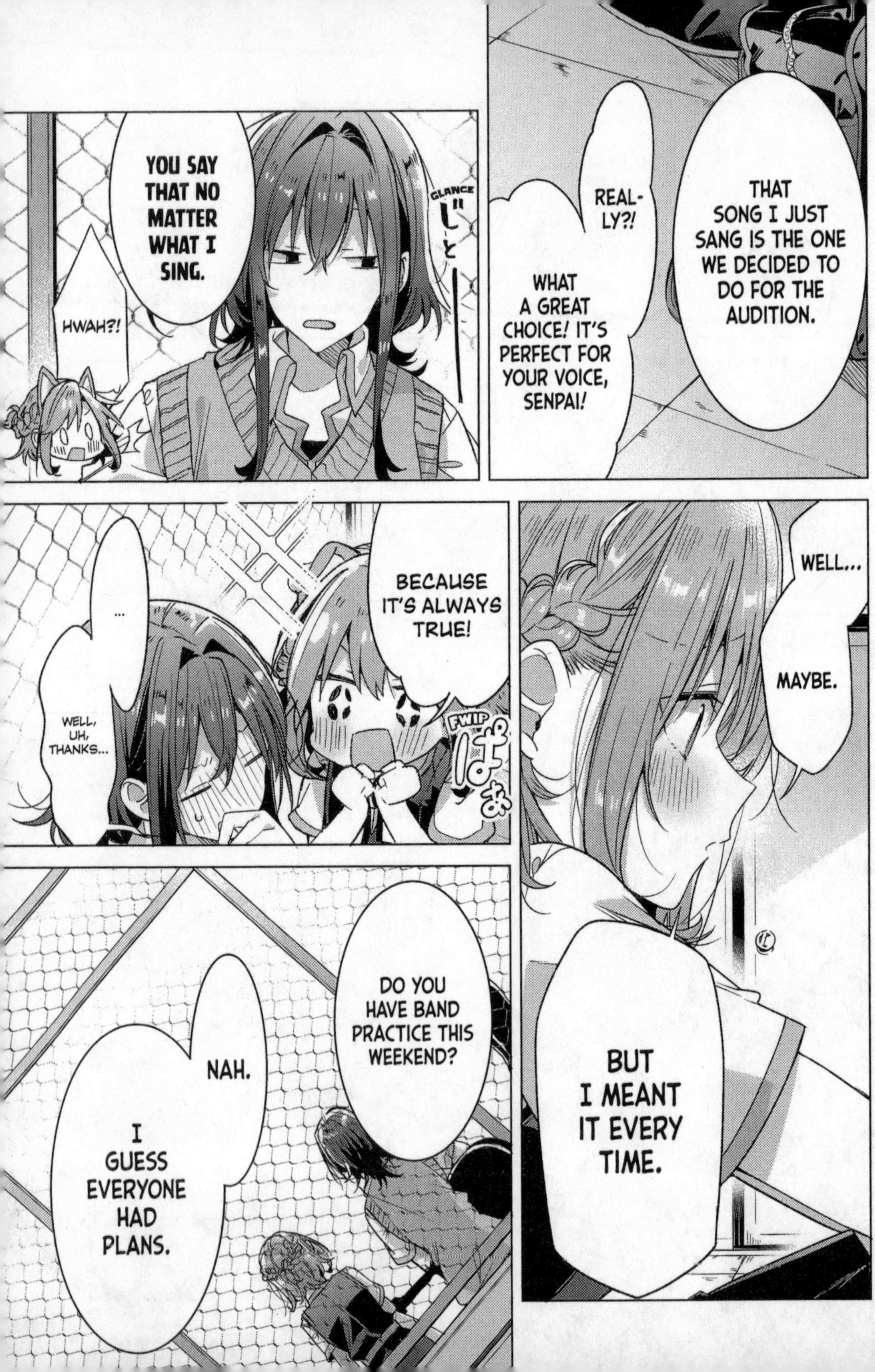
THAT SONG I JUST SANG IS THE ONE WE DECIDED TO DO FOR THE AUDITION.
REAL-LY?!
WHAT A GREAT CHOICE! IT'S PERFECT FOR YOUR VOICE, SENPAI!
YOU SAY THAT NO MATTER WHAT I SING.
GLANCE
HWAH?!
BECAUSE IT'S ALWAYS TRUE!
FWIP
...
WELL, UH, THANKS...
WELL...
MAYBE.
BUT I MEANT IT EVERY TIME.
DO YOU HAVE BAND PRACTICE THIS WEEKEND?
NAH.
I GUESS EVERYONE HAD PLANS.

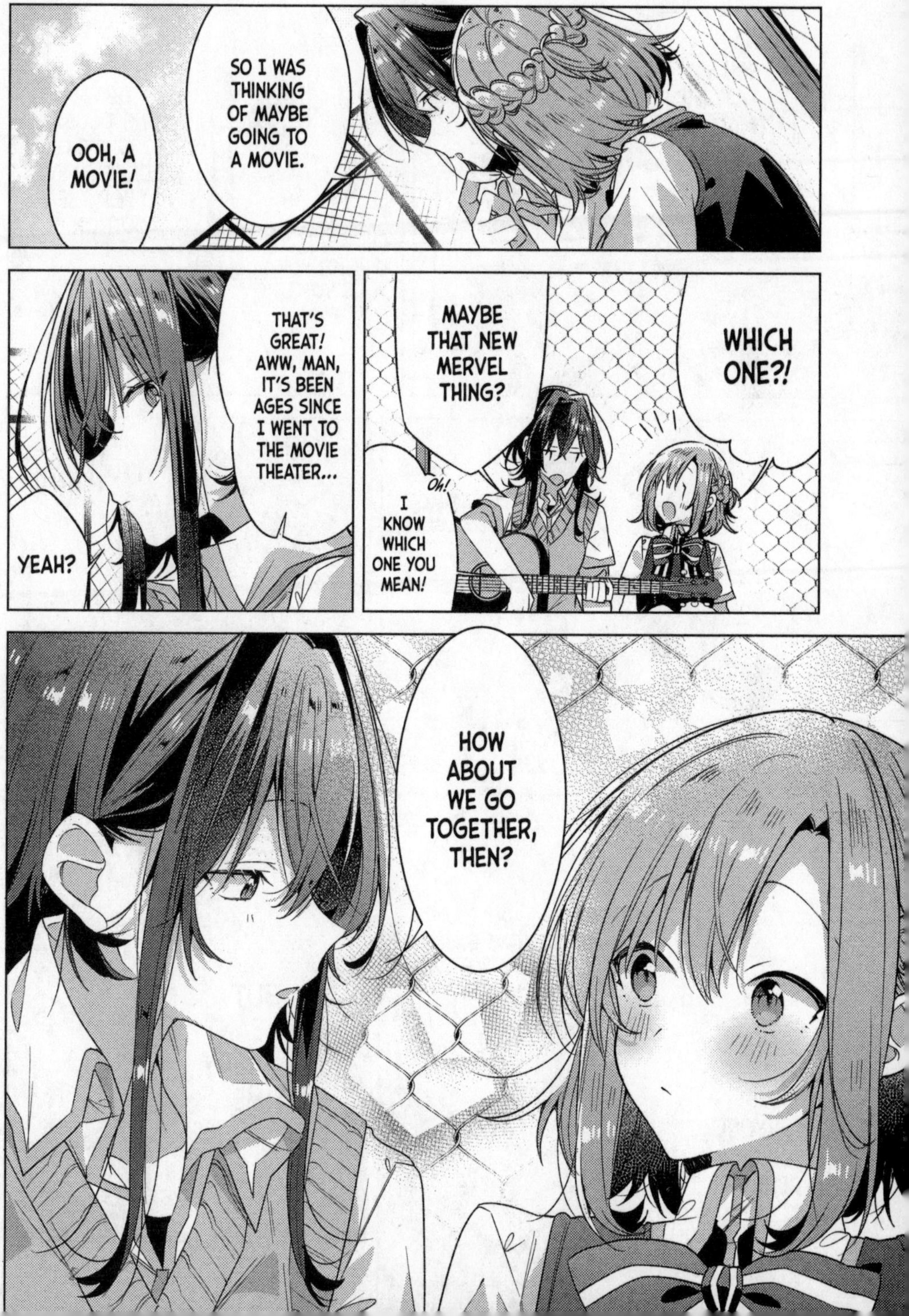
SO I WAS THINKING OF MAYBE GOING TO A MOVIE.
OOH, A MOVIE!
WHICH ONE?!
MAYBE THAT NEW MERVEL THING?
Oh!
I KNOW WHICH ONE YOU MEAN!
THAT'S GREAT! AWW, MAN, IT'S BEEN AGES SINCE I WENT TO THE MOVIE THEATER...
YEAH?
HOW ABOUT WE GO TOGETHER, THEN?

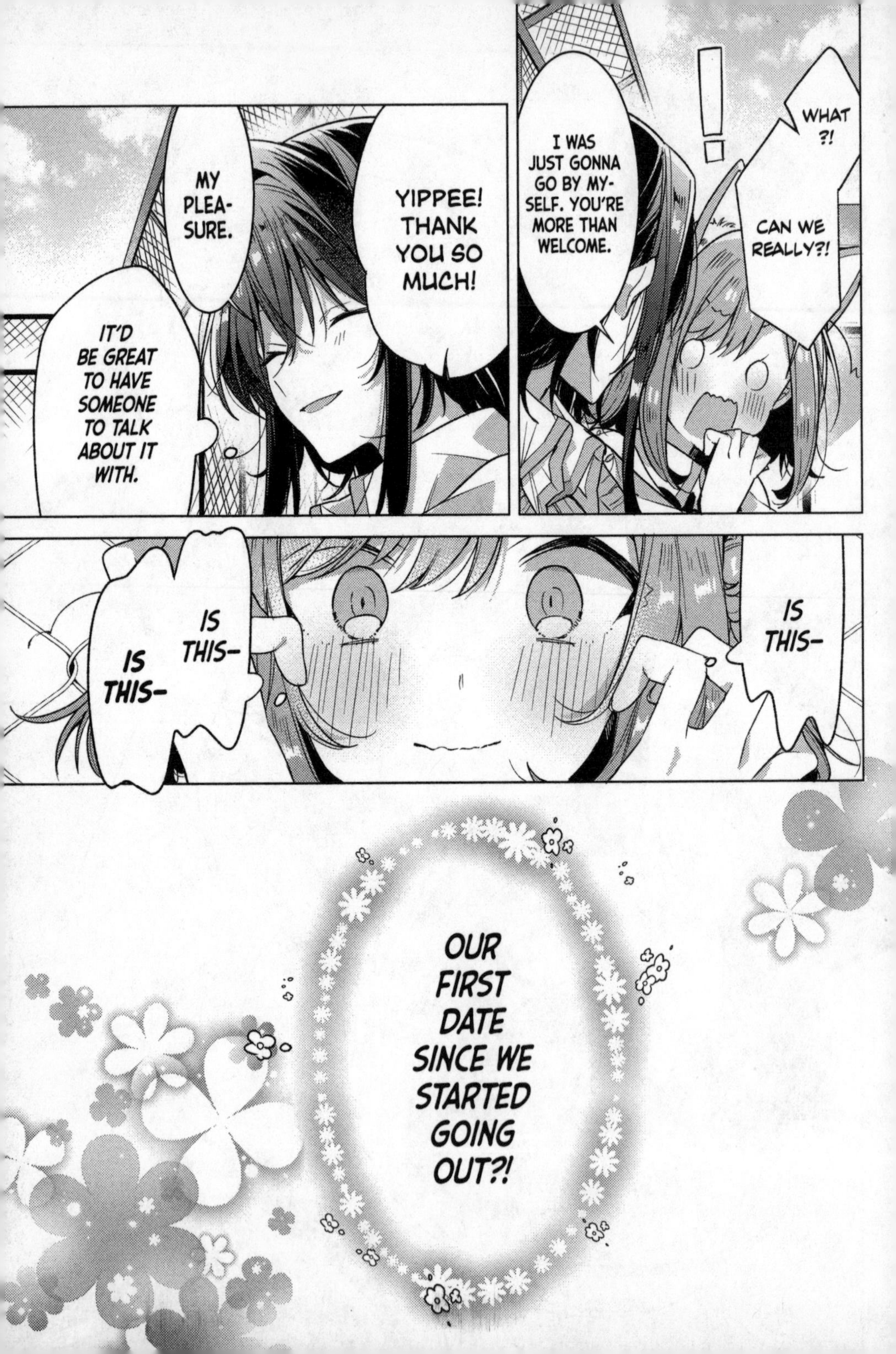
WHAT ?!
CAN WE REALLY?!
!
I WAS JUST GONNA GO BY MY-SELF. YOU'RE MORE THAN WELCOME.
YIPPEE! THANK YOU SO MUCH!
MY PLEA-SURE.
IT'D BE GREAT TO HAVE SOMEONE TO TALK ABOUT IT WITH.
IS THIS-
IS THIS-
IS THIS-
OUR FIRST DATE SINCE WE STARTED GOING OUT?!

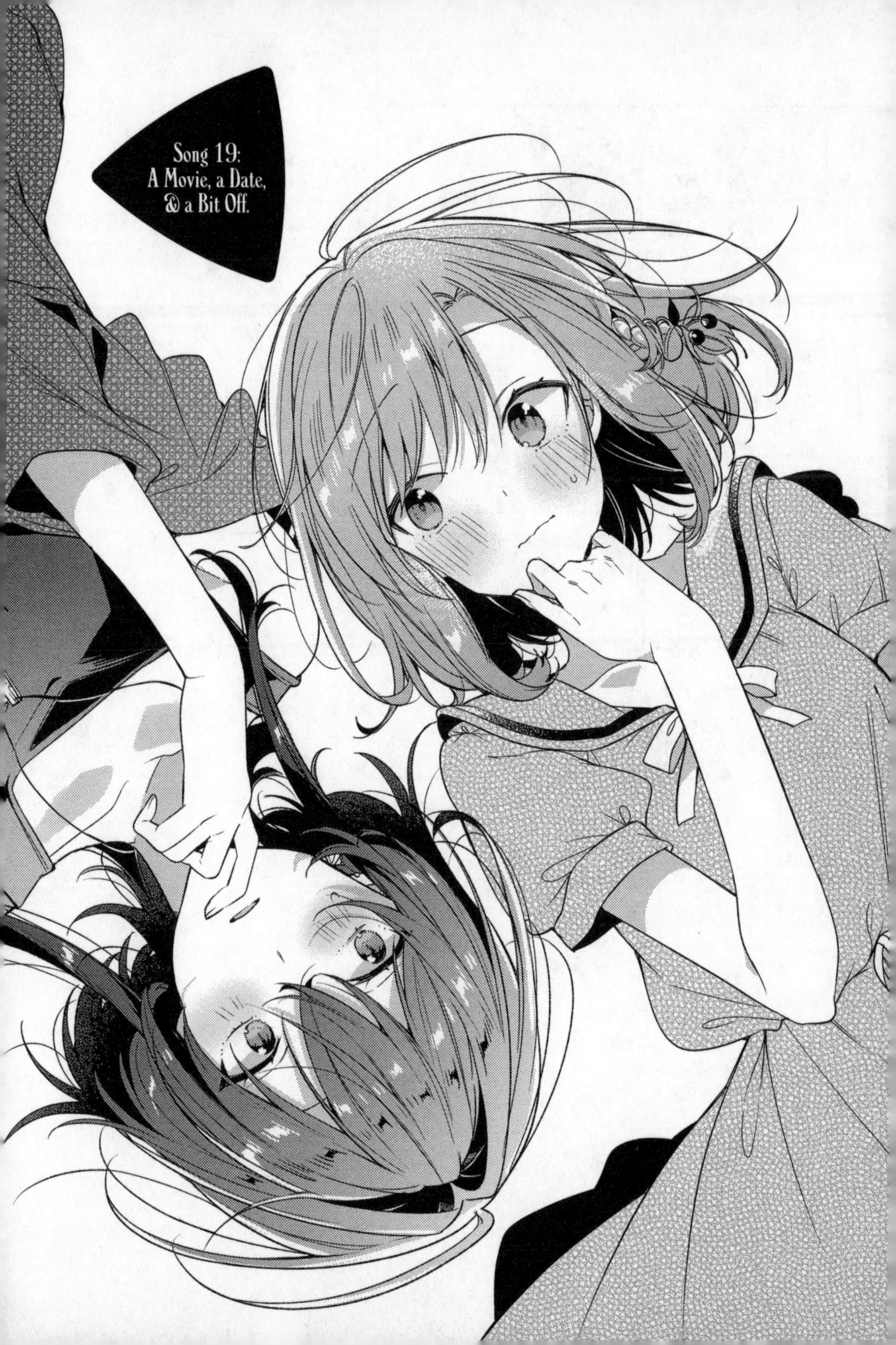
Song 19:
A Movie, a Date,
& a Bit Off.

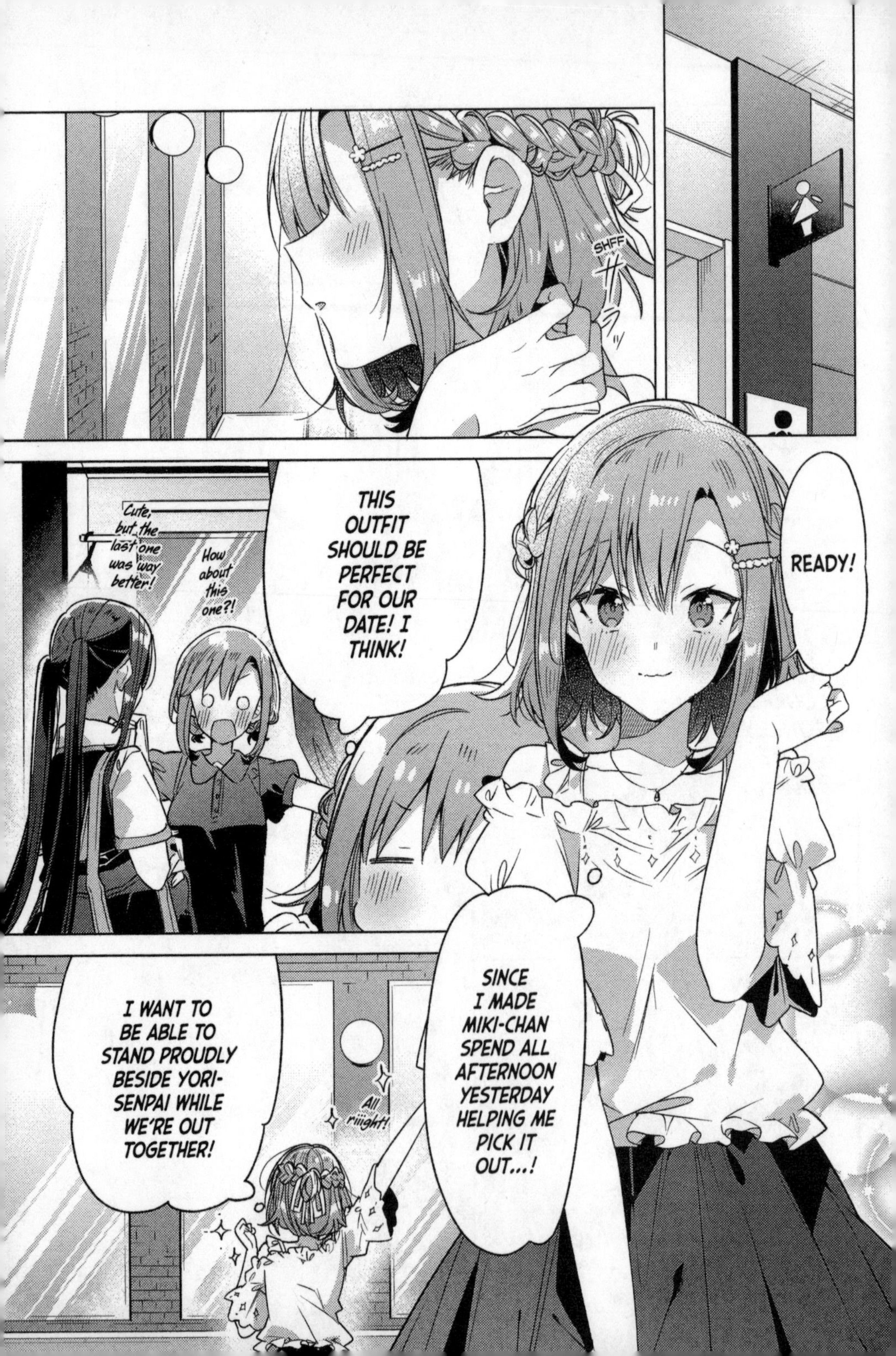
SHFF
READY!
SINCE I MADE MIKI-CHAN SPEND ALL AFTERNOON YESTERDAY HELPING ME PICK IT OUT...!
THIS OUTFIT SHOULD BE PERFECT FOR OUR DATE! I THINK!
How about this one?!
Cute, but the last one was way better!
I WANT TO BE ABLE TO STAND PROUDLY BESIDE YORI-SENPAI WHILE WE'RE OUT TOGETHER!
All riiight!

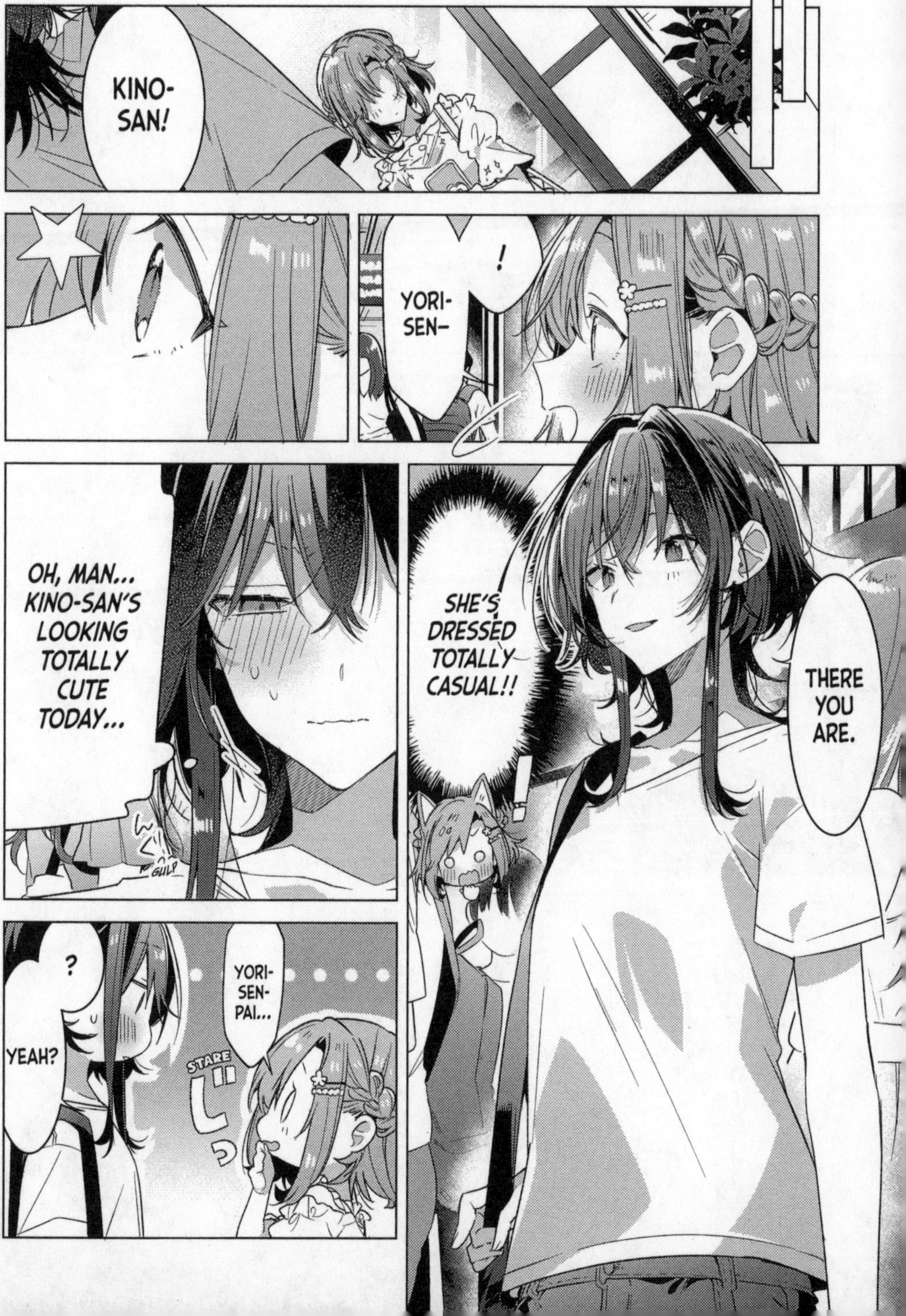
KINO-SAN!
!
YORI-SEN–
THERE YOU ARE.
SHE'S DRESSED TOTALLY CASUAL!!
OH, MAN... KINO-SAN'S LOOKING TOTALLY CUTE TODAY...
GULP
YORI-SEN-PAI...
STARE
?
YEAH?

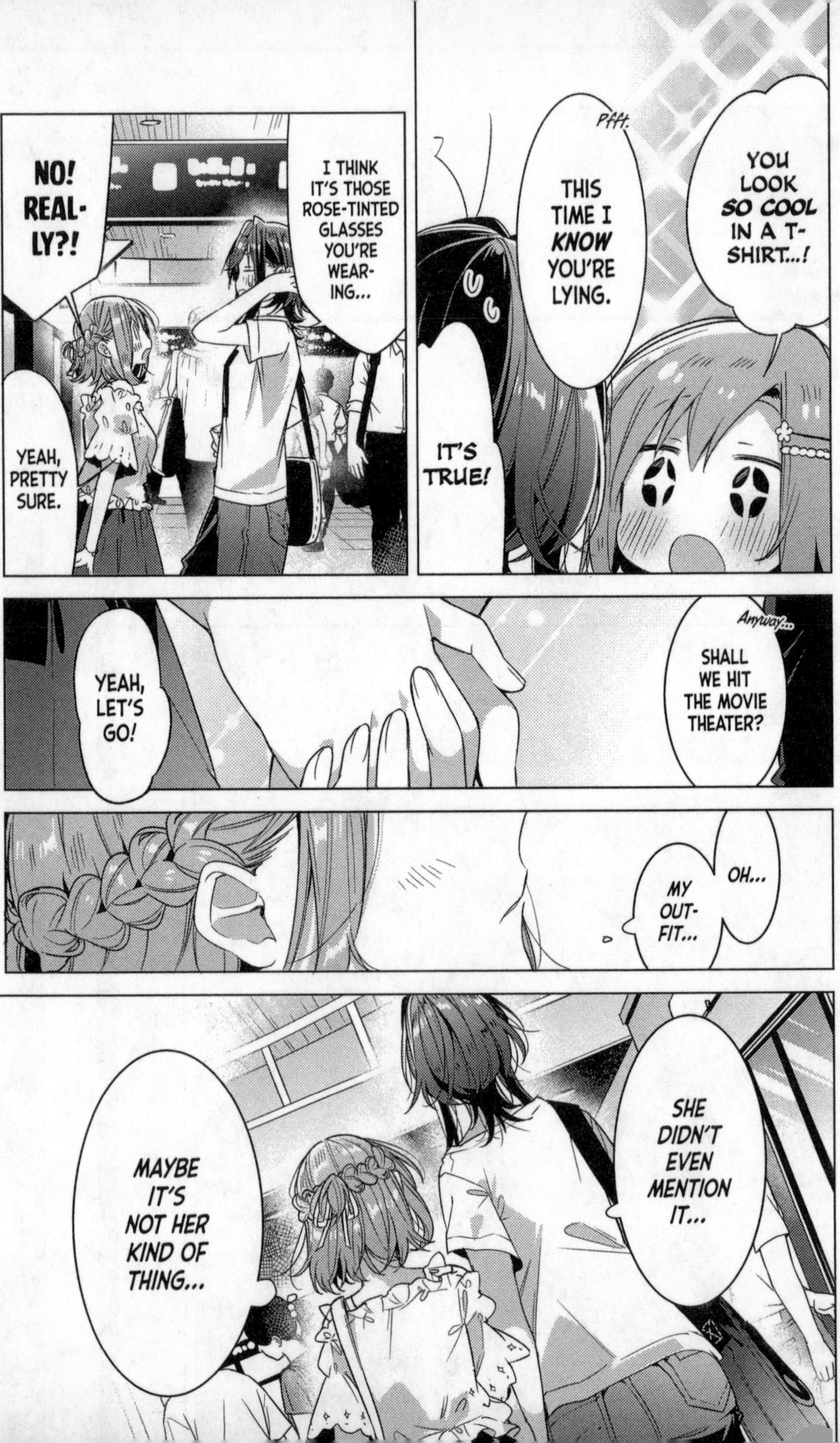
YOU LOOK *SO COOL* IN A T-SHIRT...!
Pfft.
THIS TIME I *KNOW* YOU'RE LYING.
IT'S TRUE!
I THINK IT'S THOSE ROSE-TINTED GLASSES YOU'RE WEAR-ING...
NO! REAL-LY?!
YEAH, PRETTY SURE.
Anyway...
SHALL WE HIT THE MOVIE THEATER?
YEAH, LET'S GO!
OH...
MY OUT-FIT...
SHE DIDN'T EVEN MENTION IT...
MAYBE IT'S NOT HER KIND OF THING...

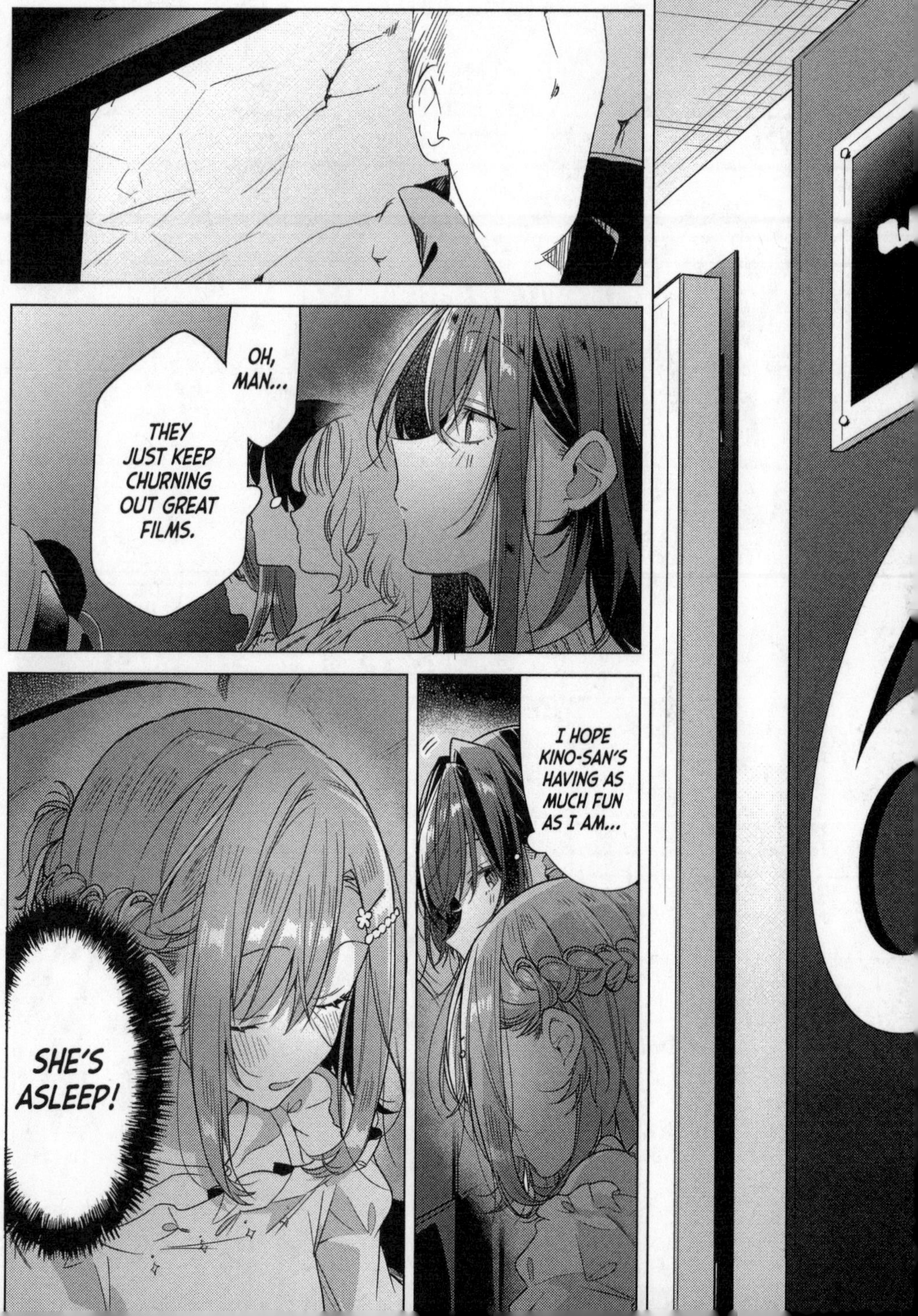
OH, MAN...
THEY JUST KEEP CHURNING OUT GREAT FILMS.
I HOPE KINO-SAN'S HAVING AS MUCH FUN AS I AM...
SHE'S ASLEEP!

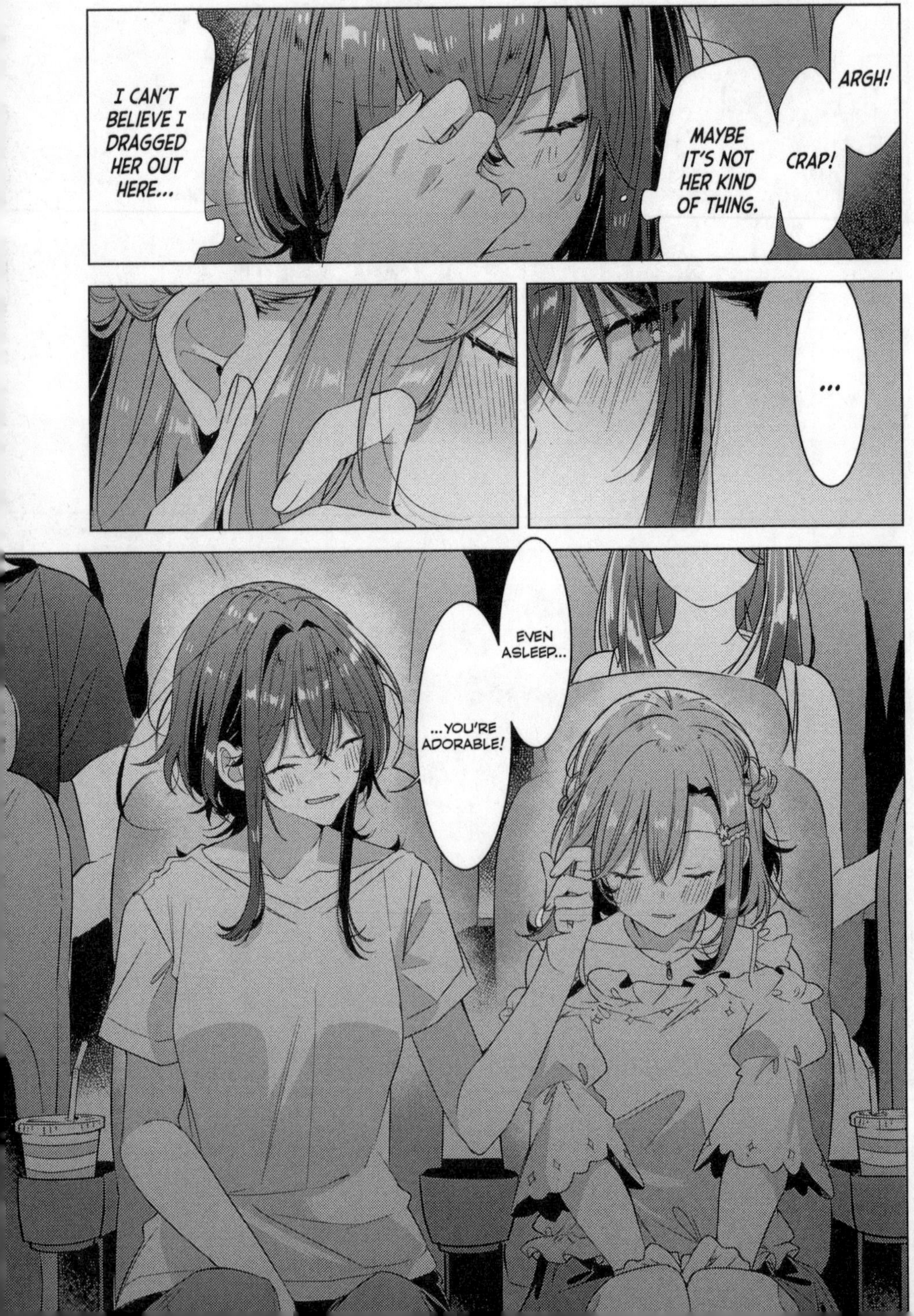
ARGH!
CRAP!
MAYBE IT'S NOT HER KIND OF THING.
I CAN'T BELIEVE I DRAGGED HER OUT HERE...
...
EVEN ASLEEP...
...YOU'RE ADORABLE!

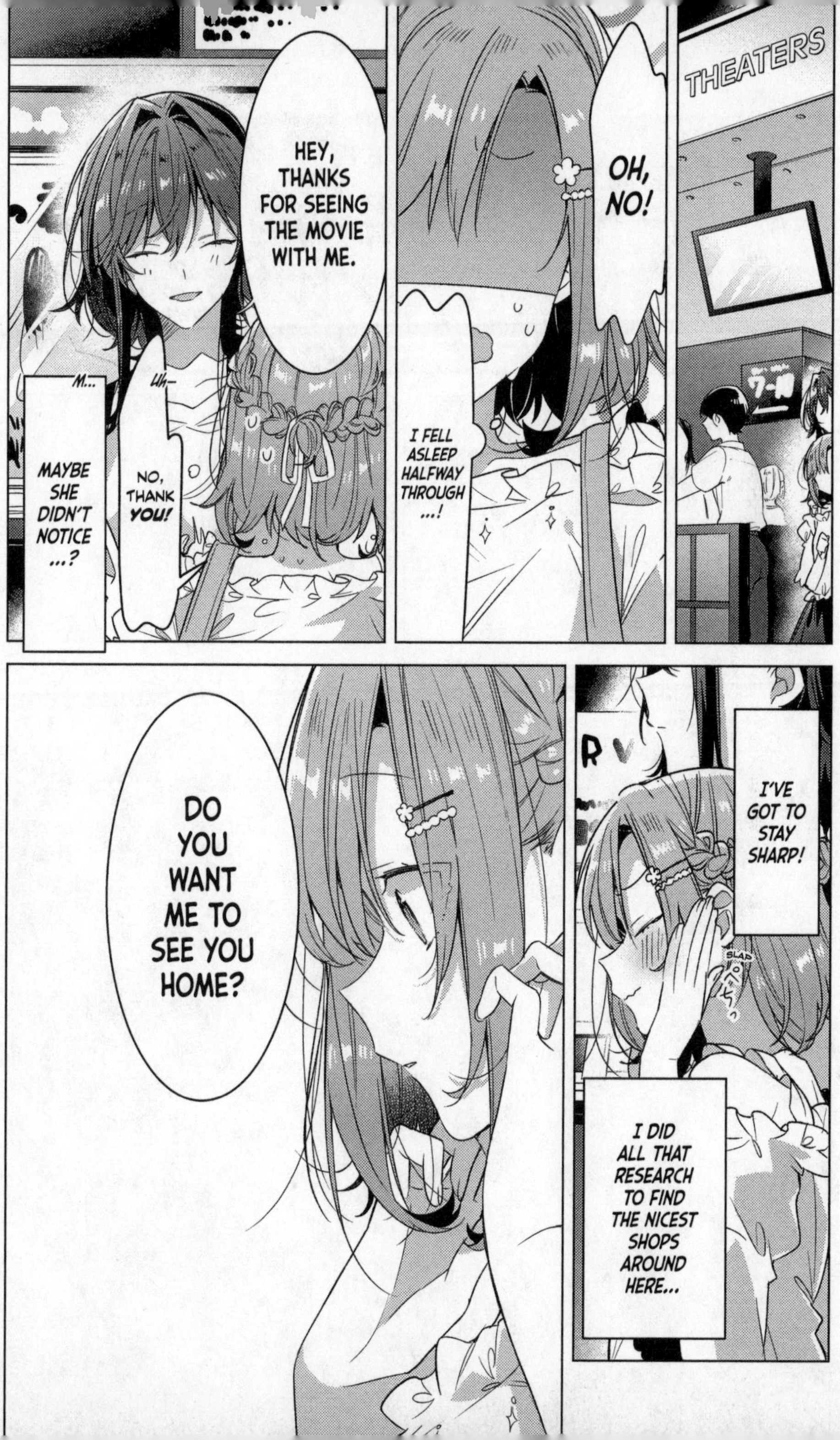
THEATERS
OH, NO!
I FELL ASLEEP HALFWAY THROUGH...!
HEY, THANKS FOR SEEING THE MOVIE WITH ME.
UH—
NO, THANK *YOU!*
M... MAYBE SHE DIDN'T NOTICE...?
I'VE GOT TO STAY SHARP!
SLAP
I DID ALL THAT RESEARCH TO FIND THE NICEST SHOPS AROUND HERE...
DO YOU WANT ME TO SEE YOU HOME?

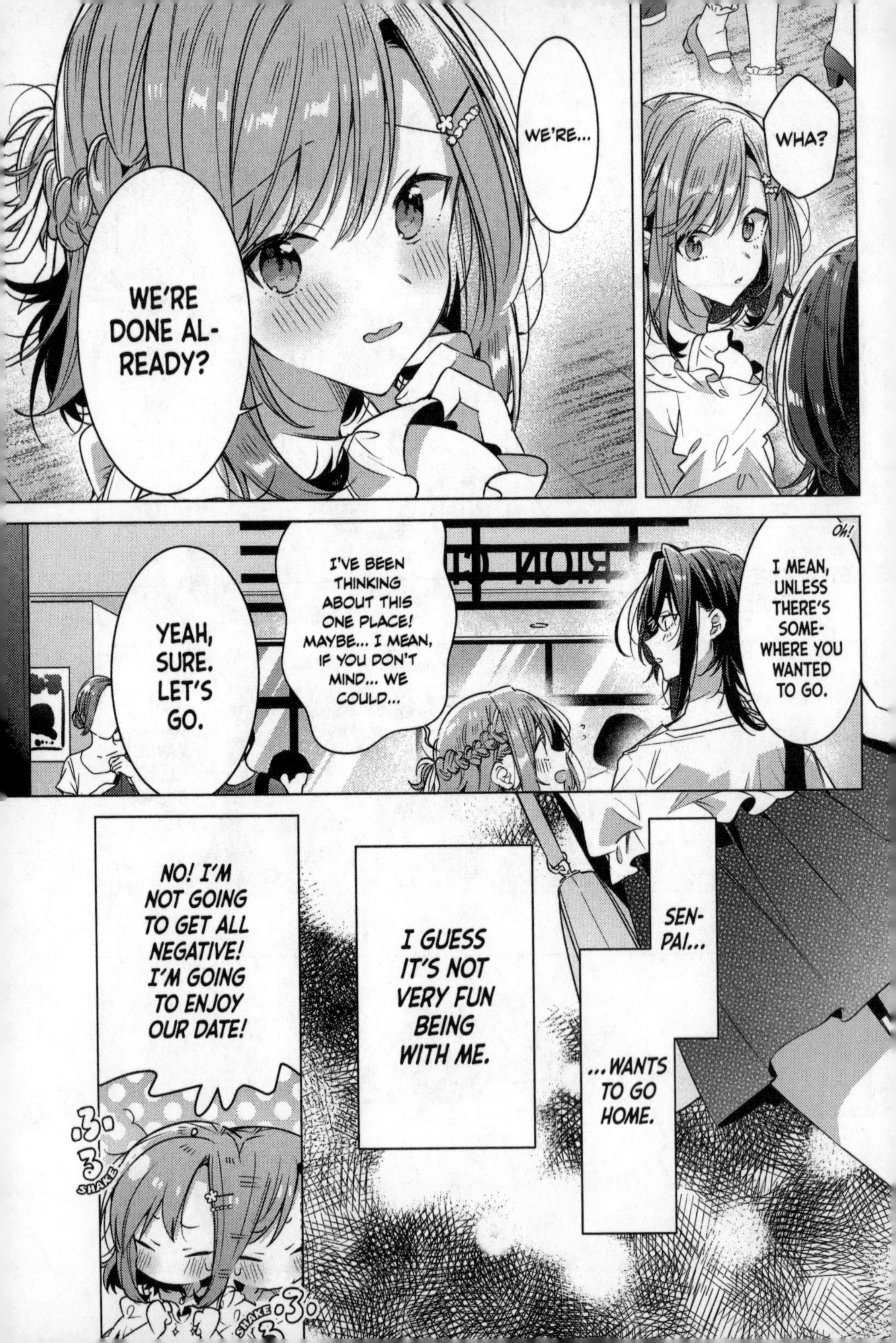
WHA?
WE'RE...
WE'RE DONE AL-READY?
Oh!
I MEAN, UNLESS THERE'S SOME-WHERE YOU WANTED TO GO.
I'VE BEEN THINKING ABOUT THIS ONE PLACE! MAYBE... I MEAN, IF YOU DON'T MIND... WE COULD...
YEAH, SURE. LET'S GO.
SEN-PAI...
...WANTS TO GO HOME.
I GUESS IT'S NOT VERY FUN BEING WITH ME.
NO! I'M NOT GOING TO GET ALL NEGATIVE! I'M GOING TO ENJOY OUR DATE!
SHAKE
SHAKE

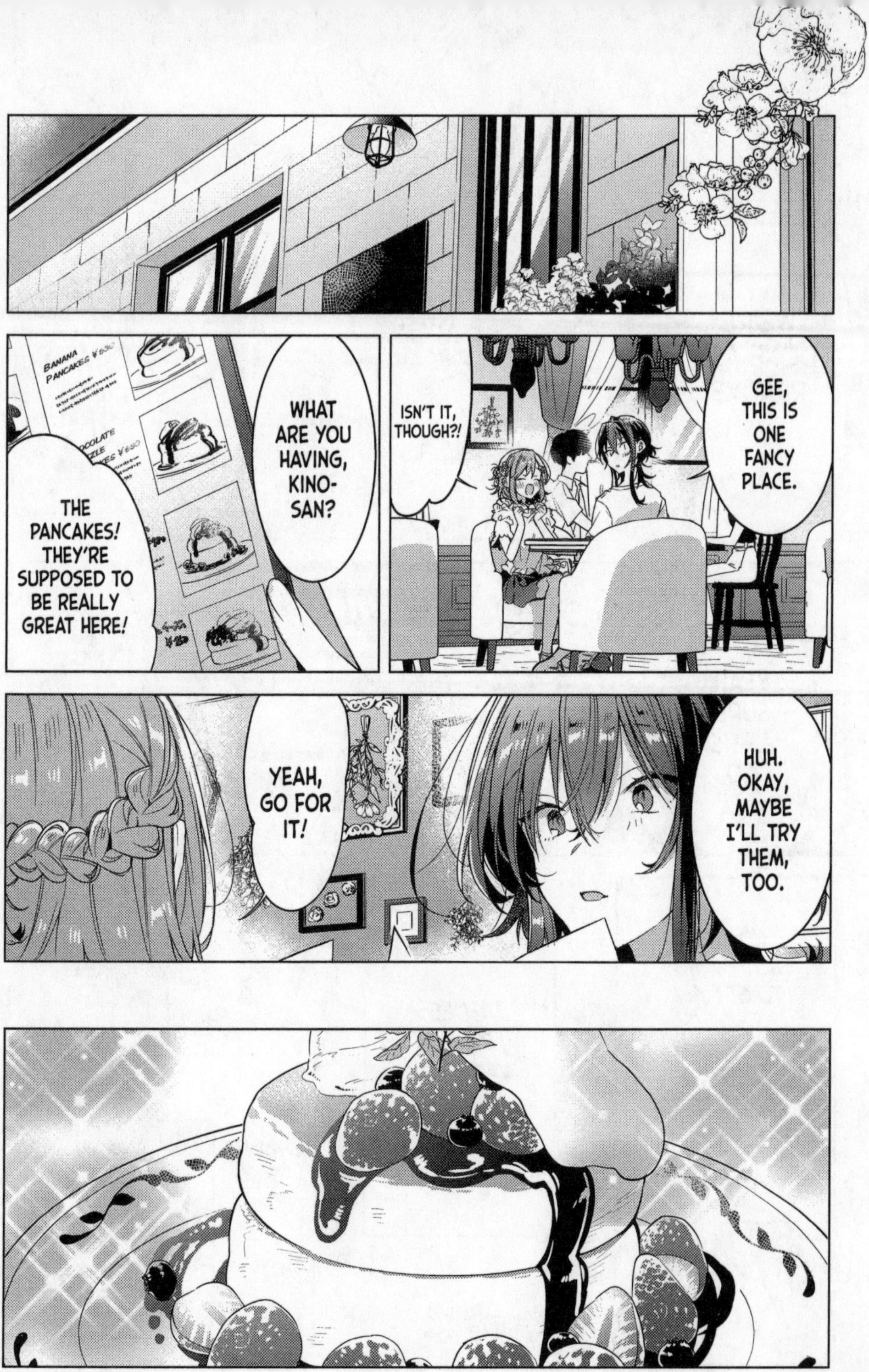
GEE, THIS IS ONE FANCY PLACE.
ISN'T IT, THOUGH?!
WHAT ARE YOU HAVING, KINO-SAN?
BANANA PANCAKES
THE PANCAKES! THEY'RE SUPPOSED TO BE REALLY GREAT HERE!
HUH. OKAY, MAYBE I'LL TRY THEM, TOO.
YEAH, GO FOR IT!

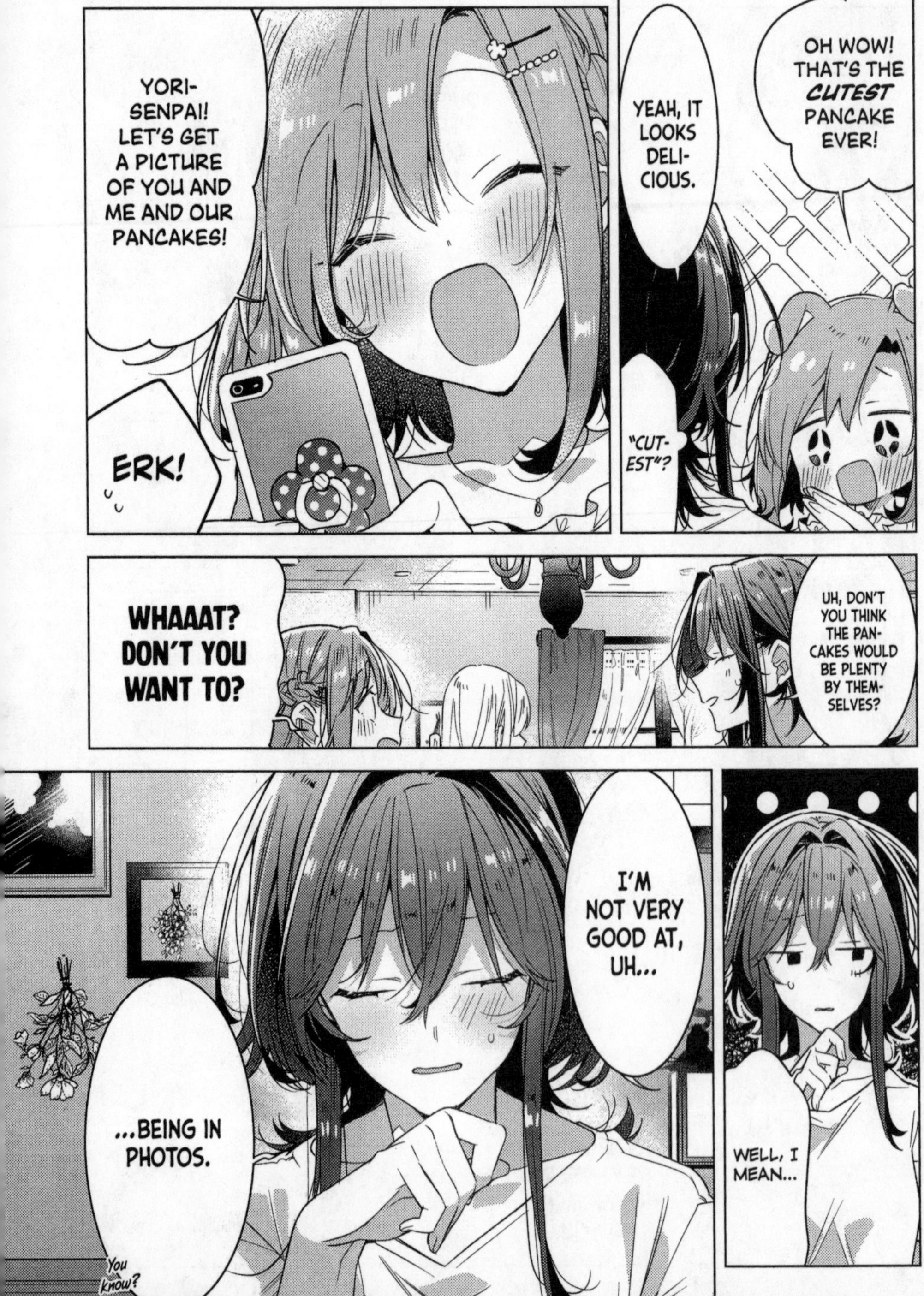
OH WOW! THAT'S THE *CUTEST* PANCAKE EVER!
YEAH, IT LOOKS DELI-CIOUS.
"CUT-EST"?
YORI-SENPAI! LET'S GET A PICTURE OF YOU AND ME AND OUR PANCAKES!
ERK!
UH, DON'T YOU THINK THE PAN-CAKES WOULD BE PLENTY BY THEM-SELVES?
WHAAAT? DON'T YOU WANT TO?
WELL, I MEAN...
I'M NOT VERY GOOD AT, UH...
...BEING IN PHOTOS.
You know?

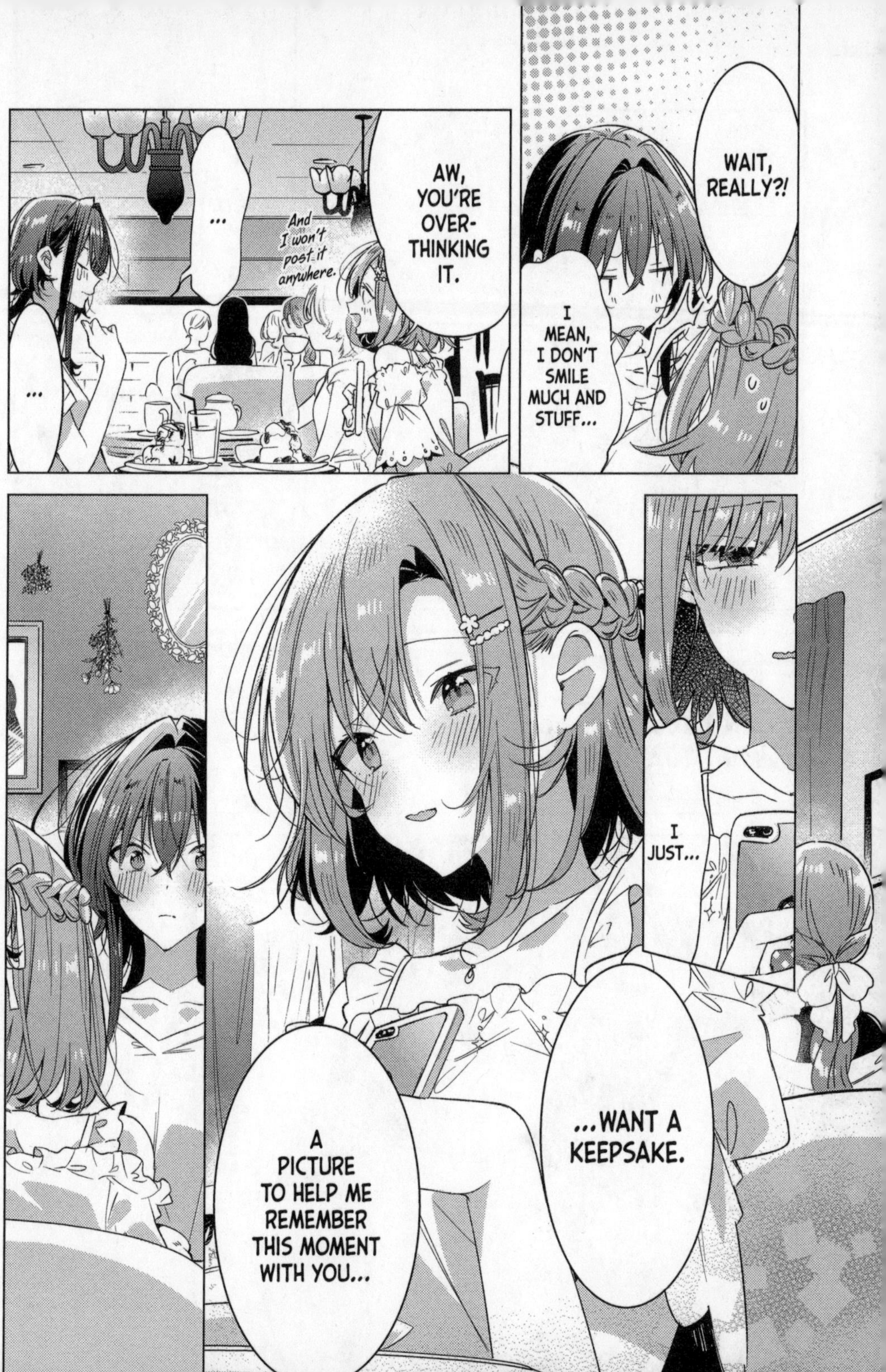
WAIT, REALLY?!
I MEAN, I DON'T SMILE MUCH AND STUFF...
AW, YOU'RE OVER-THINKING IT.
And I won't post it anywhere.
...
...
I JUST...
...WANT A KEEPSAKE.
A PICTURE TO HELP ME REMEMBER THIS MOMENT WITH YOU...

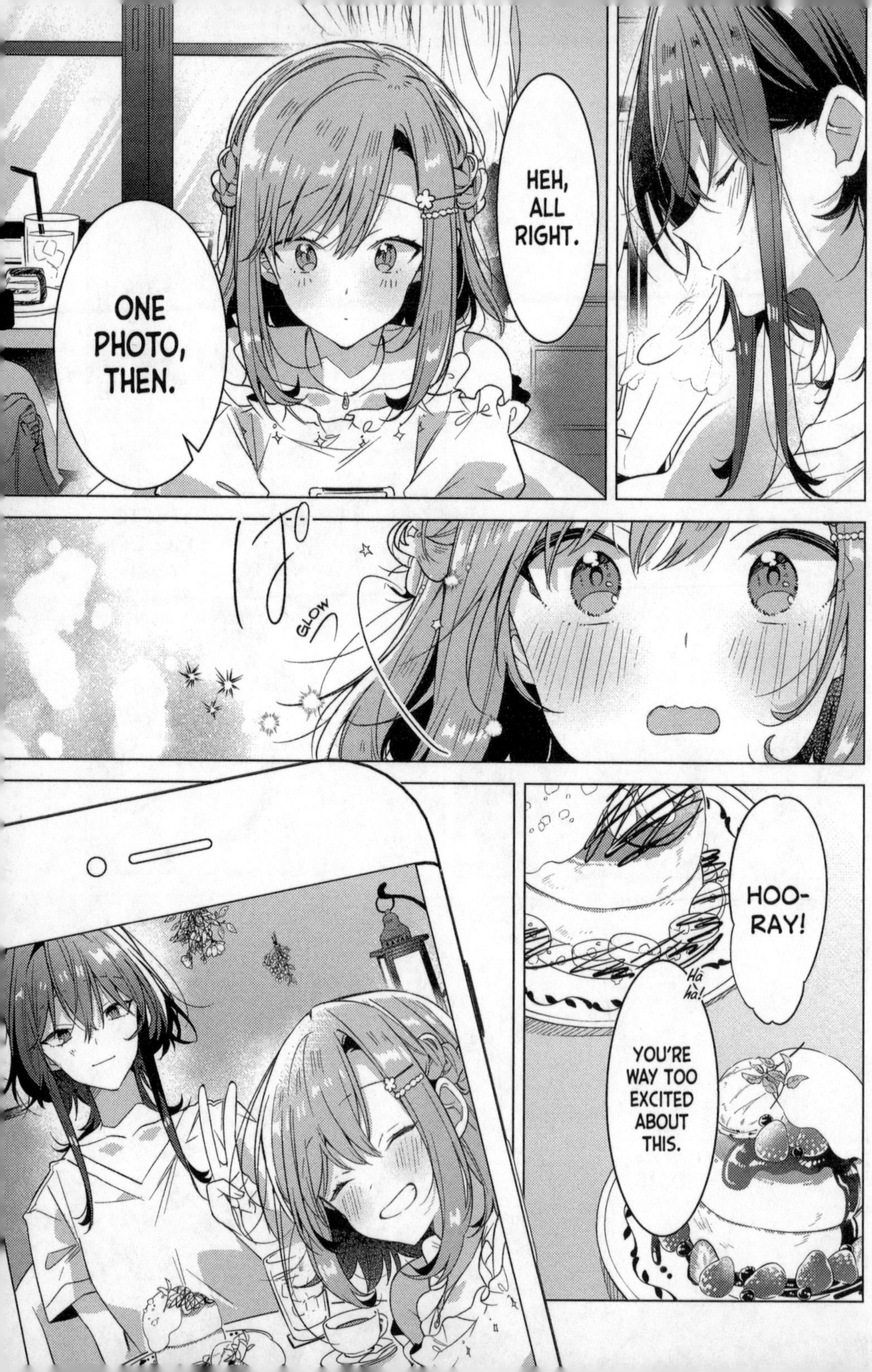
HEH, ALL RIGHT.
ONE PHOTO, THEN.
GLOW
HOO-RAY!
Hà hà!
YOU'RE WAY TOO EXCITED ABOUT THIS.

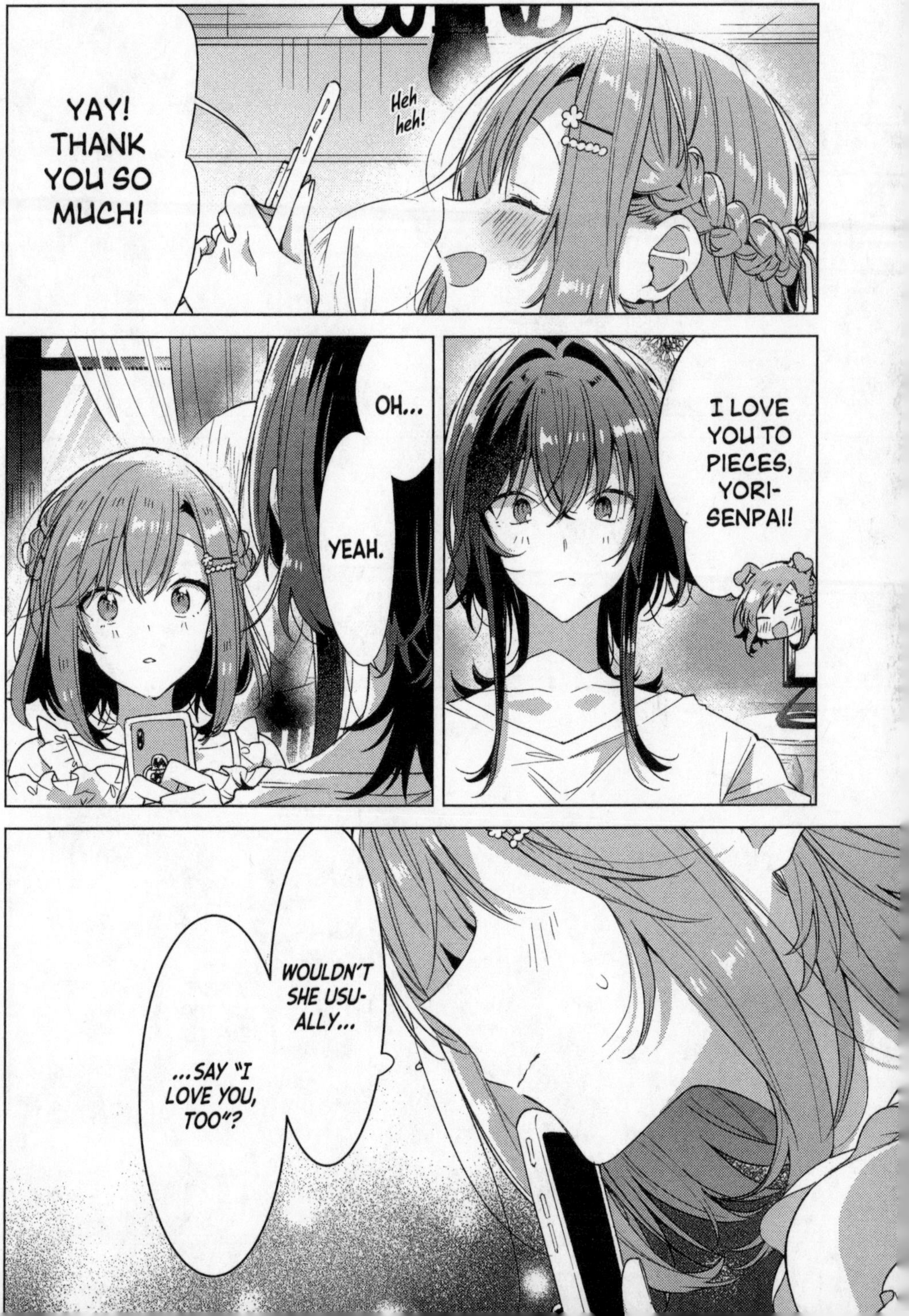
Heh heh!
YAY! THANK YOU SO MUCH!
I LOVE YOU TO PIECES, YORI-SENPAI!
OH...
YEAH.
WOULDN'T SHE USU-ALLY...
...SAY "I LOVE YOU, TOO"?

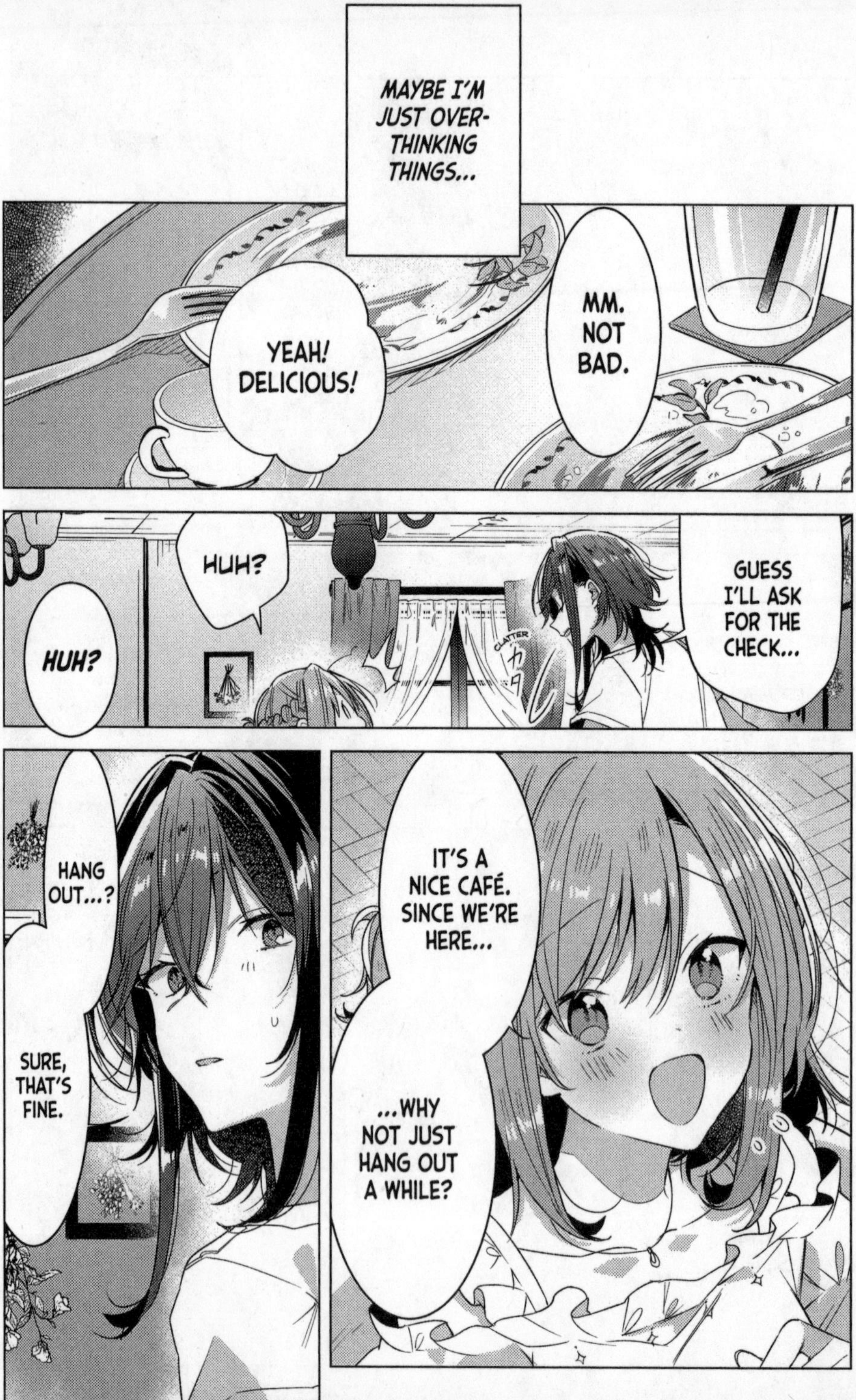
MAYBE I'M JUST OVER-THINKING THINGS...
MM. NOT BAD.
YEAH! DELICIOUS!
GUESS I'LL ASK FOR THE CHECK...
CLATTER
カタ
HUH?
HUH?
IT'S A NICE CAFÉ. SINCE WE'RE HERE...
...WHY NOT JUST HANG OUT A WHILE?
HANG OUT...?
SURE, THAT'S FINE.

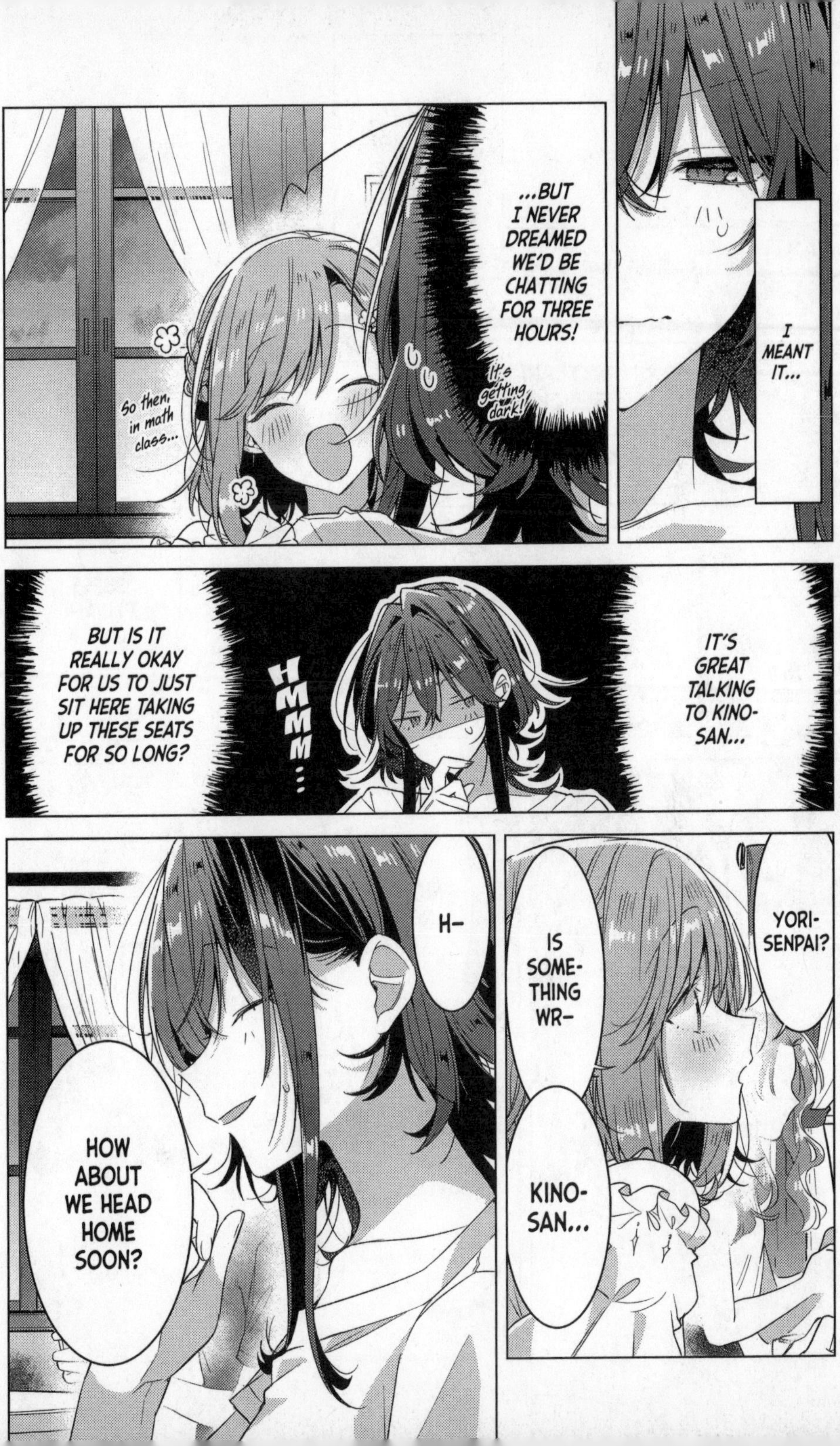
I MEANT IT...
...BUT I NEVER DREAMED WE'D BE CHATTING FOR THREE HOURS!
It's getting dark!
So then, in math class...
IT'S GREAT TALKING TO KINO-SAN...
HMMM...
BUT IS IT REALLY OKAY FOR US TO JUST SIT HERE TAKING UP THESE SEATS FOR SO LONG?
YORI-SENPAI?
IS SOMETHING WR-
KINO-SAN...
H-
HOW ABOUT WE HEAD HOME SOON?

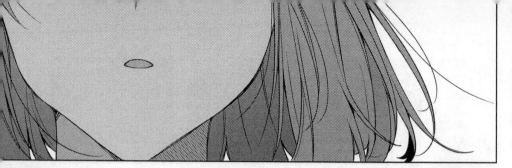

YEAH...

YOU'RE
RIGHT.

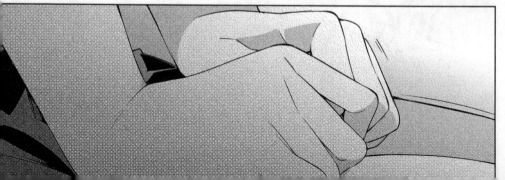

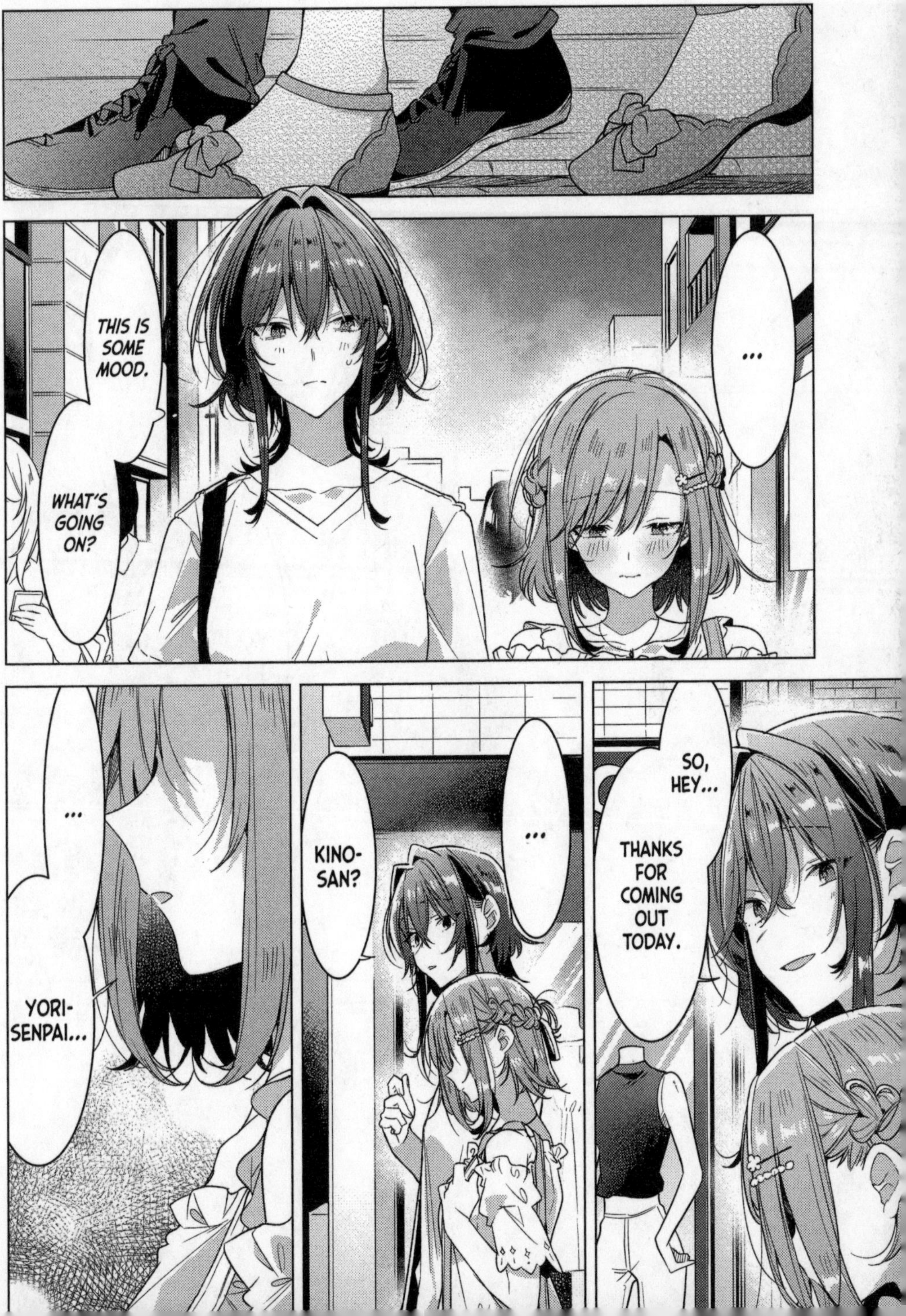
...
THIS IS SOME MOOD.
WHAT'S GOING ON?
SO, HEY...
THANKS FOR COMING OUT TODAY.
...
KINO-SAN?
...
YORI-SENPAI...

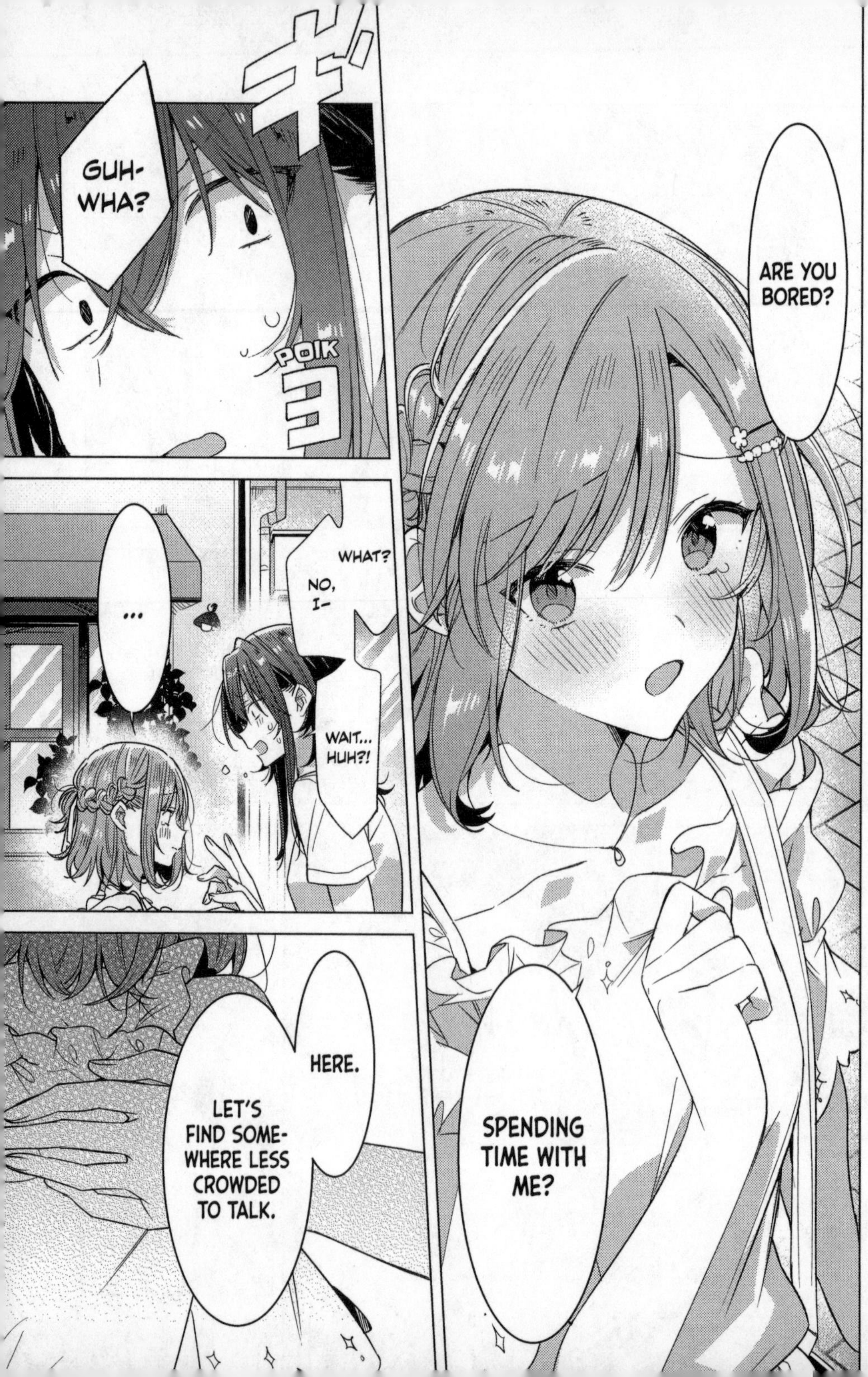
ARE YOU BORED?
SPENDING TIME WITH ME?
GUH-WHA?
POIK
...
WHAT?
NO, I-
WAIT... HUH?!
HERE.
LET'S FIND SOME-WHERE LESS CROWDED TO TALK.

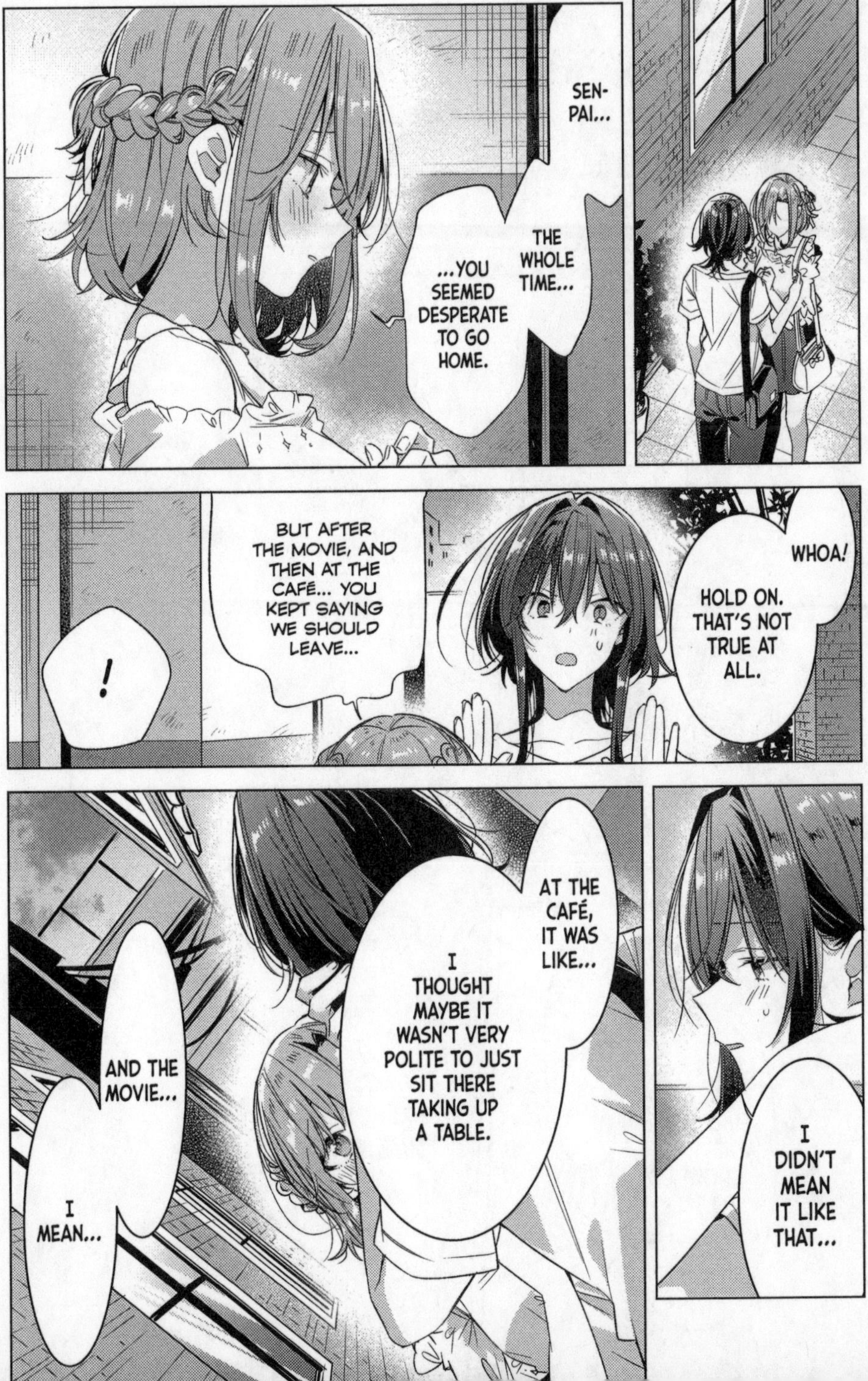
SEN-PAI...
THE WHOLE TIME...
...YOU SEEMED DESPERATE TO GO HOME.
WHOA!
HOLD ON. THAT'S NOT TRUE AT ALL.
BUT AFTER THE MOVIE, AND THEN AT THE CAFÉ... YOU KEPT SAYING WE SHOULD LEAVE...
!
I DIDN'T MEAN IT LIKE THAT...
AT THE CAFÉ, IT WAS LIKE...
I THOUGHT MAYBE IT WASN'T VERY POLITE TO JUST SIT THERE TAKING UP A TABLE.
AND THE MOVIE...
I MEAN...

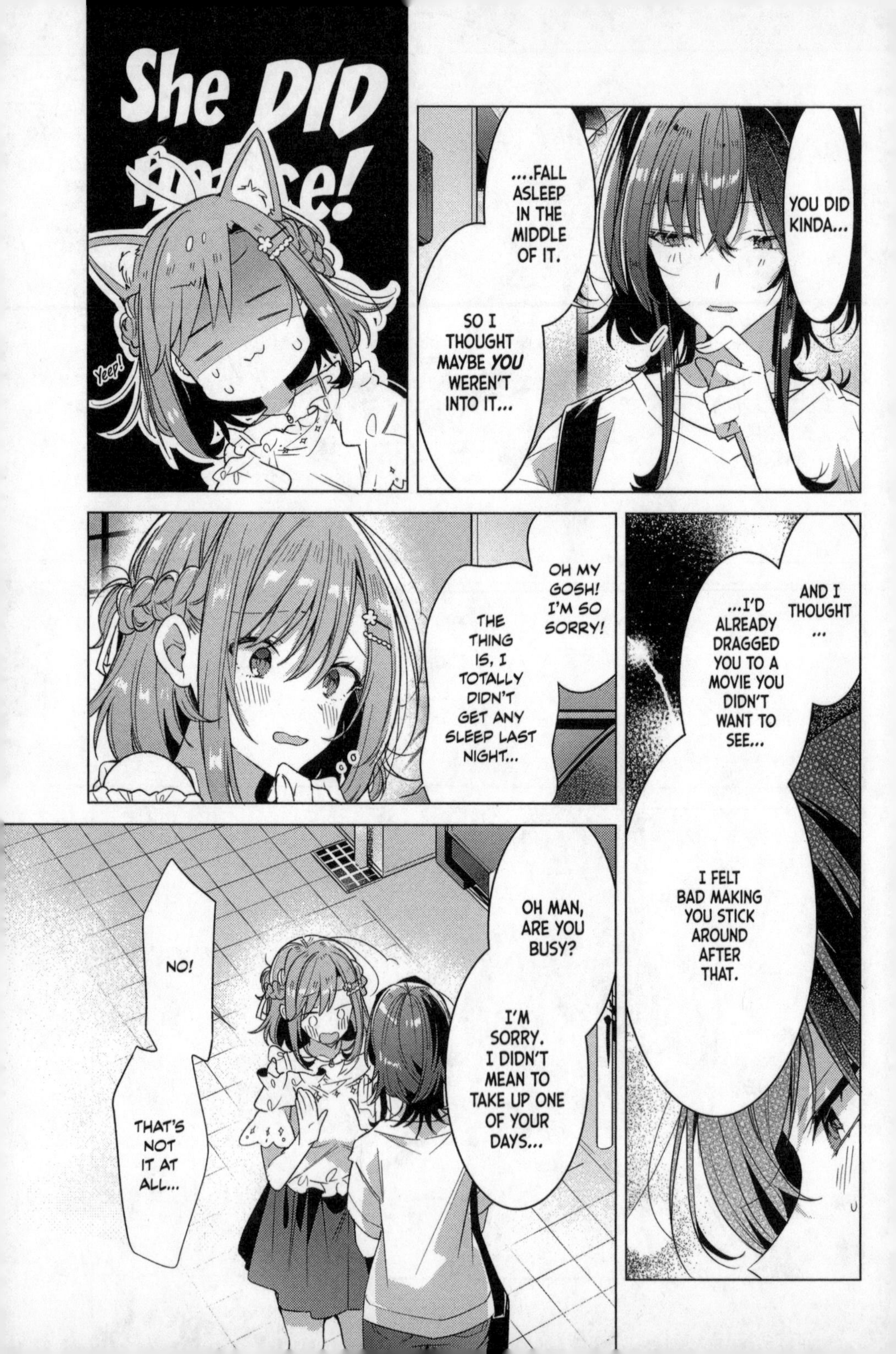
YOU DID KINDA...
....FALL ASLEEP IN THE MIDDLE OF IT.
SO I THOUGHT MAYBE *YOU* WEREN'T INTO IT...
She DID
Yeep!
AND I THOUGHT...
...I'D ALREADY DRAGGED YOU TO A MOVIE YOU DIDN'T WANT TO SEE...
I FELT BAD MAKING YOU STICK AROUND AFTER THAT.
OH MY GOSH! I'M SO SORRY!
THE THING IS, I TOTALLY DIDN'T GET ANY SLEEP LAST NIGHT...
OH MAN, ARE YOU BUSY?
I'M SORRY. I DIDN'T MEAN TO TAKE UP ONE OF YOUR DAYS...
NO!
THAT'S NOT IT AT ALL...

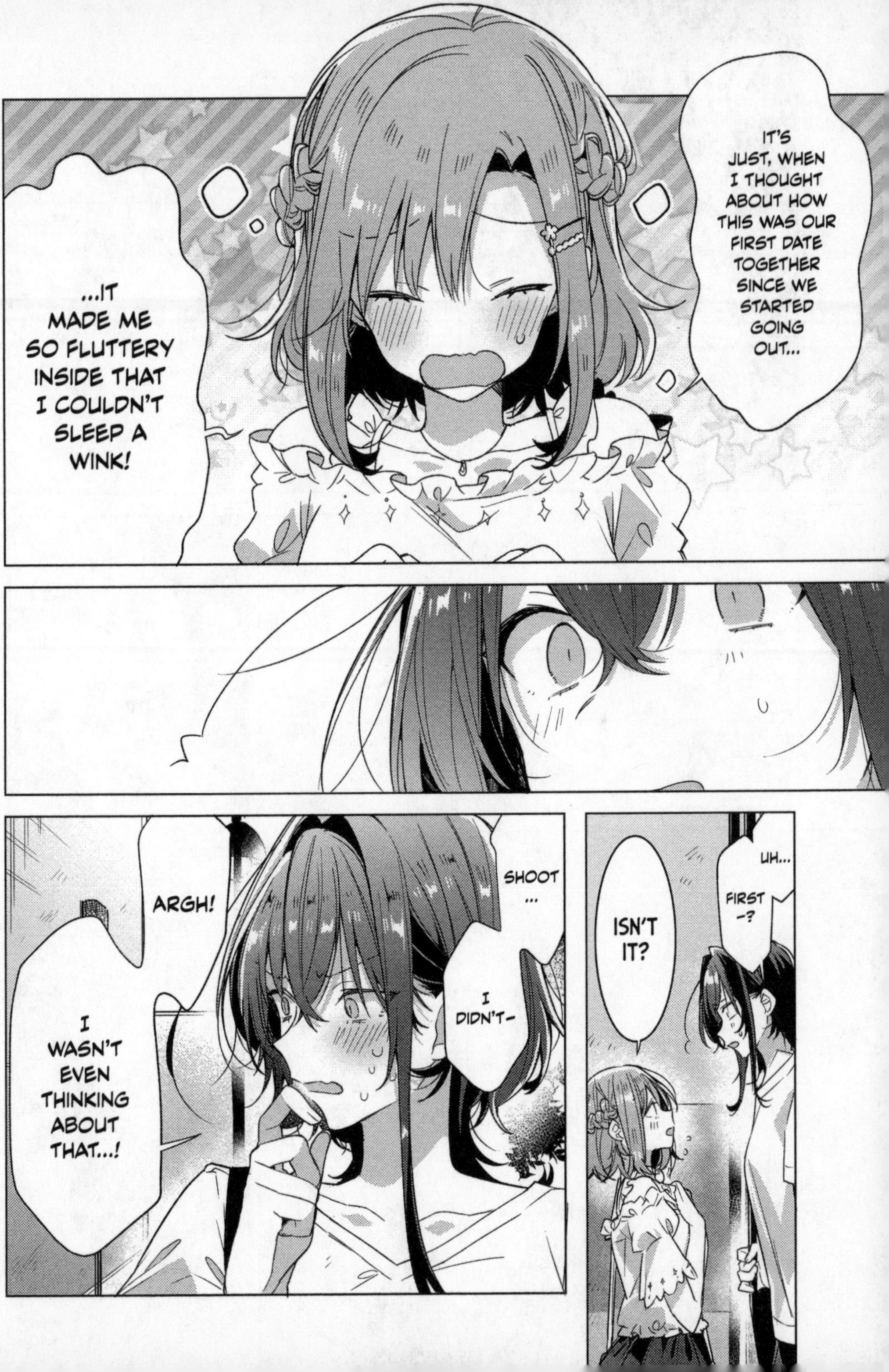
IT'S JUST, WHEN I THOUGHT ABOUT HOW THIS WAS OUR FIRST DATE TOGETHER SINCE WE STARTED GOING OUT...
...IT MADE ME SO FLUTTERY INSIDE THAT I COULDN'T SLEEP A WINK!
UH... FIRST—?
ISN'T IT?
SHOOT...
I DIDN'T—
ARGH!
I WASN'T EVEN THINKING ABOUT THAT...!

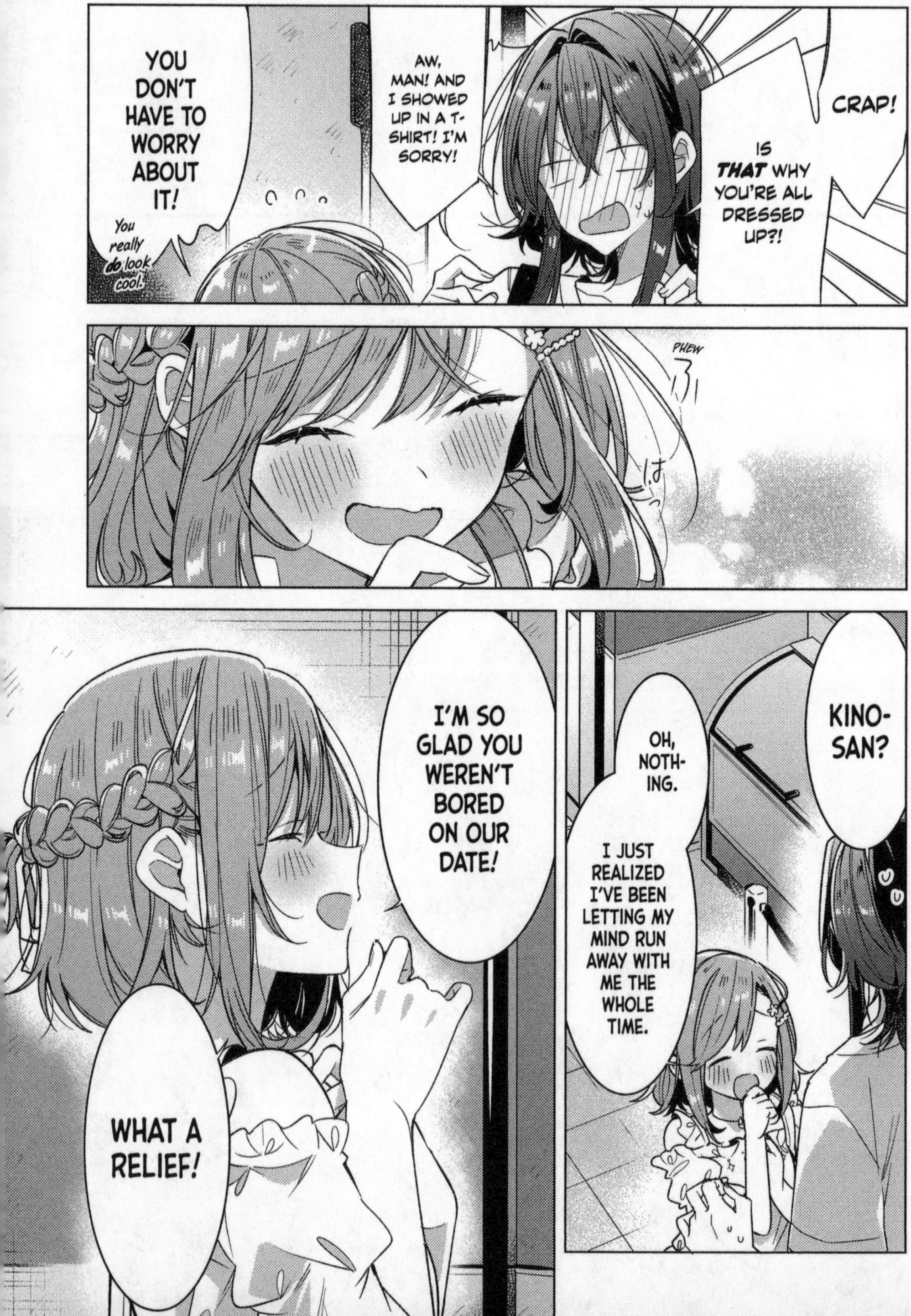
CRAP!
IS THAT WHY YOU'RE ALL DRESSED UP?!
AW, MAN! AND I SHOWED UP IN A T-SHIRT! I'M SORRY!
YOU DON'T HAVE TO WORRY ABOUT IT!
You really do look cool.
PHEW
KINO-SAN?
OH, NOTHING.
I JUST REALIZED I'VE BEEN LETTING MY MIND RUN AWAY WITH ME THE WHOLE TIME.
I'M SO GLAD YOU WEREN'T BORED ON OUR DATE!
WHAT A RELIEF!

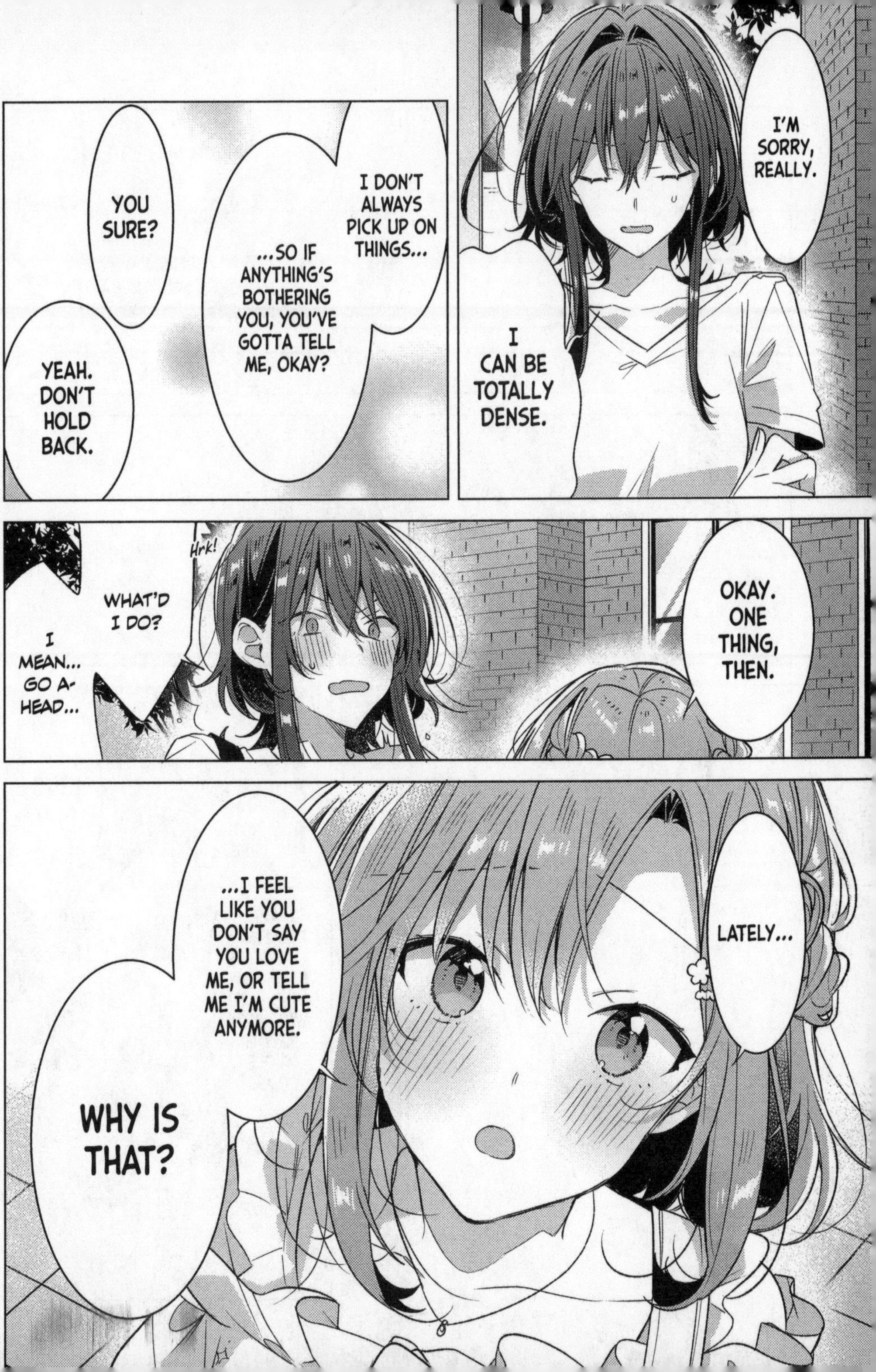
I'M SORRY, REALLY.
I CAN BE TOTALLY DENSE.
I DON'T ALWAYS PICK UP ON THINGS...
...SO IF ANYTHING'S BOTHERING YOU, YOU'VE GOTTA TELL ME, OKAY?
YOU SURE?
YEAH. DON'T HOLD BACK.
OKAY. ONE THING, THEN.
Hrk!
WHAT'D I DO?
I MEAN... GO A-HEAD...
LATELY...
...I FEEL LIKE YOU DON'T SAY YOU LOVE ME, OR TELL ME I'M CUTE ANYMORE.
WHY IS THAT?

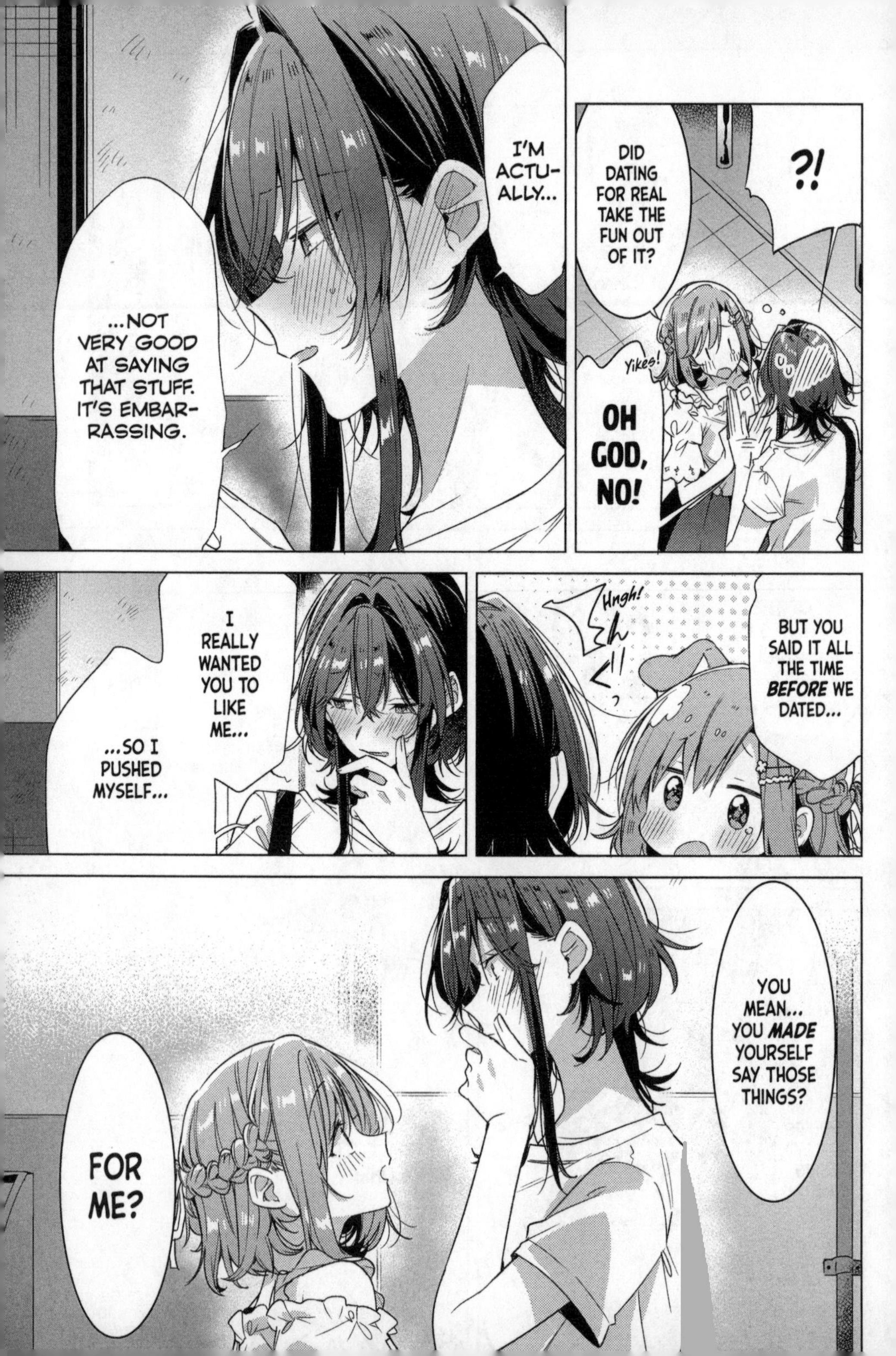
?!
DID DATING FOR REAL TAKE THE FUN OUT OF IT?
Yikes!
OH GOD, NO!
I'M ACTU-ALLY...
...NOT VERY GOOD AT SAYING THAT STUFF. IT'S EMBAR-RASSING.
BUT YOU SAID IT ALL THE TIME *BEFORE* WE DATED...
Hngh!
I REALLY WANTED YOU TO LIKE ME...
...SO I PUSHED MYSELF...
YOU MEAN... YOU *MADE* YOURSELF SAY THOSE THINGS?
FOR ME?

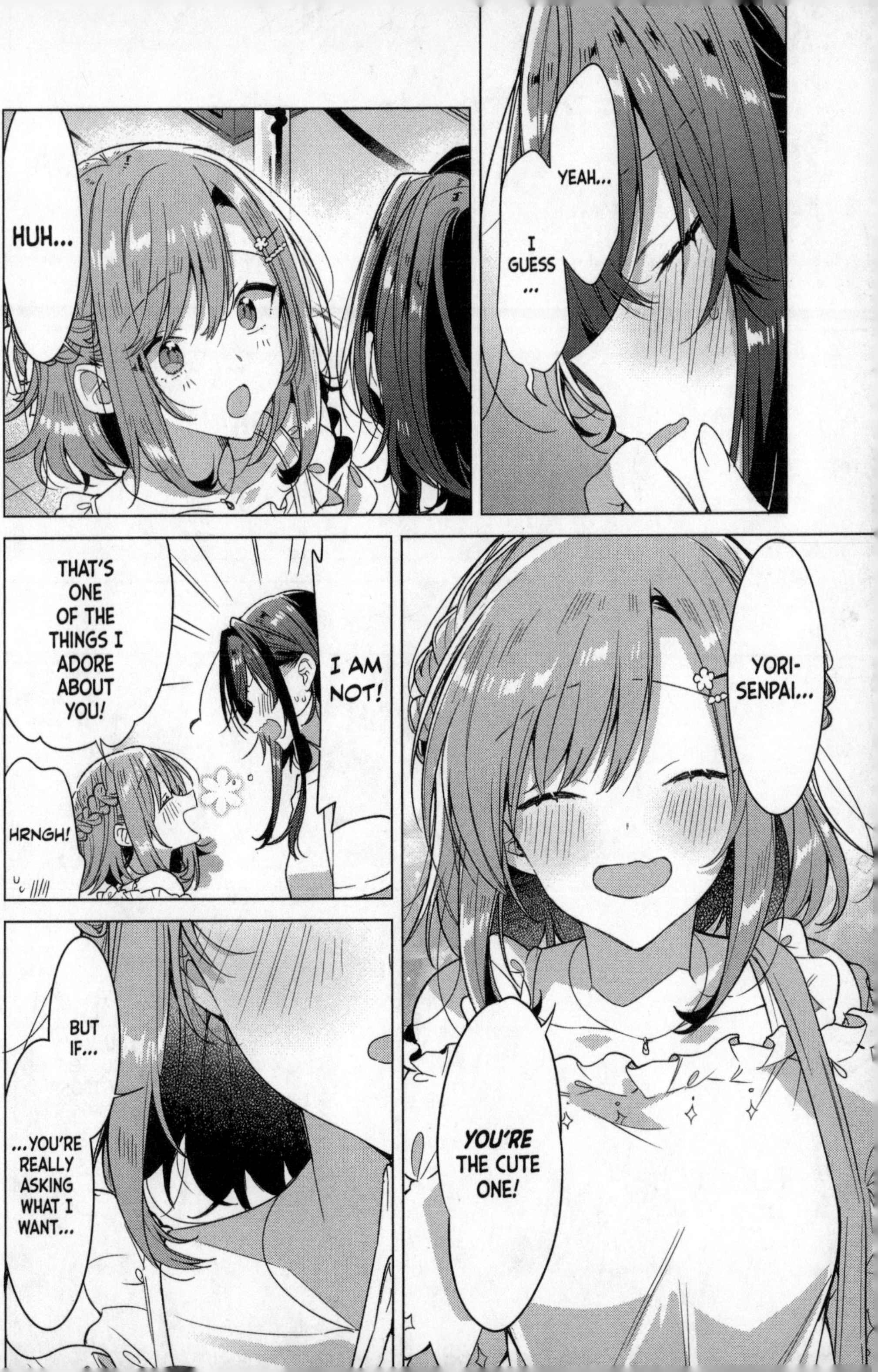
YEAH...
I GUESS ...
HUH...
YORI-SENPAI...
*YOU'RE* THE CUTE ONE!
I AM NOT!
THAT'S ONE OF THE THINGS I ADORE ABOUT YOU!
HRNGH!
BUT IF...
...YOU'RE REALLY ASKING WHAT I WANT...

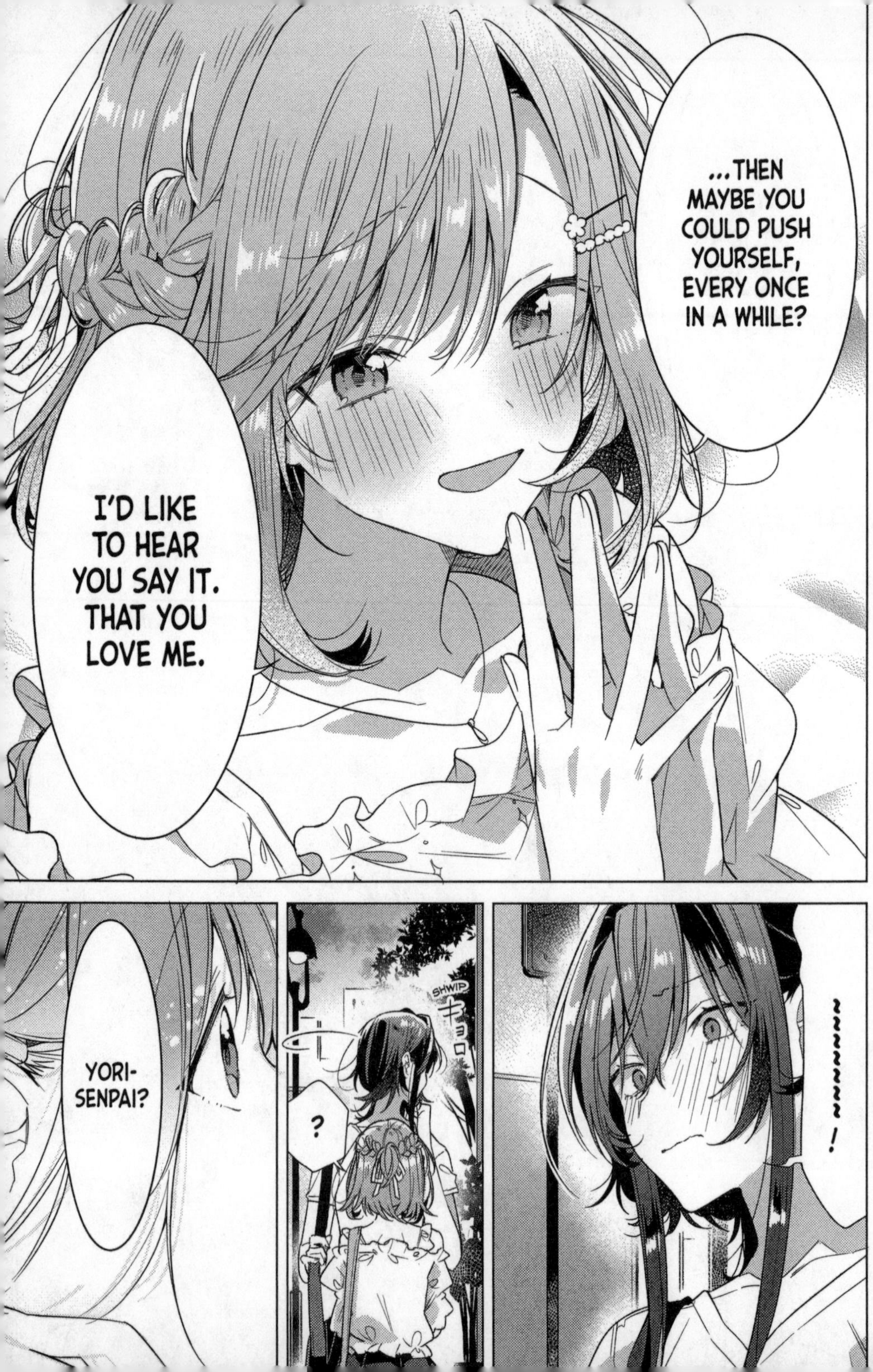
...THEN MAYBE YOU COULD PUSH YOURSELF, EVERY ONCE IN A WHILE?
I'D LIKE TO HEAR YOU SAY IT. THAT YOU LOVE ME.
~~~~~~~~!
SHWIP
キョロ
?
YORI-SENPAI?
~~~~~~~~

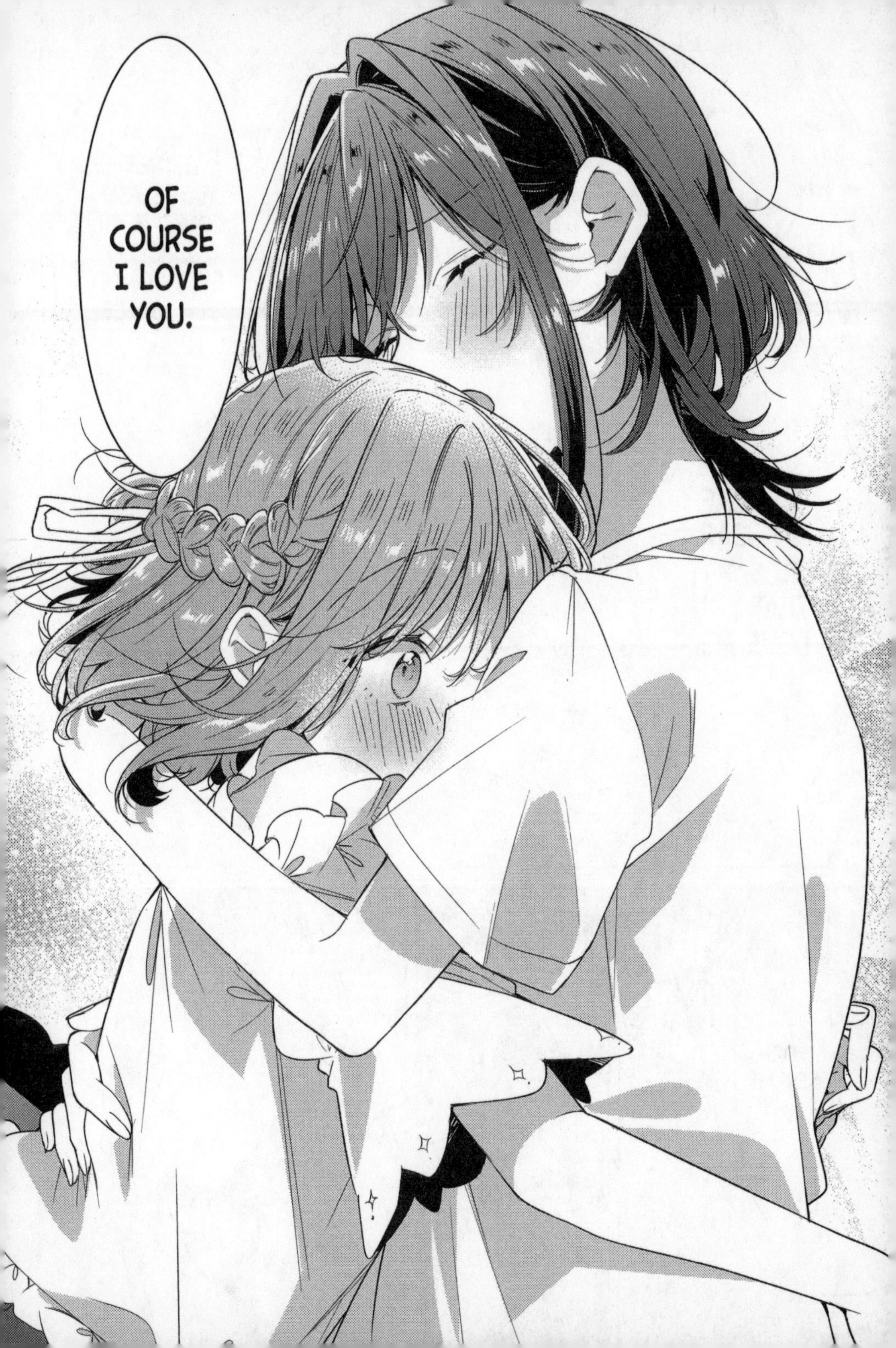
OF COURSE I LOVE YOU.

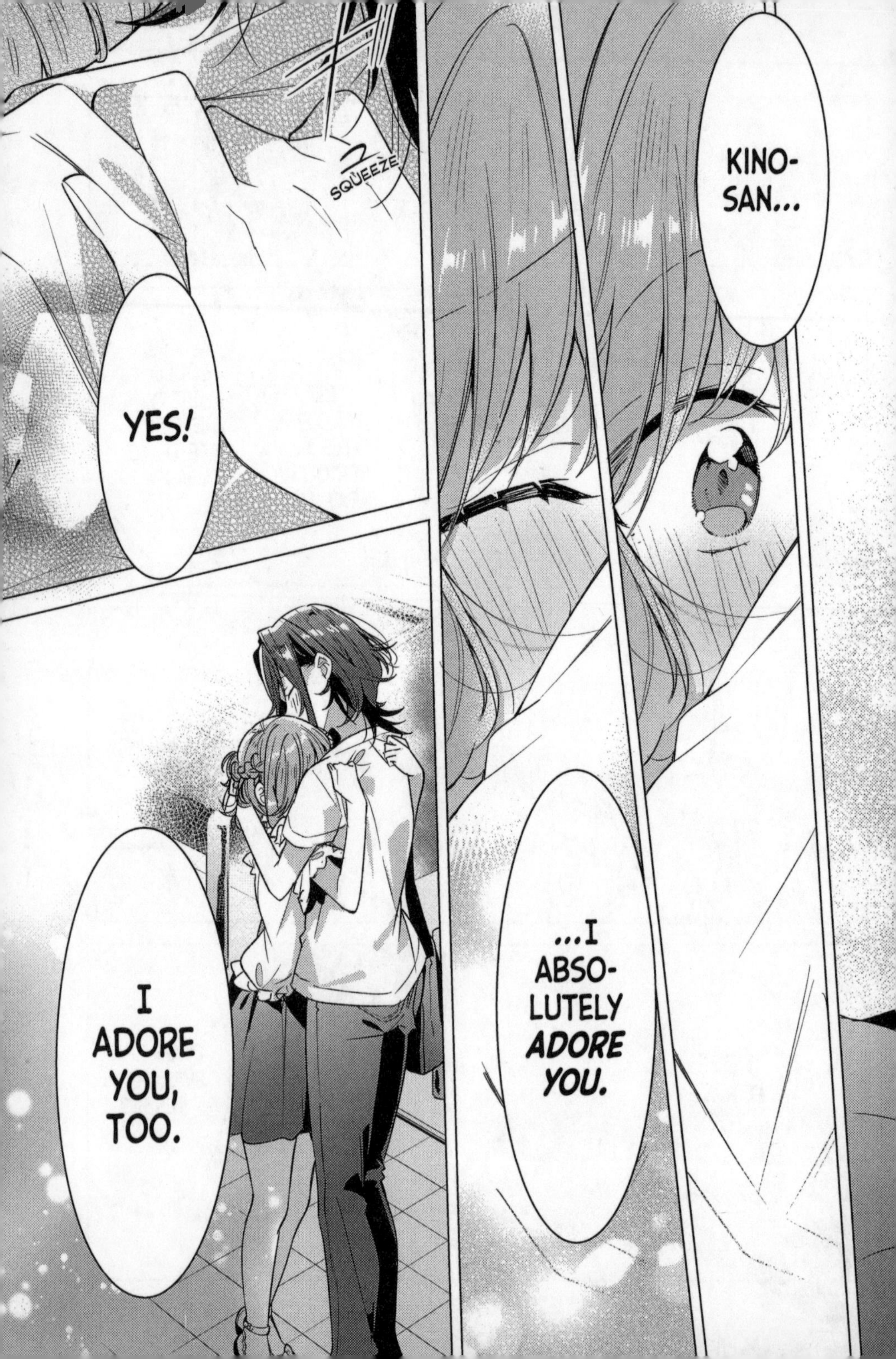
KINO-SAN...
...I ABSOLUTELY ADORE YOU.
SQUEEZE
YES!
I ADORE YOU, TOO.

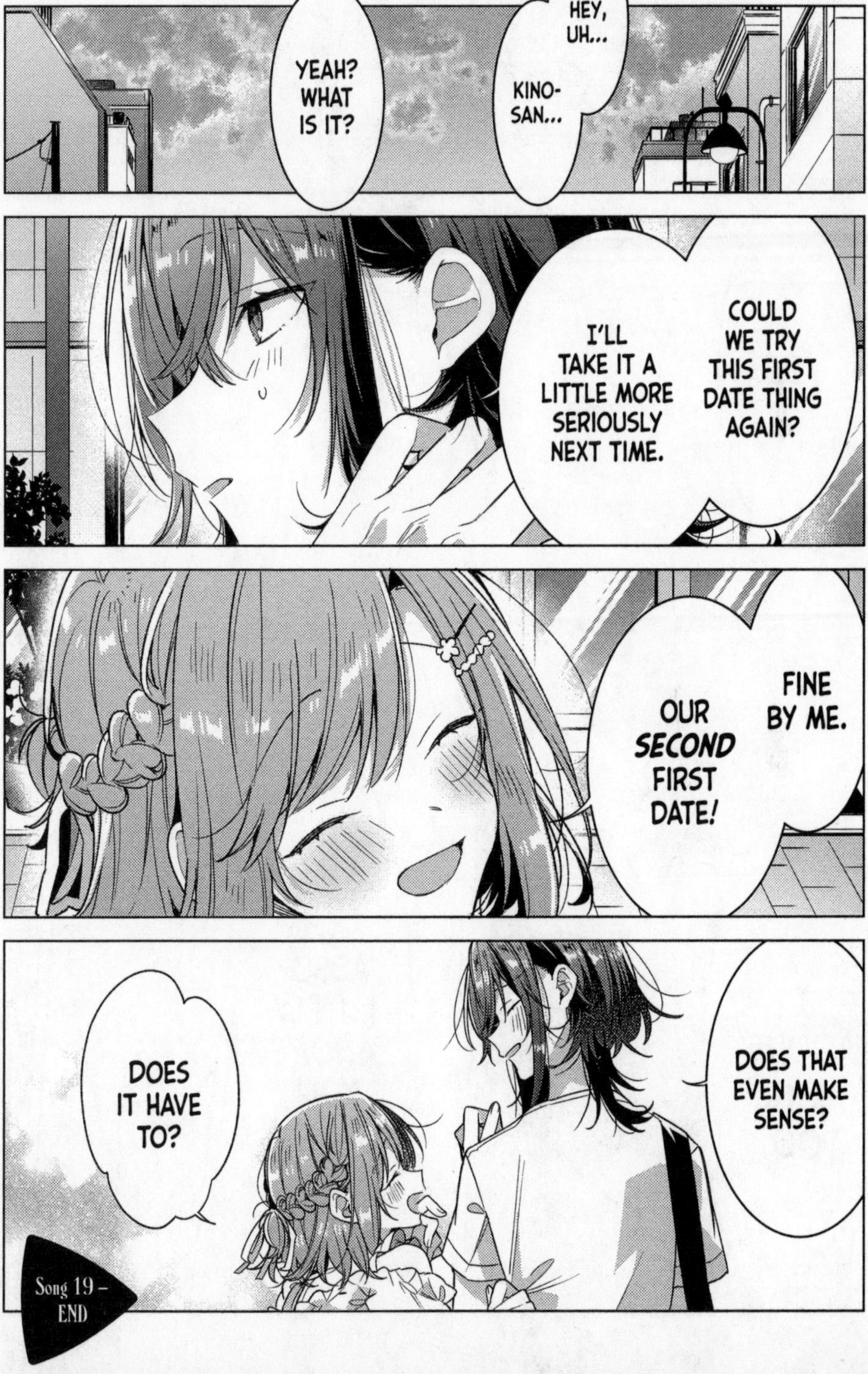
HEY, UH...
KINO-SAN...
YEAH? WHAT IS IT?
COULD WE TRY THIS FIRST DATE THING AGAIN?
I'LL TAKE IT A LITTLE MORE SERIOUSLY NEXT TIME.
FINE BY ME.
OUR *SECOND* FIRST DATE!
DOES THAT EVEN MAKE SENSE?
DOES IT HAVE TO?
Song 19 – END

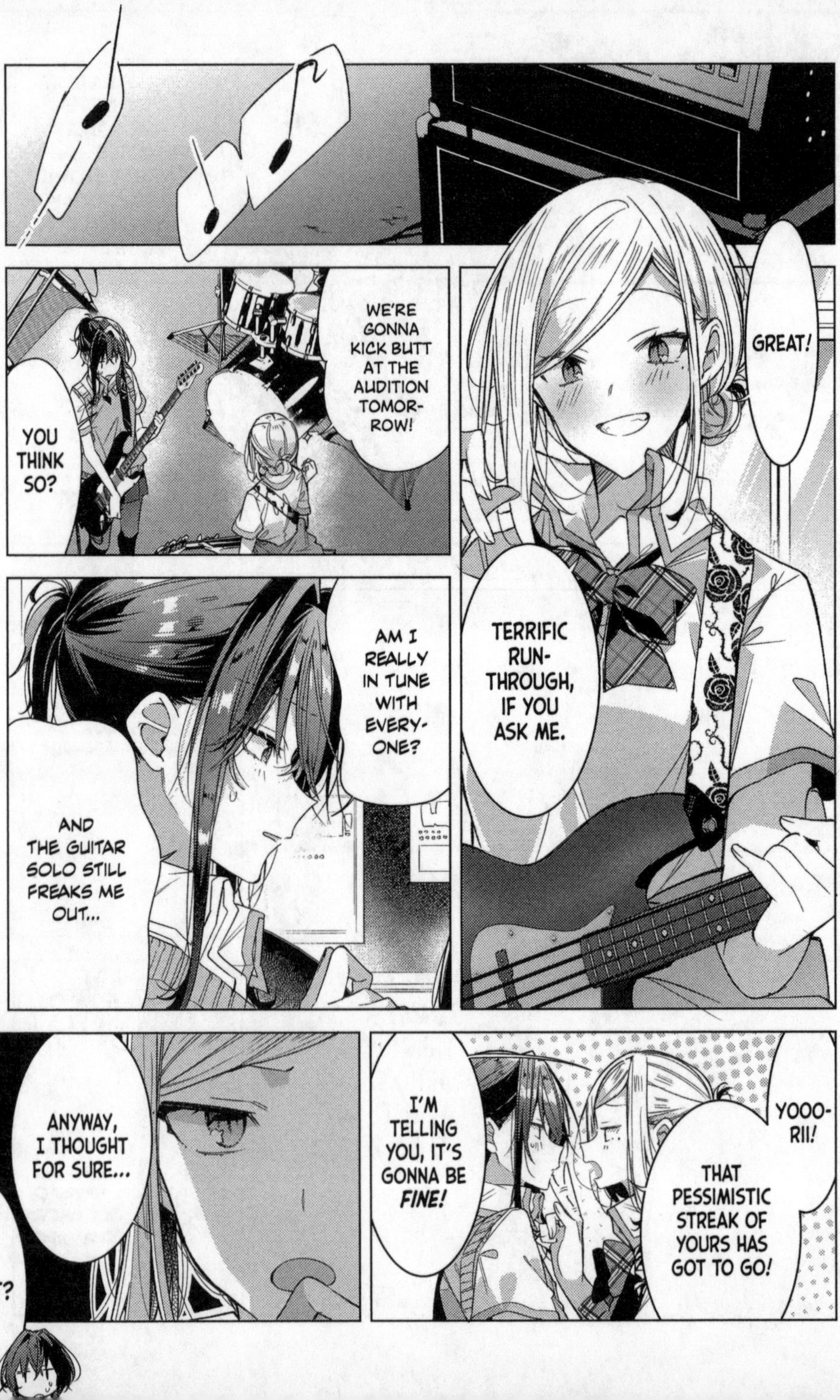
GREAT!
TERRIFIC RUN-THROUGH, IF YOU ASK ME.
WE'RE GONNA KICK BUTT AT THE AUDITION TOMORROW!
YOU THINK SO?
AM I REALLY IN TUNE WITH EVERYONE?
AND THE GUITAR SOLO STILL FREAKS ME OUT...
YOOO-RII!
THAT PESSIMISTIC STREAK OF YOURS HAS GOT TO GO!
I'M TELLING YOU, IT'S GONNA BE *FINE!*
ANYWAY, I THOUGHT FOR SURE...
WHAT?

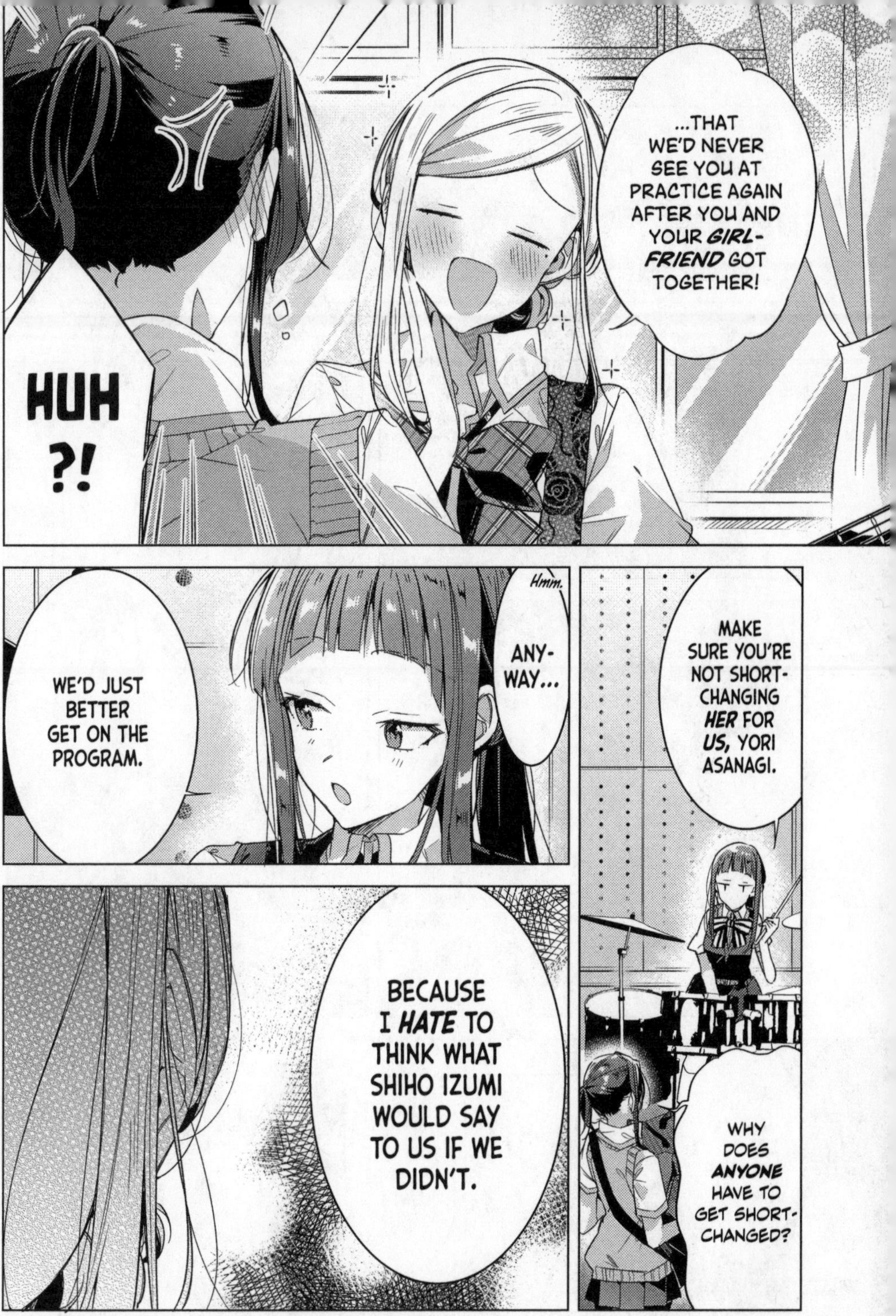

...THAT WE'D NEVER SEE YOU AT PRACTICE AGAIN AFTER YOU AND YOUR GIRL-FRIEND GOT TOGETHER!
HUH ?!
MAKE SURE YOU'RE NOT SHORT-CHANGING HER FOR US, YORI ASANAGI.
WHY DOES ANYONE HAVE TO GET SHORT-CHANGED?
Hmm.
ANY-WAY...
WE'D JUST BETTER GET ON THE PROGRAM.
BECAUSE I HATE TO THINK WHAT SHIHO IZUMI WOULD SAY TO US IF WE DIDN'T.

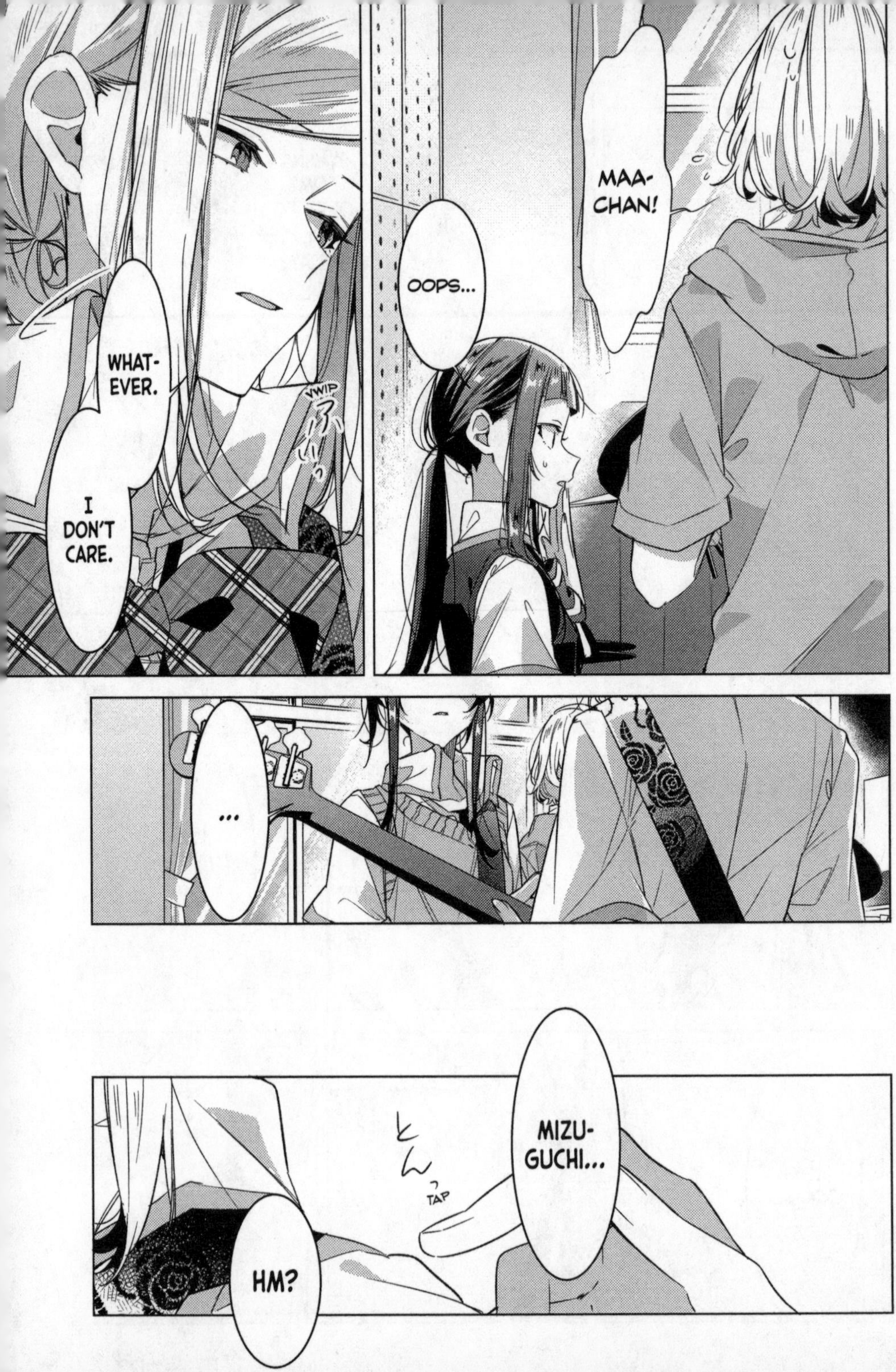
MAA-CHAN!
OOPS...
WHAT-EVER.
VWIP
I DON'T CARE.
...
MIZU-GUCHI...
TAP
HM?

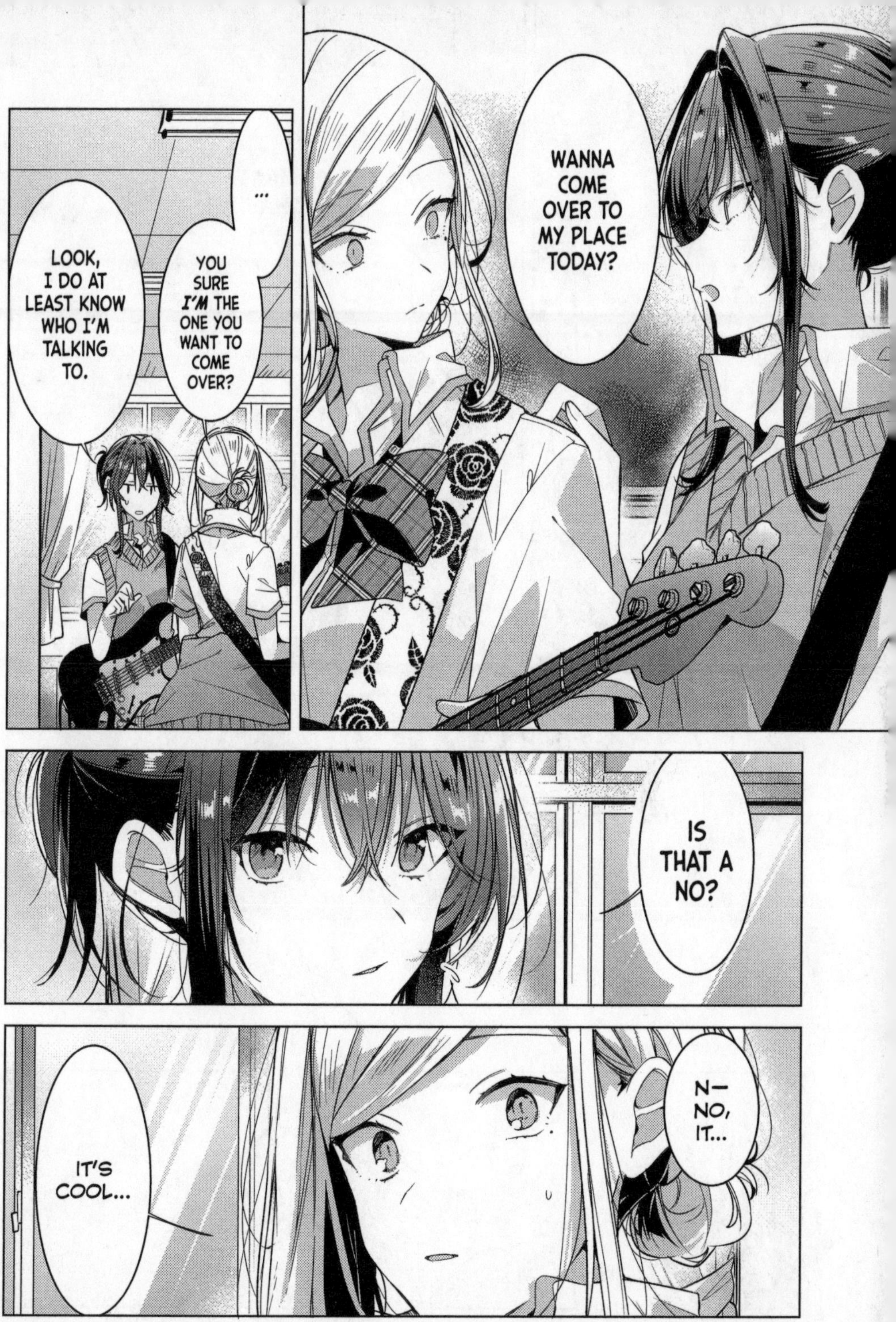
WANNA COME OVER TO MY PLACE TODAY?
...
YOU SURE *I'M* THE ONE YOU WANT TO COME OVER?
LOOK, I DO AT LEAST KNOW WHO I'M TALKING TO.
IS THAT A NO?
N—NO, IT...
IT'S COOL...

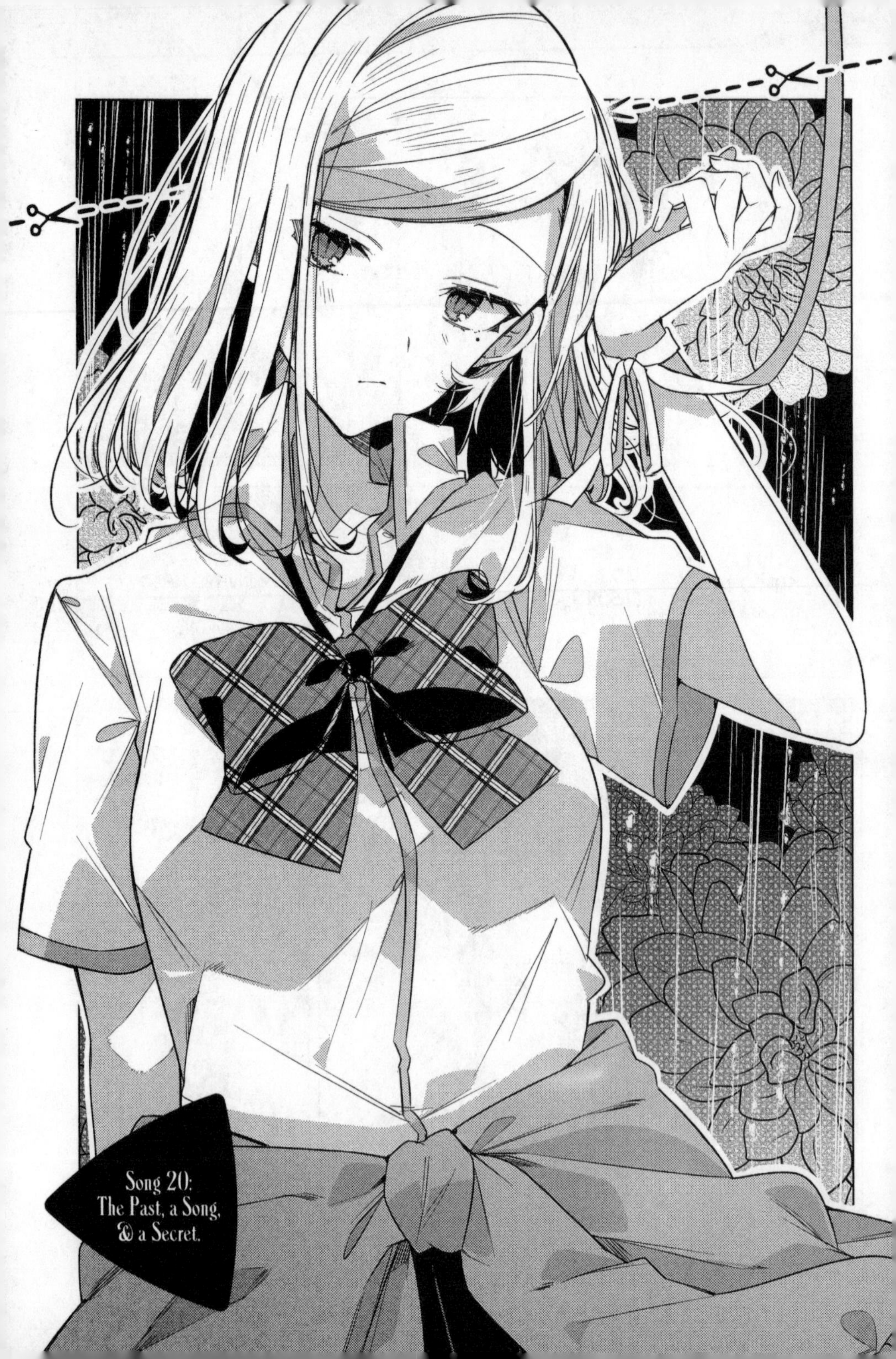
Song 20:
The Past, a Song,
& a Secret.

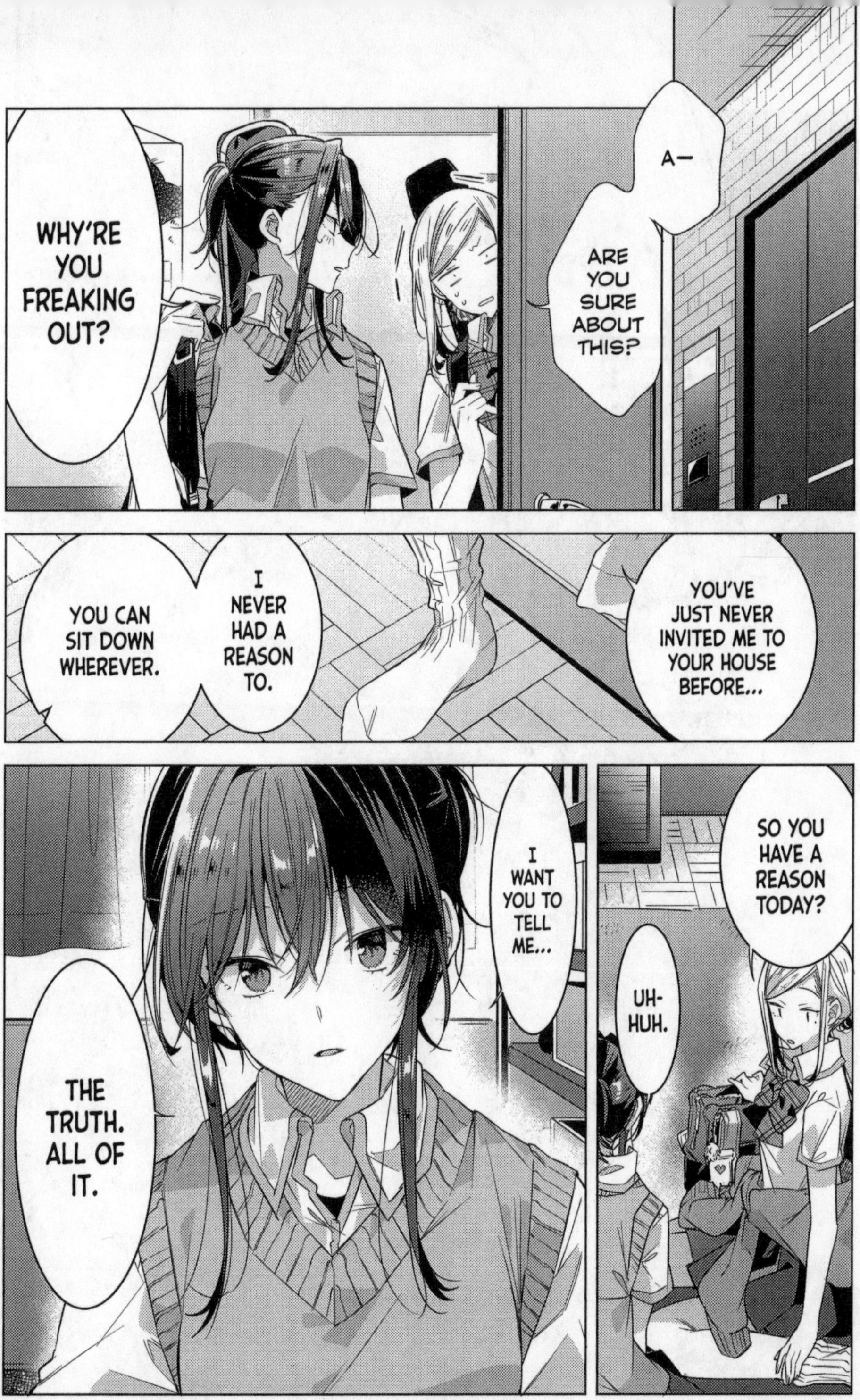
A—
ARE YOU SURE ABOUT THIS?
WHY'RE YOU FREAKING OUT?
YOU'VE JUST NEVER INVITED ME TO YOUR HOUSE BEFORE...
I NEVER HAD A REASON TO.
YOU CAN SIT DOWN WHEREVER.
SO YOU HAVE A REASON TODAY?
UH-HUH.
I WANT YOU TO TELL ME...
THE TRUTH. ALL OF IT.

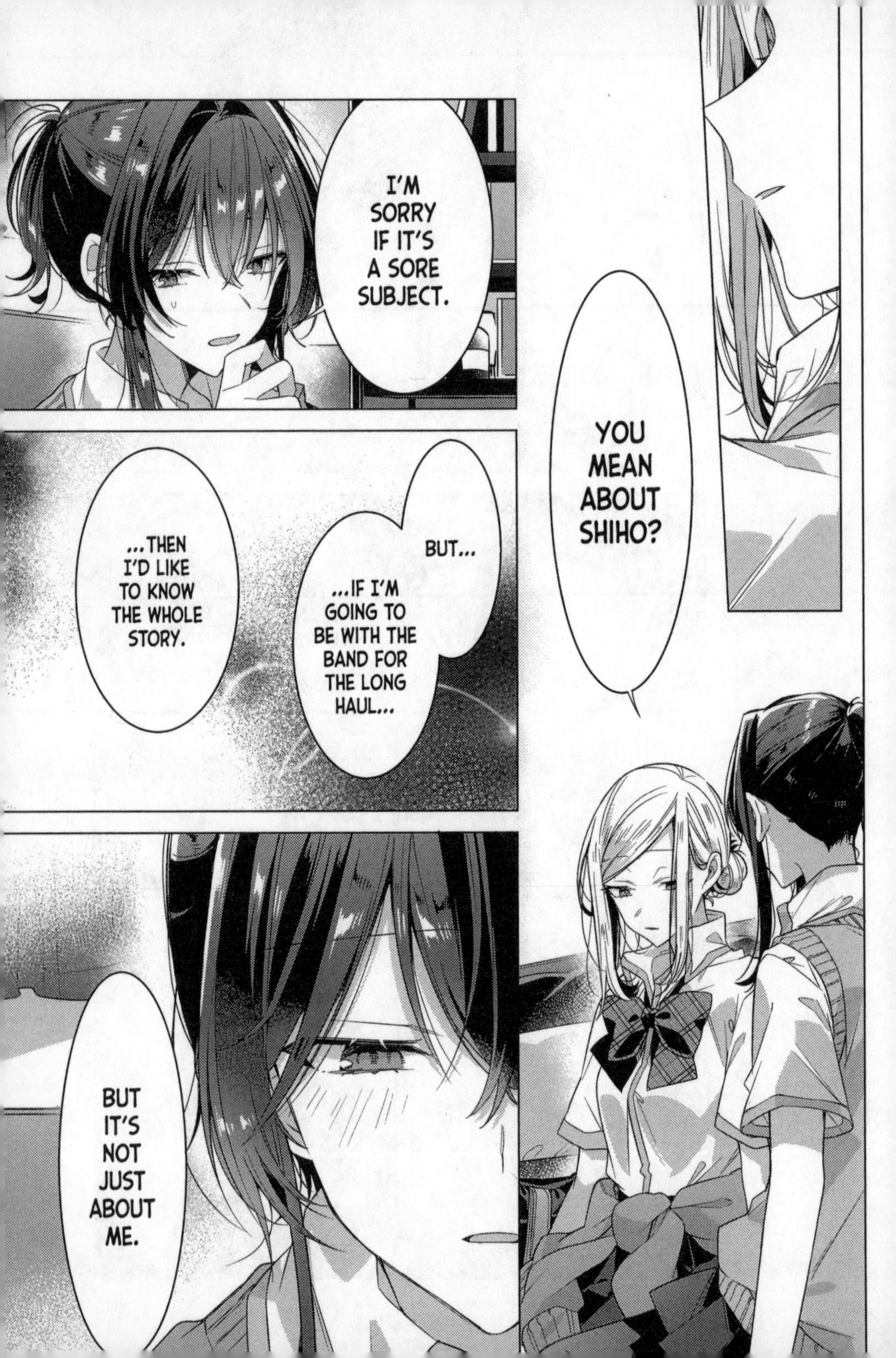
YOU MEAN ABOUT SHIHO?
I'M SORRY IF IT'S A SORE SUBJECT.
BUT...
...IF I'M GOING TO BE WITH THE BAND FOR THE LONG HAUL...
...THEN I'D LIKE TO KNOW THE WHOLE STORY.
BUT IT'S NOT JUST ABOUT ME.

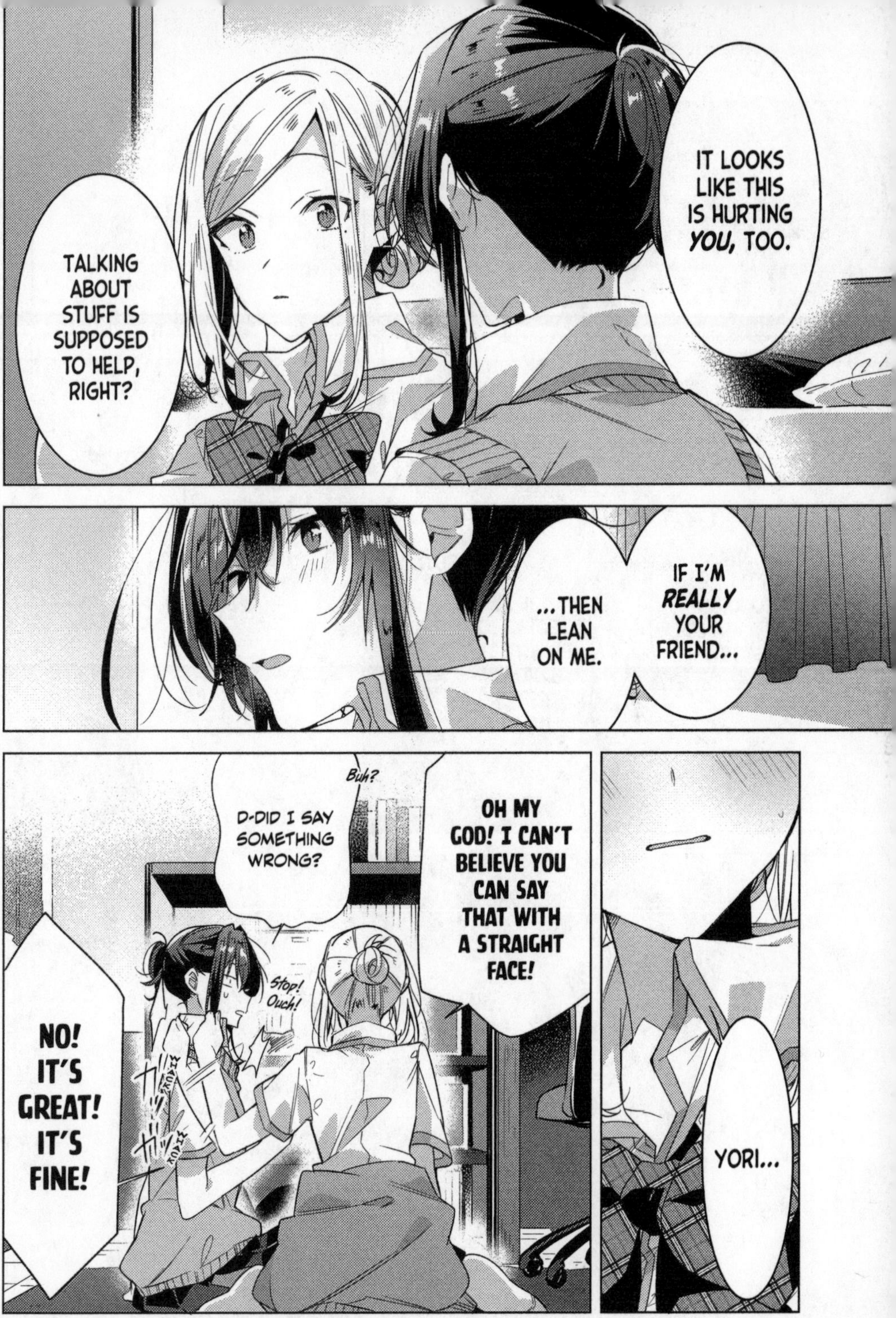
IT LOOKS LIKE THIS IS HURTING *YOU*, TOO.
TALKING ABOUT STUFF IS SUPPOSED TO HELP, RIGHT?
IF I'M *REALLY* YOUR FRIEND...
...THEN LEAN ON ME.
YORI...
OH MY GOD! I CAN'T BELIEVE YOU CAN SAY THAT WITH A STRAIGHT FACE!
Buh?
D-DID I SAY SOMETHING WRONG?
Stop! Ouch!
NO! IT'S GREAT! IT'S FINE!

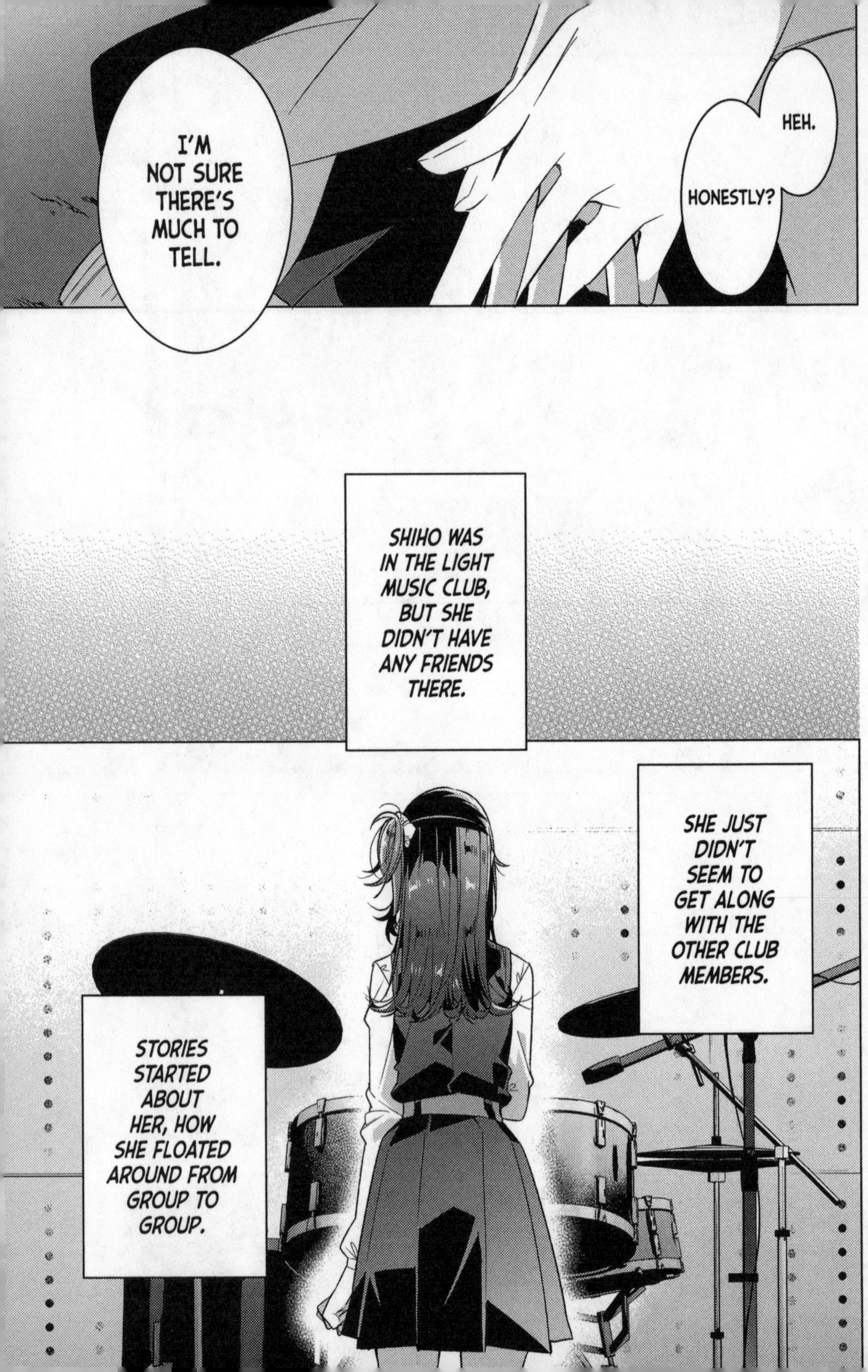
HEH.
HONESTLY?
I'M NOT SURE THERE'S MUCH TO TELL.
SHIHO WAS IN THE LIGHT MUSIC CLUB, BUT SHE DIDN'T HAVE ANY FRIENDS THERE.
SHE JUST DIDN'T SEEM TO GET ALONG WITH THE OTHER CLUB MEMBERS.
STORIES STARTED ABOUT HER, HOW SHE FLOATED AROUND FROM GROUP TO GROUP.

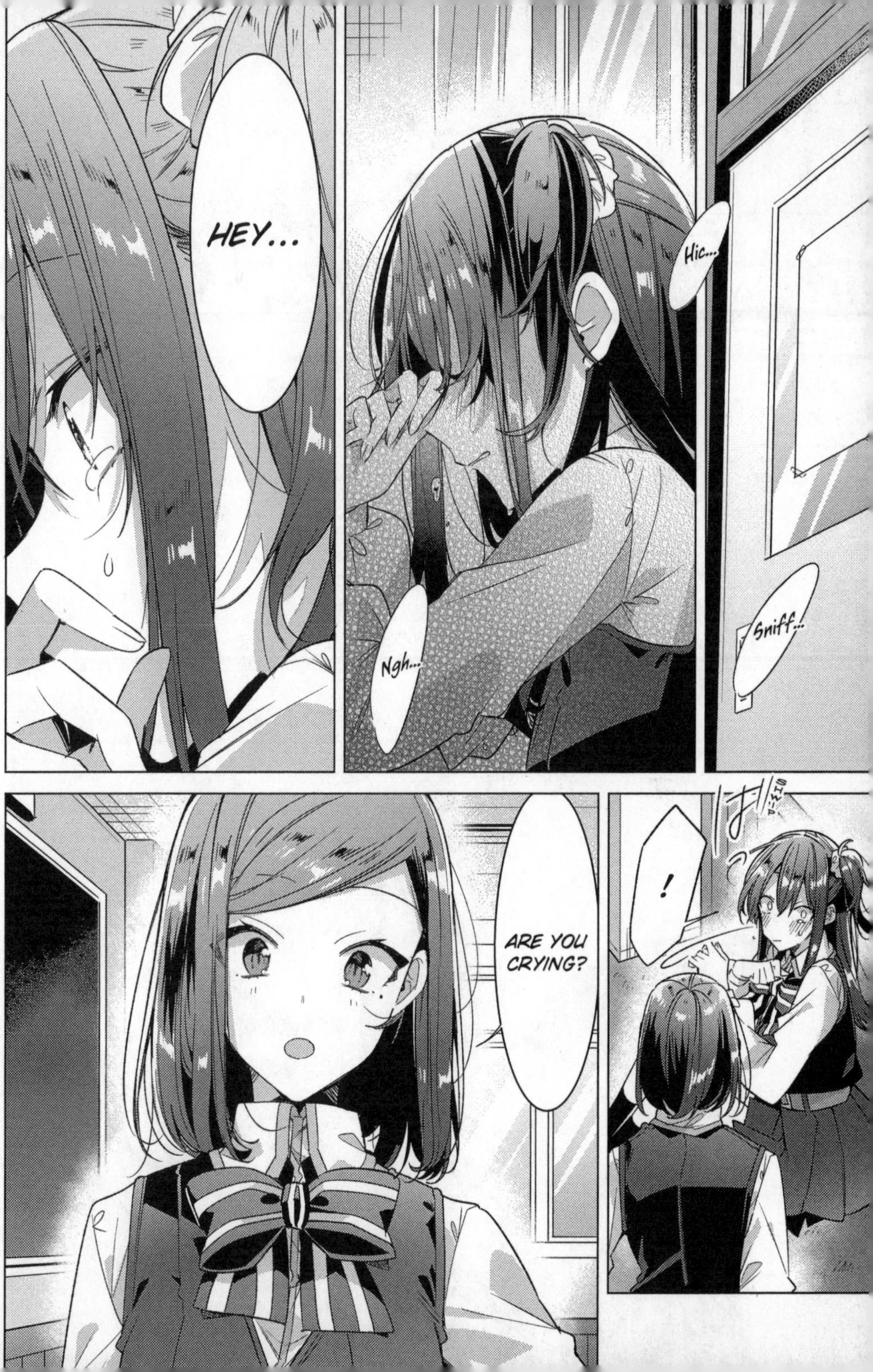
Hic...
Sniff...
Ngh...
HEY...
SWIP
!
ARE YOU CRYING?

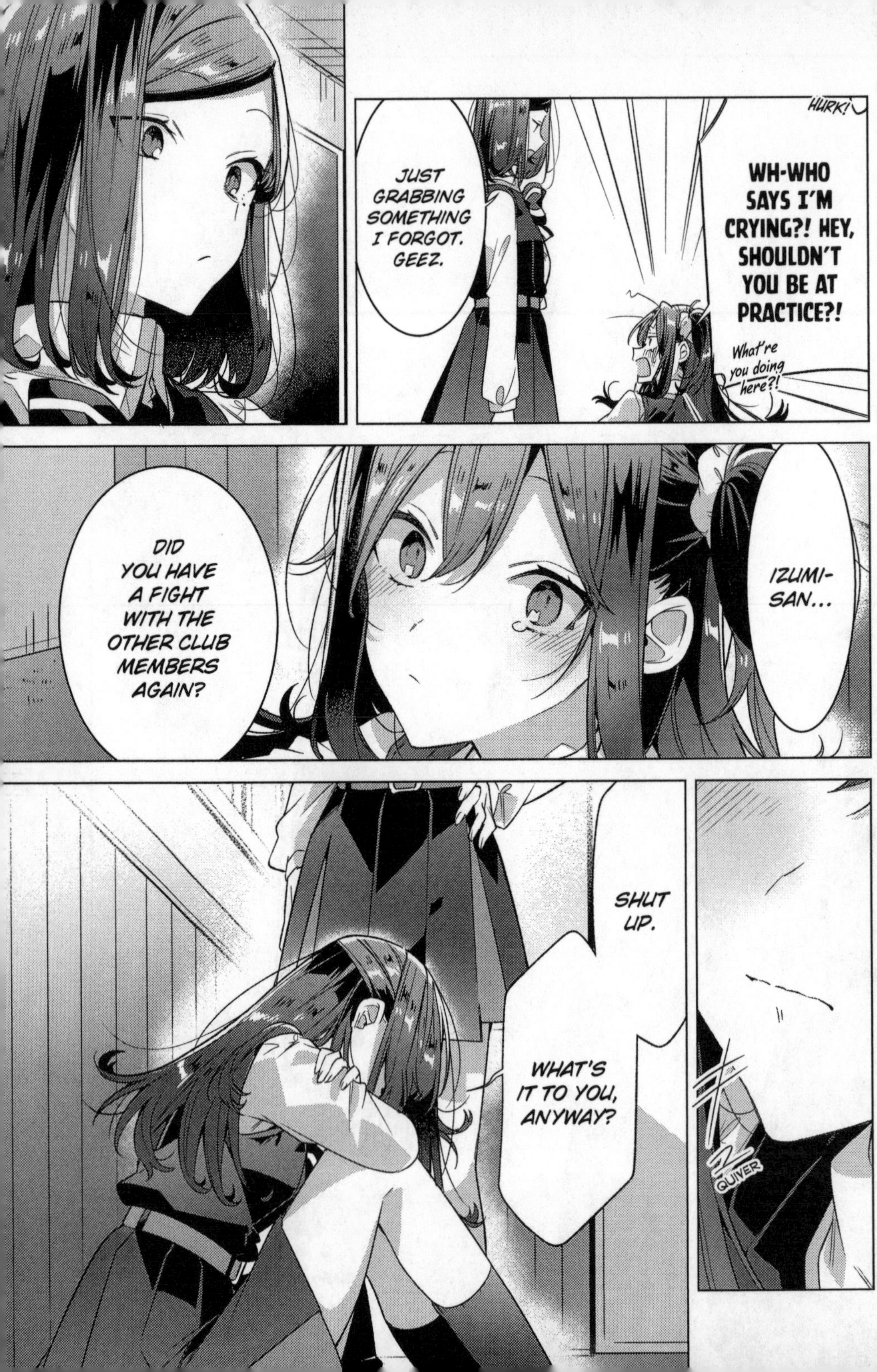
HURK!
WH-WHO SAYS I'M CRYING?! HEY, SHOULDN'T YOU BE AT PRACTICE?!
What're you doing here?!
JUST GRABBING SOMETHING I FORGOT. GEEZ.
IZUMI-SAN...
DID YOU HAVE A FIGHT WITH THE OTHER CLUB MEMBERS AGAIN?
QUIVER
SHUT UP.
WHAT'S IT TO YOU, ANYWAY?

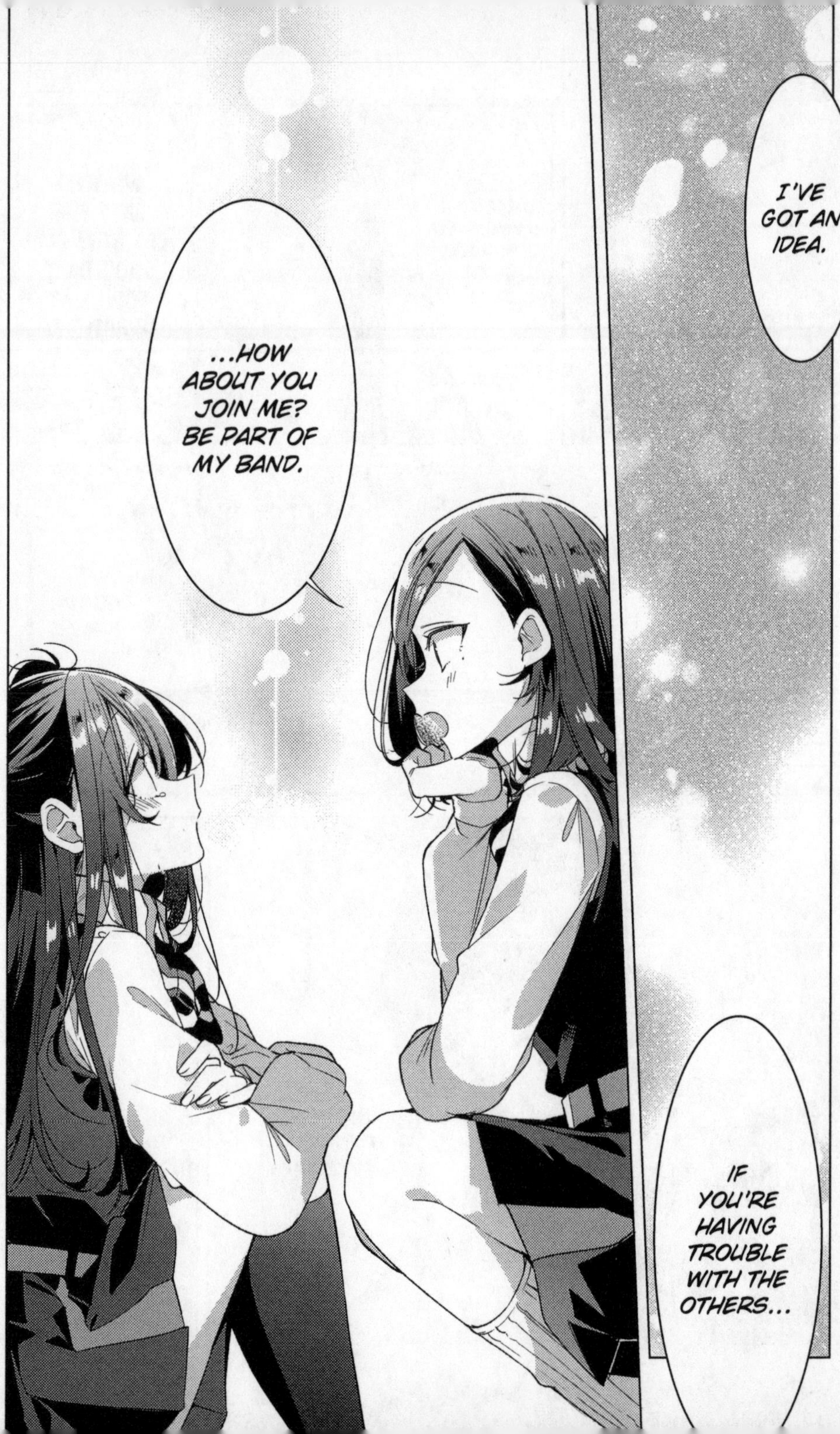
I'VE GOT AN IDEA.
IF YOU'RE HAVING TROUBLE WITH THE OTHERS...
...HOW ABOUT YOU JOIN ME? BE PART OF MY BAND.

WE WERE ACTUALLY JUST LOOKING FOR A GUITARIST!

YOU PLAY GUITAR, RIGHT?

FWIP?

I CAN'T.

IF I'M GOING TO BE IN A BAND...

...THEN I WANT TO DO IT RIGHT.

WHA?

131

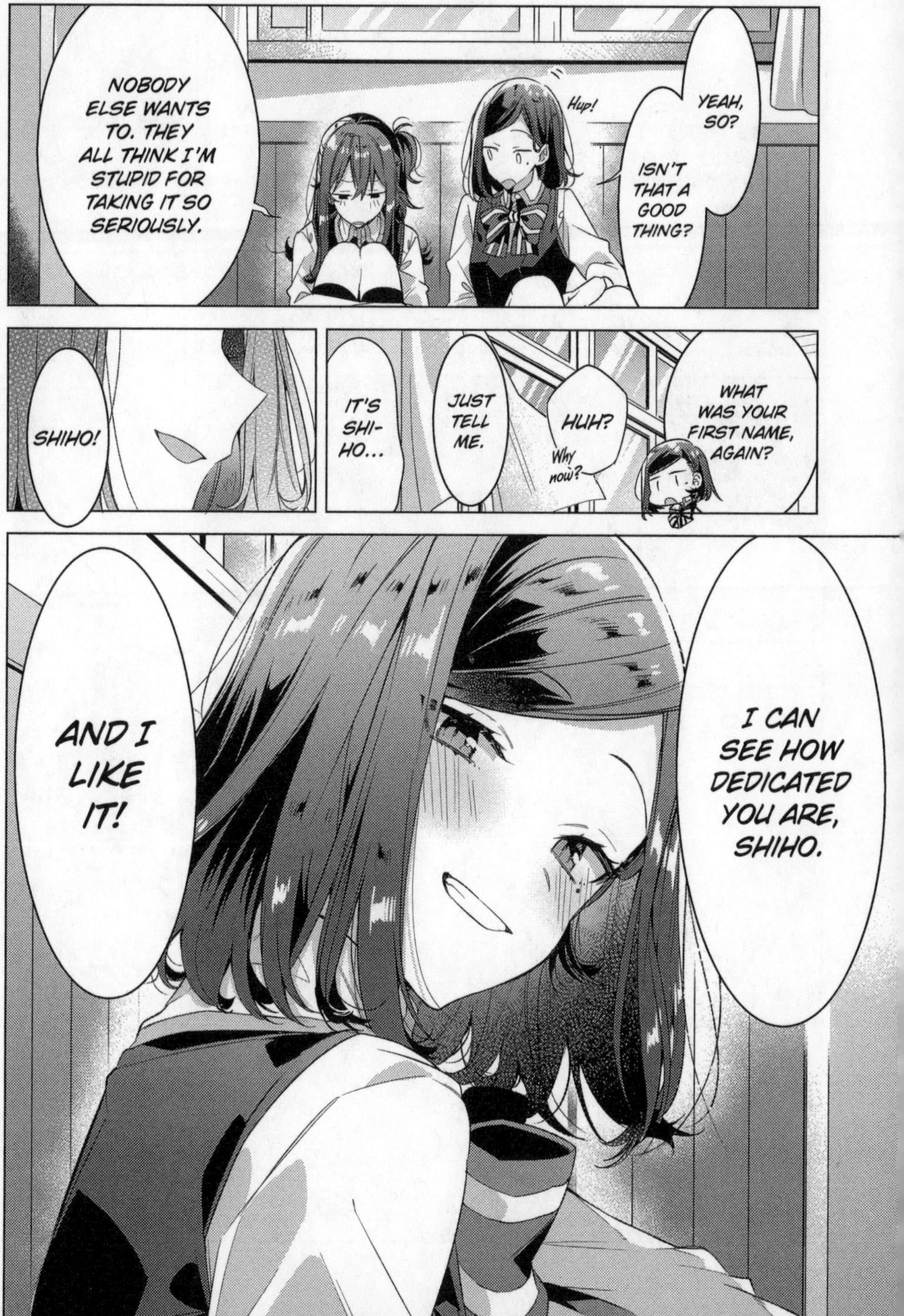
YEAH, SO?
ISN'T THAT A GOOD THING?
Hup!
NOBODY ELSE WANTS TO. THEY ALL THINK I'M STUPID FOR TAKING IT SO SERIOUSLY.
WHAT WAS YOUR FIRST NAME, AGAIN?
HUH?
Why now?
JUST TELL ME.
IT'S SHI-HO...
SHIHO!
I CAN SEE HOW DEDICATED YOU ARE, SHIHO.
AND I LIKE IT!

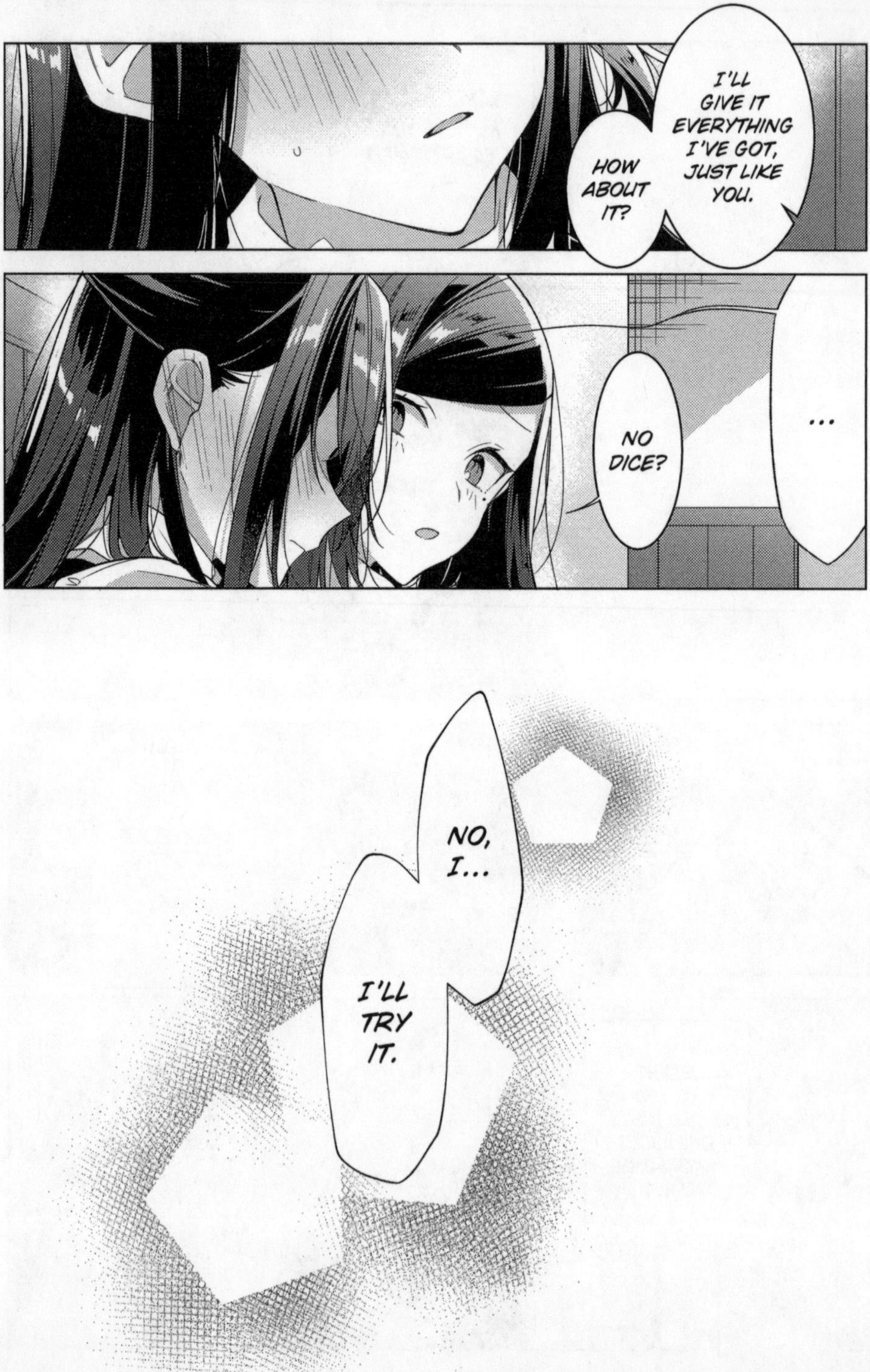
I'LL GIVE IT EVERYTHING I'VE GOT, JUST LIKE YOU.
HOW ABOUT IT?
...
NO DICE?
NO, I...
I'LL TRY IT.

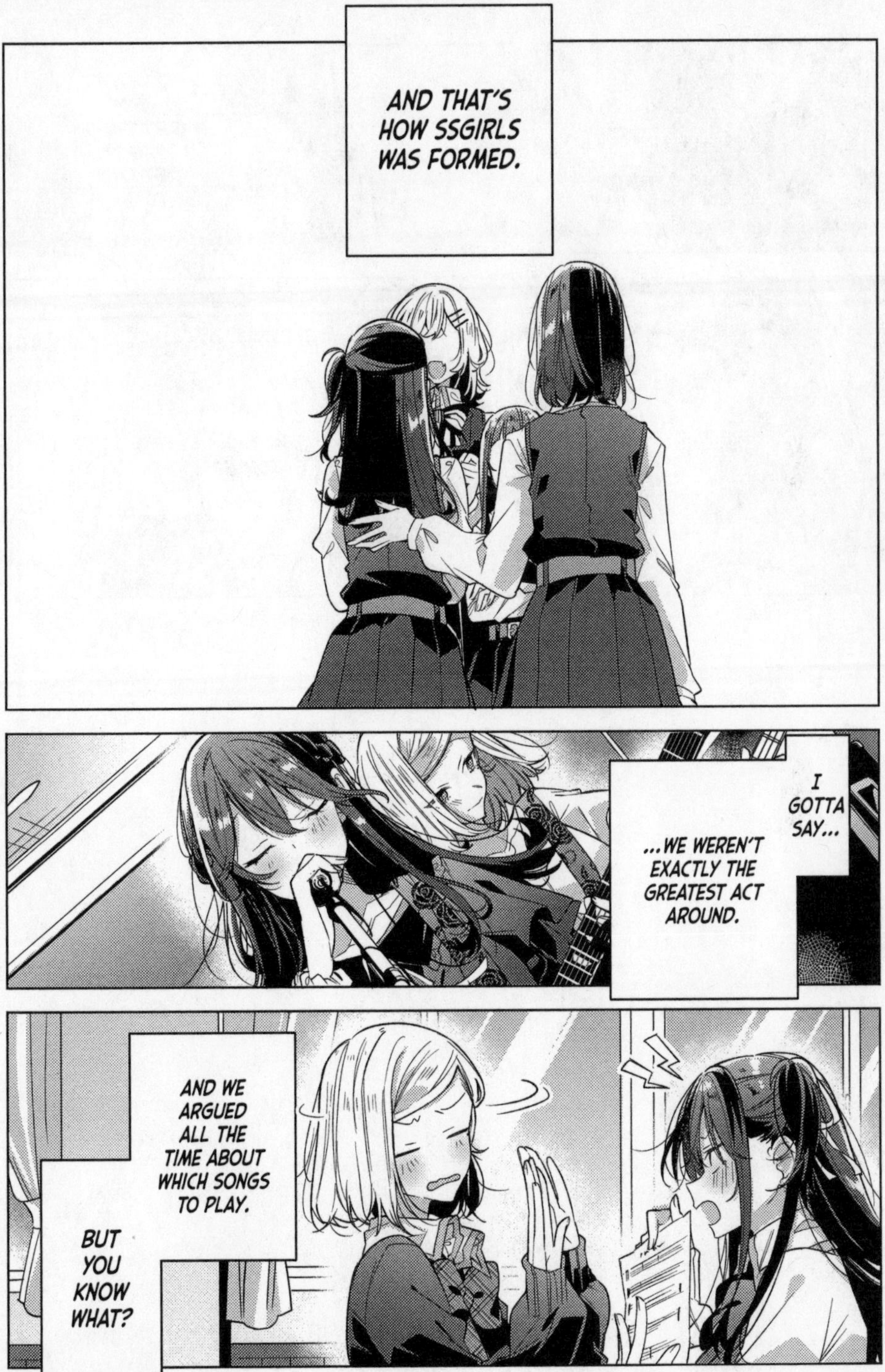
AND THAT'S HOW SSGIRLS WAS FORMED.
I GOTTA SAY...
...WE WEREN'T EXACTLY THE GREATEST ACT AROUND.
AND WE ARGUED ALL THE TIME ABOUT WHICH SONGS TO PLAY.
BUT YOU KNOW WHAT?

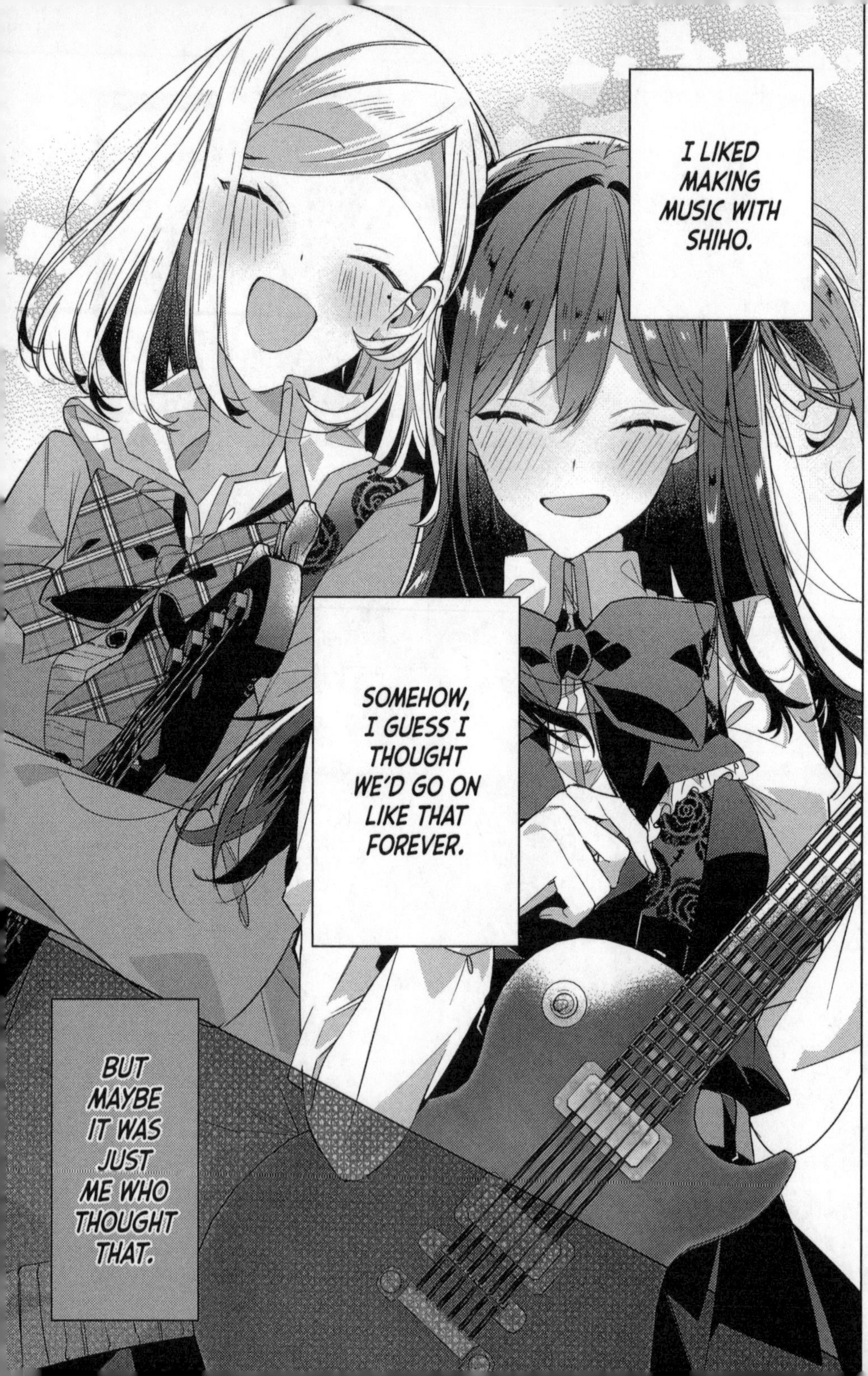
I LIKED MAKING MUSIC WITH SHIHO.
SOMEHOW, I GUESS I THOUGHT WE'D GO ON LIKE THAT FOREVER.
BUT MAYBE IT WAS JUST ME WHO THOUGHT THAT.

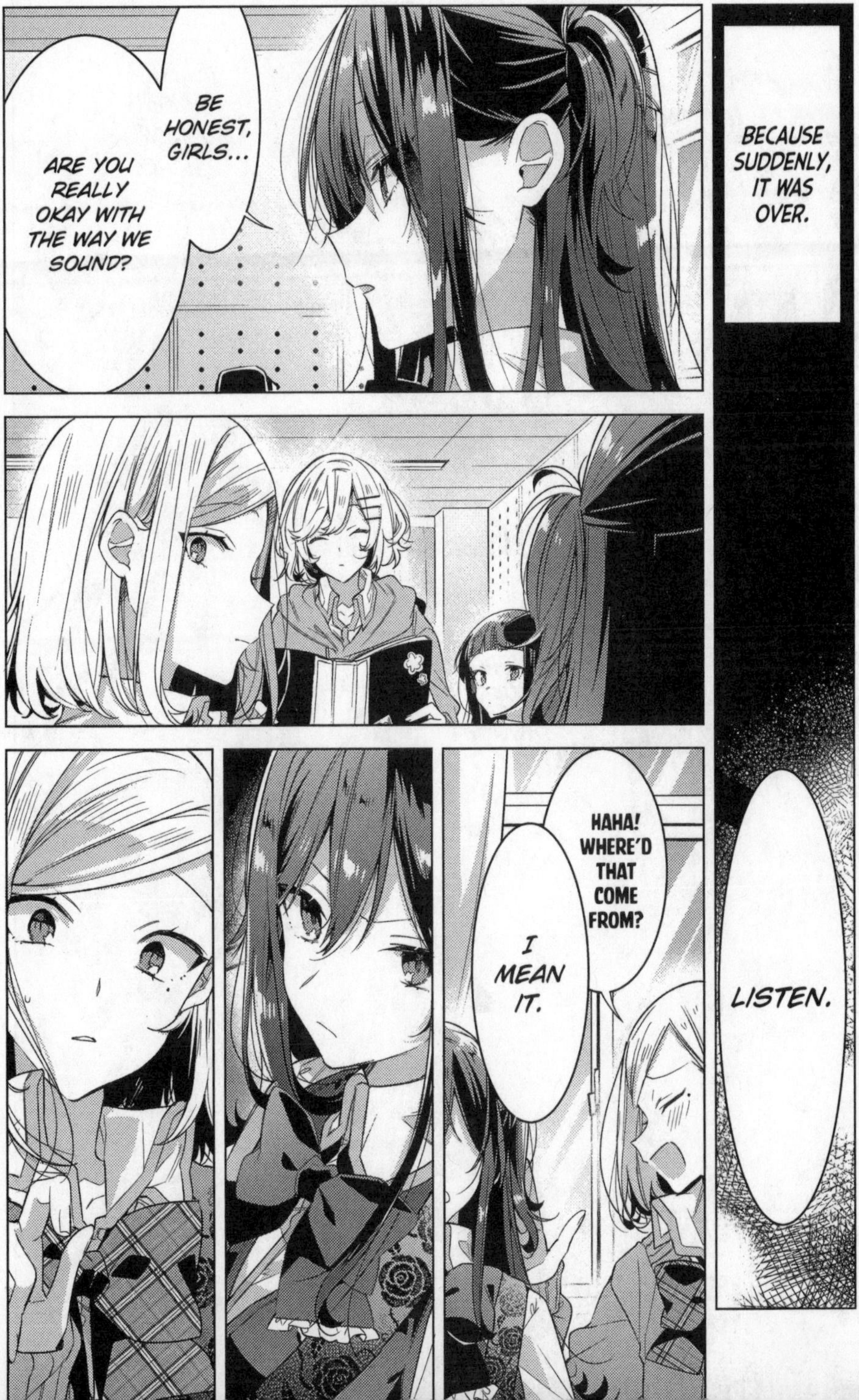
BECAUSE SUDDENLY, IT WAS OVER.
LISTEN.
BE HONEST, GIRLS...
ARE YOU REALLY OKAY WITH THE WAY WE SOUND?
HAHA! WHERE'D THAT COME FROM?
I MEAN IT.

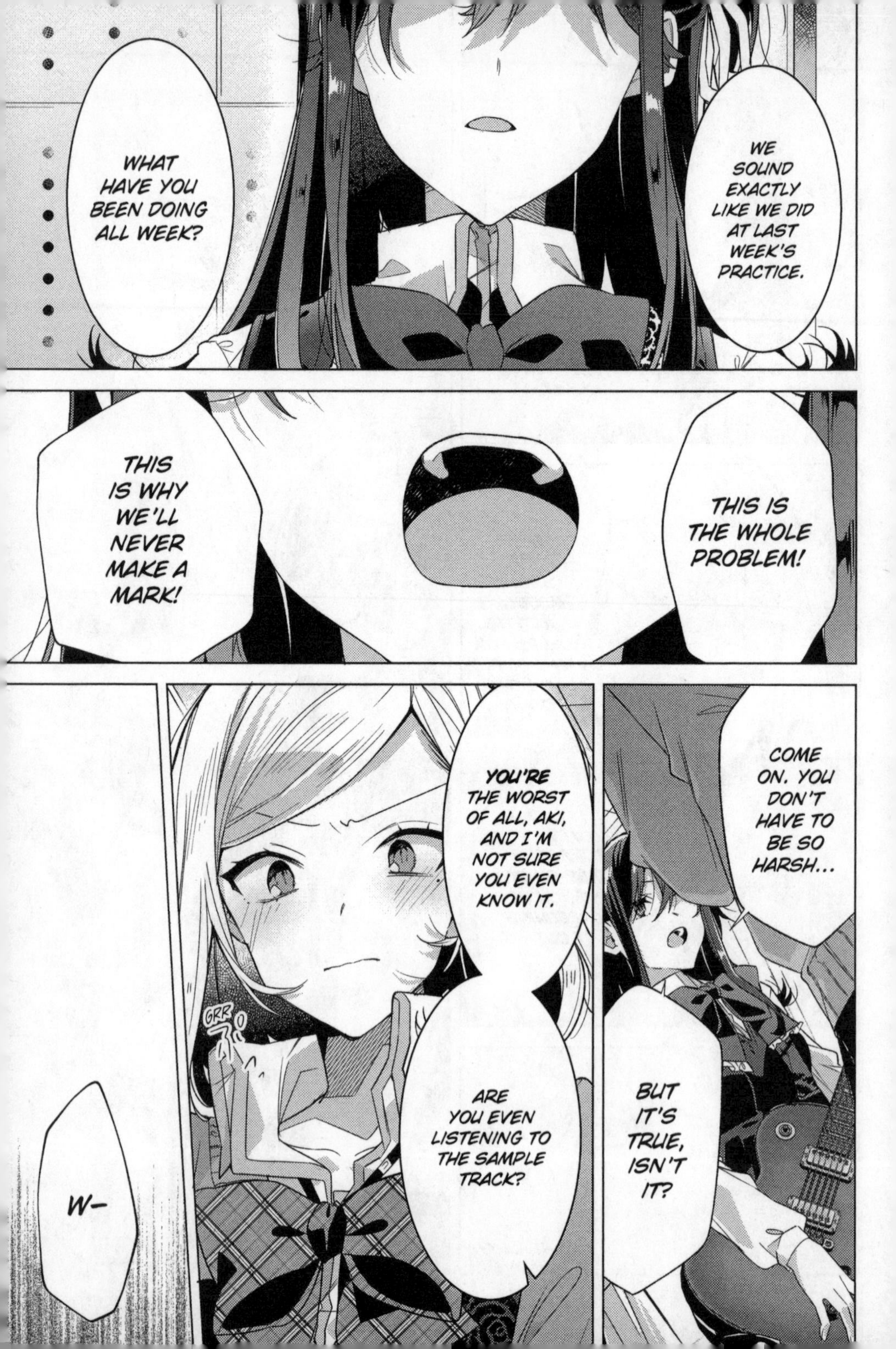
WE SOUND EXACTLY LIKE WE DID AT LAST WEEK'S PRACTICE.
WHAT HAVE YOU BEEN DOING ALL WEEK?
THIS IS THE WHOLE PROBLEM!
THIS IS WHY WE'LL NEVER MAKE A MARK!
COME ON. YOU DON'T HAVE TO BE SO HARSH...
BUT IT'S TRUE, ISN'T IT?
YOU'RE THE WORST OF ALL, AKI, AND I'M NOT SURE YOU EVEN KNOW IT.
ARE YOU EVEN LISTENING TO THE SAMPLE TRACK?
GRR
W–

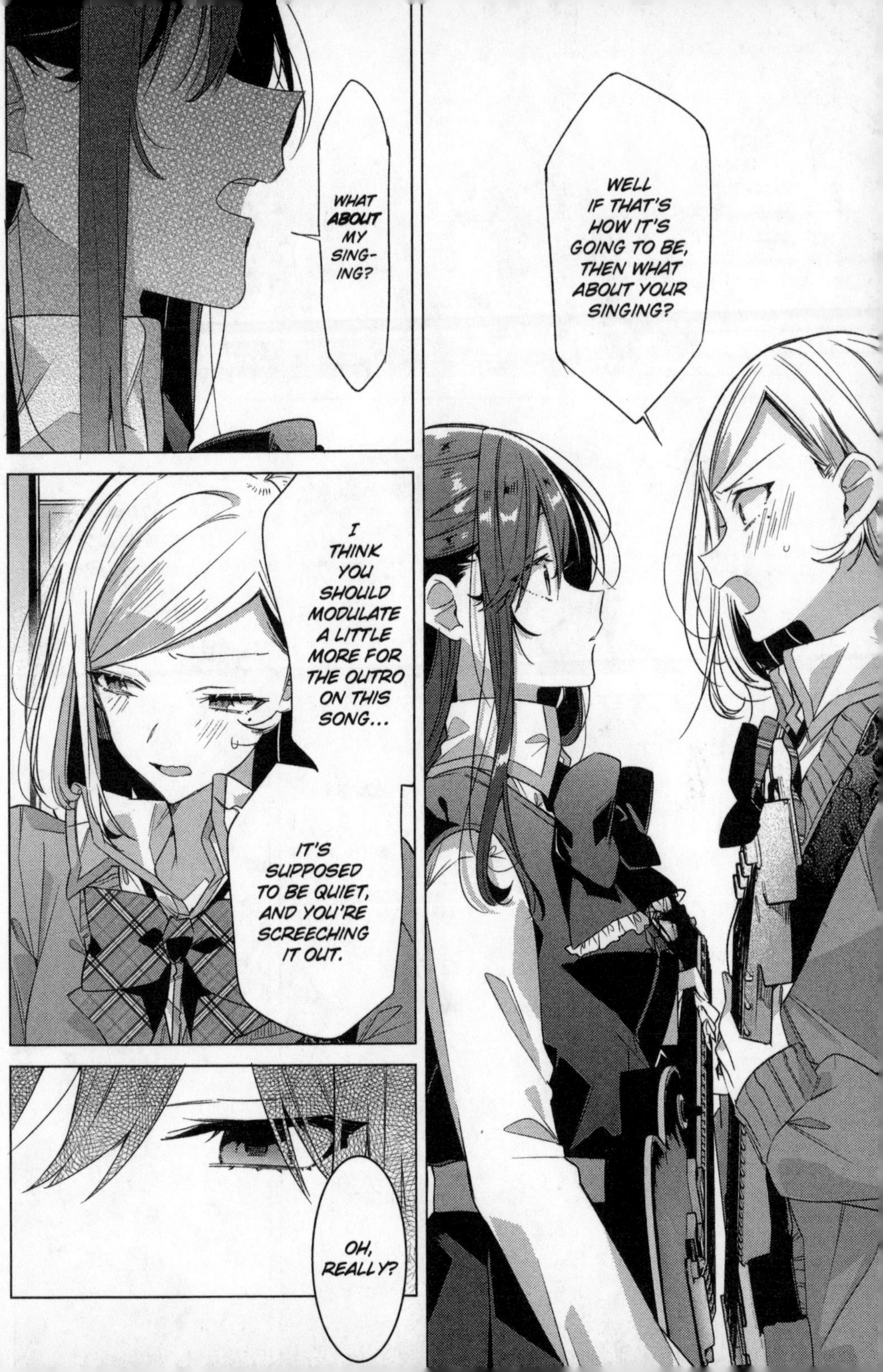
WELL IF THAT'S HOW IT'S GOING TO BE, THEN WHAT ABOUT YOUR SINGING?
WHAT **ABOUT** MY SING-ING?
I THINK YOU SHOULD MODULATE A LITTLE MORE FOR THE OUTRO ON THIS SONG...
IT'S SUPPOSED TO BE QUIET, AND YOU'RE SCREECHING IT OUT.
OH, REALLY?

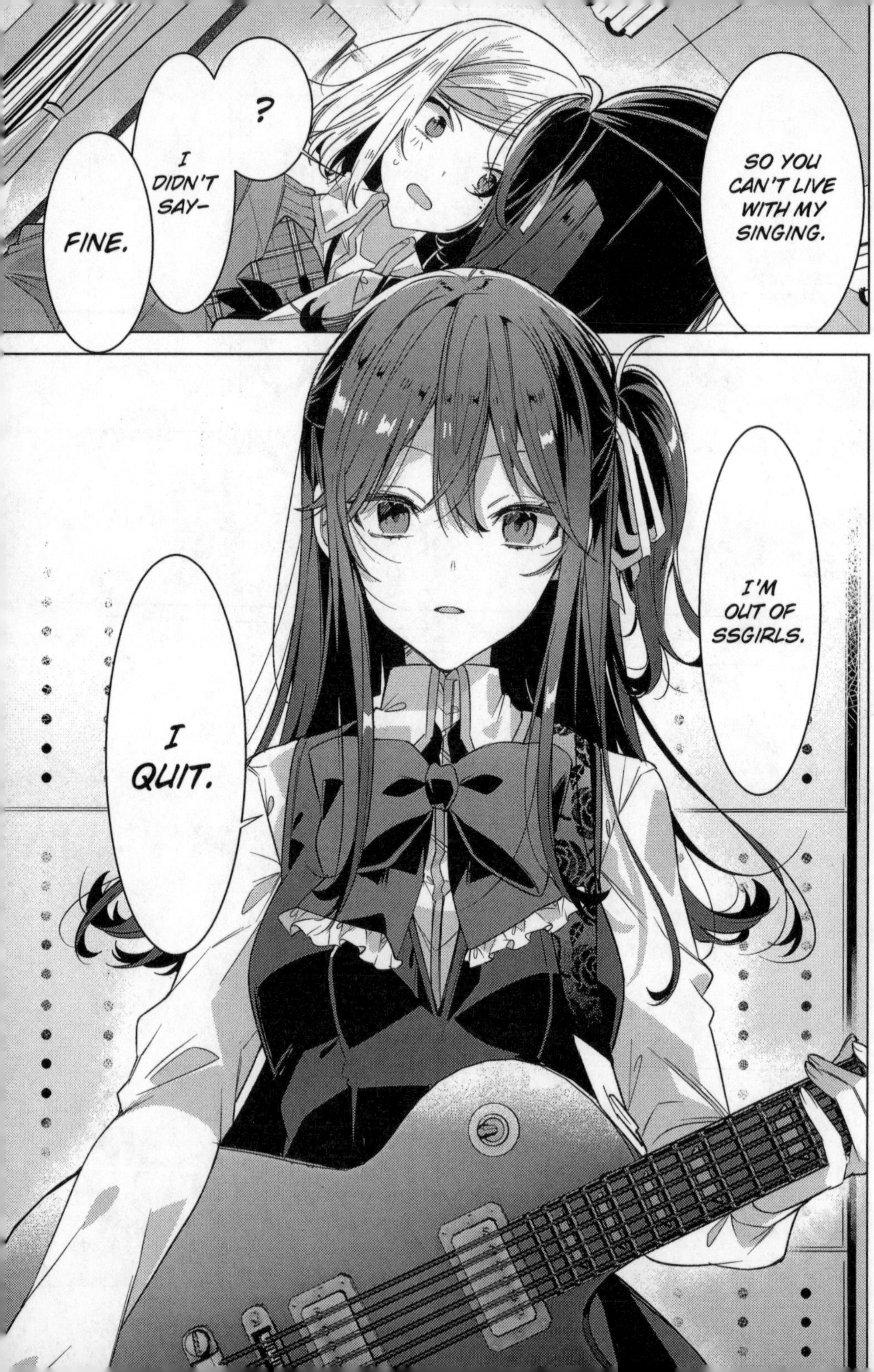
SO YOU CAN'T LIVE WITH MY SINGING.
?
I DIDN'T SAY-
FINE.
I'M OUT OF SSGIRLS.
I QUIT.

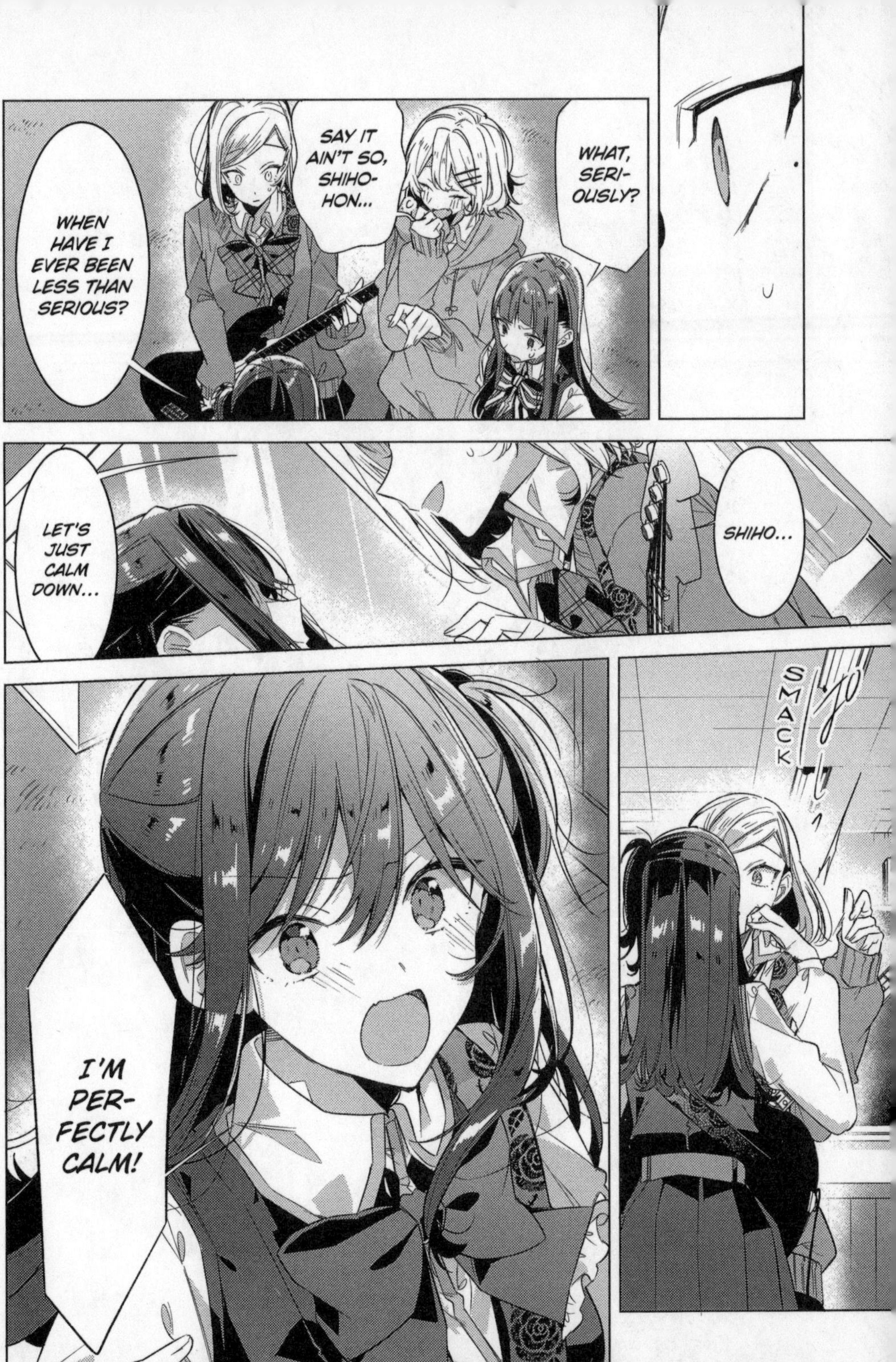
WHAT, SERI-OUSLY?
SAY IT AIN'T SO, SHIHO-HON...
WHEN HAVE I EVER BEEN LESS THAN SERIOUS?
SHIHO...
LET'S JUST CALM DOWN...
SMACK
I'M PER-FECTLY CALM!

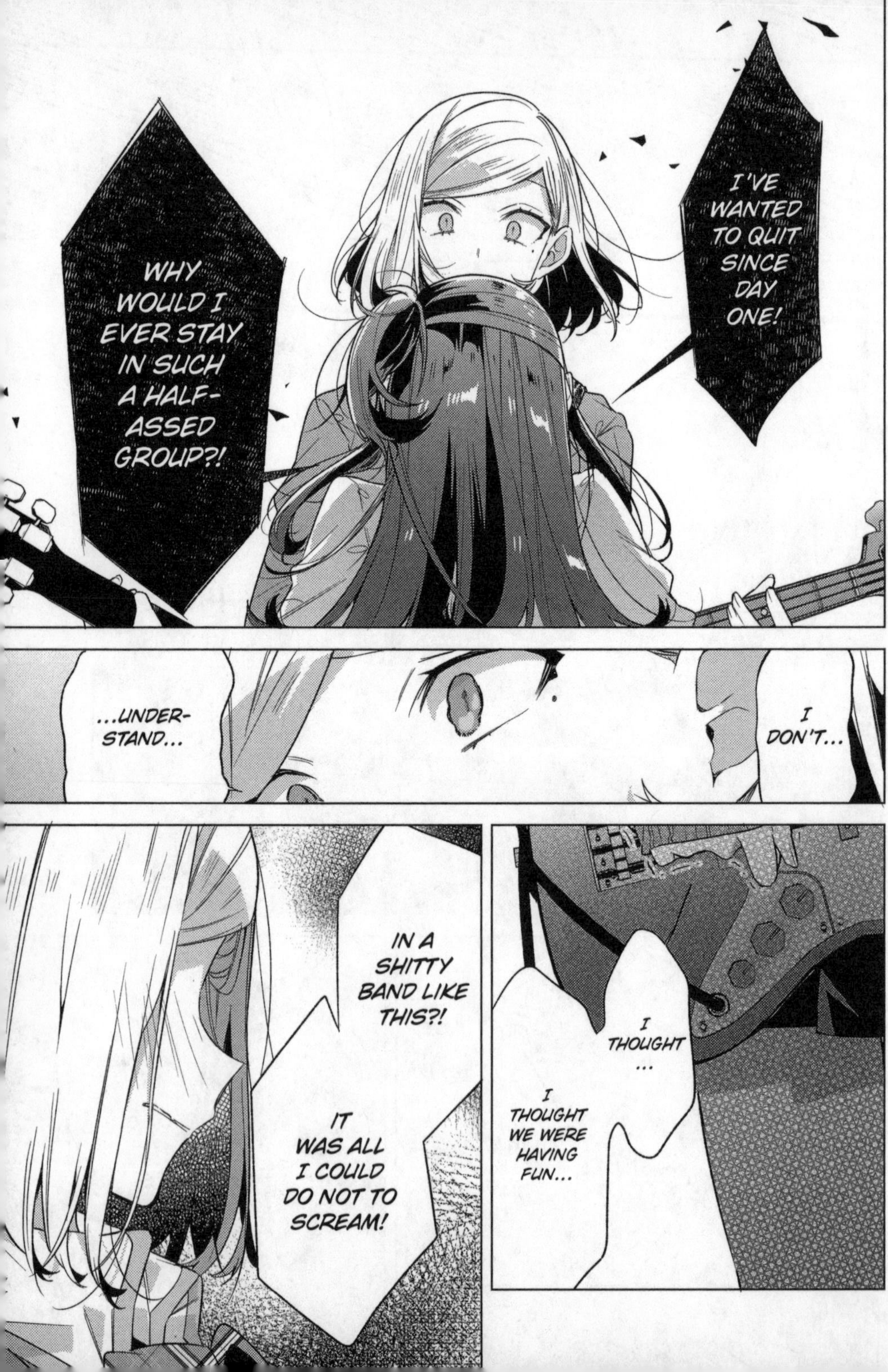
I'VE WANTED TO QUIT SINCE DAY ONE!
WHY WOULD I EVER STAY IN SUCH A HALF-ASSED GROUP?!
I DON'T...
...UNDER-STAND...
I THOUGHT ...
I THOUGHT WE WERE HAVING FUN...
IN A SHITTY BAND LIKE THIS?!
IT WAS ALL I COULD DO NOT TO SCREAM!

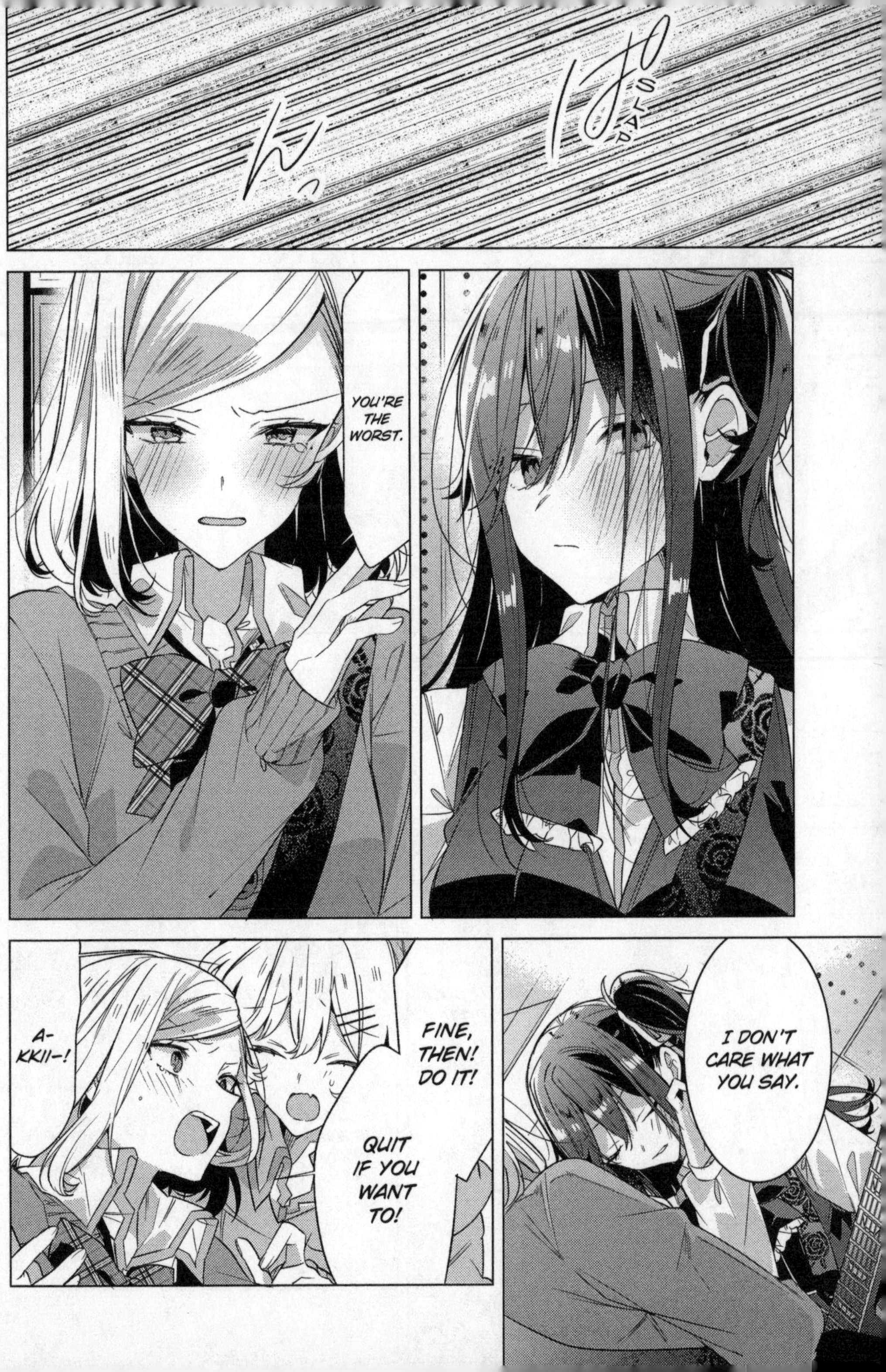

ぱん
SLAP
YOU'RE THE WORST.
I DON'T CARE WHAT YOU SAY.
FINE, THEN! DO IT!
QUIT IF YOU WANT TO!
A-KKII-!

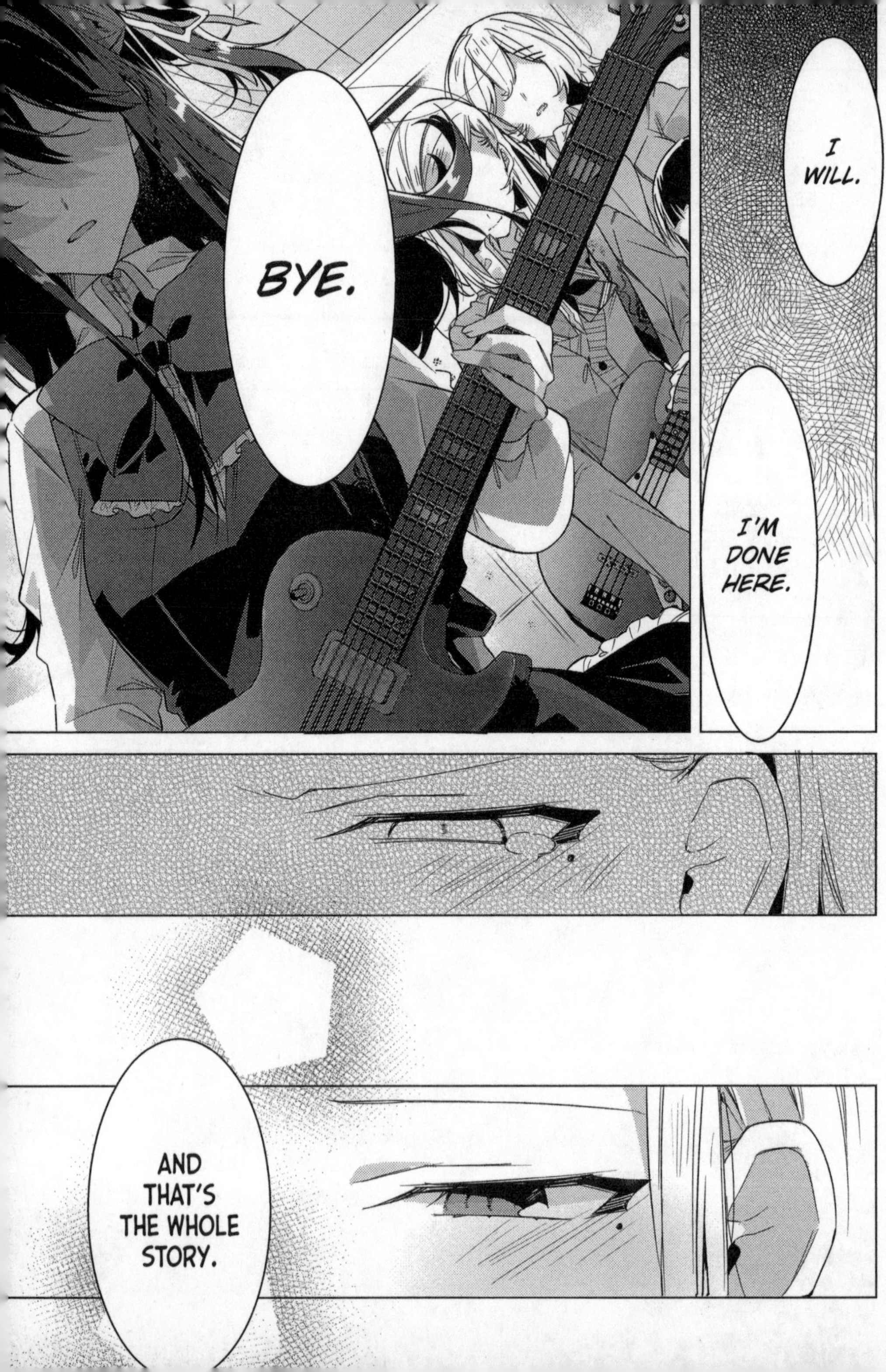
I WILL.
I'M DONE HERE.
BYE.
AND THAT'S THE WHOLE STORY.

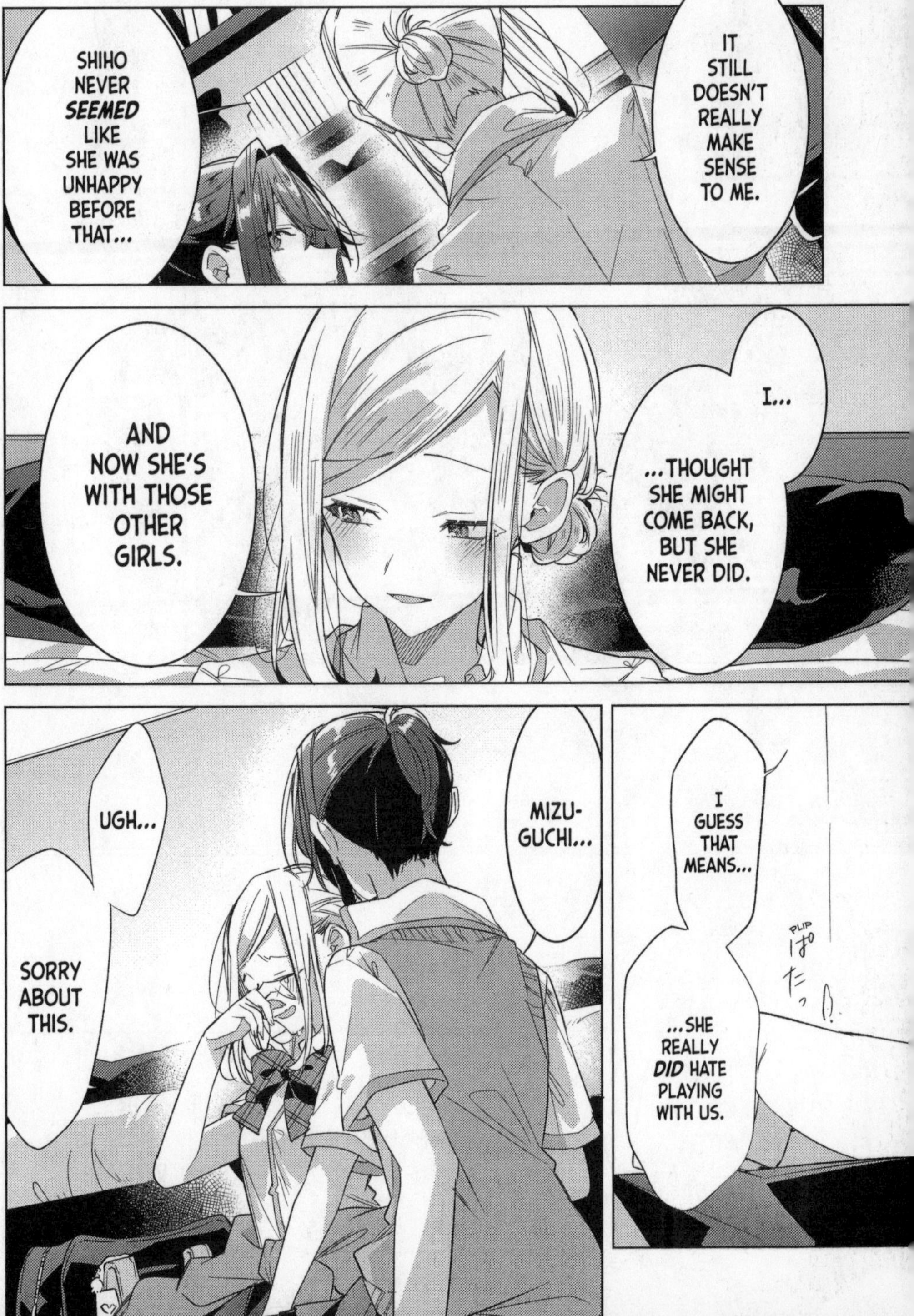
IT STILL DOESN'T REALLY MAKE SENSE TO ME.
SHIHO NEVER *SEEMED* LIKE SHE WAS UNHAPPY BEFORE THAT...
I...
...THOUGHT SHE MIGHT COME BACK, BUT SHE NEVER DID.
AND NOW SHE'S WITH THOSE OTHER GIRLS.
I GUESS THAT MEANS...
...SHE REALLY *DID* HATE PLAYING WITH US.
PLIP
ぱたっ
MIZU-GUCHI...
UGH...
SORRY ABOUT THIS.

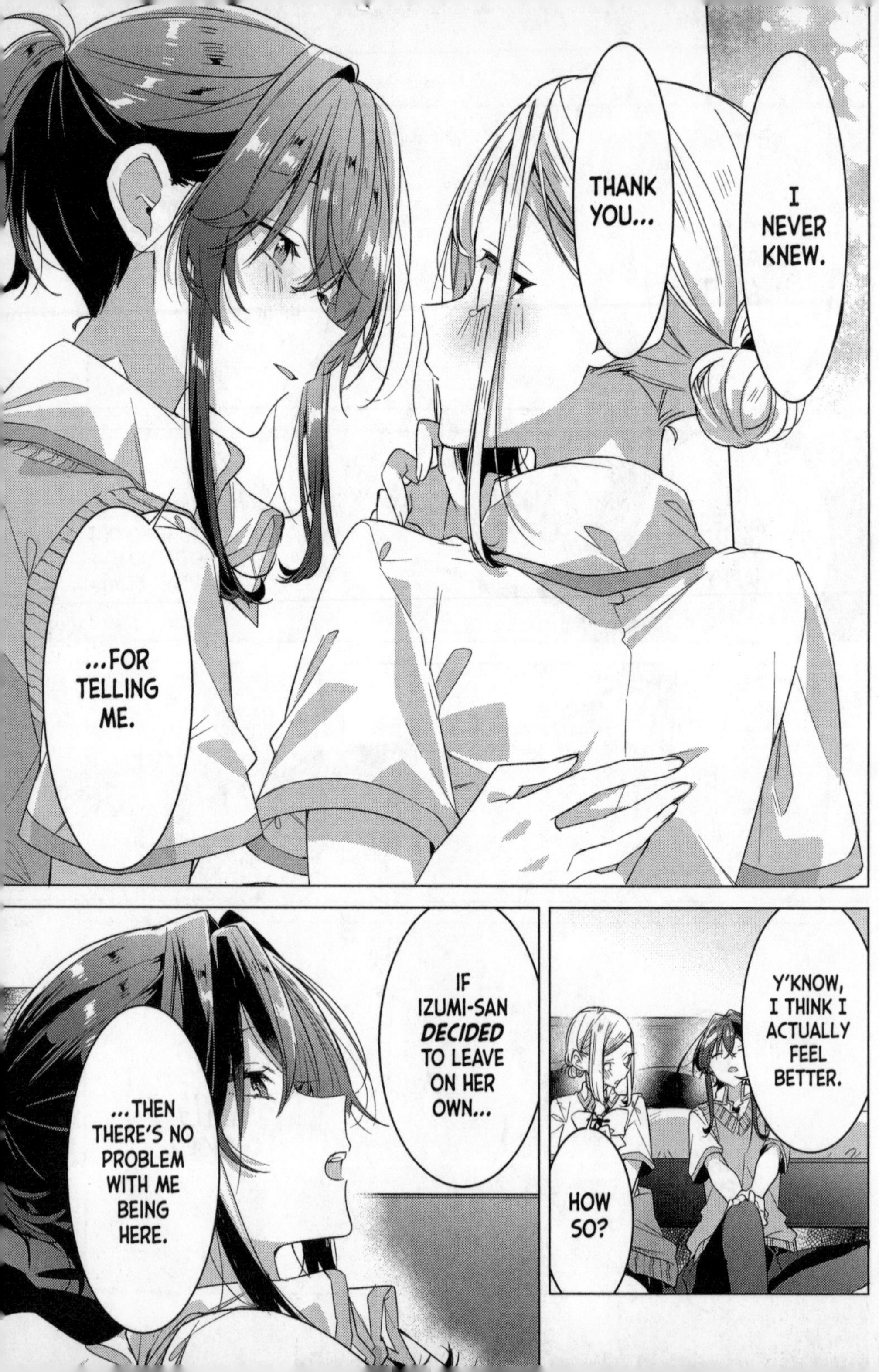
I NEVER KNEW.
THANK YOU...
...FOR TELLING ME.
Y'KNOW, I THINK I ACTUALLY FEEL BETTER.
HOW SO?
IF IZUMI-SAN *DECIDED* TO LEAVE ON HER OWN...
...THEN THERE'S NO PROBLEM WITH ME BEING HERE.

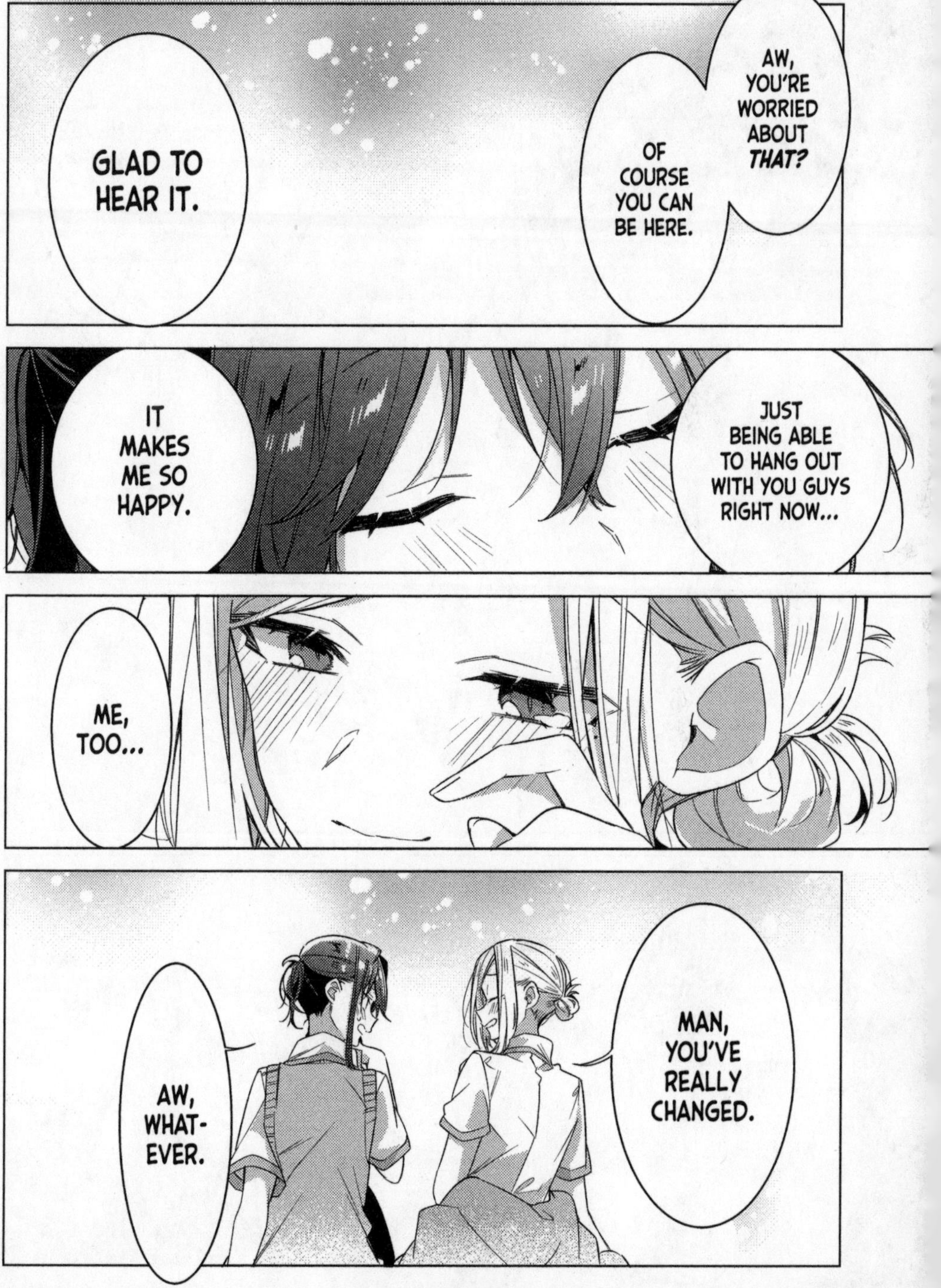
AW, YOU'RE WORRIED ABOUT *THAT?*
OF COURSE YOU CAN BE HERE.
GLAD TO HEAR IT.
JUST BEING ABLE TO HANG OUT WITH YOU GUYS RIGHT NOW...
IT MAKES ME SO HAPPY.
ME, TOO...
MAN, YOU'VE REALLY CHANGED.
AW, WHAT-EVER.

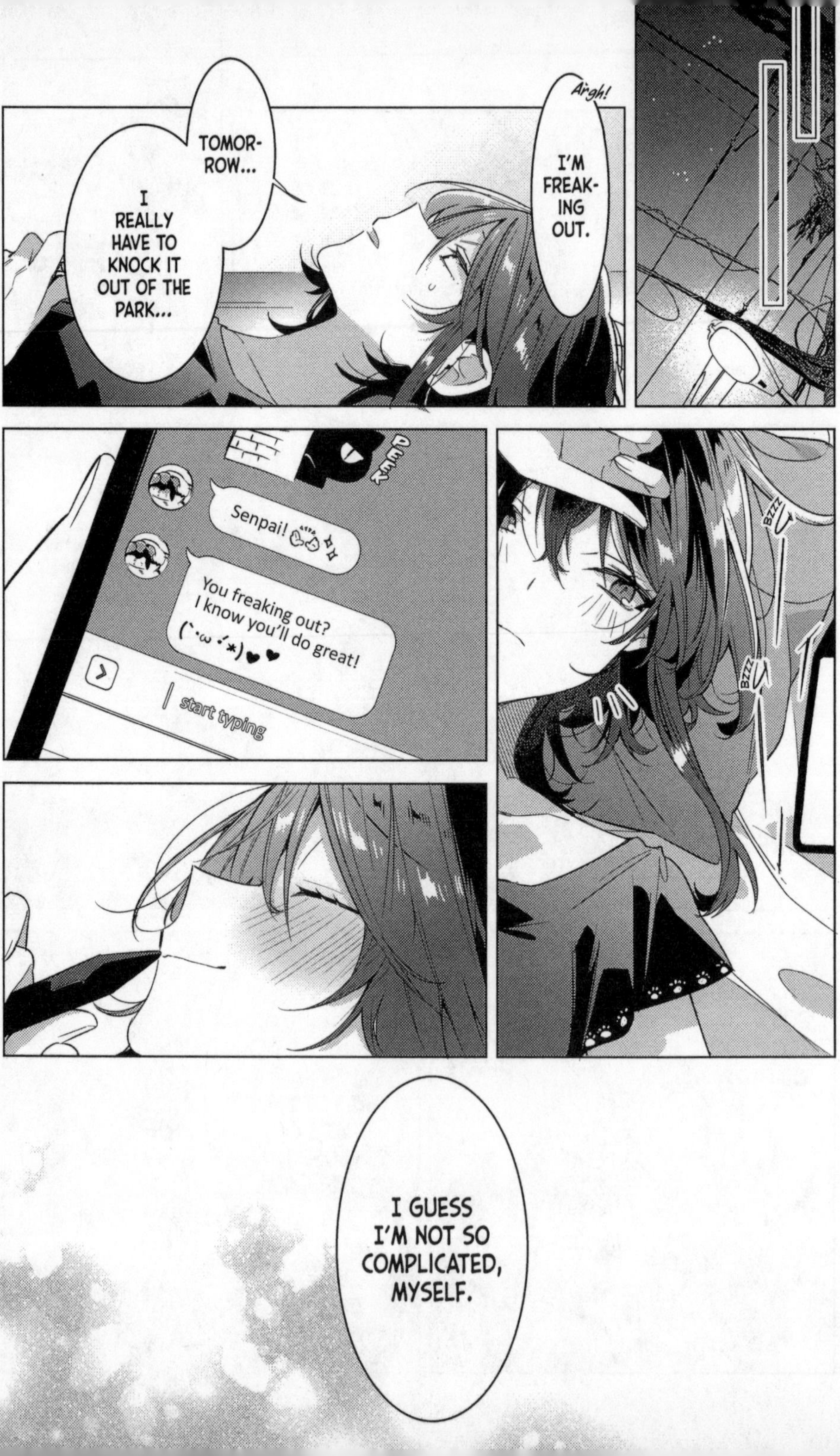
Argh!
I'M FREAKING OUT.
TOMORROW...
I REALLY HAVE TO KNOCK IT OUT OF THE PARK...
BZZZ
BZZZ
PEEK
Senpai!
You freaking out? I know you'll do great! (`･ω･´*)♥♥
start typing
I GUESS I'M NOT SO COMPLICATED, MYSELF.

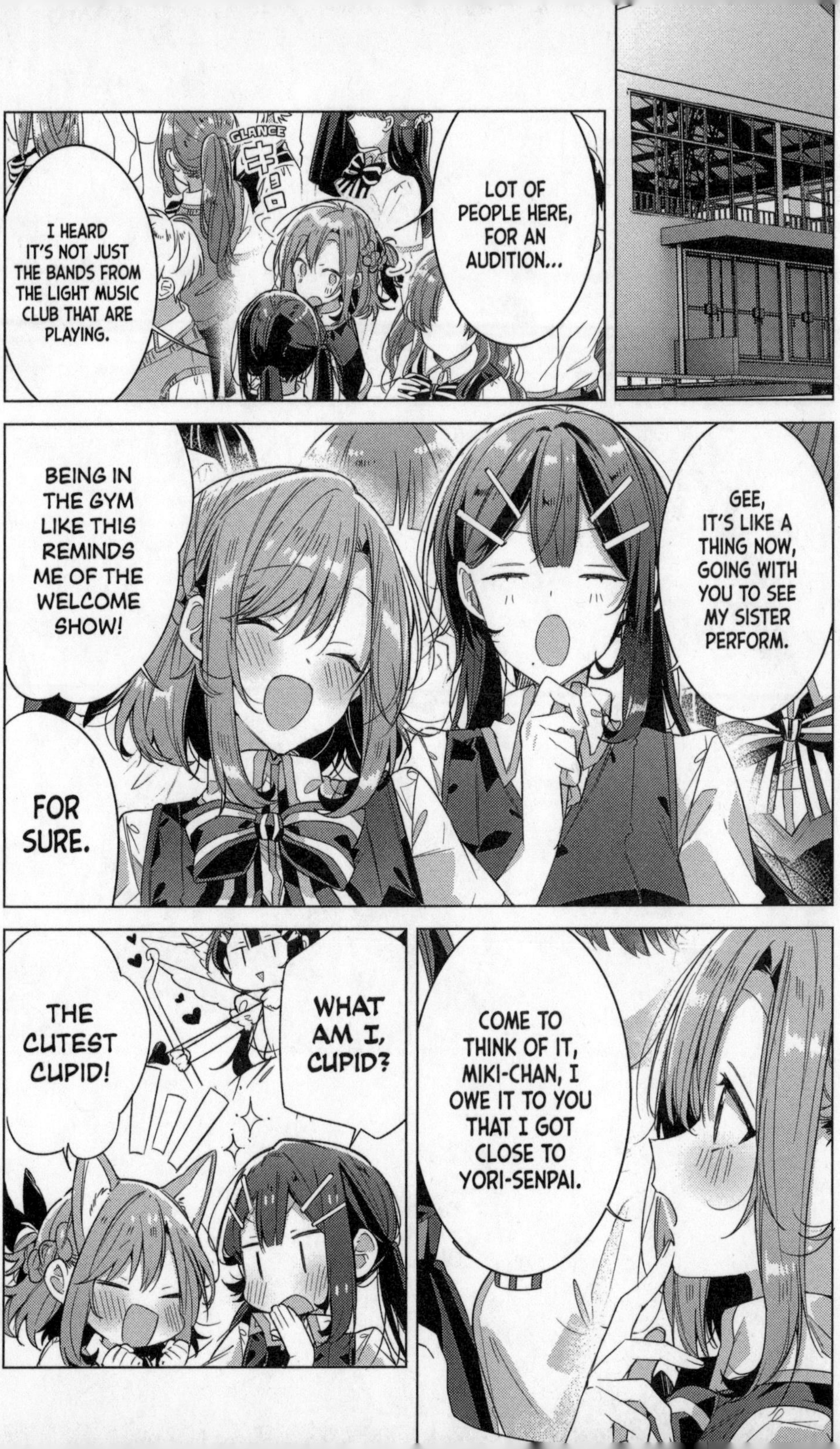
LOT OF PEOPLE HERE, FOR AN AUDITION...
GLANCE
キョロ
I HEARD IT'S NOT JUST THE BANDS FROM THE LIGHT MUSIC CLUB THAT ARE PLAYING.
GEE, IT'S LIKE A THING NOW, GOING WITH YOU TO SEE MY SISTER PERFORM.
BEING IN THE GYM LIKE THIS REMINDS ME OF THE WELCOME SHOW!
FOR SURE.
COME TO THINK OF IT, MIKI-CHAN, I OWE IT TO YOU THAT I GOT CLOSE TO YORI-SENPAI.
WHAT AM I, CUPID?
THE CUTEST CUPID!

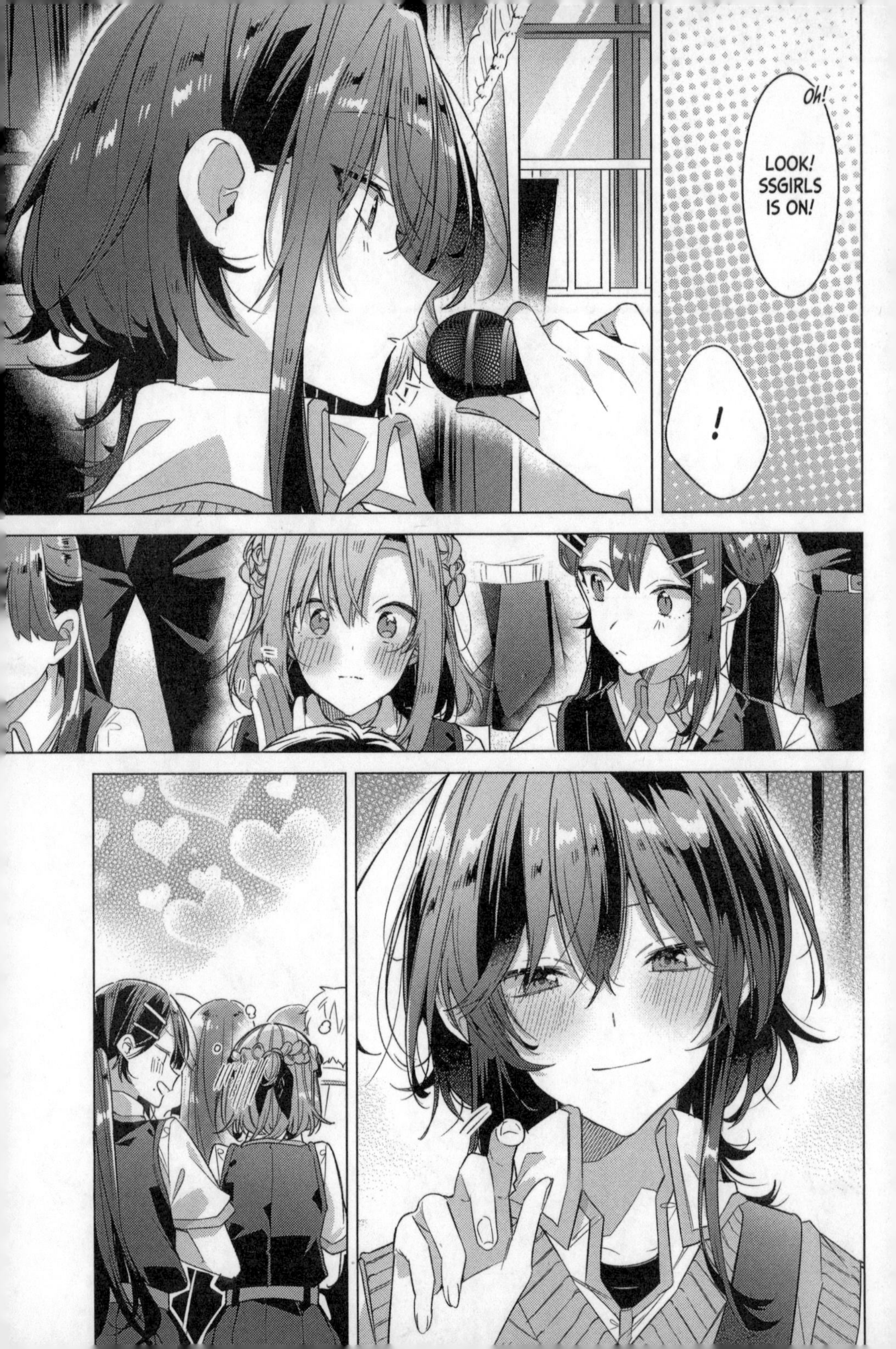
Oh!
LOOK! SSGIRLS IS ON!
!

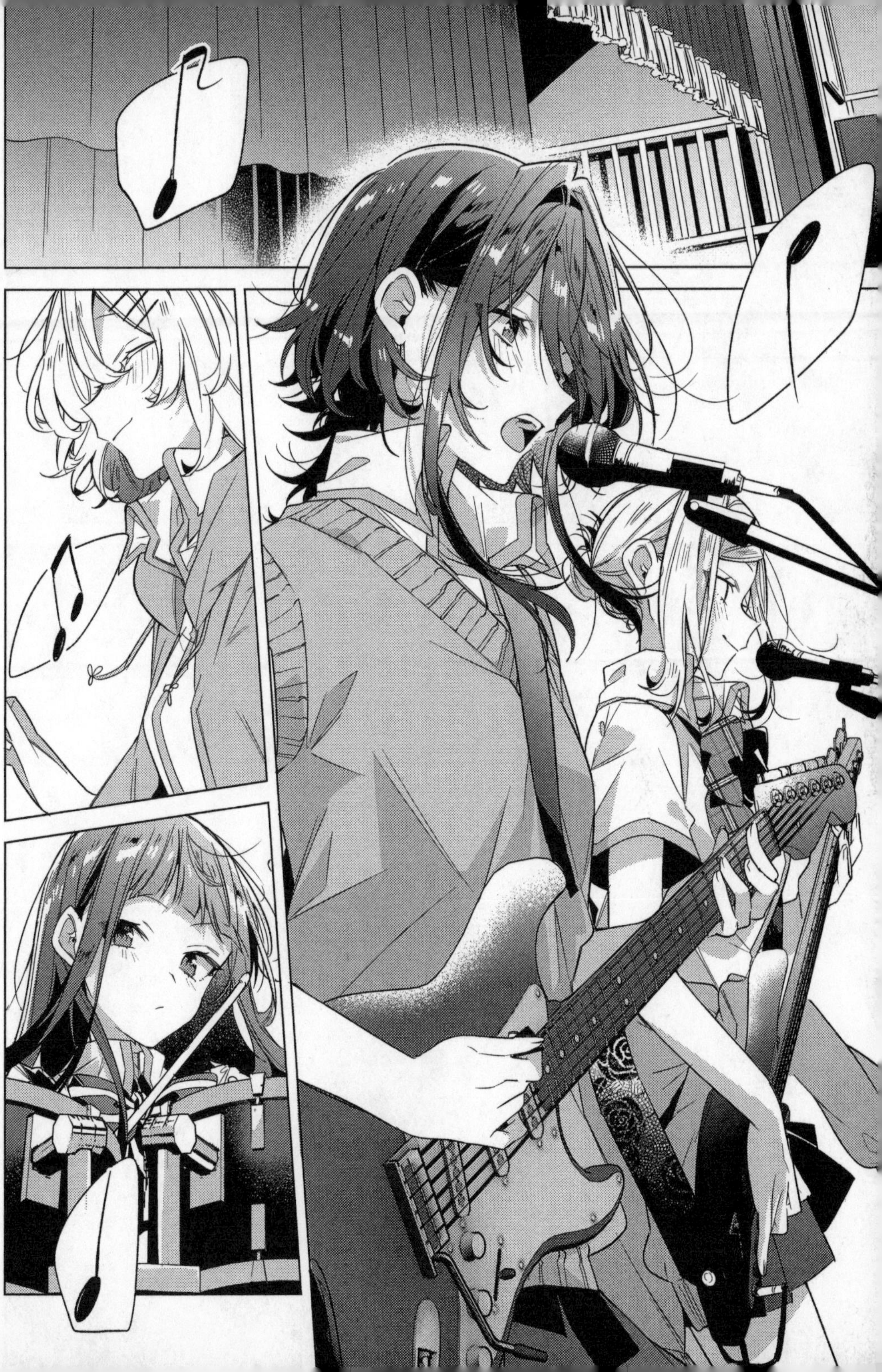

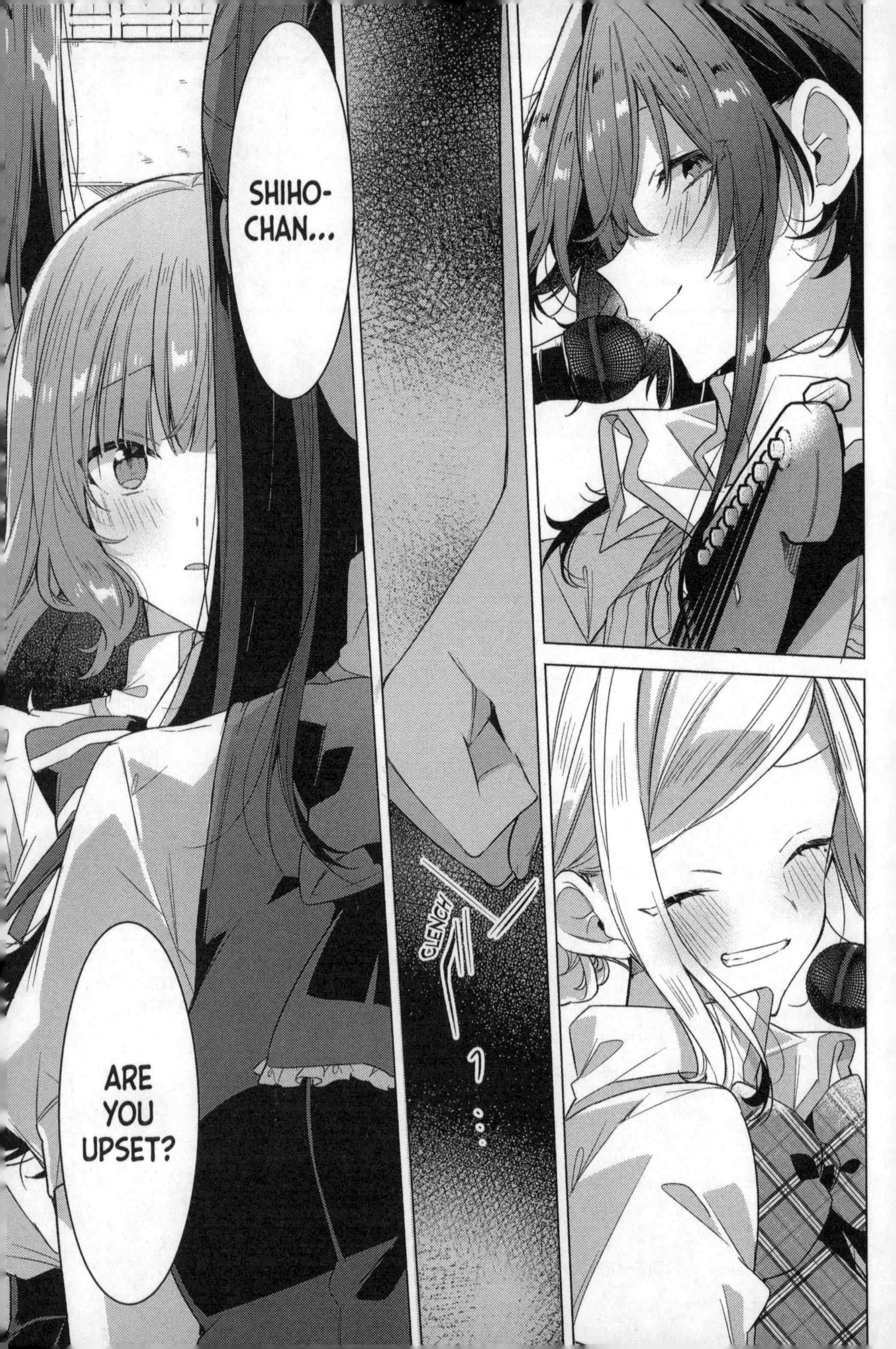
CLENCH
SHIHO-CHAN...
ARE YOU UPSET?

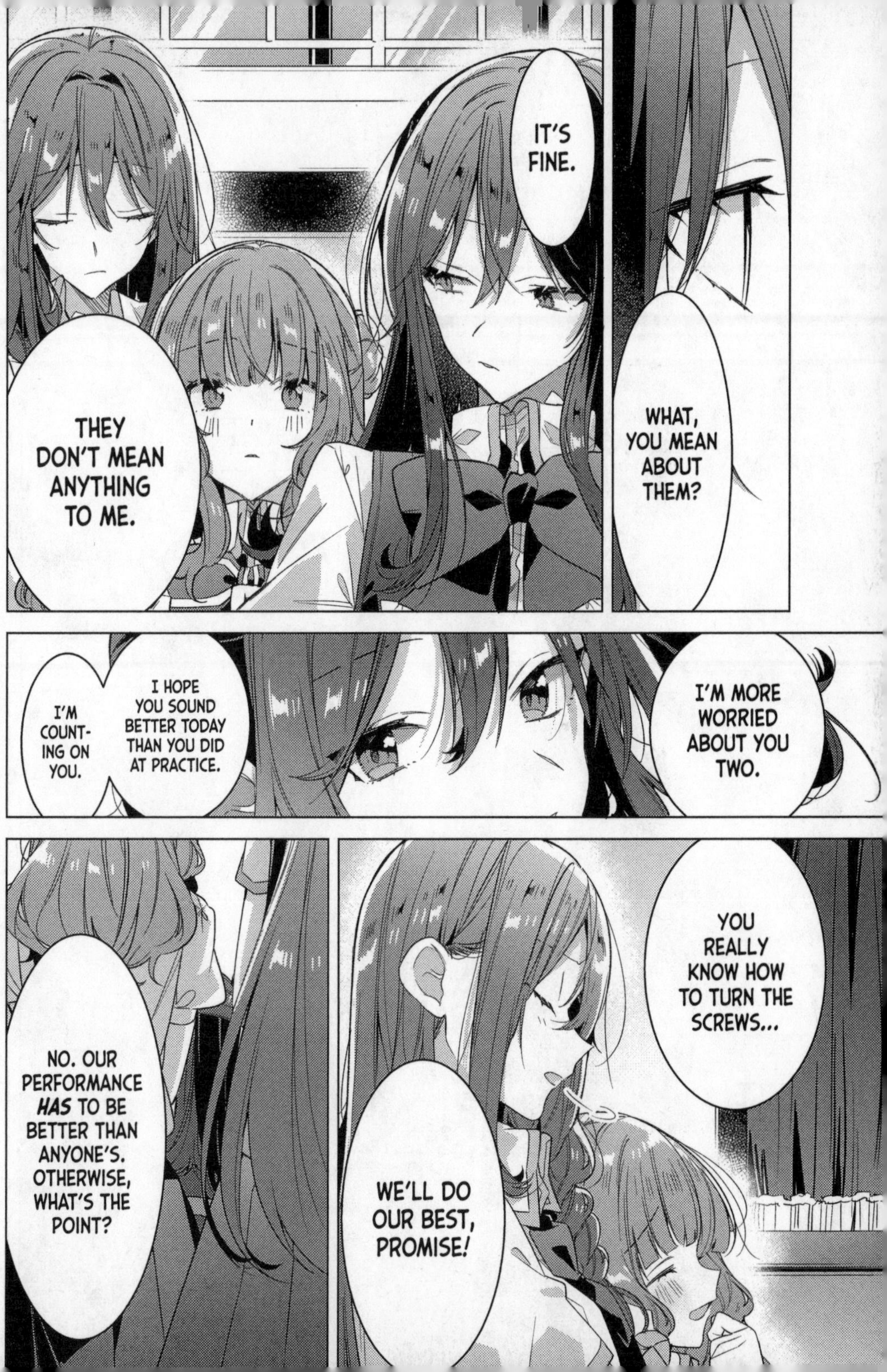
WHAT, YOU MEAN ABOUT THEM?
IT'S FINE.
THEY DON'T MEAN ANYTHING TO ME.
I'M MORE WORRIED ABOUT YOU TWO.
I HOPE YOU SOUND BETTER TODAY THAN YOU DID AT PRACTICE.
I'M COUNTING-ING ON YOU.
YOU REALLY KNOW HOW TO TURN THE SCREWS...
WE'LL DO OUR BEST, PROMISE!
NO. OUR PERFORMANCE *HAS* TO BE BETTER THAN ANYONE'S. OTHERWISE, WHAT'S THE POINT?

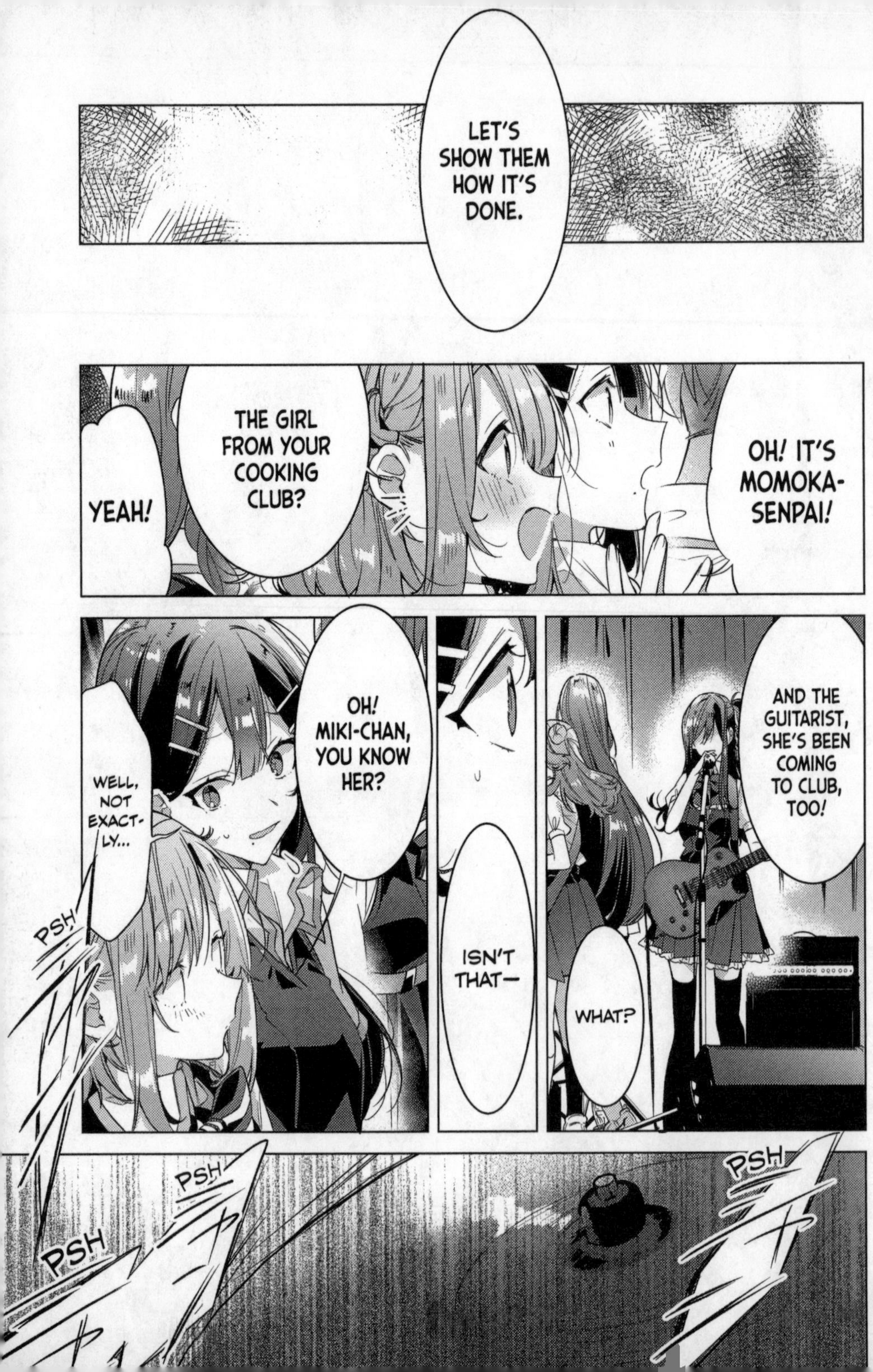
LET'S SHOW THEM HOW IT'S DONE.
OH! IT'S MOMOKA-SENPAI!
THE GIRL FROM YOUR COOKING CLUB?
YEAH!
AND THE GUITARIST, SHE'S BEEN COMING TO CLUB, TOO!
WHAT?
ISN'T THAT—
OH! MIKI-CHAN, YOU KNOW HER?
WELL, NOT EXACTLY...
PSH
PSH
PSH
PSH

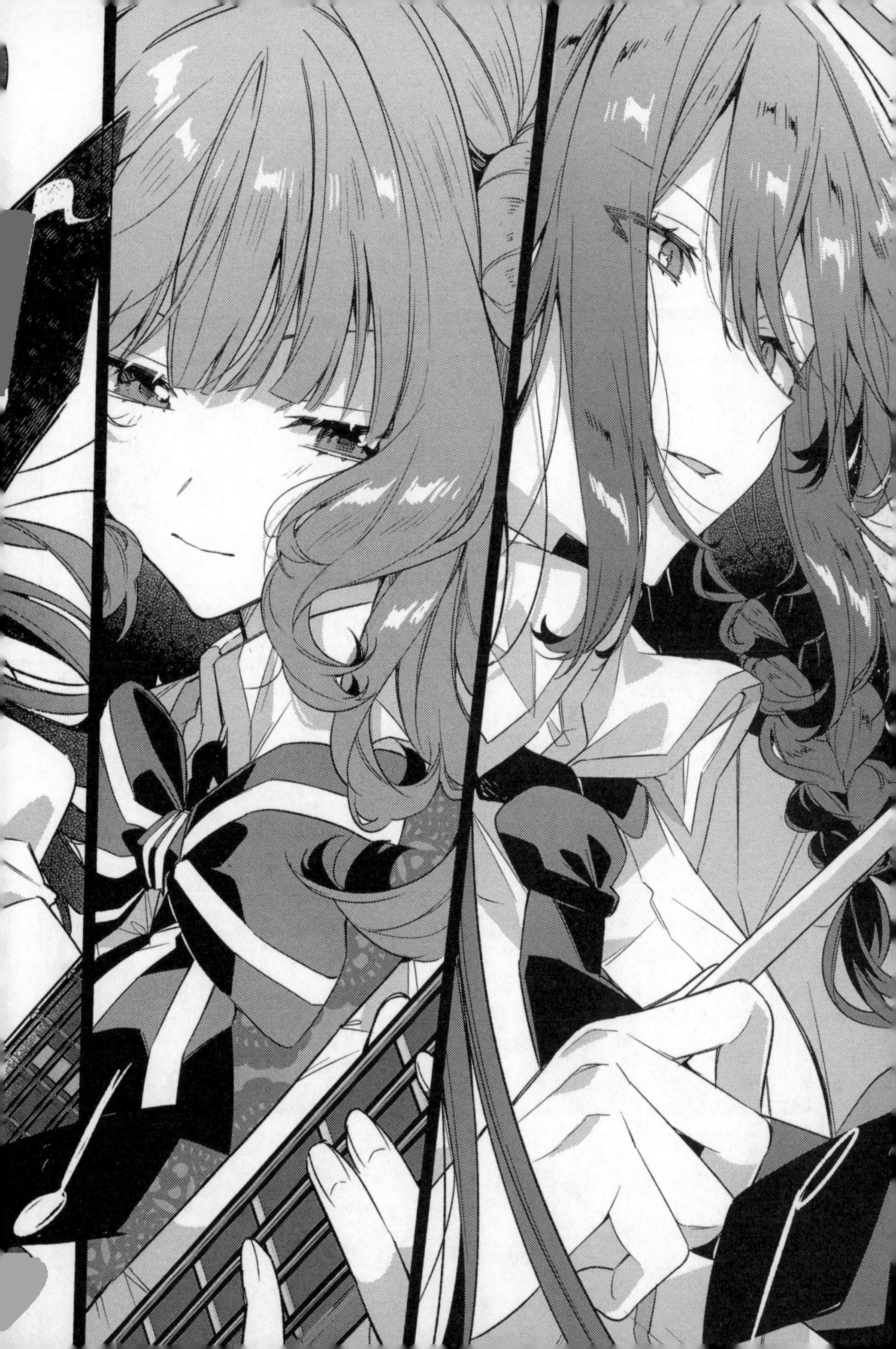

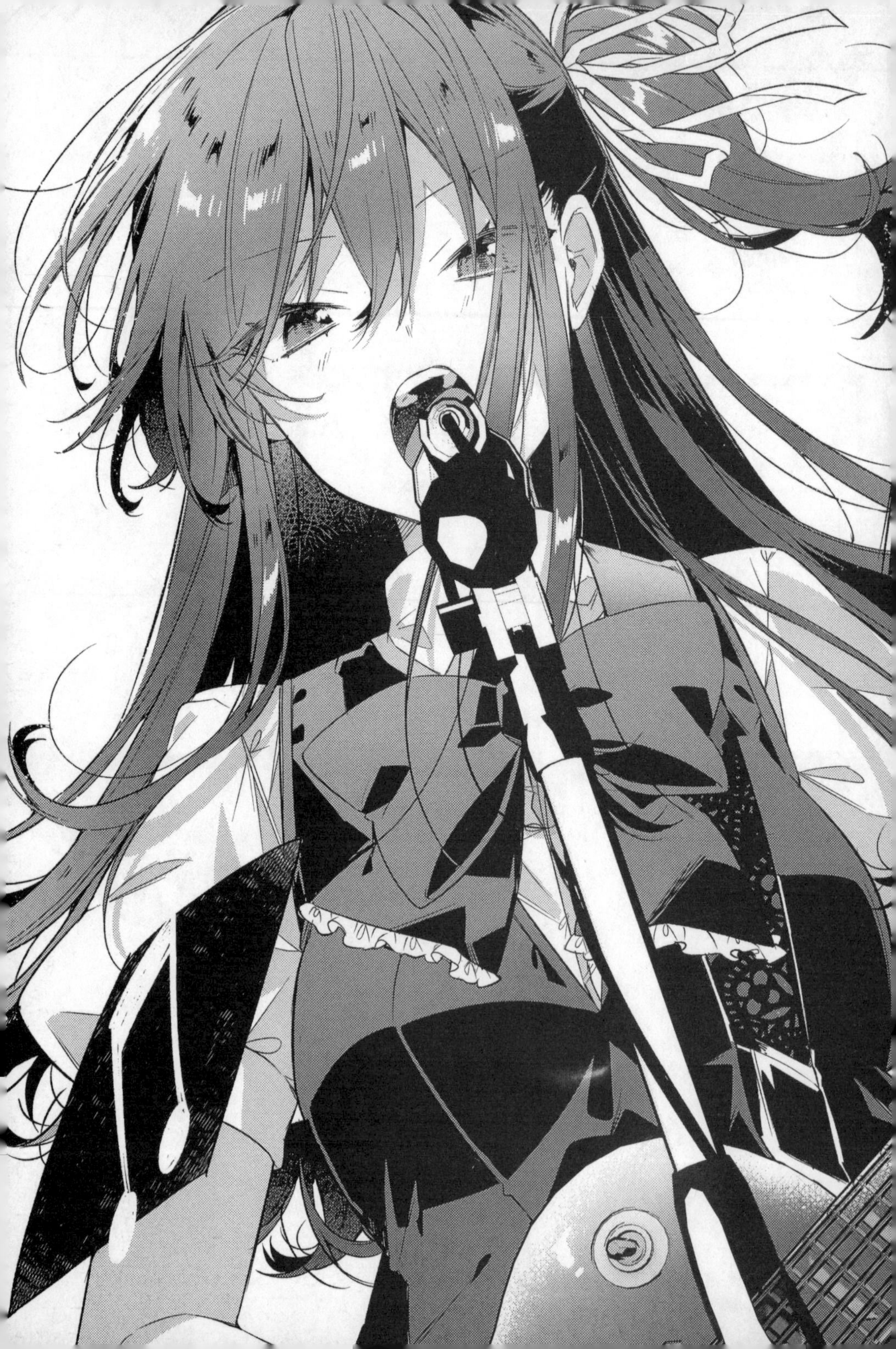

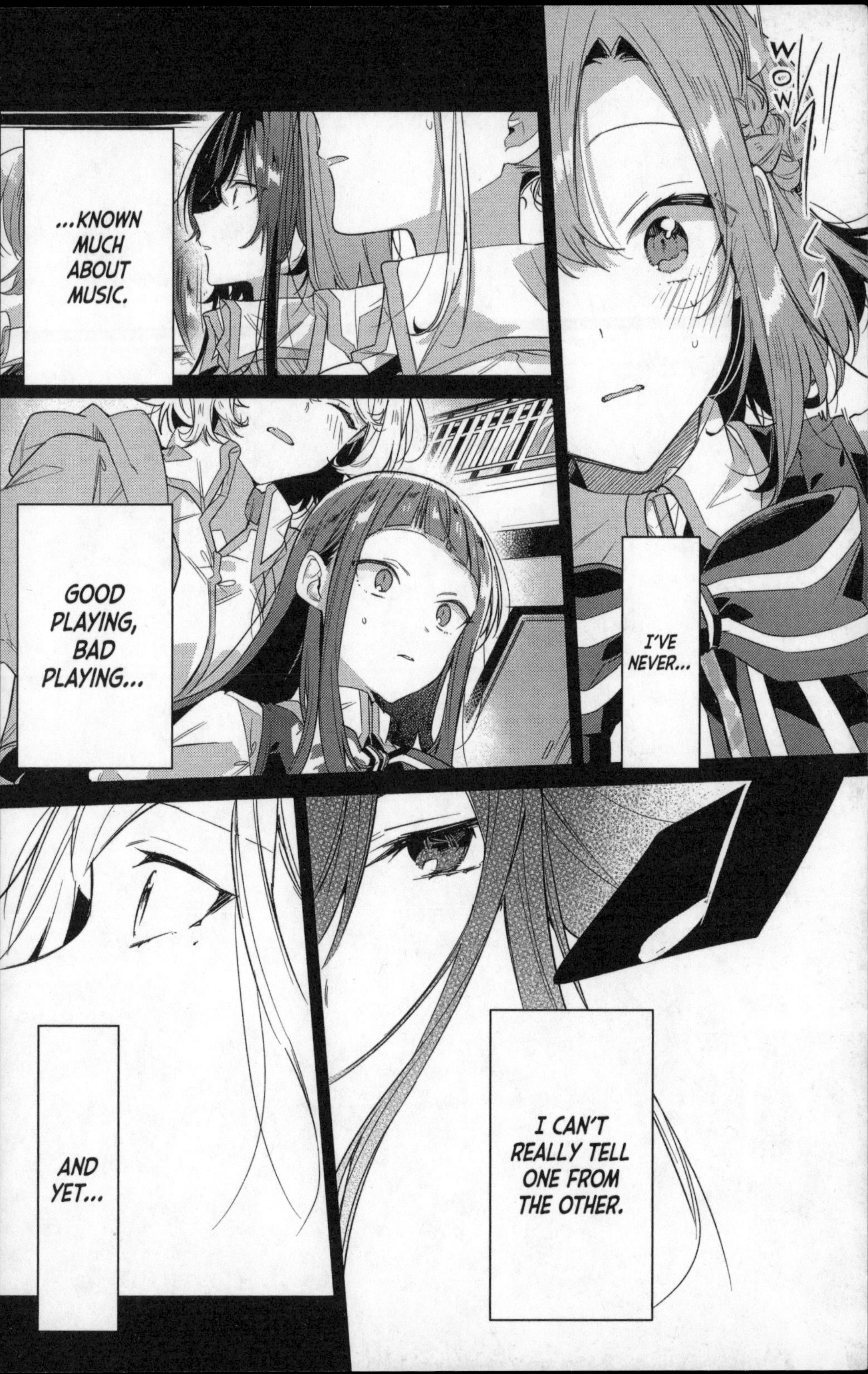
WOW
I'VE NEVER...
...KNOWN MUCH ABOUT MUSIC.
GOOD PLAYING, BAD PLAYING...
I CAN'T REALLY TELL ONE FROM THE OTHER.
AND YET...

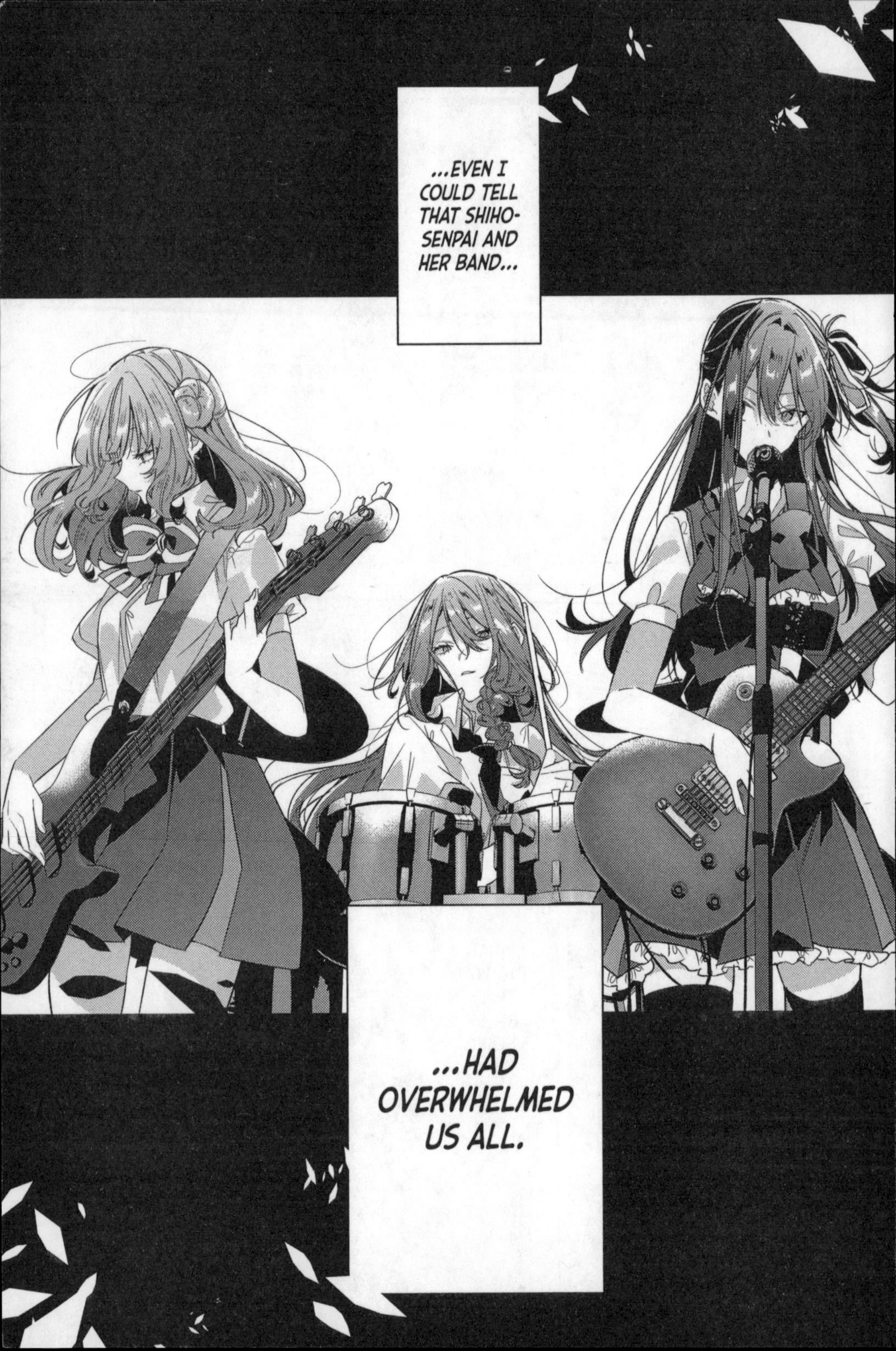
...EVEN I COULD TELL THAT SHIHO-SENPAI AND HER BAND...
...HAD OVERWHELMED US ALL.

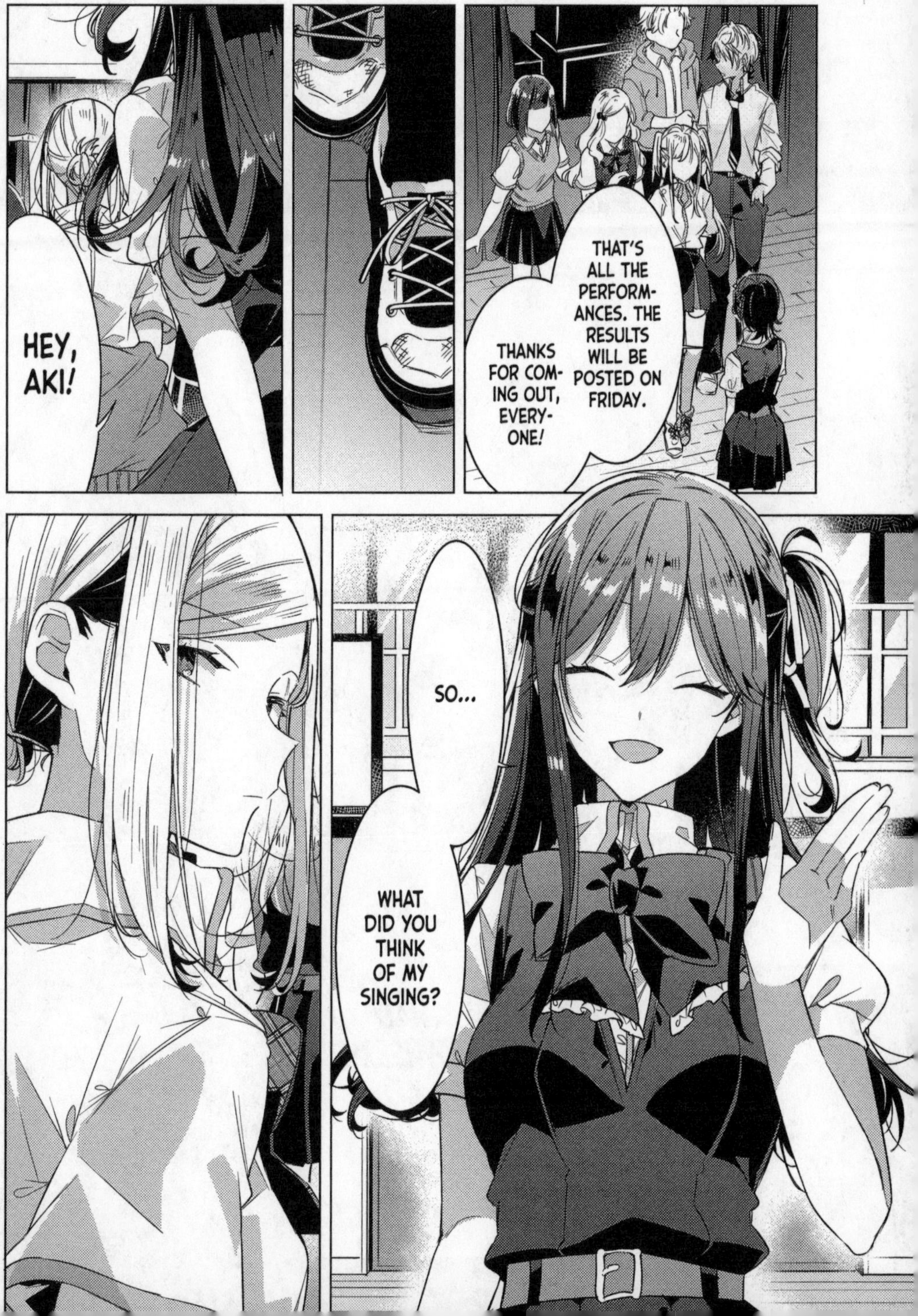
THAT'S ALL THE PERFORMANCES. THE RESULTS WILL BE POSTED ON FRIDAY.
THANKS FOR COMING OUT, EVERYONE!
HEY, AKI!
SO...
WHAT DID YOU THINK OF MY SINGING?

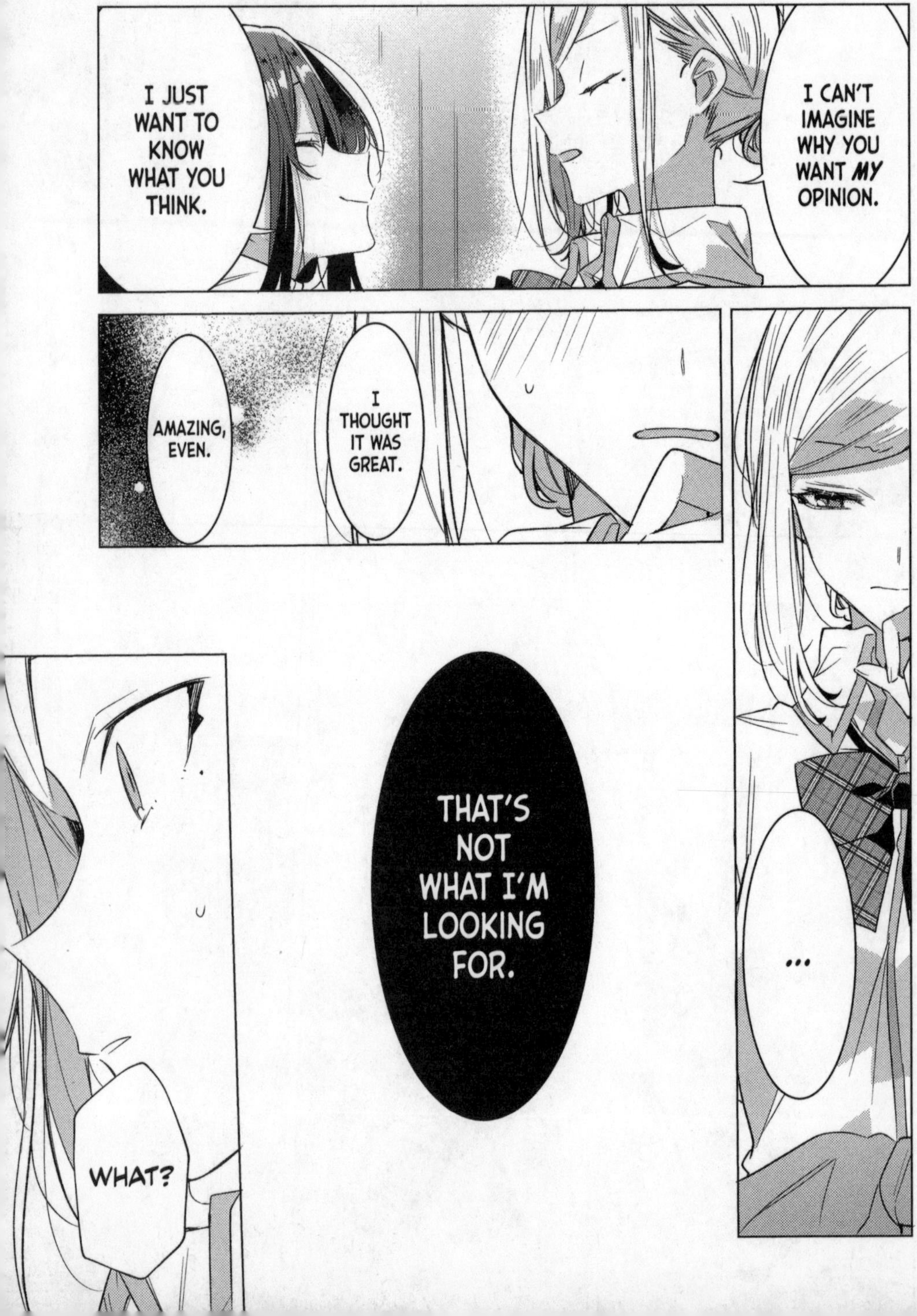

I CAN'T IMAGINE WHY YOU WANT *MY* OPINION.
I JUST WANT TO KNOW WHAT YOU THINK.
...
I THOUGHT IT WAS GREAT.
AMAZING, EVEN.
THAT'S NOT WHAT I'M LOOKING FOR.
WHAT?

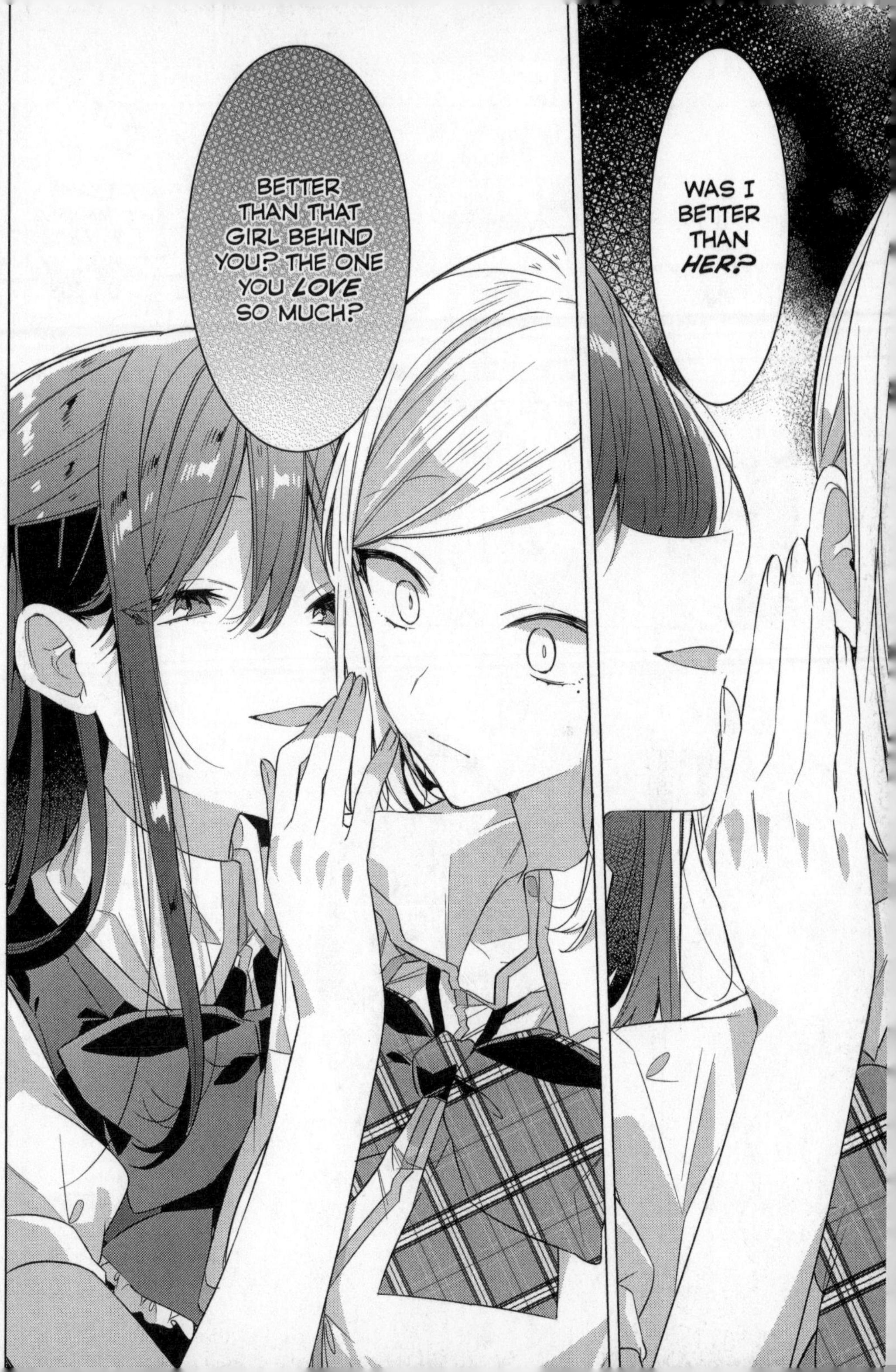
WAS I BETTER THAN *HER?*
BETTER THAN THAT GIRL BEHIND YOU? THE ONE YOU *LOVE* SO MUCH?

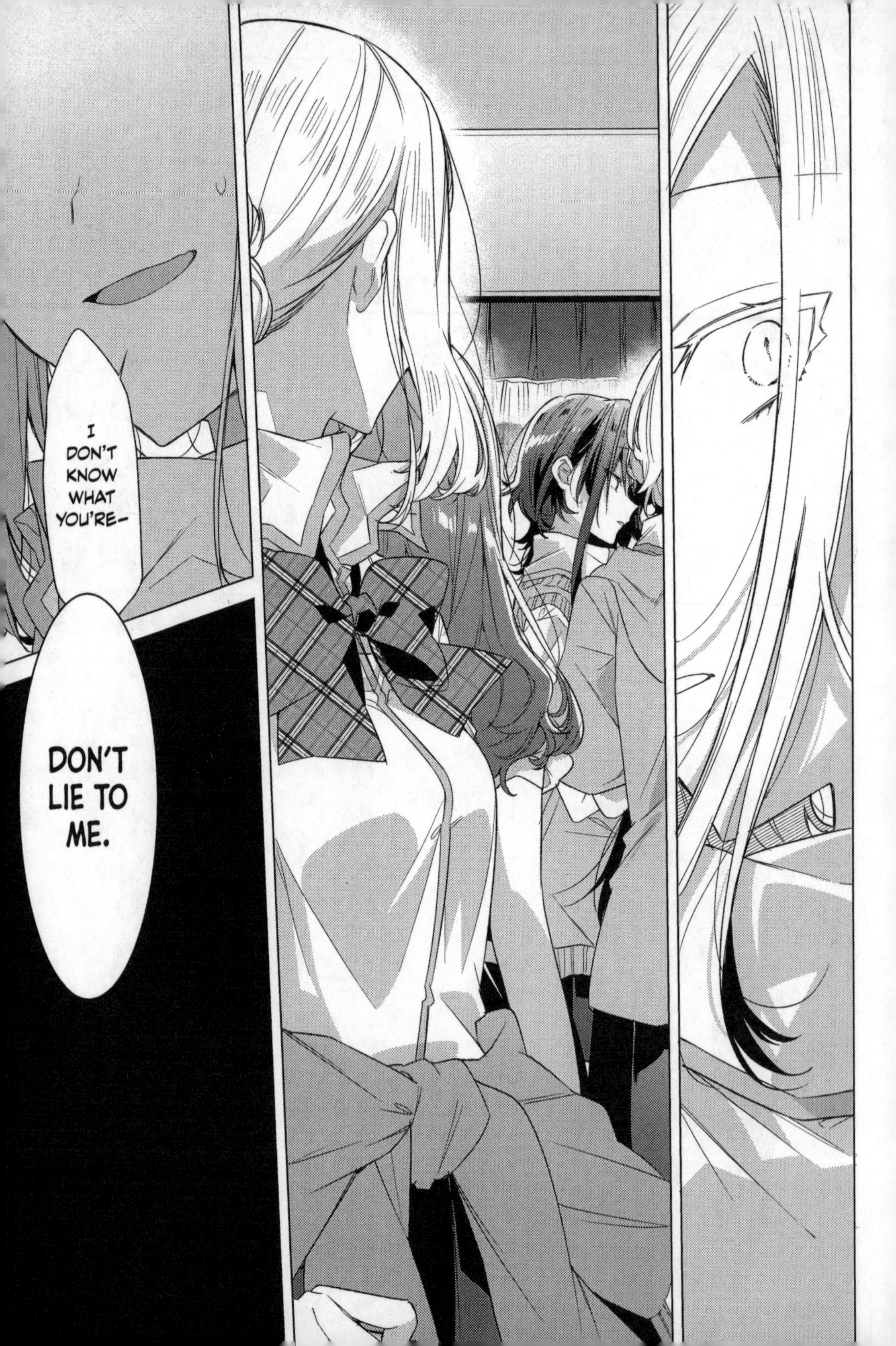
I DON'T KNOW WHAT YOU'RE–
DON'T LIE TO ME.

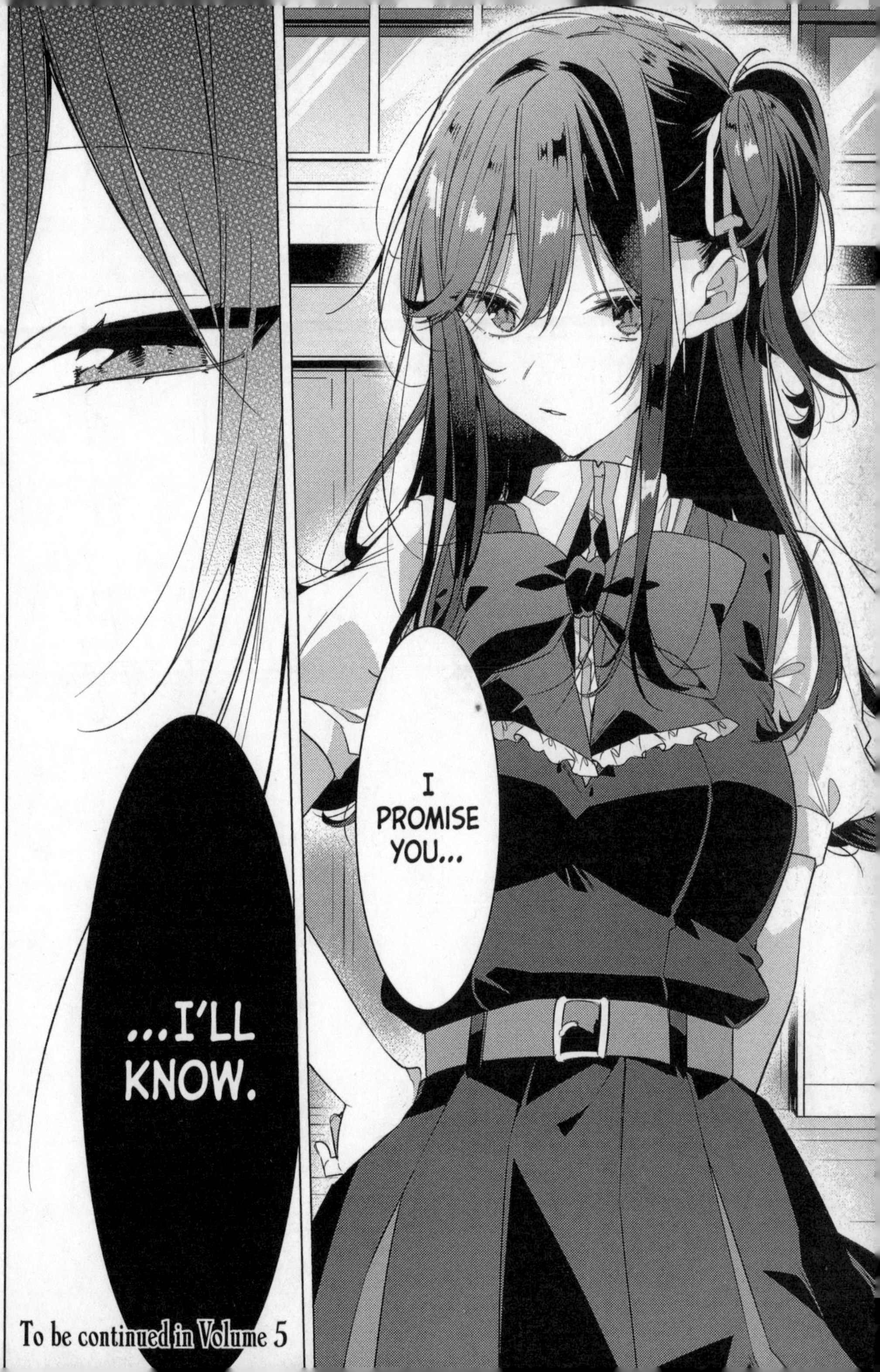
I PROMISE YOU...
...I'LL KNOW.
To be continued in Volume 5

**SPECIAL THANKS**
Editor – Ten-san
Design – SALIDAS-sama
Assistant – Hirofumi Shino-san
&
All my readers!
Thank you all so much!

# TRANSLATION NOTES

**Summer Uniforms, page 7**
Japanese schoolkids usually have two different school uniforms, one for summer and the other for winter. The winter uniform is heavier and warmer than the summer one, as you might expect. (You can see Himari, Yori, and the others are wearing long-sleeved shirts in volume 3, although their overwear seems to be more or less the same.) Across the country, students start wearing their summer uniforms on June 1, and switch to their winter ones on October 1. Japan can be sweltering by June, and is often still warm in October, so the winter uniforms can get pretty uncomfortable, but the change (called *koromogae,* or "switching clothes") always happens according to the calendar, not the weather.

**Onee-sama, page 13**
*Onee-sama* is Japanese for "elder sister," and a form of respectful address that a younger individual would use to refer to a woman who is slightly older than them. The honorific "-sama" signifies formality.

**The Street Side, page 15**
In Japan, when a guy and girl are walking along the street, it's sometimes considered gallant for the man to walk on the side closest to the passing cars, nominally in order to protect the woman. Yori is taking the protective role here, as she tries to be chivalrous toward Himari.

**Meal Tickets, page 15**
Cafeterias and fast food places in Japan frequently feature machines like the one you see here in the second to last panel on page 15, which offer meal tickets, or *shokken,* and work something like a vending machine. Each of the buttons shows a menu choice, along with the price. You give the machine your money, press the button for the item(s) you want, and the machine dispenses a small ticket corresponding to each item. You bring these tickets to the counter, where the staff takes them and prepares your meal.

**Beckoning, page 48**
Notice how Yori beckons with her palm down, motioning with all her fingers instead of just one. This is the polite way to gesture to someone in Japan. To beckon with the palm up, or worse, with just one finger, is considered very rude–hence why you so often see characters in manga starting fights that way!

**"Hustle on over to the back cover, girls!", page 167**
In the Japanese edition of *Whisper Me a Love Song,* the bonus comics on pages 167 and 168 originally appeared on the inside cover of the paperback, hidden beneath the book's dust jacket.

**Kabedon, page 168**
This is a move where one character corners another (often someone they have a romantic interest in) by a wall (*kabe* in Japanese), then places a hand firmly against the wall to prevent the other person's escape. The sound of smacking something is *don,* hence the expression "*kabedon*" (wall-smack).

# Whisper Me
# A Love Song

Eku
Takeshima

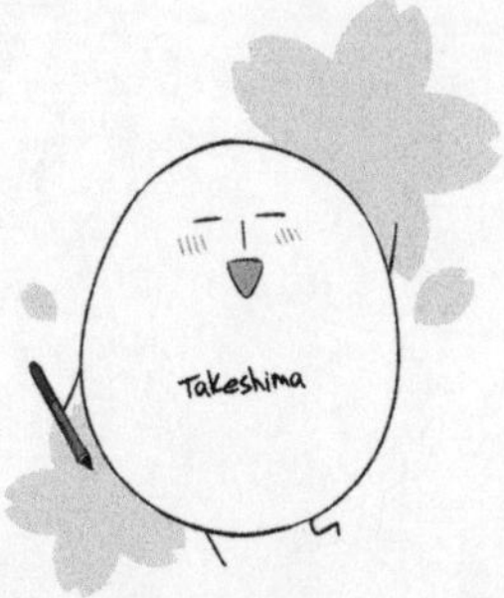
Takeshima

Wow, volume 4 already! Thanks for all the support and encouragement. It really keeps me going. I hope you enjoy reading more about Yori and Himari (who are dating now!), and the new characters who show up.

—Eku Takeshima

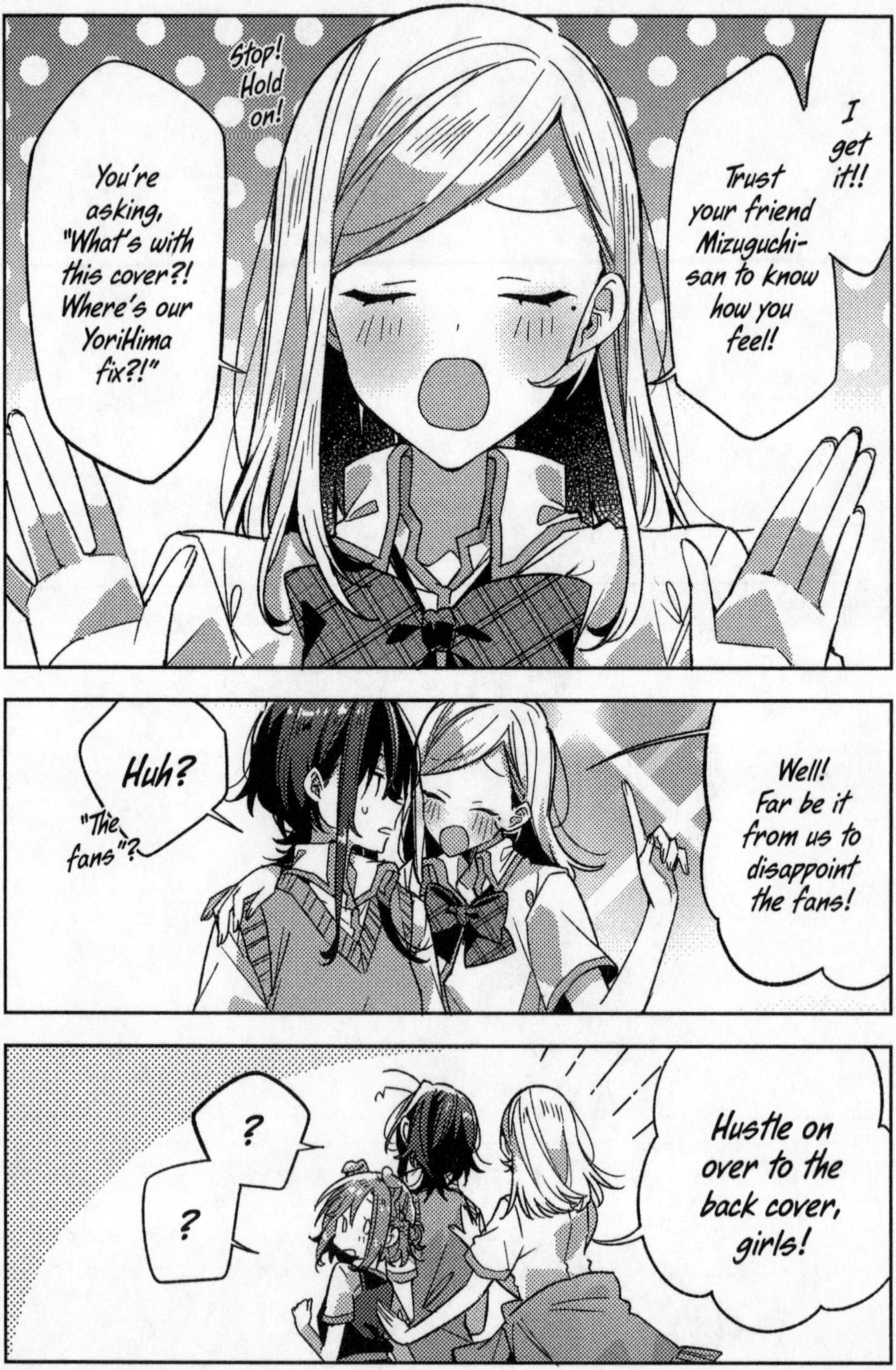
I get it!!
Trust your friend Mizuguchi-san to know how you feel!
Stop! Hold on!
You're asking, "What's with this cover?! Where's our YoriHima fix?!"
Well! Far be it from us to disappoint the fans!
Huh?
"The fans"?
Hustle on over to the back cover, girls!
?
?

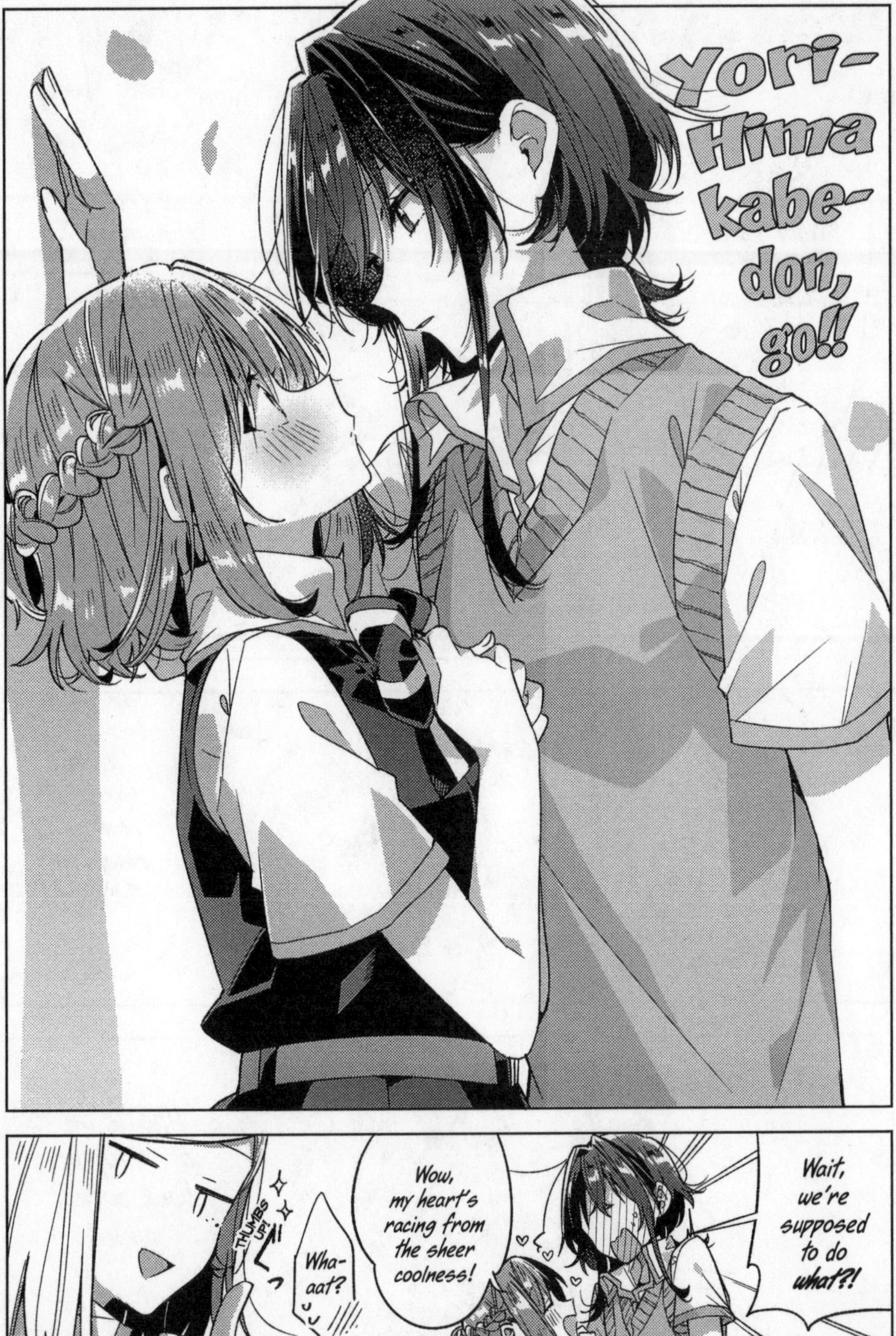
Yori-Hima kabe-don, go!!
Wait, we're supposed to do what?!
Wow, my heart's racing from the sheer coolness!
Wha-aat?
THUMBS UP!

# A SMART, NEW ROMANTIC COMEDY FOR FANS OF *SHORTCAKE CAKE* AND *TERRACE HOUSE*!

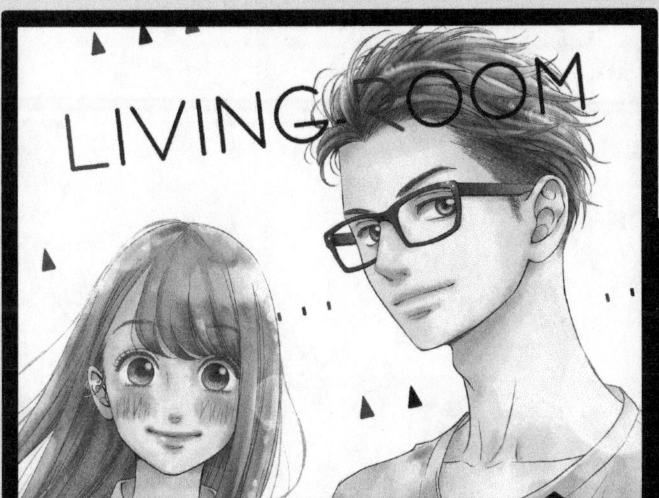
LIVING-ROOM
1
Keiko Iwashita
MATSUNAGA-SAN

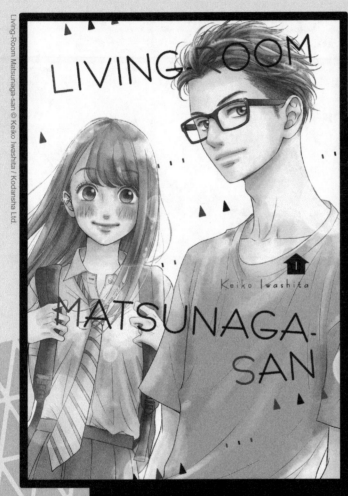

A romance manga starring high school girl Meeko, who learns to live on her own in a boarding house whose living room is home to the odd (but handsome) Matsunaga-san. She begins to adjust to her new life away from her parents, but Meeko soon learns that no matter how far away from home she is, she's still a young girl at heart — especially when she finds herself falling for Matsunaga-san.

KC KODANSHA COMICS

# PERFECT WORLD

Rie Aruga

A TOUCHING NEW SERIES ABOUT LOVE AND COPING WITH DISABILITY

An office party reunites Tsugumi with her high school crush Itsuki. He's realized his dream of becoming an architect, but along the way, he experienced a spinal injury that put him in a wheelchair. Now Tsugumi's rekindled feelings will butt up against prejudices she never considered — and Itsuki will have to decide if he's ready to let someone into his heart...

"Depicts with great delicacy and courage the difficulties some with disabilities experience getting involved in romantic relationships... Rie Aruga refuses to romanticize, pushing her heroine to face the reality of disability. She invites her readers to the same tasks of empathy, knowledge and recognition."
—Slate.fr

"An important entry [in manga romance]... The emotional core of both plot and characters indicates thoughtfulness... [Aruga's] research is readily apparent in the text and artwork, making this feel like a real story."
—Anime News Network

KC
KODANSHA
COMICS

# Something's Wrong With Us

### NATSUMI ANDO

The dark, psychological, sexy shojo series readers have been waiting for!

**A spine-chilling and steamy romance between a Japanese sweets maker and the man who framed her mother for murder!**

Following in her mother's footsteps, Nao became a traditional Japanese sweets maker, and with unparalleled artistry and a bright attitude, she gets an offer to work at a world-class confectionary company. But when she meets the young, handsome owner, she recognizes his cold stare...

The slow-burn queer romance that'll sweep you off your feet!

# 10 DANCE

## Inouesatoh presents

Shinya Sugiki, the dashing lord of Standard Ballroom, and Shinya Suzuki, passionate king of Latin Dance: The two share more than just a first name and a love of the sport. They each want to become champion of the 10-Dance Competition, which means they'll need to learn the other's specialty dances, and who better to learn from than the best? But old rivalries die hard, and things get further complicated when they realize there might be more between them than an uneasy partnership...

KC KODANSHA COMICS

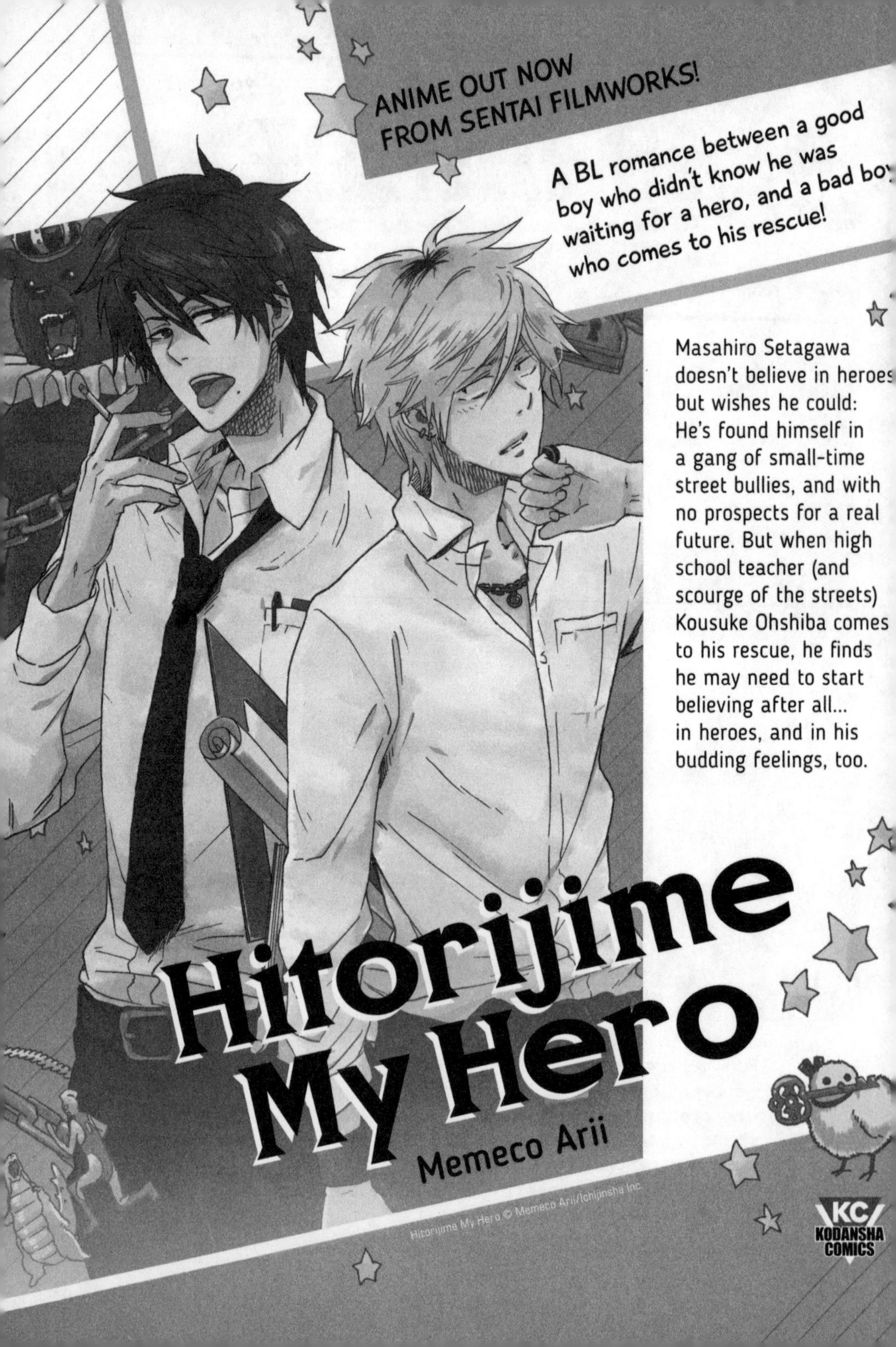
ANIME OUT NOW FROM SENTAI FILMWORKS!
A BL romance between a good boy who didn't know he was waiting for a hero, and a bad boy who comes to his rescue!
Masahiro Setagawa doesn't believe in heroes but wishes he could: He's found himself in a gang of small-time street bullies, and with no prospects for a real future. But when high school teacher (and scourge of the streets) Kousuke Ohshiba comes to his rescue, he finds he may need to start believing after all... in heroes, and in his budding feelings, too.
Hitorijime My Hero
Memeco Arii
Hitorijime My Hero © Memeco Arii/Ichijinsha Inc.
KC KODANSHA COMICS

# THE SWEET SCENT OF LOVE IS IN THE AIR! FOR FANS OF OFFBEAT ROMANCES LIKE *WOTAKOI*

VOL. 1

SWEAT AND SOAP

KINTETSU YAMADA

Sweat and Soap © Kintetsu Yamada / Kodansha Ltd.

In an office romance, there's a fine line between sexy and awkward... and that line is where Asako — a woman who sweats copiously — meets Koutarou — a perfume developer who can't get enough of Asako's, er, scent. Don't miss a romcom manga like no other!

KC KODANSHA COMICS

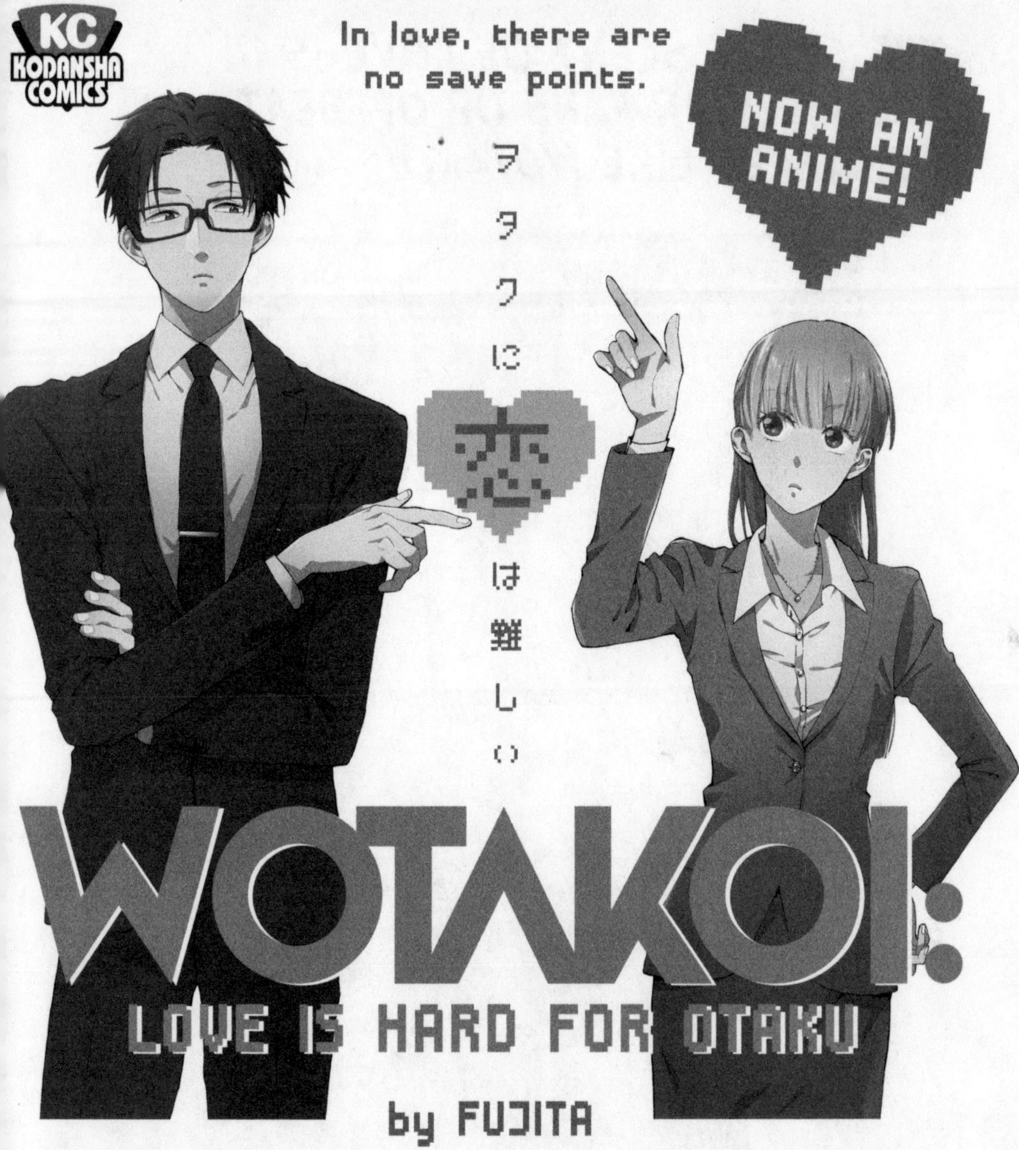
KC KODANSHA COMICS
In love, there are no save points.
NOW AN ANIME!
ヲタクに恋は難しい
WOTAKOI:
LOVE IS HARD FOR OTAKU
by FUJITA

Narumi has had it rough: Every boyfriend she's had dumped her once they found out she was an otaku, so she's gone to great lengths to hide it. At her new job, she bumps into Hirotaka, her childhood friend and fellow otaku. When Hirotaka almost gets her secret outed at work, she comes up with a plan to keep him quiet. But he comes up with a counter-proposal: Why doesn't she just date him instead?

**THE MAGICAL GIRL CLASSIC THAT BROUGHT A GENERATION OF READERS TO MANGA, NOW BACK IN A DEFINITIVE, HARDCOVER COLLECTOR'S EDITION!**

# CARDCAPTOR SAKURA
## COLLECTOR'S EDITION
### C L A M P

KODANSHA COMICS
I
DELUXE EDITION
Cardcaptor Sakura
CLAMP



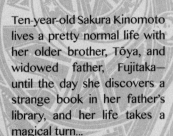

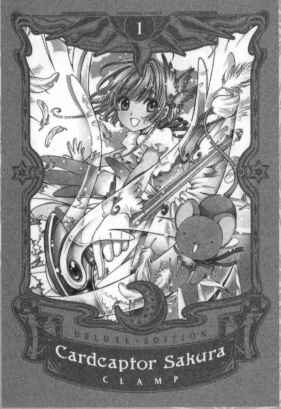

Ten-year-old Sakura Kinomoto lives a pretty normal life with her older brother, Tōya, and widowed father, Fujitaka—until the day she discovers a strange book in her father's library, and her life takes a magical turn...

- A deluxe large-format hardcover edition of CLAMP's shojo manga classic
- All-new foil-stamped cover art on each volume
- Comes with exclusive collectible art card

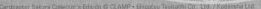

KC KODANSHA COMICS

A Kodansha Comics Trade Paperback Original
*Whisper Me a Love Song 4* copyright © 2021 Eku Takeshima
English translation copyright © 2021 Eku Takeshima

Published in the United States by Kodansha Comics, an imprint of Kodansha USA Publishing, LLC, New York.

Publication rights for this English edition arranged through Kodansha Ltd., Tokyo.

First published in Japan in 2021 by Ichijinsha Inc., Tokyo as *Sayasaku you ni koi wo utau*, volume 4.

ISBN 978-1-64651-228-7

Original cover design by SALIDAS

Printed in the United States of America.

www.kodansha.us

9 8 7 6 5 4 3 2 1
Translation: Kevin Steinbach
Lettering: Jennifer Skarupa
Editing: Tiff Joshua TJ Ferentini
Kodansha Comics edition cover design: Matt Akuginow

Publisher: Kiichiro Sugawara

Director of publishing services: Ben Applegate
Associate director of operations: Stephen Pakula
Publishing services managing editors: Alanna Ruse, Madison Salters
Production managers: Emi Lotto, Angela Zurlo
Logo and character art ©Kodansha USA Publishing, LLC

W9-AFA-445